DATE DUE FOR

<

'6

D1612979

ERRATA

The following legends were by oversight not printed below the appropriate maps and tables in the article "Segregation in the Netherlands and Turkish Migration" (pp. 253-283).

Map 1. Location of Rotterdam and Utrecht within the Netherlands.

Map 2. Mediterraneans per district in Rotterdam as a percentage of total district population (1-1-1972).

Map 3. Mediterraneans per district in Utrecht as a percentage of total district population (1-1-1973).

Map 4. Turks per district in Rotterdam as a percentage of total district population (1-1-1972).

Map 5. Turks per district in Utrecht as a percentage of total district population (1-1-1973).

Map 6. Turks per district in Rotterdam as a percentage of total Turkish population (1-1-1972).

Map 7. Turks per district in Utrecht as a percentage of total Turkish population (1-1-1973).

Map 8. Building period per district in Rotterdam.

Map 9. Building period per district in Utrecht.

Map 10. Population density (habitants/ha) per district in Rotterdam (1-1-1972).

Map 11. Population density (habitants/ha) per district in Utrecht (1-1-1973).

In the Table of Contents, *read* Nia Verkoren, *instead of* Mia Verkoren

TURKISH WORKERS IN EUROPE

1960-1975

A SOCIO-ECONOMIC REAPPRAISAL

SOCIAL, ECONOMIC AND POLITICAL STUDIES OF THE MIDDLE EAST

ÉTUDES SOCIALES, ÉCONOMIQUES ET POLITIQUES DU MOYEN ORIENT

VOLUME XIX

NERMIN ABADAN-UNAT
AND CONTRIBUTORS

TURKISH WORKERS IN EUROPE
1960-1975

LEIDEN
E.J. BRILL
1976

TURKISH WORKERS
IN EUROPE
1960-1975

A SOCIO-ECONOMIC REAPPRAISAL

BY

NERMIN ABADAN-UNAT
AND CONTRIBUTORS

With 9 Figures and 11 Maps

LEIDEN
E.J. BRILL
1976

Comité de rédaction — Editorial committee

The series is designed to serve as a link between the international reading public and social scientists studying the contemporary Middle East, notably those living in the area. Works to be included will be characterized by their relevance to actual phenomena and problems: whether social, cultural, economic, political or administrative. They will be theory-oriented, problem-oriented or policy-oriented.

Le but de la collection est de faciliter la communication entre le grand public international et les spécialistes des sciences sociales étudiant le Moyen-Orient, et notamment ceux qui y résident. Les ouvrages sélectionnés porteront sur les phénomènes et problèmes contemporains: sociaux, culturels, économiques et administratifs. Leurs principales orientations relèveront de la théorie générale, de problématiques plus précises, et de la politologie: aménagement des institutions et administration des affaires publiques.

ISBN 90 04 04478 7

PRINTED IN THE NETHERLANDS

TABLE OF CONTENTS

IMPACT OF TURKISH MIGRATION ON EUROPEAN ECONOMIC AND SOCIAL STRUCTURES

PREFACE

Economists, social scientists and historians, who are analyzing the entrenching and lasting consequences of the Second World War, are getting nowadays more and more interested in the international labour migration movement. First looked upon as a short term economic solution to overcome labour shortage in industrialized countries, it evolved in the 1960's both in sending and receiving countries as a major phase, leading to long term socio-economic structural changes and proper historical dimensions. Today international migration is no more considered as a transitional phenomenon. Furthermore economists and social scientists in addition to exploration of its multifaceted effects, attempt to formulate independent migration theories, instead of deriving key concepts from existing macro and micro level theoretical frameworks.

It is under the light of these major changes that the content of this volume has been conceived. Thanks to the broadminded support of the editor of this series, Professor C.A.O. van Nieuwenhuijze, the interdisciplinary and crossnational character of this volume permits the reader to become aware of the interrelated, mutually interacting factors, effecting external migration. Authors of various nationality (Turkish, German, Dutch, American) have contributed to a more objective, less egocentric, comparative evaluation of facts, issues and problems. Furthermore the mixed professional background of the various contributors (academicians, national and international civil servants) permits a balanced appraisal of theoretical and practical issues connected with migration.

My greatest debt in the completion of this volume for stimulation, inspiration and sincere critic is to my husband, Professor Ilhan Unat, whose patience and encouragement has been invaluable. I also would like to acknowledge sincere gratitude for the tolerance and moral support of our children, son Mustafa Kemal Abadan and daughters Ayşe and Oya Unat, who had to endure the painful months of gestation every book publishing activity requires.

Sincere appreciation goes to Mr. Fomerand from the City

University of New York, who kindly re-edited certain manu-
scripts. Special thanks are due to Mr. Talât Sait Halman for his
kind cooperation in the selection and translation of related Turkish literature. I owe thanks for gracious help from Dr. Erika
Wolf, member of the Bundestag, for her coordinating efforts.

Typing of several versions of many chapters was done with
amazing patience and courtesy by Mrs. Serpil Şaylan. Miss Melek
Erman kindly helped to complete the authors and subject index.
Responsibility for the interpretations and conclusions of the
intermediary chapters rests entirely on me.

Over the years I have been working on this subject my con-
vinction that the smaller the world becomes and the closer communities of different origin are bound to live together, the more
cross-cultural, comparative investigations and studies will be
needed, got stronger. I believe that this modest volume will certainly be only a small part of a long and continuous chain of
scientific endeavours, aiming to understand better the mankind
of tomorrow.

Ankara, July 1975   Nermin Abadan-Unat

TURKISH MIGRATION TO EUROPE (1960-1975)

A Balance Sheet of Achievements and Failures

NERMIN ABADAN-UNAT

1. *What kind of migration?*

Migration has been such a universal phenomenon that it can only be systematically categorized and evaluated from a long-term historical perspective. The major types of human migration may be conceptualized as *creeping expansion* movements, such as the Slavic and German pressure; thin and sharp *oversea thrusts*, such as the move of the Greeks to Syracuse; bold *mass movements* of people, such as the move of the Etruscans to Italy, of the Turks to Anatolia and the creation of the United States by a one-sided oversea migration wave. Next to these broad movements, *forced migration*, such as the expulsion of the Huguenots, *conquest migration*, such as the herds of Cengiz Khan, and *group religious migration*, such as the Crusades or the partition of India have equally fascinated social scientists. Today, however, migration have definitely acquired a new character. As Franklin D. Scott correctly observes, the days of individually motivated, uncontrolled international migrations have passed. Nationstates carefully select the immigrants they admit. Hence present day migrations adapt themselves to *economic fluctuations* and *nationalistic demands* of the receiving countries.[1] "Laissez faire" no longer regulates these large-scale migratory movements. On the contrary, all their aspects and phases have now become a permanent source of negotiations and mediation for the Governments involved.

The mass migrations now taking place from Southern Europe to Northern Europe and from the heart of Africa, to the shores of the Mediterranean can be compared to the movement from Southern and Eastern Europe to the United States between 1880-1913. In both cases cheap labour fed economic growth by holding down wages and maintaining high rates of profit, invest-

---

[1] Franklin D. Scott, *World Migration in Modern Times*, Prentice Hall, 1968, p. 2-3.

ment and expansion. In both cases migrants have been taking up
strenuous, unpleasant, mostly unqualified jobs (mining, construction and heavy industry), thus permitting the labour force of the
recipient country to move up into skilled or semi-skilled jobs.
However, the postwar large-scale European migration movement,
similar to the counterpart in the Caribbean, is characterized by a
number of particular features.

1.2. *The New "European South"*

The Turkish external migration, similar to the extensive labour
movement from all the Mediterranean countries, cannot be discussed as a single case-study, illustrating a number of specific
structural disfunctions of the Turkish economy, but must be
evaluated both within the general framework of an enlarging dis-
parity between the rich and the poor countries as well as a
changed conception of the "European South".

Among the countries of this geographical new "European
South", one can distinguish the following groups; first, the countries of Southern European proper (Portugal, Spain, Southern
Italy, Greece). To the second group belong Turkey and Yugoslavia: the former has deliberately determined its national boundaries after the liquidation of its empire, the latter emerged as an
independent state after the dismantling of two empires. The third
group consists of countries that have been in fact dominated as
colonies under different political forms by European countries:
Algeria, Marocco, Tunisia, Syria and Lebanon by France; Cyprus,
Israel, Iraq, Jordan, Egypt and Great Britain; Libya by Italy.[2]

At present the most striking and relevant post-war phenomenon must be found in the recent structural changes of the EEC
countries, which have permitted the emergence of a new kind of
European capitalism. These changes include, in chronological order: the attainment of a high level of concentration and central-
isation of capital, the internationalisation of capital, and a recent
growing tendency of this capital to move out of the centre of
Europe towards its peripheral areas in countries which might
provide higher profit rates.

Parallel to this change in the northern part of Europe, the
countries of South Europe, too, have gone further in their strug-

---

[2] Marios Nikolinakos, *Politische Ökonomie der Gastarbeiter*, Rowohlt Verlag 1973,
p. 142-143.

gle for industrialisation. While the southern part of the Mediterranean seeks to industrialise more rapidly some countries, such as Italy, have slowed down their migratory movements and others, like Greece, have started to import additional manpower from Africa. Thus, certain Southern European countries no longer provide potential manpower resources and this function—as long as conjunctural factors, such as the energy crisis, rationalisation of industries, etc. are not slowing down—has been taken up by peripheral countries, such as Yugoslavia, Turkey, Tunisia, Marocco and even nations south of the Sahara in Africa.

1.3. *Underdevelopment and Migration*

As a result of its growing integration within the European Common Market, Western Europe tends to become more and more—as did the United States and Canada in the first quarter of the twentieth century—a genuine immigration region. The "pull" effects of this economic expansion leads undoubtedly to a considerable impoverishment and depletion of the sending countries. As J. Galtung rightly points out, *asymmetrical interaction* relations between nations grow as a result of a certain type of division of labour, creating *new forms of dependency*.[3] Thus "centre nations" tend to require a higher level of skill and education, knowledge and research, whereas "periphery nations" continue to supply raw materials, markets and surplus labour force.

In the so-called "Southern Europe", a high rate of growth (6-7% per year) is not in itself sufficient to break away from the spiral of disequilibrium and in fact, there is at the same time a minimal increase in employment (0.2-1.0%). This creates endemic unemployment, with the consequence of a growing migratory flux. The strong increase of remittances, secured by the migrant workers, is in reality connected to a subordinated pattern of industrialisation and does not permit to break the spiral of underdevelopment.

In brief, it can be said that on one side, the major "pull" factors have been: an expansive economic growth; an unfavourable demographic situation (declining birth rate); a steady upward mobility of the indigenous worker, supported by additional vocational training, thus leaving undesirable jobs to the alien

---

[3] Johan Galtung, "A Structural Theory of Imperialism", *Journal of Peace Research*, Vol. 8, 1971, p. 81-117.

working population; and the closing up of the East German boundary. On the other side, the major "push" factors in the sending countries are: unemployment, poverty and economic underdevelopment, all of which mean retarded industrialisation.[4]

Thus, the unequal relationship between centre and periphery nations and the ineffective socio-economic structure of the latter, cannot be explained solely in terms of a given national policy. Each of the sending and receiving country, actually represents a small stone in a huge mosaic, covering the new amalgamation of an economic unit: Europe, which again partly also includes a substantial share of the activity of American economic enterprises. This economic interdependence between Europe and the United States on the one hand, and the Mediterranean countries on the other, becomes even more relevant, when the oil reserves supremacy of the United States and its dominant position among the oil producing countries are taken in consideration.[5] This pattern of interdependence became most blatantly evident during the 1973 energy crisis, when due to the rise of oil prices, the majority of the not self-sufficient European labour importing countries such as West Germany, the Netherlands, Switzerland and France abruptly put an end to their foreign labour import policy.

It is in this context that the various phases and particular problems of Turkish external migration will be examined. Nevertheless, like any other country study, there are a number of specific topics, stemming from certain particular historical and social factors, which need further interpretation. The intrusion of a large, unskilled labour force, the growing presence of social groups adhering to the Islamic faith in the midst of a predominantly Christian setting, the lack of migratory traditions, the inability to make better use of social welfare institutions (where they exist) and the impact of their absence in many cases, the rural background of the majority of Turkish workers, the short history of the Turkish trade-union movement are only a few of these particular characteristics which will be dealt at length. There is no doubt that each of these problems can, in the long

---

[4] S. Castles and G. Kosack, *Immigrant Workers and Class Structure in Western Europe*, London 1973, Oxford University Press, p. 67.

[5] Dankward A. Rustow, *Leverage, Oil and the Nex Pax Americana*, Unpublished manuscript 1974, p. 22.

run, only be solved by deep socio-economic structural changes in Turkey and by the creation of a new relation of interdependence between Europe and the rest of the world.

2. *Major General Features of the Turkish Migration*

2.1. *Intensive Demographic Pressure*

Unlike some other Mediterranean countries with a colonial past, such as Spain and Portugal or Italy, with its long history of overseas migratory flux, the beginning of a mass exodus from Turkey can be traced back only to the early 1960's, when the number of Turkish workers in Federal Germany suddenly jumped from 7,000 in October 1961 to 18,500 in July 1962 and culminated in the figure 615,827 in mid-1974.

The basic reason for this extraordinarily rapid increase must be primarily found in the demographic pressures resulting from Turkey's explosive population growth. Turkey, with a population of 36.5 million in 1972 has one of the world's highest birth rates, which reached its highest point—44 per thousand—in 1960 and has shaped the age distribution of the Turkish population.[6] It is quite obvious that such a fast population growth, generating a high percentage of dependents in a country with already widespread disguised and open unemployment, while increasing the labour supply, creates acute problems of job supply and unemployment. The official estimate in 1971 for unemployment has been calculated as 1.6 million, the unofficial one for hidden unemployment has been 1.5-3 million.[7] Even if the present day growth rate was reduced to 2%, the estimated population for the year 2000 would reach 62.7 million. This would still mean a continuous need for labour export or a substantial degree of industrialisation within the country.

---

[6] At present Turkey has an annual population growth of 2.6%. The estimation of Turkey's population for 1987 is 55.2 million and for 2000, 77 million. To this fast increase has to be added the age composition; in 1965 51.7% of Turkey's total population was between 0-18, out of which 30.4% was between 0-9. Baran Tuncer, *The Impact of Population Growth on the Turkish Economy*, Ankara, Hacettepe University Publ. No. 3, p. 56, Table 3.

[7] DPT, *Yeni Strateji ve Kalkınma Planı*, Üçüncü Beş Yıl Plan, 1973-1977, Ankara 1972, p. 79, Table 12; Ekmel Zadil, Die Auswirkung der Arbeitskräftewanderung in der Türkei, in R. Lohrmann und K. Manfrass, *Ausländerbeschäftigung und Internationale Politik*, München 1974, R. Oldenburg Verlag, p. 255-256.

2.2. *Turkey's Dependence on Federal Germany*

Historical links between the Ottoman Empire and the German Reich stretching back to the days of "defensive modernization", when Prussian military advisers exercised a noticeable advisory role in the reorganization of the army, the fact that no belligerent action took place between the two countries until the end of the Second World War, contributed in the creation of a favorable climate of opinion in regard of new forms of collaboration between Turkey and Federal Germany. In addition the relative geographical nearness and a high potential of Western Germany to acquire quasi-monopolistic position in the recruitment of Turkey's excessive labour force.

Some German semi-official institutions have suggested two additional political justifications for the preference of Turkish workers: from the point of view of foreign policy, it has been stressed that in order to strengthen the southern flank of the North Atlantic alliance the foreign labour market should be enlarged to the detriment of the Italians. Also, it has been argued that West Germany's presence would decrease growing anti-American feelings in Turkey. From a social economy point of view, the fact that most Turks are reputed for their highly praised military qualities (discipline, modesty, willingness to adjustment and easy manipulation) seems also to have played a certain role in the allocation of larger contingents for Turks.[8]

2.3. *Planning the Export of Excess Manpower*

Beginning with the First Five Year Plan, governmental agencies, mainly the Turkish Employment Service, have been encouraged to "export" "surplus manpower" by way of bilateral agreements. Thus the major bulk of Turkish migrants, unlike many of their predecessors in the Mediterranean basin, did not embark on this venture on a purely individual basis. True, decisions to emigrate have been made freely, but attempts to secure jobs outside of the national boundaries, almost from the very beginning, were mediated through administrative means and based upon bilateral agreements. Turkey signed its first bilateral agreement with Federal Germany on October 30, 1961; this agreement was followed

---

[8] Klaus Manfrass, *Entstehung, Ursachen und Antriebskräfte der Arbeitskräftewanderung* Institut für Auslandspolitikforschung, Bonn 1973, Manuscript, p. 25.

by a series of treaties with Austria (May 5, 1964), France (April 8, 1966), Sweden (March 10, 1967) and Australia (October 5, 1967).

Turkish governmental agencies have thus sent between 1961-1973 about 790,000 workers to Europe, 80.2% of them were placed on the West German labour market. In 1971, 84.3% of the Turkish workers were gainfully employed in Federal Germany.

The overall distribution of the Turkish labour force outside of Turkey at the beginning of 1974 was as follows:

Table 1

Distribution of the Turkish workers according sex and countries
(13.12.1973)

Country	Women	%	Men	%	Total	%
Federal Germany	135,575	91	480,252	75	615,827	78
France	172	0	33,720	5	33,892	4
Austria	2,622	2	27,905	4	30,527	4
Netherland	2,700	2	27,391	4	30,091	4
Australia	2,710	2	17,619	3	20,329	3
Switzerland	2,710	2	17,000	3	19,710	3
Belgium	220	0	13,809	2	14,029	2
Denmark	210	0	6,040	1	6,250	1
Sweden	1,922	1	3,139	1	5,061	0
Great Britain	131	0	1,880	0	2,011	0
Others	117	0	8,627	1	8,744	1
Total	149,089	100	637,382	100	786,471	100

Source: Turkish Employment Service (I.I.B.K.) *Statistics on Turkish Migrant Worker* Ankara 1974, Publ. No. 111, p. 19.

2.4. *Illegal Migration*

The great attractiveness of employment abroad together with the inadequacies of the home labour market—every year 700,000 people enter the labour market, while only 400,000 are able to find jobs—have led almost one million persons to register for placement in a foreign country by the end of 1973.[9] Since the trend to work abroad produced a very encouraging public

---

[9] In June 1973, 828,168 male and 110,772 female worker, constituting a total of 939,940 workers had registered at the Turkish Employment Service. 290,234 of these applicants were qualified workers. *Milliyet*, June 14, 1973.

opinion, minimum restrictive measures were brought in the form
of administrative limitations. Thus since 1972 the age for official
placement has been reduced from 20-40 to 25-35. Due to the
very high number of applications, the average waiting period for
unqualified male worker has been running in recent months as
high as 6 to 7 years. This situation has of course, largely contributed to an increase in illegal emigration. All European countries
employing foreign workers have a considerably high number of
so-called "tourist workers", who legally leave their home country
as tourists and then take up abroad any employment offered
without a work permit. The situation bears a striking similarity
with the position of the "wet backs" in the United States,
workers of Mexican origin, who, after crossing the Rio Grande
River, take up jobs in the States without the required residence
permits. Most of these "tourist workers" in Federal Germany are
concentrated in large cities such as West Berlin, Cologne, Frankfurt, Stuttgart, Munich, where control is preluded by the very
size of the urban agglomeration and the easily obtained assistance
of fellow countrymen. Illegally migrated workers are deprived of
all legal protection accorded to officially recruited foreign
workers. The trade unions of the host countries strongly oppose
this practice, which "de facto" pushes wages down and allows for
a complete exploitation of a defenseless group. But it is estimated that in Federal Germany alone there are approximately 80
to 100,000 illegal migrant workers. [10]

2.5. *Regional and Urban Concentration*

Like other large national contingents, the Turkish workers
abroad—in Federal Germany, the Netherlands or elsewhere—tend,
for reasons of job opportunities, feelings of belongingness, expectations of assistance from their fellow countrymen, etc.—to concentrate in certain large cities. These major centres of concentration are in chronological order Cologne and Stuttgart, followed
by Munich, many times described as the 68th Turkish province
and in recent years West Berlin. Indeed, the Turkish labour population of West Berlin has shown a dramatic rise since 1967, when
the total number of Turks was stationed around 4,553. Within
one year—1972 to 1973—the Turkish population registered an

---

[10]   Oğuz Gökmen, *Federal Almanya ve Türk İşçileri*, Ankara 1972, p. 202-204.

increase of 22.2% (12,100) and reached the figure of 66,521. An equally interesting development is the high number of female workers. There were in January 1973 37,760 male, 28,761 female, thus a total of 66,521 Turks in West Berlin, with an outspoken concentration in the districts of Kreuzberg and Wedding. [11]

The concentration of Turkish workers in West Berlin is so high that an average of 15 Turkish babies are born and two Turks get married each day.

3. Major Characteristics of Turkish Migrant Workers

3.1. Sex and Age Distribution

At the beginning of the heavy migration toward Europe, the Turkish migrant population was almost entirely composed of men (in 1960: 2,495 men, 173 women; in 1961: 5,193 men, 430 women). Its structure has substantially changed in the last years. Especially from 1967 on, the ratio of women has grown steadily from an initial 8% and reached 24.4% of all Turkish workers in 1973. [12] In 1973 alone, out of a total of 135,820 recruited Turkish workers roughly one fifth (18,654) were women. [13] This change can be primarily explained as a result of the fact that certain industrial activities such as textile, electronics, food processing attract predominantly women workers, whose wage scale is considerably lower than that of men. [14] This discrimination became especially obnoxious during the relatively short 1966/67 recession, when most of those who were fired by industrial enterprises employing Turks were men. [15] Since Ger-

---

[11] In addition to an almost equally balanced male and female population West Berlin also indicates a very high proportion of dependents: 27.5% of the school age population 31.3% of the 0-6 age group carries Turkish citizenship. *Berliner Statistik*, 1973, Heft 5, p. 220.

[12] Bundesanstalt für Arbeit, *Ausländischer Arbeitnehmer 1972/73*, p. 28.

[13] Turkish Employment Service, *Work and Manpower Bulletin*, July 1974, No. 163, Table 21.

[14] In Autumn 1968 the percentage of male workers receiving less then 3 DM per hour was nil, 15% received 3-4 DM, 56% 4-5 DM, 20% 5-6 DM. The distribution among female workers was showing a quite different pattern. 14% were receiving less then 3 DM, 53% were receiving 3-4 DM, 15% 4-5 DM and only 2%, 5-6 DM. Bundesanstalt für Arbeit, *Ausländische Arbeitnehmer*, p. 80.

[15] Nermin Abadan-Unat, La Récession de 1966/67 en Allemagne Fédérale et ses repercussions sur les ouvriers turcs, *The Turkish Yearbook of International Relations, 1971*, p. 45.

man immigration laws allow for family reunion only after a working period of two years, and the availability of suitable housing, a great number of men, figuring on the waiting list of the Turkish Employment Agency, have been encouraging their actually much more traditionally oriented and less independent-minded spouses or even daughters to take up work abroad, in order to secure the highly coveted legal permit of residence abroad which automatically makes them also available for employment.

In regard to age distribution, both the limitations imposed by the Turkish government, which tries to prevent any further increase of potential candidates on the waiting lists and the nature of the demands of German employers, whose specifications have to be taken into account by the placement agency of Federal German, explain why the great majority of Turkish workers constitutes an active manpower group whose members are in the most productive years, of their life. The age distribution of the men working in Federal Germany was in 1972 the following: 9% under 25, 21% between 25-30, 33% between 30-35, 22% between 35-40 and only 10% over 40 years old. [16]

Although a great number of Turkish workers are married, many are living single. In 1972, 82% of Turkish workers were married, but only 46% were living with their wives in Federal Germany. Women are in diametrically opposed situation: in the same year only 22% of them were married; among those who were married, 88% were accompanied by their husbands, who made up 98% of gainfully employed workers. These figures show that Turkish couples in Germany tend to be jointly employed. [17]

As far as the size of Turkish workers children's population goes, it is extremely difficult to give exact figures, because the German Aliens Act (Ausländergesetz) does not require a residence permit for persons under the age of 16. In order to make a reliable assessment, one can attempt to examine the number of recipients of children's allowance. However, it should be kept in mind that before the adoption of the new tax law, entering into force on January 1, 1975, the first child was not entitled to any allowance. This has been completely changed. [18] In 1973,

[16] Bundesanstalt für Arbeit, *Repräsentativ-Untersuchung 1972*, p. 16.
[17] Bundesanstalt für Arbeit, *Repräsentativ-Untersuchung*, 1972, p. 19, 20.
[18] Bundesanstalt für Arbeit, *Ausländische Arbeitnehmer, 1972/1973*, p. 36-37.

215,000 Turkish workers were entitled to receive an allowance for their second and consecutive children. The total number of these children were 560,640; 515,161 of these children were living at that date in Turkey. [19] The size of the school age population (6-16) of Turkish children was estimated for Federal Germany about 110,000, for other European countries as 115,000. [20] The dual nature of children allowances, as determined by the new tax law, which requires from recipients to live with their offspring on Federal German soil or accept a differently scaled indemnity allowance, will show in the future whether Turkish parents want to bring their children to their working place or prefer to leave them as before with relatives in Turkey.

3.2. Qualification and Social Mobility of Turkish Workers

One of the major reasons for Federal Germany's preference for Turkish workers has been, until the recent interruption of recruitment, the fact that Turkey in spite of some restrictive administrative measures, such as a ban on the recruitment of miners from the province of Zonguldak, has continued until 1973 to export the highest percentage of skilled workers abroad. While other Mediterranean countries were much more reluctant to give up their skilled labour force, Turkey has exported in 1968— 26.4%, in 1969—28.2%, in 1970—34% and in 1971—46.3% of its qualified manpower. [21]

This policy—which has been sharply criticized in recent years by the Turkish Union of Chambers of Commerce, the Ministry of Industry, the State Planning Organization among others—has been continued for obvious reasons of short-term payoffs such as the assurance of a continuous flow of remittances.

As to social mobility, external migration has undoubtedly provided both upward and downward mobility, thus provoking deep-seated social changes in the socio-economic structure and stratification pattern of Turkey itself. Upward mobility is most discernable in the form of intragenerational mobility and is producing sharp swings from agrarian occupations toward jobs in the industrial sector. In spite of the relatively high percentage of

---

[19] Bundesanstalt für Arbeit, *Ausländische Arbeitnehmer, 1972/1973*, p. 36.

[20] Turkish Ministry of Education, *Yurt dışında çalışan Türk İşçilerinin (0-16) çocuklarının eğitimi sorunları*, Yayın No. 74-20, p. 6.

[21] Bundesanstalt für Arbeit, *Ausländische Arbeitnehmer 1971*, p. 35.

qualified Turkish labour force in Federal Germany, downward
mobility is most strikingly represented by a shift from white
collar to blue collar jobs, such as in the case of teachers and civil
servants taking up industrial employment. The fact that as many
as 9,000 former primary school teachers are mostly engaged in
industrial jobs, indicates the strong attraction of high wages.

Downward mobility, a dominant characteristics of agrarian
societies, while producing partial status consciousness, may also
produce intense job dissatisfaction. But even in the case of upward mobility, a rather important phenomenon presents itself:
status inconsistency, which will increasingly affect Turkey's stratification pattern. [22]

In summary, the major characteristics of the Turkish external
labour population are the following: it is predominantly male
(mostly due to the deliberate separation of family members);
young, with an average 5-year primary school education; rather
isolated, not integrated into German society, living in ghetto-like
dwelling units (Heims-dormitories); showing great solidarity between countrymen, with little interest in language learning and
vocational training; a faster social adjustment degree among female workers; and a very strong motivation for money-earning
and saving in both sexes.

4. *Phases of Turkish Migration*

Although migration, stretching from brain drain to brawn
drain, has become in present day Turkey a commonly accepted
alternative for employment, generally speaking, this tendency has
a very brief history. Actually it can be argued that Turkey after
1960, experimented for the first time in its history large scale
migration. The fact, that at the end of 1973, about 1.5 million
Turks were gainfully employed in about thirty countries shows
the rapidity with which this new type of behaviour has been
adopted. This becomes even more significant if one considers
that at the beginning, migration was rather considered as a form
of apprenticeship, a kind of training in service through a system
of rotation. Only later did the idea of prolonging the duration of

---

[22] Nermin Abadan-Unat, Turkish External Migration and Social Mobility in P. Benedict, E. Tümertekin, F. Mansur, Turkey, *Geographic and Social Perspectives*,
E.J. Brill, Leiden 1974, p. 397.

work abroad win a general approval. Under these conditions one can distinguish between three major phases of the Turkish external migration, beginning from 1960 on.

4.1. *Experimental, Initial Phase of the Late 1950's and Early 1960's (1956-1962)*

This phase is characterised by the attempt of semi-official institutions trying to organise an exchange of trainees (Praktikanten), while in reality this already constituted at the time a temporary form of industrial manpower recruitment. The Institute of World Economy of the University of Kiel, applied in 1956 for the first time to the Turkish Ministry of Foreign Affairs, requesting an arrangement for the exchange of vocationally trained volunteers for the purpose of facilitating German capital investment in Turkey. [23]

The first agreement following this request was signed by the Ministry of Labour of Schleswig-Holstein and led to the arrival of 12 craftmen on April 1, 1957 in Kiel. The event was advertised under the slogan "The middle class helps the middle class". The entire programme was sponsored by the Chamber of Artisans of Hamburg. Thus, until the legitimate intervention of the Germany Federal Agency of Employment in Nurnberg, the "Research Institute of Turkish-German Economic Relations", founded by Dr. Salahattin Sözeri, carried on a constant labour recruitment activity, charging DM 15,-- per worker for each placement. Only after the German and Turkish authorities made it clear, that recruitment and placement activities would have to remain definitely under governmental control,—in other words that there was a monopoly over the recruitment of available labour, to be exercised only by public authorities—, did the activity of the so-called private "Translation Bureaus" in Turkey and similar organizations in Federal Germany begin to disappear.

Among those skilled workers from Turkey who were the first to be asked to participate in this limited industrial apprenticeship, a rather high percentage quickly experienced a bitter disappointment, when they found out that their vocational training in Turkey, which was primarily based upon theoretical teaching and little practical work, was not acknowledged in Germany, that

---

[23] Nermin Abadan, *Batı Almanya'daki Türk İşçileri ve Sorunları*, Ankara 1964, DPT, p. 35.

they were not put on an equal footing with their German counterparts and that they were primarily employed as semi-skilled
workers in fields no more attractive to the German labour market. Nevertheless, these early comers remained in Federal Germany and established themselves primarily in the Northern part
of the country, in ports such as Hamburg, Bremen and Kiel,
where they worked predominantly in the dockyards. Unlike their
successors, who were recruited on the basis of a bilateral agreement with restrictive conditions, they were able to settle down
with their families and this largely accounts for the high degree
of income and status satisfaction they expressed later. [24]

4.2. *The Second Phase: Explosive Growth, Governmental Mediation, Adjustment to Industry and Social Life (1963-1967)*

This second phase is marked by an important change in the
size and structure of Turkey's migratory wave. While external
migration remained at the beginning limited to individual or
mostly group initiative, its size was small and it was sporadic and
relatively unknown. This situation changed drastically with the
signing of a bilateral agreement with Federal Germany in 1962.
This coincides on one side with the after-effect of the building of
the Berlin Wall, which brought to an end the flow of additional
labour force from the Democratic German Republic, and on the
other side, the initiation of the First Five Year Development Plan
(1962-1967) in Turkey. This plan contains, together with a significant section about the "export of excessive manpower", projections about the population growth for the coming decades and
strong recommendations to accelerate Turkey's industrialisation.
The constantly growing demands of West Germany's employers
for additional labour force—preferably a skilled one—in order to
meet the conjunctural growth of Germany's economy, lead very
rapidly to an extraordinary rapid growth both of West Germany's
foreign labour population and of Turkey's external migration. In
1960: 2,700 workers left Turkey; in 1963, they were 27,500. In
1960: 258,466 foreign workers were employed in Federal Ger-

---

[24] Nermin Abadan, *Batı Almanya'daki Türk İşçileri ve Sorunları*, Ankara 1964,
DPT, p. 121 Table 108.

many; in 1963: 828,743 of the gainfully employed workers in Federal Germany were alien. [25]

In these early years of mass migration, measures were taken to extend a comprehensive, effective social work organisation, which was provided mostly through the auspices of the *"Arbeiterwohlfahrt"*, an auxiliary branch of the German Social Democrat party. The special organisation which was set up for the exclusive use of the Turkish workers was called "Türkdanış".

In order to avoid the establishment of a permanent black market, the workers' earnings, were converted into Turkish money according to a special foreign currency rate. During this period, semi-official German funds assisted Turkish workers in setting up their own cultural associations and helped them to obtain centres of communication and social activities. In 1963 the number of these Turkish associations was about 20 and meanwhile this activity had reached quite remarkable dimensions. In 1973 there were a total of 112 Turkish workers' associations in Federal Germany alone. [26]

This phase also witnessed the beginning of a special broadcasting programme in Turkish, which soon was functioning daily. Finally, special staffing policies for Turkish consulates and the establishment of new consulates helped to facilitate contact between Turkish and German authorities about the problems of Turkish workers.

Although already during this period we were able to find the seeds of ghetto-like communities (cases of relative isolation and the Turks' difficulty to fraternize with Germans), these problems were not yet important to German public opinion. The question of family reunion was at this point relatively not very significant, nor were schooling problems recognized as a major subject of long-term policies. All of these developments came to an abrupt end with the emergence and disappearance of the relatively brief economic recession of 1966/67, which effected about 70,000

---

[25] Bundesanstalt für Arbeitsvermittlung, *Erfahrungsbericht 1961*, p. 3; *Erfahrungsbericht 1964*, p. 5.

[26] Outside of FRG there are 26 Turkish workers association in Switzerland, 3 in Bern, 23 in Zürich; in Austria there are 7 in Vienna, again 7 in Bruxelles, Belgium, 4 in Copenhagen, Denmark. The total number of Turkish workers associations in Europe is 156. Turkish Employment Service, *Sayılarla Yurtdışındaki İşçilerimiz ve Sorunlarına ait İstatistikler* (Statistics on Turkish Migrant Workers) Ankara 1974, Publ. No. 111, p. 59.

Turkish workers and brought the discussion about foreign labour under critical appraisal.

In spite of their discharge, the great majority of Turkish workers did not return home and most of them tried to shift to other sectors or to find employment in neighbouring European countries, such as the Netherlands, Belgium, Denmark. [27] In the spring of 1967 almost all of the discharged Turkish workers were again back to work. This date marks also the beginning of a mass influx of Turkish workers into FRG as well as more public articulation of clashing group interests. The question whether foreign labour represents a reserve labour army or is a basic element of any given highly industrialised society began to be largely discussed.

4.3. *The Third Phase: Consolidation, Redefinition of the Goals in the Employment of Foreign Workers, Policy of Integration (1968-1973)*

This phase is marked by the fast growth of Turkish workers employed abroad, in 1973 alone 103,793 Turks were placed in the FRG, the growth of the female percentage within the Turkish worker population (in 1973, 24,267 Turkish women workers were sent abroad), the fast increase of remittances (over one billion dollars in 1973) which greatly helps Turkey's balance of payments. It is also characterized by newly emerging family patterns with far reaching consequences, the crystallisation of the grave issue of vocational training for young adults, active participation in worker's strike, and the urgent schooling problems for the workers' children. Finally during this phase, the question of political participation in Turkish elections through absentee ballot, as proposed by the People's Republican Party, the activity of Turkish workers in German trade unions, the verbalisation of their demands at home and abroad, all become acute.

On the German side, important new points of view appeared and were partly put into action. The consensual opinion shared until the middle of the 60's by government, employers and trade unions in the FRG, according to which the employment of a foreign labour force represents a temporary solution

---

[27] Nermin Abadan-Unat, La Récession de 1966/67 en Allemagne Fédérale et ses répercussions sur les ouvriers turcs, *The Turkish Yearbook of International Relations, 1971*, p. 59.

against labour shortage, began to dissolve after the recovery from the recession of 1966/67. The German Employer's Association, BDA, on the one side, sharing the concern of communal organizations that their infrastructure (hospitals, social security system, schools, etc,) is overburdened, began to support the principle of "rotation", according to which any recruitment would only be for a limited period. [28] Continuing labour shortages could be remedied by replacement of former workers. The major worker's organisation, DGB, on the other side, anxious not to lower wage levels by permitting to range foreign labour in low paid job categories and desirous to oppose the endeavour of some employers to encourage further illegal immigration, started to attack after 1968, the discriminatory Aliens Act and to promote the principle of "full integration" of foreign workers into German society. [29]

This discussion led to an important modification of FRG official labour policy. Following a widely diffused working paper, drafted by the *Arbeiterwohlfahrt* organisation, aiming to achieve a far reaching reform in the employment of foreign labour, [30] the Federal Minister of Labour and Social Affairs, made public the government decisions of June 6, 1973. Accordingly to these decisions, the ultimate goal in the employment of foreign labour is to achieve a harmony between the needs for continuity in production and a full integration of foreign manpower in society. Thus, (1) the recruitment procedure for each new foreign worker will depend upon the availability of adequate and decent housing facilities, to be provided by the employer in conformity to the standards established in April 1974; (2) the permission for new comers to settle in already heavily concentrated regions depends on the absortive capacity of the existing social infrastructure; (3) employers will have to pay a considerably higher sum for recruitment services, this said sum being meant to be used for vocational and language education; (4) any obligatory or coercive measures tending to terminate abruptly prevailing employment ar-

---

[28] Rolf Weber, Rotationsprinzip bei der Beschäftigung von Ausländern, *Auslandskurier* Heft 5, Okt. 1970, p. 10.

[29] Max Diamant, Bemerkungen zur sozialen und rechtlichen lage der ausländischen Arbeitnehmer, *Studentische Politik*, 1/1970, p. 48.

[30] Zur Reform der Ausländerpolitik, *Theorie und Praxis der Sozialen Arbeit*, Sondernummer Z 21441 F, April 1973.

rangements of foreign labour, are to be rejected on "social and humanistic" grounds. [31]

It can be said that the third phase represents both for Turkey and the major European host countries the achievement of gaining "consciousness" in regard of the mannifold problems of foreign workers. This explains also why a much more extensive public interest was attracted during these recent years. This trend is also evidenced by the high number of articles which were published in the European and Turkish press, as well as the efforts of the audio-visual mass media to make the large public familiar with the magnitude of labour shortage, imported foreign labour, alienation, xenophobia, etc. Finally the impact of this process has reached considerable depth also in the domain of the arts, external migration becoming a recurrent theme in Turkish literature and drama.

The major issues discussed during this period are the following ones:

1. The inflated size of waiting lists—an average of about one million potential migrant workers—which indirectly encourages illegal forms of behaviour.

2. The debilitating and impoverishing impact of the constant outflow of highly skilled and skilled manpower from Turkey, its negative effect on the development of Turkey's industries, with special reference to its associate membership in the Common Market.

3. The growing concern about the emergence of "bilingual illiterates" the usage of Turkish teachers, sent by Ankara or employed by Turkish authorities versus Turkish teachers recruited among workers in Germany and employed by German authorities, the problems of equivalence of diplomas.

4. The threat to future employment abroad due to the acceptance of the "rotation" principle in Bavaria and Schleswig-Holstein against the "integration" principle, favoured and endorsed officially by the ruling party, SPD.

5. The efforts displayed by Turkey's major political parties to secure for Turkish workers employed abroad the right of voting by proxy at general elections. The special provisions in the German Aliens Act which prevents Turkish workers from

---

[31] Walter Arendt, Aktionsprogramm für Ausländerbeschäftigung, *BULLETIN*, Presse und Informationsamt, No. 70/S. 689, Bonn, June 8, 1973, p. 693.

taking a more active role in local politics. Since they can neither participate in the politics of their home country, the question of cultivated apolitization of the Turkish workers abroad and its repercussions have been during the recent years a source of debate and grievance. [32]

6. The struggle to prevent a substantial brain drain from the mother country represents and additional serious problem. Turkey, like Yugoslavia, Korea and Taiwan, suffers from a severe emigration of highly skilled personnel to the United States and Europe. This is especially true for scientists, physicians and engineers. Their choice means that the total expenditure of a free higher education heavily weighs on the shoulders of the Anatolian peasant, while the gain accrues to the individual and to the foreign employer and country. This trend also causes severe regional disequilibria. [33]

These problems have in recent years preoccupied almost daily Turkey's public opinion and they have also contributed to an enrichment of the language. The term "Almanya beyleri"—the lords of Germany—reflects the dual and controversial status of this new stratum in Turkish society. It indicates also its perennial dilemma: to be envied by their countrymen, while being looked down and discriminated in the host country.

As Turkey, together with all other Mediterranean countries, has entered a new phase in its external migration process which carries the imprint of the energy crisis and its inevitable consequence—limitation of external migration—it looks as if the dichotomy between the ins and the outs will lead to more acute, more intense social tensions and struggles.

5. Contributions and Shortcomings of the Turkish Migration

5.1. Growth of Population and Manpower

It has been often claimed that external migration contributes to alleviate the excessive population pressure in the large cities

---

[32] Ayşe Kudat, *International Migration to Europe and its Political and Social Effects on the Future Turkish Society*, Mimeographed Paper, presented at the Hacettepe Conference, Ankara, June 1974, p. 17.

[33] Peter Goswyn Frank, "Brain Drain from Turkey", in The Committee on the International Migration of Talent, *The International Migration of High-Level Manpower*, Praeger, New York 1970, p. 299-369.

and to diminish employment in urban areas. This thesis can not be verified since Turkey's urbanisation rate is rising constantly [34] and unemployment is higher in large cities than in the countryside. [35] In this context, the example of Greece seems, however, to be relevant to Turkey. As A. Pepelasis has rightly pointed out, "it is not the excessive population which is permitted to migrate; on the contrary, the Western industries are looking for the best qualified and most suitable elements, exactly those who are most needed by the home industry". [36] This is an observation repeated by other Greek and Turkish authors. According E. Vlachos "the lack of abundant and cheap labour hinders investment in industry which in turn contributes to a deteriorating economy". [37] An almost identical observation is made by A. Aker, who states that "Turkish external migration has followed the trend of internal migration: qualified manpower migrates from impoverished regions to more developed and richer ones. In terms of external migration it leads to regional disequilibrium". [38] It might be significant to state here that the Chambers of Commerce of the new burgeoning industrial centres such as İzmir and Eskişehir, have dealt in depth with the problem and have informed and repeatedly warned Turkish public opinion. [39] This argument has been validated by the most recent survey carried out by the DGB in 1973, which reveals that 46% of the Turkish workers were employed in Turkey as factory worker, 32% were active as artisans and only 21% came from the agrarian sector.

---

[34] The rate of urbanization in metropolitan areas was between 1940-50, 5.2%; in 1950-60, 9% and in 1960-70 around 11%. Ruşen Keleş, *Socio-Economic Aspects of Urbanization in Turkey*, Mimeographed Paper presented at the University of Chicago Seminar, November 3-5, 1973, p. 9.

[35] The Third Five Year Plan states that in urban areas 750,000 persons are unemployed or underemployed. In 1987 it is estimated that this figure will rise up to 2 million. *Yeni Strateji ve Kalkınma Planı*, Üçüncü Beş Yıl Plan, 1973-1977, Ankara 1972, p. 146-147.

[36] A. Pepelassis, "Les Problèmes de la Main d'Oeuvre de la Grèce dans le Cadre du Marché Commun", in J. Cuisenier (Ed.) *Problèmes du développement économiques dans les pays méditerranéens*, Paris, Mouton, 1963, p. 322.

[37] Evan Vlachos, "Worker Migration to Western Europe: The Ramifications of Population Outflow for the Demographic Future of Greece", *Comparative Interdisciplinary Studies Section*, Working Paper No. 22, July 1974, University of Pittsburgh, p. 38.

[38] Ahmet Aker, *İşçi Göçü*, Istanbul 1972, Sander Yayınları, p. 115.

[39] Türkiye Odalar Birliği Ekonomik Raporu, *Cumhuriyet*, May 26, 1972.

5.2. *Learning New Skills and Qualifications*

Innumerable responsible politicians, economists, social workers have repeatedly boasted that even a limited stay abroad in a highly industrialized society contributes to the acquisition of technical and vocational skills. However, almost all empirical research—whether dealing with Turkish, Algerian or Spanish workers—shows a quite different pattern. Due to their extreme mobility, resulting in major changes of social stratification, almost all dirty, physical exhausting, dusty, noisy, low prestige, repetitive jobs in highly industrialized countries are relegated to foreign workers. This tendency has been more than demonstrated by the experience of Turkish workers, who are predominantly concentrated in the fields of iron and metal industry (22.9%), manufacturing (21%) and construction (18.1%). Turkish workers employed in services amount to 11.7%. [40]

Comparative aggregate data further bolsters this view. Metal production and engineering heavily rely on all male immigrant groups and most particularly on Yugoslavs, Greeks, Spaniards and Turks. Yugoslavs are most frequently employed in building, where there are also high ratios of Italians and Turks. No doubt this concentration also leads substantially to an overwhelming concentration in unattractive, monotonous, repetitive, partly dirty and exhausing jobs which offer little if any opportunity to acquire new skills.

Entire production lines solely operated by Turks or street building carried out by Turkish workers' teams are not rare and it is obvious that semi-automatic or purely manual labour will not offer any further educational opportunity. In addition, one should not forget that this type of employment, which requires heavy physical efforts weakens the individual's will and motivation, thus reducing his ability to benefit from additional educational opportunities after the completion of a regular work day. Furthermore, the usage of such educational opportunities becomes meaningful only if the social structure of the sending country undergoes deep changes, allowing for faster industrialization. This type of thinking among the workers is confirmed by various studies. R. E. Krane's major conclusion is that "socioeconomic mobility engendered in Turkish society by cyclical

---

[40] Bundesanstalt für Arbeit, *Ausländische Arbeitnehmer 1971*, p. 10.

international migration manifests itself primarily in terms of moderately elevated earning power and improved living standards. Occupational mobility in and of itself would appear marginal for in most instances the educational opportunities essential to substantially augmented skills are not present in the migration cycle". [41] Thus it is by no means certain that daily industrial work actually contributes to the learning process of workers.

Already in 1963, the findings of empirical research proved that the nature of work performed by foreign workers is of extreme simplicity. The Abadan survey [42] indicated that 40.3% of the Turkish workers in FRG learned their work within 1 to 24 hours, 10% in one to three days, 13.6% within one week, 20.2% within two to four weeks and only 9% within six months or more. The same research also indicated that in 1963, 40.8% of Turkish workers did not use a single tool (not even a shovel), another 45.3% did not operate any machine. In other words, the work carried out was predominantly purely manual, requiring mostly three qualities: physical endurance (47%), sharp eyesight (13%), a quick grasp (8%). [43]

The fact that Turkish workers, whose conditions are similar to that of all other foreign workers coming from the Mediterranean basin, are primarily interested in a very speedy accumulation of savings, but not in the acquisition of industrial skills has been extensively documented by similar comparative empirical research such as the one conducted by R. Reitschel and his colleagues in Cologne. [44] as well as the study of U. Mehrländer. [45]

Thus it seems to be the rule that migration, instead of promoting new interest for additional learning, pushes people rather to a mentality of accelerated saving. This prevailing attitude explains also the ambigous trend in Turkish society: external migration appeals to a large section of the active manpower population

---

[41] R. E. Krane, Effects of Cyclical International Migration upon Socio-Economic Mobility, *International Migration Review*, Vol. 7, No. 4, Winter 1973, p. 436.

[42] Nermin Abadan, *Batı Almanya'daki Türk İşçileri ve Sorunları*, Ankara 1964, DPT, p. 116, Table 99.

[43] Nermin Abadan, Studie über die Lage und die Probleme der türkischen Gastarbeiter in der BDR, in *Arbeitsplatz Europa*, Europa Union Verlag, Köln 1966 Europäische Schriften des Bildungswerks Europäische Politik, Heft 11, p. 111.

[44] R. Reitschel et al., *Die Integration der ausländischen Arbeitnehmer in Köln*, Tabellenband, Köln 1968, p. 19.

[45] Ursula Mehrlander, *Soziale Aspekte der Ausländerbeschäftigung*, Bonn 1974, Verlag Neue Gesellschaft.

because it opens new employment opportunities. However, migration also lures employed and qualified workers who look for better wages and/or better job opportunities. This tendency is best expressed in G. Lenski's concept of "status inconsistency", which indicates, among other factors, that a shift from a white collar to a blue collar occupation occurs under such circumstances much more frequently. While the Turkish workers' upward mobility is most discernable in the form of intragenerational mobility and sharp swings from agrarian occupations toward jobs in the industrial process, downward mobility has been mostly observed among teachers, clerical workers and artisans, who opted for blue collar jobs. Downward mobility, a dominant trait of agrarian societies, while producing partial consciousness of status, may also produce intense job dissatisfaction. This is remarkably true in the case of Turkish workers. But even in the case of upward mobility a rather important phenomenon presents itself: status inconsistency. The great discrepancies between the social status of migrant workers abroad and at home, together with slowly evolving socio-economic structures, make the evolution of choices and decisions related to future projects and forms of investment rather difficult, unpredictable and vague. [46]

Authors dealing with the European situation as a whole and conducting country studies such as Zolotas (1966), Dietzel (1971), Nikolinakos (1973) have all confirmed and provided ample empirical evidence of this phenomenon.

To sum up, it is exaggerated to say that one of the indirect results of migration is the "training of untapped industrial skilled manpower". Such a contention seems to be much more wishful thinking and much more a convenient social and political myth than a quantitativly measurable assertion.

5.3. Remittances of Turkish Workers

The existing literature on international labour migration, which is widely discussed in this volume, attempts to evaluate from various points of view the economic impact of large-scale human migratory movements. It is generally stated that remittances have two kinds of effects; firstly, an internal effect in terms of potential purchasing power of dependents and return-

---

[46] Nermin Abadan-Unat, La migration turque et la mobilité sociale, *Studi Emigrazione* June 1973, Year X, No. 30, p. 252.

ees. Secondly and indirectly, an external effect in terms of hard foreign currency at the disposal of governments or central banks. Indeed, during the last years, Turkey has been able to bridge its payments deficit through constantly and steadily rising workers remittances.

Table 2

Transfer of Remittances of Turkish Workers in Federal Germany
(in Million Dollars)

1964	1965	1966	1967	1968	1970	1971	1972	1973
45	70	115	73	107	273	471	740	1.100

Source: Bundesanstalt für Arbeit *Ausländische Arbeitnehmer 1969*, p. 5; 1970, p. 4; 1972, p. 6; 1973, p. 9.

However, the crucial question is not, as W.R. Böhning states is correctly that remittances are used under everybody's praise to cover payments deficits, but how they are used. [47]

In the first instance remittances constitute an importation of demand. At the beginning, they are used to cover immediate personal family needs, later they go primarily to the improvement of dwellings. This process leads to the following undesirable consequences: a) Inflationary pressure, b) Increased imports, c) Increased skill needs, d) Disproportionate infrastructural outlays.

This generalized trend applies, of course, to Turkey, too. As it is pointed out by R. Lohrmann and K. Manfraas, the so-called "boomerang effect" of highly industrialised countries induces a re-export of these remittances to the host country in the form of importation of consumer goods, machinery, etc. [48] The foreign trade balance between Turkey and Federal Germany exemplifies this trend:

---

[47] W. R. Böhning, *Making Emigration a More Positive Factor in the Development of Mediterranean Countries*, ILO-WEP, March 1974, 2-26-02, p. 29.

[48] Karl Kaiser, Transnational Politics: Towards a Theory of Multinational Politics *International Organisations*, Year 25, No. 4, 1971, p. 8213.

Table 3

Foreign Trade of Federal Germany with Turkey, 1961-1963
(in Mil. DM)

	1961	1972	1961-1973 (in %)
Export	376	1,035	+ 175,3
Import	311	594	+ 91,0
Difference	+ 65	+ 441	

Source: For 1961, *Statistisches Jahrbuch 1962*, p. 328; for 1972, *Statistisches Jahrbuch 1973*, p. 316.

5.4. *Private and Publicly Supported Investment Patterns: Acquisition of Real Estate, Village Development Cooperatives, Worker's Enterprises*

– The dominant investment form of Turkish migrant workers—as discussed in greater length by Ruşen Y. Keleş and other authors— remains to the present day the acquisition of houses, condominium, land, as well as the setting up of small independent business. This trend maintains its attractiveness and continuity through the years.[49] However, the saturation of certain economic activities such as the operation of taxicabs, while not reducing the longing for an independent economic activity, increasingly motivates the workers to set up conventional and popular small enterprises such as barber shops, beauty parlours, restaurant, coffee houses, etc. Since all these investment forms have a very reduced capacity to create new employment opportunities, except the indirect impact which is derived by an intensified construction boom, the Turkish government and its major planning body, the State Planning Organisation (DPT), attempted to channel the high degree of willingness to migrate into some new administrative and economic alternatives. These alternatives were conceived with the idea to prevent the continuous blowing up of the informal sector[50]—which contrary to the conclusions of the

---

[49] N. Uphoff and W. W. Ilchmann, "Beyond the Economics of Labour Intensive Development: Politics and Administration", *Public Policy*, Vol. XXII, Spring 1974, No. 2 p. 193.

[50] Informal activities are characterized by: a) ease of entry, b) reliance on indigenous resources, c) family ownership of enterprises, d) small scale of operation, e)

UN expert team working in Kenya—does not seem to offer any real beneficial solutions for the industrialisation of the country.

Village Development Cooperatives

One of the imaginative formulas to decrease the disproportional size of waiting lists for employment abroad was the creation of "village development cooperatives". The idea was launched by the first incumbent of the Ministry of Rural Affairs toward the end of 1963 and represented both a new form of economic activity as well as a criterion for the exemption of figuring on the normal waiting list,[51] which had reached in 1973 a total of 466,108 candidates, out of which 110,000 were registered in Istanbul.

At the beginning the goals and work programmes of these coops were left to the imagination, initiative and discretion of the rather uninformed villagers and no administrative guidance whatsoever was furnished. Between 1963-1966, the only requirement for an official recognition of such a cooperative which them became the basis for privileged recruitment, was a membership pledge for a financial contribution of 8,000 TL, out of which only 2,000 TL actually was demanded as a down payment.

During this first period these coops were almost uniquely used as administrative "pretext" organisations for the obtainment of jobs outside of the country. The first obligatory installment was looked upon by the adhering members rather as an administrative bribe—an understanding which helps to explain the reluctance of their members in regard to further payments once abroad. Following a critical appraisal of the DPT in 1965, the fast proliferation of these so-called "German" or "Nylon" cooperatives was

---

labour-intensive and adapted technology f) skills acquired outside the formal school system and g) unregulated and competitive markets. Informal-sector activities are largely ignored, rarely supported, often regulated and sometimes actively discouraged by the Government. ILO, *Employment, Incomes and Equality*, A Strategy for increasing productive employment in Kenya, Geneva, 1972 p. 6.

[51] Aside of becoming member of rural cooperatives in order to benefit from the exemption of waiting ones turn on the official list, there is a second category, which served also to avoid excessive long waiting periods. Inhabitants of areas subject to natural disasters such as earthquake, flood, drought could also apply on an exceptional basis. So far 22,209 applicants of this category were sent abroad, another 25,390 are still registered on this preferential, special waiting list. Oğuz Gökmen, "Die türkischen Gastarbeiter in Europe", Colloque Européen sur la Migration, Louvain-La-Neuve, January 31-February 2-1974 Mimeographed paper, p. 6.

stopped by freezing their number early in 1966 at 298. However, since this setup enables political forces to enter into a bargaining dialogue with the administration, the ban was lifted in 1968 and the establishment of such cooperatives was again encouraged. During this second phase the requirements became more speci-fied. The financial participation was first raised to 12,000 TL, later to 20,000 TL and most recently to 32,000 TL. In addition, the Ministry of Rural Affairs compelled each of these coops to present a detailed feasibility project, which has to be approved by the interministerial committee dealing with external migration matters.

Since the concept of "village development cooperatives" was less developed in the mind of their members whose major motiva-tion has rather been to seek ways and means for a speedier proce-dure of migration, a new kind of intermediary institution began to prosper. The required feasibility projects were mostly carried out by private "consulting firms" such as *Tümas, Opa, Tümtaş*, usually established by former civil servants. Thus the obtainment of a job abroad on the basis of a recognized membership in a village development cooperative actually turned out to be a rath-er expensive way to secure a job abroad. Additional problems of these cooperatives are related to the difficulty to obtain the com-pletion of the pledged financial contribution, the pressure which comes from those members of the cooperative who are not re-cruited abroad, and the control of these cooperatives. At present some 10,000 cooperatives have been registered in almost every Turkish province, but only 740 of these cooperatives are in pos-session of ratified projects. The table below is indicating the actual size of these coops, the number of their members and those members employed abroad.

Table 4

Number of Village Coops which were Given Priority to Jobs in Foreign Countries by Years and by Membership (1965-1974)

Years	Number of coops	Total number of members	Number of members sent to foreign countries
1965-1973	779	32,606	21,361
1974 (Jan.-July)	181	5,884	1,162

Source: Employment Service, *Work and Manpower Bulletin*, Ankara 1974, Table 25.

This table shows that administrative guidance, technical expertise and individual financial contribution have helped to find
industrial jobs abroad for almost two thirds of the acknowledged
coop members. Thus the function of becoming a basis for privileged recruitment seems to overshadow the basic function of
cooperatives.

The experiences of the past years indicates that the greatest
change for a successful operation of such village development
cooperatives lies in the direction of some kind of "agro-industrial" type of institution, requiring a minimum capital of about
5 Million TL. In addition its employment generating capacity
depends from the degree it will become interrelated with an overall governmental policy based upon a nationwide cooperative
movement. Otherwise the vitality of such projects remains confined to individual talents in organising and realising local initiative. In other words such an organisation, instead of securing to
the community involved some additional economic opportunities, enhances the leaders of such projects with more social prestige and status. The vehicle for community development actually
becomes an elevator for increased individual social mobility.

Workers Enterprises

One of the most relevant impacts of the recent migratory wave
is the growing awareness among Turkish workers in regard to the
potential possibilities of industrialisation. This explains the growing tendency to invest their savings in industrial enterprises. Yet,
prior to the energy crisis only a very small percentage of Turkish
workers were ready to invest their savings in such enterprises.
The explanation lies probably in the ambivalent attitude Turkish
workers are sharing with other migrant workers from the Mediterranean: on one hand, they express an outspoken reluctance to
settle definitely in the host country, while on the other hand,
they are not willing or able to determine the time of return. The
scarcity of satisfactory employment conditions at home and individual reasons such as the education of the children or the intention to pursue vocational training explain this ambivalent attitude and foster a typical mentality, which can be best qualified
as the rationalization of the international permanent commuter.
The sudden increase of unemployment in 1974 in FRG must

obviously have led to some serious modifications of opinion in this regard.

So far, there seems, however, to exist a certain form of investment which appeals to a greater extent to the Turkish workers and may represent the precondition for an earlier return to the home country. Before discussing this particular form, which has been vigorously fed by feelings of regional belongingness and local patriotism, it seems important to point out what sort of an investment is definitely rejected by Turkish workers. Various official and private actions have proven that Turkish migrants are not interested in placing their savings in (a) shares of economic state enterprises, (b) participation in the setting up of joint ventures, (c) acquisition of shares of Turkish private firms. The attitude toward the last group seems recently to have considerably changed in favour of a participation in such shareholding corporations. The most important reasons for this outspoken reluctance is the conviction that, (a) state economic enterprises are centres of political nepotism and function permanently at a deficit, (b) there are not sufficient safeguards and guarantees to protect shareholders from the waste, risks and speculative action of private firms. The fact that some foreign companies such as ISO (Investment Overseas) and Intercontinental Turkish Mutual Fund, after have attempted to induce Turkish workers to place their savings in bonds, went bankrupt in 1970, has reinforced the prevailing sceptical attitudes.

This may partly explain why so far only a relatively small number of Turkish workers—about 30,000, roughly 5% of the total population of Turkish workers in FRG—decided to participate in the establishment of workers enterprises. [51] However, the spreading of large scale unemployment exercises doubtless an important impact on the mentality of migrant workers. It can be assumed that the unfavourable economic conjoncture does motivate more and more migrant workers to seek for practical solutions which enable them to find in their home countries permanent employment outlets.

A recent survey of ISOPLAN [52] confined its analysis to 26 workers' enterprises, established in FRG, out of which 11 were, at the time of the survey still in the preparatory phase. A

---

[52] ISOPLAN, Institut für Entwicklungsforschung und Sozialplannung. Hrbg. *Türkische Arbeitnehmergesellschaften in der BRD* Saarbrücken and Bonn, 1973, p. 129.

more recent survey of the Turkish State Planning Organisation [53] indicates that the number of workers' enterprises has officially risen to 88, but actually has passed over 100. However, similar to the German survey, it points out that at present only 13 of these enterprises have so far been able to realise their projects and start production, while another 23 are still in the planning phase. The nominal capital of these enterprises ranges between 500,000TL—10 Million TL, the largest capital recorded being about 31 Million TL. Only one of these enterprises has been able to increase about 43% of its production within one year and only four of these enterprises have so far published their balance sheets.

The majority of these workers' enterprises are located around Istanbul (12), about 8 are scattered in various provinces of Central Anatolia (Kırşehir, Yozgat, Karaman, Çorum, Kütahya, Konya, Niğde, Kayseri) and some others are in the Marmara and Aegean region. So far no investment project has been realized in the less developed Eastern provinces. The entrance of workers' enterprises into Turkey's economic system has not contributed to reduce sharp regional disparities.

The largest segment of these enterprises are dealing with the production of construction materials, food processing and metal manufacturing. Paper, electrical equipment, chemical products and touristic sites are occupying a secondary place. These choices have been induced by factors such as: (a) the availability of a ready market in Turkey, (b) the relative simple technology required, (c) the need of various stratas of the population for better housing.

The most relevant obstacles preventing a further increase of these enterprises seems to be: (a) poor credit facilities, unwillingness of major banks to reinforce the nominal capital of these enterprises, (b) lack of a stock market, (c) shortage of managerial skill and technical advice, (d) difficulty of elaborating feasibility projects fitting the regional and local preferences of future shareholders, (e) excessively restrictive customs regulations preventing the import of technical equipment. The assumption that solely the goodwill of a group of workers desiring to invest, the backing

---

[53] İsmail Karaman, *III. Beş Yıllık Kalkınma planında gönderileceği tahmin edilen edilen işçi dövizleri ve bunların yurt içinde yatırıma kanalize edilebilmesi için alınması gerekli tedbirler*, DPT-SPD, Araştırma Şubesi July 1974, p. 67.

of one or two innovative and energetic group leaders, as well as modest starting capital is sufficient to overcome the hurdles of an underdeveloped economic system is doubtless extremely naive. [53] Dynamic economic systems owe their increased productivity not to an enlarged informal sector which rests mainly upon repair and maintenance, transport and catering functions, but to the high number of large, complex industrial organisations. Innovative enterpreneurs are the product of a certain level of economic growth and technological progress. Mixed economies, such as the Turkish system, are demonstrating that investment tendencies of private enterprises are oriented toward short-term, profit-ensuring projects, while long-term projects aiming at significant socio-economic structural changes are almost inevitably shouldered by the public sector. Indeed, as Dietzel has observed [54] the encouragement of innumerable small industries is only going to damage the competitive capacities of the underdeveloped home industry vis-a-vis Western Europe and its giant industries. The bourgeois aspirations of Turkish workers predominantly leads them to the establishment of small scale firms and workshops, which basically have little chance of survival.

Thus the most rational and effective way to attract the estimated 3 billion DM savings or Turkish workers, deposited at present in German banks, as well as, the additional savings in other European countries, lies in the ability to conceive, design and realize a bold, motivating, promising public policy, which combines the worker's initiative with the expertise, knowledge, and backing of the government. Such a policy could be realised by establishing a bank for worker's savings and by creating a largely government sponsored polyglot holding in which present and former migrant workers will constitute the largest shareholding group. This type of holding, representing a semi-public "entrepreneurial/labour sector", would have to coordinate its investment activities according to the priorities indicated by the Third Five-Year Development Plan and to benefit extensively from tax exemption.

It appears to be undeniable that only nation-wide policies based on a clear conception of the interrelationship between mi-

---

[54] K. D. Dietzel, "Die Rolle der rückkehrenden Arbeit in der Entwicklungsstrategie des westdeutschen Imperialismus", Das Argument, 68, 9/10 December 1971, p. 764-781.

gration and economic underdevelopment or stagnation can constitute a sound basis for the launching of a counter process against the impoverishing effects of migration.

5.5. *Problems Related to the Legal and Social Security of Turkish Workers*

Turkish workers, similar to the major contingents of European migrant workers in regard to social security, are covered, in accordance to the fundamental principles elaborated by supranational organisations such as the Council of Europe, the EEC and ILO, by a series of bilateral agreements. The first of these agreements was signed between Turkey and Federal Germany (30.4.1964), it was followed by agreements with the Netherlands (5.4.1966), with Belgium (4.7.1966), with Austria (12.10.1966), with Switzerland (14.1.1970), with Sweden (10.3.1967) and with France (20.11.1972). These agreements are based upon the recognition of the principle of absolute equal treatment of workers of both countries in matters related to sickness, accident, unemployment, old age insurance as well as children's allowances.

In principle, workers of both countries are placed legally on an equal footing. However, a number of specific conditions have been functioning in favour of the host country. The most important of these conditions is the principle of territoriality [55] inherent in almost all clauses of social security legislation and the discretionary power allocated to the German Federal and State administration through the Aliens Act. In addition, the following characteristics of migrant workers also contribute to decrease the burden of social security measures:

— their relative low age structure,
— the low degree of sickness,
— the insufficient knowledge of social legislature in regard of claims concerning tax exemption, tax return, other benefits accruing from social security, etc.,
— the special provisions of the Aliens Act enabling the administration to suspend the right of residence in cases of persistent unemployment.

---

[55] Frank Woltereck, "Sociale Sicherung, Besteuerung" in Tuğrul ANSAY and Volkmar Gessner, *Gastarbeiter in Gesellschaft und Recht*, C. H. Beck, 1974 p. 134.

The principle of territoriality is based upon the idea of granting any legal right to everybody, citizen or foreigner, residing in the territory of a given national state. The major consequences which arises from the application of this principle for Turkish workers are the following:

1. *Sickness insurance* for the Turkish worker and his spouse and children are only paid in case of residence in the FRG. For separated families and their dependents the insurance premiums are paid in Turkey according the scale adopted by the Turkish social security laws.
2. *Accident insurance* is only paid if the Turkish worker involved takes up permanent residence in the FRG—a situation which deprives the disabled worker from the assistance of his family and is only applicable if the beneficiary continues to maintain his residential permit.
3. *Unemployment insurance* is also distributed according the same rule. Especially during the recession of 1966/67 differences of opinion among administrators created major handicaps for discharged Turkish workers. Some Länder authorities decided to extend this right only to workers "permanently available for recruitment", a category which automatically discarded foreign workers depending on residential permits. Later, this formula was interpreted in a more liberal way, but the cited legal definition and its inbuilt discrimination still retains its validity.
4. *Old age insurance* is not applied within the context of the principle of territoriality, but the present scheme has been for years a source of grievances. The reason of dissatisfaction lies in the fact that in Turkey any person subject to the Social Insurance scheme may apply for his retirement pension after reaching the age of 55, while most of the European countries have adopted an age limit starting at 63 and stretching until 67. Thus any Turkish worker, who is eligible for retirement according to Turkish law and whose contributions to the German retirement fund have accumulated through the years, is obliged to wait at least seven years if he wants to benefit from the German scheme or accept a lump sum indemnity after a waiting period of at least two years. This situation presents an open example of inequality.

5. Actually the most widely discussed application of the principle of territoriality concerns the allocation of _children's allowances_. Whereas Turkish workers, similar to all other migrant workers, could obtain until the end of 1974 children's allowances irrespective of whether their dependents were living with their parents or staying in the home country, a tax reform act, entering into force on January 1, 1975 and aiming to realise a drastic cut-down of social welfare expenses, is making a clear-cut distinction between children living in the FRG or in their home countries. The new legislation is affecting Turkish workers most, for they display the highest percentage of marital status (86%), with the lowest percentage of united families—only 46% are living with their wives in the FRG. While Turkish workers have received in the past the highest amount of children allowances—357 Million DM in 1973 for 515,161 children—the average amount paid to foreigners and Germans does not indicate a similar magnitude. Statistics indicate that the average German family has 2.1, foreigners 2.5 children. The major differencce lies in the fact that in 1973, 60.5% of the total sum of children allowances was paid to Turkish workers. Thus, by applying in this field the principle of territoriality, it is possible to achieve drastic savings. In addition, the new law introduces a double standard in the field of tax reduction. Since Turkish workers whose children remain in Turkey are not eligible to claim any tax deduction, their tax share automatically increases. The following table indicates solely the difference in matter of the old and new allocation of children's allowances.

This table shows clearly that while the impact of fast growing inflation has lead to more than doubled allocation for children residing inside FRG, the newly signed agreement between Turkey and FRG represents an open case of deliberate discrimination. The deeper reasons have to be found in the recent governmental policy, which in spite of the rising rate of unemployment has not been changed and rests upon the principle of partial integration. This means on the one hand, a generous financial support in matters such as housing, etc., tending to reduce or at least to minimize sharp discrepancies between national and settled foreign workers, and on the other hand, reducing the scope of ex-

Table 5

Monthly Children's Allowances in DM, Paid According Nationality,
prior and after 1975

Number of	Allowance for German and foreign children, irrespective residence, 1964-1974	Allowance for Turkish children residing outside FGR from 1975 on	Allowance for German and foreign children, residing inside FGR from 1975 on
1	—	10	50
2	25	25	70
3	50	60	120
4	60	60	120
5	70	70	120

Source: Metal Haberler, Frankfurt, December 1974, No. 12 p. 3.

tended financial aid to fragmented families, thus reducing the attractiveness of single migration. The modification of Art. 33 of the Turkish-German Social Security Agreement of 1964 no doubt represents an open violation of the principle of equal treatment of migrant workers' children such as it is formulated in Art. 25 of the Universal Declaration of Human Rights, in Art. 4 and 6 of the ILO Social Convention of 1962 and in Art. 51 of the European Economic Community.

The first reaction to this change in the German social security policy seems to develop a rather undesired trend: increasingly more Turkish workers are bringing their children to the FRG. Of course this new wave of "minors migration" applies solely to already united families. Whether this move will slow down with the rise of unemployment remains to be seen.

Permit of residence

The German Aliens Act, which generated hot debates during the last years within Germany's political parties, trade unions and other public opinion forming centres, represents the most effective tool for the manipulation of migratory policies. The criteria inherent in the law permit the issue or denial of the prolongation of permit of residence according to "personal, political and economic factors, as well as the interests of the labour market". Although this law has been vigorously challenged by alternative drafts [56] it still remains in action. Thus very high numbers of Turkish workers—about 25,000 Turkish workers in the FRG have been refused such a permit, while almost all Turkish workers invited for one year contracts to Denmark are facing the same situation—might take more and more refuge in evasion of the law, such as through the performance of "pseudo marriages". Such a practice, which received a widespread echo especially in Denmark is nowadays also an issue of administrative and judicial inquiries. Since mixed marriages performed in Denmark automatically guarantee a residential permit of up to six months, investigations attempt to determine whether such marriages indeed represent genuine partnerships.

5.6. *Educational Problems of Migrant's Children*

The most relevant attitudinal change in Turkey during the last decade is doubtless the intensive desire to migrate aborad. This desire can be represented both as a search for more income and at the same time as a propensity to minimize the family's living costs. This has produced in general widespread fragmentation of the family. However, with the increased tendency of Turkish workers to bring their families to the FRG, two major features began to be noted: (a) Due to the high fertility trend, each year, more Turkish children are born and represent a potential new population group to be educated, (b) Elder children, between the age group of 6-16, first left behind, are also brought over to the FRG. They represent an even more problematic aspect of school enrollment and placement. A survey carried out in 1972, indicates that among the Turkish workers 42% were living with one child, 32% with two, 20% with 3 or 4 and 6% with 5 or 6 children. [57]

This new development has produced two types of children: acculturated and unintegrated children. Those children who have migrated at early ages, who have acquired an adequate command of the German language, have also acquired a special role in the family and neighbourhood circles. They are resorted to for help in translating letters, are taken as interpreter to stores, the police etc. even at the ages of 8-10. On the other side, especially young

---

[56] Franz/Heldman/Kaspzyk, Majer, Paetzold, Ausländergesetz, Alternativentwurf 70, Kiritik und Reform, *Studentische Politik*, 1/1970.

[57] Bundesanstalt für Arbeit, *Repräsentativuntersuchung '72*, p. 25.

girls who deliberately have not been sent to school in order to assume the care of younger siblings, represent a group of totally alienated youngsters, pre-adolescent and adolescent, who may be qualified as "bilingual illiterates". These children have an extremely restricted vocabulary both in Turkish an the respective host country language and they are hardly able to communicate not to speak of becoming adjusted in school whenever an attempt is made to enroll them. Thus a very important group among the Turkish workers' dependents are subject to an incomplete process of socialization, which makes them unable to prepare for an active participation either in the host country or in the home country.

Unfortunately, the exact number of Turkish children still remains an unvalidated estimation, due to the fact that there is no legal obligation for registration of foreign person under 16. While the German Labour Bureau indicated already in 1972 a Turkish children population of 195,000 with 46% under 6, 22% between 6-11, 17% from 11-16 and 15% born prior to 1955, the Turkish Ministry of Education gave in June 1974 for the FRG total figure of 175,000. Parallel to these estimates, the Turkish Ministry of Labour Published an estimated figure of 205,371 children abroad, while the Turkish Federation of Labour (Türk-İş) mentions about 230,000 children. [58] The Netherlands comes in second place with a children population of about 10, 619, Belgium ranks third with 6,540, Switzerland is the host of about 5,715 and Sweden of about 2,03 Turkish children.

It should be noted that so far international documents such as the recommendation proclaimed by UNESCO at its eleventh General Assembly in December 1960 against discrimination in education have so far only been adhered to by Baden-Württemberg. Actually, the fact that all educational issues are subject in accordance with the federal system to the jurisdiction of the various Länder parliaments has given way to a great variety of educational models.

The major concern on the part of the sending countries is to equip the growing generation abroad with the language and culture of the home country, and to provide equal access to all educational institutions while the host country desires a friction-

---

[58] Ministry of Education, *Yurt dışında çalışan Türk işçilerinin (0-16) yaş çocuklarının eğitimi sorunları*, Ankara 1974, p. 6-7.

less adjustment of foreign children within the national school system, a smooth transition of these children toward technical vocations and a relatively small contingent desirous to continue higher education. These contradicting goals resulted in a dual strategy of education—integration as well as segregation—and in political rivalry—teaching of the mother tongue under the control of German authorities in some Länder, but submission to consular control in other Länder.

Thus in Bavaria and West Berlin, educational activities are authorised but not subsidized by the responsible authorities of education, while in Hessen, Niedersachsen and Nordrhein-Westfalen the realization of Turkish instruction is carried out under the direct supervision of local German authorities, who also exercise full control.

a) This practice has led to the emergence of two locally different types of teachers: professionals, recruited in Turkey and paid by the Turkish Ministry of Education; b) former primary school teachers, who due to downward mobility were recruited first as blue collar workers, later returned to their initial profession and are receiving their payment from German authorities.

In 1974 about 249 Turkish teachers, attached to the Ministry of Education are holding supplementary Turkish classes in history, Turkish for about 11,607 Turkish children. In Belgium official Turkish teachers are shouldering the heavy job of teaching about 1,544 children in 28 classes.

The Turkish teachers employed by German authorities are teaching in so-called "transitional" classes, their duty being to help Turkish children to adjust their linguistic knowledge to the class level in German schools.

Since this issue has become a real concern in various circles of Federal Germany's public opinion, two opposed practice became the major focus of discussion.

The "Bavarian" model is based upon the principle that parents are given a free choice: they may decide to educate their children either predominantly in Turkish or in German. In schools with a minimum of 25 foreign children, instruction is given—upon request—up to two thirds in the respective mother tongue. The second alternative called the "social integration" model does not accept the principle of free choice for parents, but attempts to integrate foreign children fully in German society. Under this model Turkish children are either first instructed in transitional classes with the purpose of teaching them basic German or, if their command of German is sufficient, they may join regular classes in German schools.

It should be noted that while Bavaria from the beginning stood firm on the provisional nature of foreign labour employment and insisted on keeping the rotation principle, the Länder with larger industrial concentration fought for a complete integration and recruitment without restriction. Thus it becomes clear that the shaping of educational policies is determined by the degree of industrial absorption of foreign labour rather than pedagogical or humanistic considerations.

An additional complicating factor arises from the fact that a number of Turkish workers have been asking for the creation of exclusive "Koran schools". Such demands have been vigorously criticised by the Association of Turkish teachers in FRG in a paper stating "the real function of such clerical schools is not to transmit religious education. They are often exercising an open criticism against the republican form of state of Turkey while defending the creation of an Islamic state. Their programme is conceived in contradiction to modern civilisation and progress ... Their method is solely based on memorising". [59]

The discussion of whether a dual system of equal weighted acquisition of language is necessary for the socialisation process of the child or whether such a demand is psychologically an overburdening of the child, continues to rage. Meanwhile the decision in various countries has been following the economic conjuncture: France, Belgium, Sweden are still following a policy of absolute integration while Switzerland, desirous to send back their foreign labour force after a given period, is at present experimenting with a so-called "Scuola a due uscite-School with double exit", based on equally weighted bilingual teaching.

Summing up, it appears clearly that each of the major actors involved in the process of educating migrant's children is confronted with a myriad of educational and political problems, which can be grouped as following:

---

[59] Verband Türkischer Lehrer in der BRD und in Westberlin, *Zur pädagogisch-politischen Funktion der türkischen Priester und Koranschulen in der Türkei und im Ausland*, Paper presented at the workshop in April 1-4, 1971, Th. Heuss Akademie, Gummersbach.

a. *Parents*. 1. The relationship of foreign workers to the school
system is largely determined by the conditions and traditions of
the home country. Especially, Turkish workers of rural background, similar to Italians from the South and very much unlike
the Greeks and Yugoslavs, are by and large only encouraging the
school attendance of their gifted male children, while trying, in
spite of an absolute prohibition of juvenile employment, to obtain illegal jobs for the less eager boys of the family. In regard to
the daughters of Turkish migrant workers two important factors
are playing a decisive role in their non-attendance: (a) The imperative necessity of supervision for the younger members of the
family, especially in those cases where the mother also works
outside of the home. (b) Dominant negative value judgements in
regard to the permissive, co-educational education in Europe,
which leads either in non-enrollment or early dropping out. The
real number of Turkish children in Europe who are growing up
outside regular schooling remains at the present day a "sacred
scandal".

2. Housing difficulties also play an indirect role in non-enrollment. Many parents are disinclined to register their children because the size and quality of their lodging does not meet the
obligatory requirements demanded by the administration.

b. *Pupils*. 1. The various organisational handicaps migrant
workers' children are confronted with, has its heaviest impact on
Turkish children. Lack of interest, inability to evaluate the role
of pre-school education, fear of religious indoctrination, results
among Turkish children in the lowest percentage of kindergarden
attendance among foreign workers.

2. During primary school years a major handicap for the success or failure of Turkish children seems to stem from the inability
to get access to the free distribution of books. In many cities Turkish children are asked to buy the special books at a price of
14.— DM, which seems too high to many parents. [60]

3. After completion of the obligatory 9 years long schooling,
only 3% of the Turkish children continue their education in voca-

---

[60] Gerhart Mahler, *Zweitsprache Deutsch*, Donauworth 1974, Auer Verlag,
p. 154-155; Herbert R. Koch, *Gastarbeiterkinder in deutschen Schulen*, Königswinter
1970, p. 173.

tional institutions. There is an almost complete reversal between the expectations and hopes of the parents and the choices opted by the teenagers. Lack of proper guidance and information, attractiveness of early money earning, as imbued by the consumption society, plays in this regard an important role.

c. *Teachers*. 1. Neither German nor Turkish teachers are linguistically and professionally prepared to cope with the additional burden resulting from the setting up of preparatory classes or Turkish classes conducted in a foreign environment.

2. There is deep cleavage between former Turkish primary school teachers, at present employed by German authorities and required to prepare Turkish pupils for an adjustment to the German curriculum and Turkish teachers attached to the Ministry of Education in Ankara, whose primary obligation is to foster the pupils attachment to their home country and whose classes, except in Bavaria, are scattered and based upon voluntary participation.

3. In contrast to Spanish, Greek and Italian teachers, there has been so far no serious attempt to organise periodical seminar and workshops for Turkish teachers permitting them to acquire new educational and methodological insights.

In addition to the complexity of problems related to the different value judgements and preferences of parents, and teachers of Turkish migrant's children, the inconsistency of public policy has to be considered too. For years the most vital issue which preoccupied the mixed Turkish-German cultural committees was the degree of control which official representatives wanted to retain in order to secure a proper amount of diffusion of Turkish culture. After the emergence of the energy crisis, the policy adopted was changed drastically: comprehensive measures for complete integration of the Turkish pupils became the demand of official representatives.

In reality both sides of the coin deserve equal attention. The Europe of tomorrow will largely depend on the versatility of its enlarged community. This requires equal access to all educational vistas in both countries for its growing young generation.

Conclusion

The multifaceted aspects of Turkey's external migration reflect only one case-study of a series of transitional processes, affecting both agrarian and industrial countries. The degree of interdependence of such a complex relationship can be measured under different lights: terms of trade, transfer of certain technologies, flow of monetary and human capital as well as information, impact of multinational corporations. It is impossible to evaluate the migratory movement as an independent variable. On the contrary, this process represents a dependent variable, subject to cyclical economic movements. The most relevant feature of this process lies in its undeniable asymetric character. The validity of this assertion can be tested by considering the following types of interaction:

— Interaction between labour markets of sending and receiving countries
— Impact of educational systems
— Transfer of foreign currency
— Conception of economic development plans
— Determination of migratory policies.

Starting to consider the demands of European labour markets suffering from acute shortage of manpower, both the increase of migration—in case of Turkey it reached roughly 100,000 per year during 1968-73—as well as its abrupt call-off has been determined by the FRG, France and the Netherlands. The existence of a foreign labour army reserve facilities the manipulation of recession trends. Factors like long-lasting friendship ties, common membership in a defence alliance such as NATO are not decisive. [61]

In regard of the impact of educational systems, it is easy to explain the sudden change of policy under the light of the absorptive capacity of Turkey's economic structure, should a massive return of migrant workers and their dependents become a living reality. The fact that Turkish technical and vocational

---

[61]   Reinhard Lohrmann, "Wechselseitige Ein-und Auswirkungen zwischen Industrie und Herkunftsländern durch die Arbeitskräftewanderung hervorgerufene Abhängigkeiten", in R. Lohrmann and Klaus Manfrass *Ausländerbeschäftigung und Internationale Politik*, Wien 1974, R. Oldenburg Verlag, p. 368.

schools are more and more shaping their curriculum and criteria of qualification according to German standards indicates, too, the one-sided dependency between the two countries.

Maybe only cultural activities, such as special broadcasting and TV programmes for Turkish workers display a more equally weighted character, yet these programmes too have originally received their official blessing in order to present an increased exposure to East European indoctrination among the massive group of foreign workers in the FRG. Attempts to utilize these means of enlarged communication to increase the political education of Turkish workers and to supply them with a certain degree of critical appraisal has been repeatedly vigorously objected to both by German and Turkish official representatives.

The transfer of remittances appears to represent the most powerful process where the initiative is taken by Turkish workers. But there too it should be kept in mind that these large sums, which overshadow the modest income secured by tourism, are actually enjoying a deliberate encouragement of the host countries, who are anxious to stop a further proliferation of inflation. It is easily predictable that, similar to the tax reform act of 1975, in case of shortage of hard currency, the major European labour employing countries could take sharp decisions to curtail or prohibit the export of savings.

Considering the possibilities enabling countries like Turkey to implement their development plans, it should be reminded that both the outflow of qualified industrial manpower as well as the brain drain will continue as long as these highly industrialized countries are ready to absorb them. Thus the degree of competiteveness with the founding members of the Common Market, depend, aside from the technological gap, to a large extent on the interest or disinterest toward the human capital which could realise the various phases of Turkey's development plans.

The shaping of migratory policies is another clear cut example of interdependence/dependence relationship. Although Turkey's conservative government of Melen in 1972/73 adopted a rather critical approach toward the growing number of oppositional minded Turkish workers in the FRG and a number of Turkish politicians charged the FRG with encouraging among its countrymen the spreading of communist and subversive ideas, the same government did not resort to stopping recruitment. On the contrary, when the FRG government decided to reorganise its foreign labour policy and opted against rotation, Turkey did not object, although it was predictable that with an increased amount of family reunion the flow of remittances might grow smaller. However the grave decision taken consequently by the FRG, France and the Netherlands at the end of 1973, declaring a complete stop of further recruitment, was taken unilaterally. Turkey was not consulted at all.

To sum up, the asymetric, interaction of Turkey as a manpower exporting country with a number of European industrial countries indicates the existence of an undeniable degree of economic dependency. Acceptance as full member to the Common Market may solve certain legal aspects related to the free circulation of labour, but will not essentially change the nature of the centre's domination over the periphery.

The handling of this administratively organised mass exodus will continue to be planned and implemented by elites of both countries, who in spite of the delineated conflicts, are basically in a state of harmony of interests. Thus the solutions to satisfy the urgent needs of developed and developing economies will continue to be solved by the compromising proposals of cooperating bureaucracies. A real change on the macro level of migration implies an entrenching change in the socio-economic structure of the sending countries. The implications of this permanent labour exchange on the micro level have so far not been sufficiently studied. Whether the pioneers of the postwar dualistic labour market will perform after their return to Turkey the role of active opinion leaders demanding more comprehensive, new organizational forms in order to articulate better the defense of their demands or whether this new stratum will be submerged within the growing ranks of the new middle classes can only be measured within its historical dimension.

FACTORS INFLUENCING EXTERNAL MIGRATION

"Why stay behind? For a thousand green marks a month,
Let's go and spread out from eagle Anatolia, to the face of the earth.
Those foreign gentlemen are about to wake from their golden sleep,
  Come on, let's sweep their streets,
Huge brooms, towering garbage,
Feeling no shame in the face of the crimson sun.
  Hands filthy, hearts filthy.
My forefathers were too mighty for today and tomorrow;
I fell, I flounder, a servant for foreigners now."

From "Our Street-Sweepers in Germany"
FAZIL HÜSNÜ DAĞLARCA
Translated by Talât Sait Halman

Individual scholars and a considerable number of expert teams working for international organisations have based their analysis concerning factors influencing external migration on the hypothesis that emigration relieves a country's unemployment. However, this explanation is neither sufficient in itself nor as unequivocal as it appears at first sight. Receiving countries are naturally interested in engaging only the best workers available. This entails a "Skimming off" effect (W. R. Böhning) that may not touch at all the hard-core unemployment. Actually emigration has deprived every sending countries of an important segment of its better educated and skilled active population. As long as sending countries are unwilling or unable to limit the scope of emigration, not to speak of forbidding it, which would mean a denial of the basic human rights,—they are losing within their newly developing industrial sectors experienced workers who are sometimes difficult to replace.

Furthermore, any emigration intensifies regional disparaties and accentuates intellectual erosion. Any large-scale emigration of skilled industrial labour force and highly qualified manpower entails a heavy loss in educational expenditure which has to be met by the taxpayers in addition, increased emigration also leads to a widespread disdain for domestic products and a higher value placed on foreign goods. This trend for conspicuous consumption with an open preference for foreign goods might even worsen, rather than improve, the underlying balance of payment problem. Thus, there is an undeniable need for more coordination and cooperation between emigration and immigration. Furthermore, only comprehensive planning, both in terms of attempting to overcome the bottlenecks of regional underdevelopment, as well as in terms of creating new employment opportunities can only be overcome by national development plans. All the three papers included in this section attempt to focus attention on these major issues.

O. Neuloh challenges the theory of social market economy and tries to show why a dysfunctional labour market—even if migration concentrates on partly skilled and mostly employed labour force—can only be modified by the elaboration of a new labour market policy build upon interlinking ties between labour market, migration and social planning.

T. Oğuzkan deals with the most important human resource problem related to the right use of high-level manpower. The facts presented in his paper are new evidence that the substance of poor nations is being used to educate people for the rich nations. Actually, in order to avoid a large scale drain, there are four possible ways to stop educating Turks for the rich West: one would be to stop emigration; another would be for the West to stop all immigration, the third would be to reduce the output of the education system and the fourth would be to rationalize and adjust the output of universities to the economic and social needs of the country. The third alternative of reducing the number of graduates is theoretically possible, but would, in practice, be most difficult. As a matter of fact, the opening of all doors to higher education by addition of higher education through correspondence has played in recent Turkish politics a paramount role. This explains also why it is so difficult to relate educational output with national needs. Decisions relating to the supply and to the demand of this problem require the kind of planning, information, organization, conviction and structure for implementation that few countries possess. Oğuzkan's paper only points out which professional groups are apt to suffer the greatest losses—normally, medical doctors, engineers and scientists—but also why international migration of talent is a highly complex phenomenon. Its threefold dimensions: pull forces in the country of destination; push forces in the country of origin and the perception of these forces by the potential emigrant implies also an interplay of a whole series of relevant socio-economic factors, as well as psychological forces leading to migratory behaviour.

İ. H. Aydınoğlu analyses the major priorities accorded in each Five Year Plan and discusses the choices for speedy industrialisation in relationship to the transfer of agricultural surplus labour into non-agricultural sectors. This paper discusses on a comparative basis the unbalanced distribution of available skilled manpower among various sectors and its inefficient utilization. The conclusion indicates the wrong emphasis on capital instead of resource endowment of the country and also explains why all the three Five Years Plan have left emigration of manpower as the only possible alternative without attributing sufficient attention to conjunctural tendencies. In this sense, Aydınoğlu's paper not only furnishes an explanation for the style of Turkey's migration, but also supplies a new case study for the manpower shortage/ surplus dilemma faced by a great number of developing countries.

STRUCTURAL UNEMPLOYMENT IN TURKEY
Its Relation to Migration
OTTO NEULOH

1974 seems to be the beginning of a new phase of migration inside Europe between undeveloped countries and industrial societies. The past ten years of dynamic economic development were characterized by a very high rate of unlimited and nearly uncontrolled migration mobility. This time is for most European countries over. The government of the German Federal Republic has recently put an end to the exchange of foreign workers because of new trends in the economic and social development in Germany which include not only the crisis in oil production and transportation, but also the result of many difficulties in German economy and social relations. The three million number of foreign workers, the so-called "guest-workers", is understood as the limit capacity of the labour market. Also there is much resistance against the unlimited migration on the part of the German people. It is not necessary to summarize all the reasons of this unexpected change, but it is very important to keep in mind that this new phase may bring up tensions, and thus original reasons and motivations of dynamic migration may be forgotten.

The following analysis of the relations between structural unemployment in Turkey and migration of Turks will be focused on the co-ordination of economic and social rationality in the migration policy of a very important migration country. Therefore it seems necessary to briefly survey the employment situation in Turkey and the motivations of Turkish migrants into foreign countries. The purpose of this analysis is a long-term investigation of the problem of rotation or integration of Turkish migrants and some repeated studies in German industrial areas. Three major questions, will be raised here:

1. the objective reasons of the large scale/migration of Turks into foreign countries;
2. the subjective motivations of Turkish migrants;
3. Turkey's perspectives on the relation between structural unemployment and migration.

1. The Objective Reasons of the Large Scale Migration of Turks into Foreign Countries

There are different kinds of objective reasons; economic, financial, psychological, social and a few others, f.i. labour law and social insurance. Our analysis is primarily concentrated on sociological and social reasons, although the others can be very important. Sociological and social questions in the field of migration are connected with labour market problems in Turkey and the social situation of the Turkish people.

1.1. Unsufficient theory of labour market

We don't find labour market and unemployment relevant sociological theories in European social science. The methods of labour market research in particular have still not been clarified. The oldest publications started with the thesis, that only modern industrialism could be the basis for the development and differenciation of the labour market in the sense of social economy and occupational structure. The labour market in industrial society will be determined by the percentage of labour fource depending on renumeration in wages and salaries. It is not quite sure, that both theses can be used in relation to the underdeveloped countries with the criterias of completeness or uncompleteness of the labour market structure. This has to be proved in the economic and social situation of Turkey. We find the same problem in the definition of unemployment as a "lack of occupation of working people depending on wage and salary."[1] This means, that self employed people are not recognized as unemployed, although they have no occupational income. A definition like this can not include all unemployment situations in underdeveloped countries. A theory of a functioning labour market must consider not only economic, but also non-economic factors. Traditional economic theory did not take into account differences between the single kinds of markets, i.e. mercantile, financial and so on. It portrayes the market mechanism of offer and demand as a self-regulating system, and applied the same conception to labour market. Two more progressive theories: the full employment theory of J. M. Keynes and the theory of social

---

[1] Eduard Willeke, Arbeitslosigkeit, in *Handwörterbuch der Sozialwissenschaften*, Vol. 1, p. 305.

market economy of A. Muller-Armack, challenged this statement. The first author developed the theory of equilibrium between economic, non-economic factors and indicators like population growth, mobility readiness, working mentality, social relations, industrial relations and others. It was the first approach to
deviate from the theory of full employment and unemployment
by very close combination between the economic rationality of labour market with criterias of social rationality. The theory of social
market economy was based on the recognition of the necessity of
social measures and institutions to overcome the social shortcomings of free market competition. A social market economy
entails a highly differenciated and elaborate system of social organizations to protect workers and consumers full employment,
secure work-places and a stable monetary situation. It is inas-
much as possible a progressive regulator of economic policy.
Both theories, full employment and social economy, may be understood only as models and measures for evaluating the degree
of economic and social deviation in the undeveloped and disfunctional labour market. We will try to use these theories in the
analysis of the Turkish labour market and the objective reasons
of large scale migrations.

1.2. *The social and cultural causes of unemployment in Turkey*

If the Turkish economy would be an industrial system with half
of the economic and social structure of industrial countries like
West Germany, Belgium or England, then no problem of expansive migration would exist in the situation and mentality of the
Turkish people. In contrast to Italy, Spain and Greece, the Turks
in the past did not get used to a workplace in foreign countries.
They are not a society of migrants and mobility. Until recently,
there were no large Turkish communities in the USA or other
immigration countries. Therefore, we must ask what have been
the special causes leading to the massive migration of Turks in
the last ten years. In view of the different factors arised by
various disciplines we have to limit the following analysis to four
main points in the social and cultural situation: the disfunctional
structure of the labour market, the gap between population
growth and the labour market, the lag of educational and professional training and unemployment as a permanent social situation.

1.2.1. *Disfunctional structure of labour market*

The two labour market theses mentioned before: modern industrialism and high percentage of wage and salary earning people, are not applicable to Turkey. Only 12% of about 14 million labour force are occupied in industry, only 25% of the labour force are employees, all other are selfemployed and unpaid family workers. This does not mean, that the self-employed don't try to get salaried positions, because of their poor situation, but this is exactly a further test of uncompleteness and disfunctional structure of Turkish labour market. Yet in the long-term distribution of the labour force we can observe some progressive changes in the economic and social structure during the last 25 years in Turkey.

Table 1

Distribution of Labour Force by Major Economic Sectors

	1955	1960	% 1965	1970
Agriculture	77.4	74.0	71.4	67.0
Industry	8.1	9.6	10.2	12.1
Services	4.0	5.4	11.1	11.4
Others	10.5	11.0	7.3	9.5
	100	100	100	100

Source: State Institute of Statistics. Cited from: Sunday Uner, The population of Turkey. 1974 World Population Year C.I.C.R.E.D. Series (in press).

The table shows three major directions in the process of change: the decreasing numbers of people working in agriculture (about minus 13%), the growing number of workers in industry (plus 50%) and in the tertiary sector (services) from 4% to more than 11%, (nearly threefold). Although these tendencies are significant for the development toward an industrial society, the typical trend in underdeveloped countries is the enormous growth of services. There are two reasons for this: first, underdeveloped countries need a lot of planning and administrating offices and employees, because of the disfunctional structure of the labour market; on the other side the population of those countries does not like to be engaged in handicraft and heavy

industrial work but prefers employment in offices and similar
positions. It is very significant for this reason, that in the Turkish
bureaucracy from the ministry down to the local Government we
find many clerks waiting in lobbies to be summoned to carry
out letters or bring tea. The 12% of the labour force engaged in
industry is mainly concentrated in the manufacturing industry
and construction both rose from 6% to 8.4% and 1.6% and 2.8%
respectively between 1955 & 1970. ([2] Uner, Sunday) Nevertheless the general structure of the labour market in Turkey is characterised by a predominant agriculture and the very small size of
handicraft and salesmen. It is disfunctional in several aspects:
First, in the general living standard, influenced by the poverty of
the rural people and by the low standard of industry and commerce; secondly by the high percentage of self-employed and
unpaid family workers without sufficient educational and professional background.

1.2.2. *The gap between population growth and labour market*

Turkey has 38 millions inhabitants. This is nearly 3 times more
than the findings of the first census after the foundation of the
Turkish Republic in 1927, which was 13.5 millions. The present
growth rate would rise the number of inhabitants to more than
50 millions in the next ten years and to about 70 millions in the
year 2000. The quantitative development of the Turkish population is one of the most dynamic of all countries in the world. It is
influenced not only by a high birth-rate, but also by declining
mortality trend. One of the most important results of the high
birth-rate is, that more than 40% of the population is younger
than 15 years, nearly twice the figure of industrial societies. This
means that the potential labour force between 15 and 65 years
cannot exceed 50% of population. Consequently the population
with an earning capacity, but in a disfunctional labour market,
has to care for the half of all Turks (youth and old). From a
regional perspective the problem varies because of different birth
—and mortality-rates in urban and agrarian areas, and because of
the concentration of industry in West Turkey and the lack of
workplaces and earning possibilities in the highland Anatolia.

---

[2] State Institute of Statistics. Cited from: Sunday Üner, The Population of Turkey.
1974 World Population Year C.I.C.R.E.D. Series (in press).

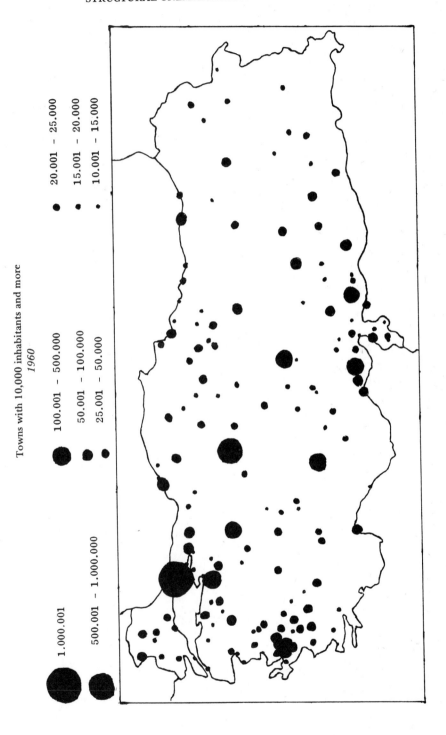

The development of urban population in Turkey
1960

Towns with 10,000 inhabitants and more

100.001 – 500.000
50.001 – 100.000
25.001 – 50.000

1.000.001
500.001 – 1.000.000

20.001 – 25.000
15.001 – 20.000
10.001 – 15.000

OTTO NEULOH

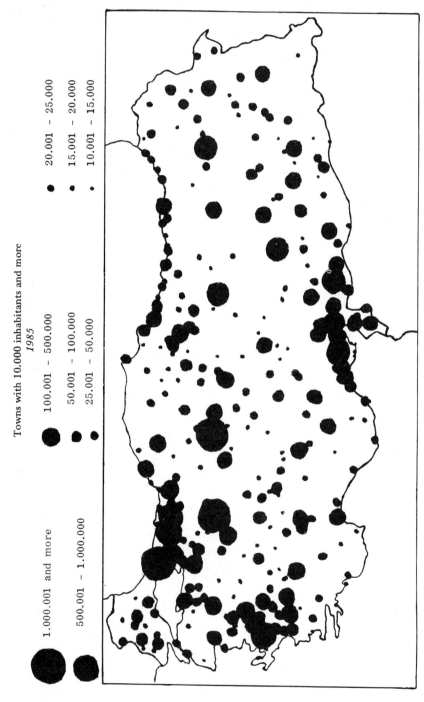

The development of urban population in Turkey

Towns with 10.000 inhabitants and more
1985

1.000.001 and more

500.001 – 1.000.000

100.001 – 500.000

50.001 – 100.000

25.001 – 50.000

20.001 – 25.000

15.001 – 20.000

10.001 – 15.000

These are the main causes of large scale migration in the non-industrial areas of Turkey, primarily in Central Anatolia and in the eastern regions. The disfunctional structure of the labour market in Turkey can therefore be demonstrated by a high birth- and mortality-rate on the one hand and a lack of employment possibilities in Central and Eastern Anatolia, while Western Anatolia is more urbanized and economically developed. This disfunctional situation may lead to explosive developments in the future and one prospective study of the Turkish Central Planning Office recognizes that the shifting of the dynamic population for the next ten years from West to East will double or triple the population of the eastern towns. (See the diagrams on the pages 55 and 56).

1.2.3. *The lag of education and professional training*

A functioning labour market system depends on high standard of education in primary schools and a differenciated and graduated professional training. Illiterates are not active members in an industrial oriented labour market. Applicants for workplaces in industry without vocational and technical background can not cope with the quality requirements of modern industry. The following table shows the educational and vocational school situation in Turkey:

Table 2

Educational Attainments of the Labour Force

	1960		1970	
	Number (Thousand)	%	Number (Thousand)	%
Educational Level Completed				
Illiterate	8,863	72.2	7,696	56.0
Primary School	2,829	23.0	4,931	35.9
Secondary School	255	2.1	407	3.0
Highschool	100	0.8	184	1.3
Secondary Vocational and Technical School	127	1.0	297	2.2
Higher Education	99	0.8	206	1.5
Unknowns	8	0.1	16	0.1
	12,281	100.0	13,737	100.0

(See Sunday Uner, loc. cit.).

More than 50% of the potential labour force in Turkey is illiterate. This means, these people have not learnt the primitive forms of communication by writing and reading and have no background for industrial work with a same lacking knowledge in mathematics and physics. The table clearly demonstrates a declining trend in the number of illiterates and a rising rate of primary school attendance, but it must be known, that children in Turkey spend only five years in elementary school and that nearly one third of the 40,000 villages have still no school, especially in the removed rural areas of Central and Eastern Anatolia, the most important recruitment regions of large scale migration. On the other hand, the percentage of illiterates is very different for men and women, as the following age structure diagram (page 59) shows.

This accounts for the inferior status of women in Turkish families and society, particularly in the agrarian sector. Also remarkable is the proportion of illiteracy varying according to the age group. It makes evident the success in fighting against illiteracy for young people. Nevertheless the consequence of educational and vocational progress is the growing number of applicants for industrial workplaces and migrants to foreign countries with possibilities of qualified work and training. This leads to the question of the development of vocational and technical schools. In the table on educational attainments we found 297,000 students enrolled in such schools in 1970 in contrast to 127,000 in 1960, about 2 1/2 time. This means not only an enlargement of professional training facilities, but also a broader diffusion all over Turkey. The data in our study of various regions suggests the existence of general standards for the vocational and technical schools, but also differences in the quality and co-ordination of theory and practice. Here it is necessary to note, that Turkey has very few apprenticeships in industrial firms as is the case in the state of Karabuk and Zonguldak near the Black Sea. Therefore we can not compare the vocational and technical school education in Turkey with the dualistic system of professional training in West Germany. It follows from our study, that a majority of responsible Turkish members in offices and schools are critical of vocational and technical training in Turkey because it is more theoretical instead of practical and industry oriented. Young people finishing school, with success, don't like to work

Illiteracy in Turkey

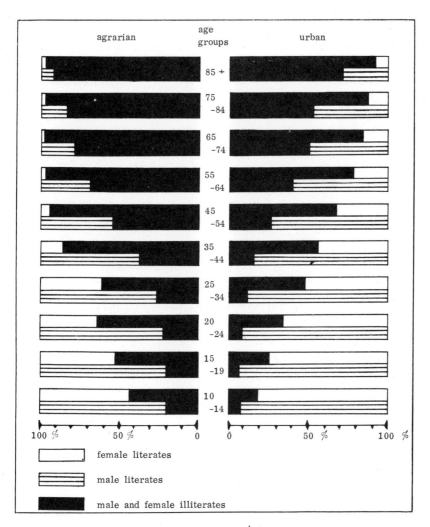

(Dates of this figure come from Z. Y. Hershlag: Turkey, The Challenge of growth, Leiden 1968)

with unskilled or demiskilled workers and demand normally higher positions without having practical experience. The German
recruitment offices have since long time special difficulties
with such Turkish migrants, who have passed this kind of theoretical vocaitional training. The Turkish government and trade
unions are quite familiar with these problems and tried to overcome the lack of practical training by special courses immediately combined with industrial work and in co-operation with the
Turkish exchange offices.

In the Third Five Year development plan of the Turkish State
Planning Organization we find the following conclusion under
the subject "Inadequate education services": "In general, the formal educational system does not conform to the need of the
economic and social development, nor is it susceptible to
changes. The informal education system also has proven inadequate to improve the manpower productivity necessary for higher production. Primary education does not provide the basic
needs either for further education or for a practical life."[3]

1.2.4. Unemployment as a permanent social situation

The result of the race between population growth, education,
vocational training and industrialization is finally deciding to labour market functions and employment. It is very difficult to get
statistical material about unemployment in Turkey with an at least
minimum of correctness. This is not a failure of the statistical administration, because all characteristics of unemployment in industrial countries are not comparable. So many social groups of
Turkish people, f.i. youth and unpaid family workers or other
disguised unemployed, can not be registered by statistical methods. Therefore estimations rely on very broad categories: The
main reason of these differences is the definition of unemployment, as we have seen before, either in the small sense of the
criterias in industrial countries or in the broader sense with disguised and latent unemployment.[4] In any case, unemployment is
outgrowth of the economic, social and regional structure, i.e. of
the disfunctional labour market. This statement could not be
disproved by some advances in industrialization and vocational

---

[3] State Planning Organization, *A Summary of the Third Five Year Development*.

[4] Nermin Abadan, Le non-retour à l'industrie, trait dominant de la chaine migratoire turque, *Sociologie du Travail*, Paris 1971, pp. 278-293, here p. 279.

training. The trends in unemployment between 1962 and 1972 can be demonstrated by an index on the basis of 1962 = 100, rising to 181 in 1972, thus nearly doubling in ten years. This rising unemployment has happened, although more than 500,000 Turks left in the same time their country for workplaces in West Germany. We see here, that in the race between population growth and labour market till now the former is the winner. All these arguments and trends confirm the accuracy or the title of this chapter: unemployment is a permanent social situation.

1.3. *Emancipation and migration*

The extensive migration as a consequence of a disfunctional labour market has different phases and goals in an internal or external direction.

1.3.1. *Internal migration*

The population growth of the towns mentioned before can be illustrated by the three steps the Turkish people went through from agrarian to urban life.

The first step is a transition from village to the next small town. It has already happened in the last 30 years and has multiplied the number of communities with more than 10,000 inhabitants (1935 = 80; 1960 = 138; 1965 = 168; Planning Officer of Turkish government). This mobility was a normal result of Turkey's growing infrastructure (road-making, building of water dams, etc.) and encouraged seasonal migration.

The second step which followed in recent years entails very often a shift from small towns to proving centres in Inner-Anatolia like Erzurum and Sivas and Eastern-Anatolia like Malatya and Van. Normally this migration phase results from the impossibility of working in the rural labour market and ends up in the final abandonment of village life. The two diagrams, based on estimations of the Turkish Planning Office, show, that till 1985 a mass migration from the country-side to the administration and industrial centres can be expected.

In the third phase these large scale population movements try to continue moving in the direction of a small number of large cities like Ankara, Bursa, Istanbul, Izmir. This is the last and very important goal of internal migration accompanied by numerous settlement problems. An important part of these internal migrants settles in the so-called "gecekondu" (squatter house) areas.

1.3.2. *External migration*

As we have mentioned earlier, the Turkish people had in earlier time no tendency to such regional mobility and migration.
The Turkish mentality is characterized by a conservative thinking,
distrust and reserve against new situations and strange people.
Religious, family and national thinking are typical of Turkish
attitude and human relations. To change this mentality by Euro-
peanization was one of the most important aims of Ataturk, the
founder of the Turkish Republic, but change was limited to West-
Turkey citizens and couldn't significantly influence Central and
Eastern-Anatolia. The famous Turkish proverb, that industrial
chimneys should be spread as "minaretts of Ataturk" all over the
country, has not been realized till now. The Turkish labour market was for a long time tight and very little influenced by internal
and external migration. The changing process of this conservatism was initiated by the exchanges with West-Germany which
began in 1961 and grew from year to year, as shown the following
table:

Table 3

*Turkish "guest-workers" in the Federal Republic
of Germany*

Time	Total Number
September 1964	85.200
September 1965	132.800
September 1966	161.200
September 1967	131.300
September 1968	153.000
September 1969	244.300
September 1970	353.900
September 1971	453.145
September 1972	511.600
January 1973	528.200

Source: Informationen zur Auslaenderbeschaefti-
gung.
Ed.: Bundesvereinigung der Deutschen Arbeitge-
berverbaende.

In the first years of the exchange policy Turks mainly from
the Western Anatolia provinces with better schooling and vocational training applied to the German recruitment offices in
Istanbul and Ankara. Later on Central and East Anatolia became

more and more important as secruitment area for foreign countries. Meanwhile responsible men of Turkish administration and economy in these regions stated, that external migration became immediately a necessity of existence for the people in the villages of Anatolia. We have seen that different push and pull factors succeed in overcoming a tight labour market and a large scale migration in Anatolia, they include the following in particular:

— a permanent structural open and disguised unemployment leading to external migration;
— urbanization and chances of better education, vocational training and social upward mobility in the city;
— growing self-consciousness and generation gap among the rural people of Turkey;
— attractive exchange possibilities for foreign countries with a preference for West Germany because of traditional friendship ties and high living standard.

Actually the Federal Republic of Germany has today a similar high attraction for Turks as in the last the United States for German people.

1.3.3. *Industrial work as a new social ideal*

The historian A. J. Toynbee[5] stated long before this large scale migration began, that: "The most remarkable and bold innovation of the young Turkish Republic may be, that Turkish people have a new social ideal: the goal of life is no longer as till now to work in agriculture and ruling on human beings, but to participate in commerce and industry". This statement seems somewhat surprising, if we consider, that the Turks prefer self-employment and no hard handwork. But the extensive migration seems to have changed the attitude to hard work and economy. This can be recognized by the answers of Turkish workers to the question: "What is the best way to rise the living standard?"

Two thirds of these answers are oriented on more work and industrialization as methods of social development in Turkey. Very few see amelioration of agriculture as the best path. We

---

[5] A. J. Toynbee, *Kultur am Scheideweg*, Berlin 1958, p. 141.

Table 4

Attitude toward work and economy

1. more work	30.1%
2. more new workplaces, diminution of unemployment	23.3%
3. industrialization	12.9%
4. wage increase, lowering of prizes	8.6%
5. establishment of social justice, further rights for the workers	4.9%
6. improvement of agriculture	3.7%
7. capital procurement, investments	2.5%
8. better policy, more political activity	1.8%
9. other answers	12.2%
	100.0%

Source: Survey carried out by the Institute of the Empirical Sociology, Saarbruecken, 1969.

know, that this is typical of underdeveloped countries all over the world, but it shows a new thinking of Turkish people in view of the conservative and stiffening mentality in the past: the Turks will become industrial-minded by push factors in their traditional life and pull factors in industrial modern life.

2. *Subjective Motivations of Turkish Migrants*

It is a common opinion in the Federal Republic of Germany, that foreign people have only one motivation in coming to work here: money making and high wages. In the chapter dealing with the objective reasons of large scale migration we tried to explain, that not only economic and social, but also cultural factors are push factors for low income people. In the case of the Turks, we know, that their mentality has many socio-cultural hindrances like family relations, religion, national consciousness and so on. These become more and more decisive with rising income and long-term involvement in industrial societies, because of the socialization effects in the working and social environment. The changing process begins by eliminating subjective considerations before the migration and lead some to the desire for integration in the new modern life and surrounding. This socio-psychological process is to be underlined briefly.

2.1. *Unemployment as social role and situation*

A disfunctional labour market with a permanent open or disguised unemployment has many consequences for the social role and life situation of the individuals in their family and neighbourhood. The attitude toward unemployment in the Turkish people is not unanimous. Some recognize unemployment as the sign of an individual destiny. This is characteristic of Muslim beliefs. Other Turks, certainly not a minority, resent this situation and the impossibility to care of the family. For them these are deep wounds in the pride of man. To be mainly dependent on relatives has an impact on self-consciousness and social relations. Generally the members of Turkish families have the special common sense to help each other not only in their own family, but also in the extended family. But this social oriented thinking will be influenced by the length of time spent in an unemployed situation and can change the norms of inter personel relations and individual attitudes. Social conflicts and daily reproaches can lead to an intolerable social climate. This is one of the reasons for the high percentage of readiness for work in any place outside of the home.

2.2. *Motivations to external migration*

The following table gives a breakdown of the special motivations concerning one's "pull and push factors" provoked by German's manpower recruitment policy.

Our study shows that unemployment is a fundamental push factor in connexion with earning chances, but some push factors are also pull factors for certain goals like saving to buy land or houses or further vocational training facilities for better work in Turkey. Other pull factors include experiences and contacts with "guest-workers" coming from Germany with remarkable changes in attitude and social situation, the desire to learn foreign languages and to know foreign countries. This makes clear, that not only unemployed people, but also self-employed, clerks, and small peasants are willing to go abroad to get a better chance for higher living standards.

Table 5

Motivations to external migration

1. unemployment		22.1%
2. money making, within:		39.9%
a) to gain money in general	30.1%	
b) saving for a fixed aim	9.8%	
3. "to secure the future"		4.9%
4. vocational training respectively continuation of vocational training		7.4%
5. other reasons, within:		19.0%
a) desire to know foreign countries	12.9%	
b) to learn foreign languages	5.5%	
c) "because it seemed, that other Turks were well in Germany"	0.6%	
6. no answer		6.7%
		100.0%

Source: Survey carried out by the Institute of the Empirical Sociology, Saarbruecken, 1969.

2.3. *The socialization effects of migration*

There are two socialization factors of external migration, which are very attractive to the Turks in contact with home-coming guest-workers. The first is the change of personal role-consciousness influenced by work and life in the foreign country, but with some difference: A Turkish migrant, who only plans to make money in any workplace, will seldom overcome the passive phase of socialization. He will re-adapt very soon to traditional norms after returning home; most of these people are unskilled workers in Germany. Other Turks who want to get vocational training and move upward in society will use the possibilities of learning new jobs and new languages. They may acquire self-criti-cal attitudes toward their original social environment and inter-personal relations. In this way they accept more active socializa-tion processes and adapt themselves to foreign customs, standard of living and thinking. A third group can develop an industrial minded and modern life personality, because they are not able to conform to the individual and social situation upon returning to their country. This third group can be the nucleus of moderniza-tion and industrialization in Turkey, although this will not go

without many social conflicts with their own family and neighbourhood. At the same time this group has the best opportunity
to be integrated in the foreign country. Socialization in this sense
very often leads Turkish migrants to compare the development
and situation of Turkey with Germany's. The question on the
causes of reconstruction and the high living standard of Germany
after the second world war was by more than 80% with "hard
work, good co-operation, planning and common sense", very few
mentioned "financial and other support from countries outside
of Germany, f.i. the United States". They emphasized in the
same vein that similar dynamic change in Turkey's economic and
social situation could be obtained by intensive work like in Germany, a more efficient administration, more economic planning,
more discipline and more social justice and fairness. They are
ready to sacrifice themselves for the development of Turkey, and
work as much ar possible, to invest part of their money and pay
more taxes.

3. Turkey's Perspectives on the Relation between Structural Unemployment and Migration

As we have seen, structural unemployment and the migration
of Turks are very closely connected. External migration is a very
important condition for remedying the shortcomings of the economic and social structure, improving social and individual situations on the background of planning activity and progressive
measures in Turkey itself. We have to consider in this respect
major sources of information about change in the next ten or
twenty years: the perspectives of the State Planning Organization
in Ankara, the integration of Turkey in international organizations such as the E.E.C. and the relations between social planning
and migration.

3.1. The Perspectives of the State Planning Organization in Ankara

The perspectives for the economic and social development in
the next twenty years are included in the Summary of the Third
Five Year Development Plan 1973-1977, published in 1973 by
the State Planning Organization in Ankara. The general outline of
this plan is portrayed as "more than just a projection into the

distant future; in fact it is a realistic statement to the goals to be achieved". (p. 38). These goals entail a fully industrialized economy, higher standards of living and more developed social institutions, comparable with higher developed industrial societies. Their terminal prospective year 1995 is the deadline when Turkey will be fully integrated into E.E.C.—these projections aim at a very high level of employment and the elimination of the disfunctional structure of the labour market. To what extent can this be recognized as a "realistic statement", under the present conditions. Let us consider the projections in detail.

We have already pointed out, that the race between population growth, industrialization and vocational training is deciding one for the economic and social future of Turkey. The Five Year Development Plan prognoses the population development for the following dates:

Table 6

Projection of population development in Turkey

	1972	1977	1987	1995
Population (in million)	37.5	42.6	55.5	65.9
urban – rural distribution (in %)				
– rural	62	53	38	25
– urban	38	47	62	75

Source: Third Five Year Development Plan, p. 54.

If we compare these figures with European countries: the expected population growth between 1972 and 1995 seems to be explosive. A similar growth rate, the Federal Republik of Germany would reach, have more than 100 million people. But Turkey is a three-times larger area than West Germany. Nevertheless the relations to the extent that between population and labour market including the age structure of Turkish people and educational standard already suggest at present the existence of so many unsolvable problems, a labour force in the size of 65,9 million population, i.e. about 30 million with an earning capacity, may simply make the situation even less manageable. Thus the

Five Year Development Plan give the following projective figures for migrants (cummulative after 1972, i.e. additional to the present number of Turkish guestworkers): 1977 = 500,000; 1987 = 1 million; 1995 = 1 million (p. 54). This is a small part of the projected labour force, but it is a high number in view of what foreign countries, and West Germany in particular will be able to absorb. The distribution of the projected rural and urban population can be considered as evidence of our thesis about the urbanization trends from internal migration. The figures show a marked decline of the rural population (62% in 1972 to 25% in 1995) and a significant growth of the urban population (38% in 1972 to 75% in 1995). One of the measures to achieve this goal is the establishment of "central villages" and small towns with more effective public services in rural areas. An other way is industrialization with the setting up of small and middle sized plants all over Inner—and East—Anatolia, till 1995.

"The three main components of population change, namely births, deaths and migration determine the general structure of population." (p. 154). The relation between birth-rates and death-rates is prognosed in the plan with the following declining figures from 37.5 in 1970 and 1975 to 26.7 in 1990-1995 for the birth-rate and 12.1 to 6.6 for the death-rate (p. 155). Thus the declining percentage for the birth rate is about 30%, while it is 50% for the death rate. Although the fertility rate in Turkey is expected to decrease, the population will increase in accordance with the difference between birth- and death-rates. Life expection at birth is estimated to be 65 years for males and more than 70 years for females in 1995 (p. 154). Today life expectation is normally 45 to 50 years. This raises the following question; what will the Turkish government do to lower the following fertility and birth-rates in order to reach better balance between births and mortality rates.

The educational and vocational perspectives of the plan are based on certain measures to develop the formal and informal aspects of education and training by means of an eight year cycle for basic education instead of five years now beyond pre-school instruction. In 1995 all children will attend the second cycle (sixth to eighth schoolyear). 45% will have the opportunity to have access to secondary education, 35% to general high school and 65% to vocational technical training (p. 58). This educational and vocational plan is grounded of the above mentioned assumptions of the plan, i.e. the coalescing of the population in villages and towns, the spreading of industrialization and the construction of thousands and thousands of buildings for the educational and professional schools of all levels. One of the most serious problems involved in the implementation of these plans is the recruitment of teachers. Since Ataturk's radical reform which substituted Latin to Arabic characters in the Turkish language many governments have tried to solve this problem not only by setting special schools for teachers, but also by inviting students and educated members of the military to teach for at least one year in the villages of central and Eastern-Anatolia. The results were not very encouraging. This means, that the educational and vocational system needs a thorough reorganization. The major principles of the Third Five Year Development Plan are:

— increase the social consciousness, knowledge and skills through education,
— adapt the educational system to manpower requirements,
— special training in modern industries using progressive technology,
— equality of educational opportunity and social justice for all individuals.

The State Planning Organization in Turkey will seek to implement these objectives by co-ordinating the various activities of ministries and institutions in the different sectors of planning and administration.

3.2. *Integration in international institutions*

Several international organizations have been willing for many years to help the Turkish economy and social development as illustrated by the recommendations and active support of for instance, the OECD in Paris, the ILO in Geneva, the European Council in Straesbourg and the E.E.C. in Brussels. They have special Turkey committees, primary under the aim to improve the economic and social structure and to fight against all forms of unemployment. Most important is the E.E.C. since Turkey has become an associated member and later will have the possibility to apply for full membership. An association contract with the E.E.C. was concluded in 1963 in Ankara and is effective since

1964. The most important parts of this contract consist of provisions for a development policy. Thus a permanent association council with members of the E.E.C. commission and the Turkish government has to prove each year the progress of industrialization and the standard of employment. It reports to the European parliament in Strasbourg. This report is normally focused on very concrete investment projects. For example, the establishment of electric power stations all over the country provide for settlements of households, waterworks, incandescent bulb plants, nylon plants, many long-term projects like bridges and road-making and other kinds of infrastructure works. A remarkably successful illustration of activities involving the co-operation with E.E.C., other international organizations and big private companies is the construction of the suspension bridge across the Bosporus for traffic between Europe and Asia. The industrialization policy of the association council encourages primarily small and middle sized factories for supplies and furniture. At another level, the association contract deals with the development of international commerce and provides for the establishment of the customs union in three phases: A five year preparatory phase; from 1964 to 1969, transitional period of twelve years. The last phase will be completed in 1991 with Turkey's full participation in customs union. The implementation of this timetable depends on Turkey's economic and social adaptation to the standards of E.C. The social policy adaptation is especially important for fighting against unemployment because it includes the opening of the Turkish labour market to all European countries. However article 12 of the Ankara contract stipulates that freedom of movement for labour will be realized step for step between 1976 and 1986. Until now only the Federal Republic of Germany has signed (in 1961) a bilateral contract with Turkey providing for an exchange of the labour force. This is not the beginning of liberalization itself, only a first step toward it. Full liberalization means the international right for Turks to take over any jobs in the European countries without special permission. At present, this liberalization has been prevented by blocking labour movements from Turkey to West Germany. Nevertheless the German government is still a partner to this agreement and remains Turkish single partner recognizing its exceptional position in the European labour market. The question is, what kind of social

policy the Turkish government can pursue inside Turkey to prepare the liberalization phase.

3.3. *Labour market migrations and social planning in Turkey*

In general the Turkish government has been in the last
20 years very planning oriented since three Five Year Development Plans were enacted in that period. The emphasis of the
three plans is very different: the first focused mainly on industry,
the second on the mechanization and productivity of agriculture.
The third combines intensively for the first time economic with
social planning. We define social planning as programming and
projecting conceptions relying on a sociological basis to achieve a
balanced social and ecological structure in the labour market.
The field of social planning can be divided in primary sector
(family planning, population planning, labour force planning),
secondary sector (education and vocational training planning, regional planning of settlements and work-places) and tertiary sector (electrification, road-making, communication—broadcasting
and television, press—last not least administration and government's activity). A centre of social planning like this in Turkey
should make projections for the economic and social functions of
the labour market. Part of social planning is conditioned by other
planning activity, beginning with family planning. The Third Five
Year Development Plan includes several goals, f.i. declining of
birth-rates, fight against childrens high mortality, progress in
modernizing the country-side, mainly East and South Anatolia.
But the plan does not spell out the nature of the means and
measures necessary to supplement the policy. Family-planning
will be especially difficult because of the national religious and
biological mentality of the Turkish people. Without an extensive
legislation it seems impossible to affect the race between population growth and labour market in the favour of the latter as well
as external migrations. In the same sense internal migrations are
the object of social planning in order to prevent the migratory
flows to feed the mushroom development of gecekondu in large
cities. All this is connected with social planning against illiteracy.
This entails not only the establishment of schools, for example, but also a greater density of mass communication through
regional and local radio and television facilities. A labour market
oriented toward social planning may be focused on the need to

fill the large lag between the possibilities and habits of life and thinking in the rural and urban parts of Turkey. This lag is the strongest push factor encouraging internal migration and increasing unemployment in the cities. So long as this goal of social planning is not reached, Turkish workers coming back from foreign countries may not be willing to readapt their life into the poor, undeveloped environment they have left. (see Nermin Abadan, loc. cit., pp. 293)

The quintessence of the analysis and arguments presented in this paper is, that the theories of full employment and social market have no chance to succeed, if the connection between labour market, migration and social planning is not reappraised to a new labour market policy in Turkey. This policy is predicated on the assumption that the Turkish population, a "sitting people" (Moltke) for a long time, must become highly mobile.

THE SCOPE AND NATURE OF TURKISH BRAIN DRAIN

TURHAN OĞUZKAN

International migration of talent could be regarded as a special feature of the over-all labor movement across national boundaries. Like the larger movement, it consists of outflow of people from their native lands to other countries in search of their fortunes elsewhere.

The impact of the two movements, however, is not entirely similar. While the international movement of labour relieves the pressure of surplus manpower for employment in one country, it adds to the productive power of the other. Hence, in spite of the existence of many serious issues associated with the movement, it is considered by and large to be beneficial to both countries supplying and absorbing the labor force.

Such a feeling of mutual benefit hardly prevails in the case of international migration of talent, and for appreciable reasons. Scientists, engineers, medical doctors and several other high-level professionals in any country form a small but strategic part of human capital for economic and social progress. They fulfill leadership positions in their professions and frequently in public life. Their contribution as a group to the quality of living is substantial. Some of them may have unusually rare qualities with which they can be instrumental in accelerating the process of development; others who are not as outstanding as the most able ones may be irreplaceable in their own ways. Finally, they all represent a large sum of investment as a result of care and education provided to them. Any large-scale and continuous flow of these professionals to other countries through migration results in the loss of brain power which could be used for purposes of national development.

What makes the problem especially serious is the acceleration of the brain drain movement itself as well as the direction of the flow. A report by the United Nations summed up the trend a few years ago by indicating that: "Highly trained personnel from many developing countries are emigrating to a few major developed countries, that the size of this flow is large and that it is increasing at a rapid rate."[1]

The attraction of foreign talent by developed countries is facilitated by a number of socio-economic factors including rapid scientific and technological advancement, continued production of new types of consumer goods, new marketing techniques, increasing purchasing power for the average worker, unprecedented growth in higher education, and massive programs of research and development. Conditions such as these at the same time have intensified the demand for selected professionals like scientists, engineers, and medical doctors. When these countries were unable to meet the rising demand through the use of their own human resources, they have turned to professionals from other lands to fill the gap.

Developing countries, on the other hand, are faced with serious socio-economic problems, aggravated by poor legacy of the past. Although many of them have made great strides toward modernization, it is a difficult struggle upward with scarce resources available to them. Therefore, unfavorable conditions continue to exist to a large extent. These conditions are reflected in the social, economic and political systems of these countries.

Booming industry and services coupled with favorable market conditions for highly trained professionals in advanced countries on the one hand, and the failure of the local labor market to absorb or to satisfy these professionals in the developing countries on the other hand foster the international movement of talent.

No less important than the socio-economic gap between the advanced and developing countries are the specific policies of some of the advanced countries to encourage the inflow of highly trained personnel from all parts of the world. The tradition of national ethnic quota systems for immigration has been replaced by a priority system on the basis of need for selected professionals.

The example of the United States is illuminating. That country attracting the highest number of talent, admitted approximately 125,200 immigrant scientists and engineers and 41,700 immi-

---

[1] Report of the Secretary General of the United Nations (UN), "Outflows of Trained Personnel from Developing Countries," General Assembly Document No. A/ 7294 (November, 1968).

grant physicians between the years 1949 and 1970. Until 1965, the bulk of these professionals came from European countries such as Germany and Great Britain due to national ethnic quota system in effect. After the 1965 revision of the basic immigration law changing the national quota system, the migration pattern shifted markedly. First, there was a substantial increase in the total volume of high-level immigrants. Second, the majority of immigrants began to flow from developing countries, especially from the Asian region led by India and Philippines. These trends and the practice are continuing.[2]

The intensity of the movement shows variation from one country to another. Not all the advanced countries serve as equally powerfull centers of attraction for the outside talent; nor do the countries with similar socio-economic conditions supply talent in similar proportions to the countries of attraction. If we take, for example, the case of brain drain from Western Europe to the United States, we see that the rate is high for Germany, Great Britain, Netherlands and Switzerland, while it is remarkably low for France. The same phenomenon was observed in a study of migration of scientists, engineers and medical doctors from Latin American countries to the United States; the rate of emigration per million population was found to be high in the case of Ecuador, Columbia and Argentina, whereas it was low for Peru, Uruguay and Brazil.[3] A recent study on high-level emigration from the Middle East to the United States gave similar results; there were wide differences among most of the countries in the rate of emigration relative to the total population.[4]

Professional variations represent another noteworthy feature of the movement. The US data show the engineers leading the inflow, followed by physicians and natural scientists. In the case of migration to England, it is felt that medical personnel is qualitatively if not in numbers are the most significant group.[5]

---

[2] Detailed information can be found in National Science Foundation, *Scientists, Engineers, and Physicians From Abroad: Trends Through Fiscal Year 1970*, Washington D.C.: The Foundation, 1972, pp. 1-3.

[3] Pan American Health Organization, *Migration of Health Personnel, Scientists and Engineers from Latin America*, Washington D.C.: The Organization, 1966, pp. 14-15.

[4] Committee on the International Migration of Talent, *The International Migration of High-Level Manpower: Its Impact on the Development Process*, New York: Praeger Publishers, 1970, pp. 261-263.

[5] For the US data, see National Science Foundation, *op. cit.* p. 1. Data on migra-

The observations above are indicative of the complexity of the international brain drain movement. They suggest also that the phenomenon cannot perhaps be explained solely on the basis of an economic analysis of supply and demand, or the theory of socio-economic gap between the advanced and developing countries. A number of intervening variables come into play, including specific policies of individual countries, historical affiliations, cultural ties, existing political and economic relations among countries, the aspirations of migrants, and several other factors. Each country, therefore, has its own unique problems and conditions deserving closer examination.

The intention of this paper is to review the scope, the direction and the nature of high-level emigration from Turkey. The plan includes a review of research findings and an analysis of factors which seem to be most relevant to the movement. Then, the recent policy attempts to control the outflow of highly trained professionals will be examined.

The Scope of Migration

Statistical Evidence

Statistics describing the scope of the international brain drain movement are far from perfect, and Turkey is no exception. One of the reliable sources is a UN document to which reference was made earlier. This document contains information about the size of brain drain from Turkey along with other developing countries. Although the information given covers emigration to a limited number of countries only, namely the United States, Canada and France, it nevertheless suggests the serious nature of the movement. According to that report, a total of 830 highly qualified persons migrated from Turkey to these three countries between 1962 and 1966. The professional distribution of emigrants was 388 engineers, 333 medical doctors, 58 natural scientists, and 14 social scientists. Out of 830 who migrated, 535 went to the United States, 161 to Canada, and 134 to France.[6]

---

tion to England can be found in a paper by Geoffrey Oldham and Oscar Gish titled "Migration of Professionally Qualified Manpower From the Developing Countries to Britain," in Committee on the International Migration of Talent, *op. cit.*, pp. 563-637.

[6] UN, *op. cit.*, pp. 60-65.

Using the UN data and the admission figures to the United States in 1967, Franck estimated the annual rate of high-level emigration from Turkey to these countries to be on the average of 172 persons between 1962-1966, and 265 in 1967.[7] Allowing for emigration to Germany, England and other countries for which no record was available, he estimated the global annual rate of emigration of high-level manpower from Turkey to be 375. Turkish State Planning Organization estimates that medical doctors made up 51.5 percent and engineers 40 percent of this 375 annual migrants during the years mentioned above, followed 5.5 percent natural scientists and 3 percent social scientists.[8]

The United States keeps a better record of the inflow of foreign talent where Turkish high-level emigrants prefer to go. For this reason, we may examine migration of Turkish talent to this particular country more closely. A recent document by the National Science Foundation gives us detailed information about the flow of talent into the United States from all countries including Turkey.[9]

Table 1 shows that a total of 1,501 Turkish scientists, engineers and medical doctors were admitted to the United States as immigrants during the fifteen years between 1956 and 1970; out of this total, 907 were scientists and engineers, and the remaining 594 were medical doctors. 1967 was a peak year when an exceptionally large number of medical doctors gained immigrant status. In spite of the fluctuations in the number of immigrants from year to year, the trend for an increase in later years is evident.

In addition to those who are admitted as immigrants, there are always a number of non-immigrants residing in the United States as exchange visitors, industrial trainees, temporary residents of distinguished merit or ability, and temporary workers performing services unavailable in that country. This particular group constitutes a potential source of immigrants. For example, it is estimated that 41 percent of the immigrant scientists and engineers in 1970 had previously worked in the United States under non-

---

[7] The study on "Brain Drain From Turkey" reported by Peter Goswyn Franck in the Committee on the International Migration of Talent, *op. cit.*, p. 301.

[8] Devlet Planlama Teşkilâtı, *Yeni Strateji ve Kalkınma Plânı: Üçüncü Beş Yıl, 1973-1977* (New Strategy and Third five-Year Plan of Development, 1973-1977), Ankara: Teşkilât, 1973, p. 687.

[9] National Science Foundation, *op. cit.*

immigrant status of one kind or the other. [10] Even if they eventually return to their homelands, all of those non-immigrants bring some increment to current manpower resources of the host country while staying abroad. There were 104 Turkish scientists and engineers, and 23 medical doctors in the United States with non-immigrant status in 1970. [11]

Finally, another category of Turkish citizens in the United States forming a potential source of immigrants is the students at various universities and colleges. Their number has exceeded 1,500 in recent years. After the completion of their studies, some of these students become engaged in full-time employment and take up permanent residence there. Since we will discuss Turkish

Table 1

Immigrant Scientists, Engineers and Medical Doctors
to the United States From Turkey As the Country
of Last Permanent Residence

Year	Scientists and Engineers	Medical Doctors	Total
1956	21	3	24
1957	40	17	57
1958	106	48	154
1959	70	19	89
1960	40	10	50
1961	30	43	73
1962	42	31	73
1963	128	55	183
1964	42	29	71
1965	37	36	73
1966	60	57	117
1967	84	111	195
1968	61	49	110
1969	64	42	106
1970	82	44	126
Total	907	594	1,501

Source: The figures are taken from National Science Foundation. *Scientists, Engineers, and Physicians From Abroad: Trends Through Fiscal Year 1970.* Washington D.C.: The Foundation, 1972. pp. 26-29, Tables B-1 and B-2.

---

[10] *Ibid.* p. 11.
[11] *Ibid.* pp. 34-41, Tables B-7 and B-8.

students abroad later in detail, here it may be sufficient to mention only this important group.

The foregoing analysis suggests that the size of emigration of high-level professionals from Turkey to the United States and to other countries may well exceed the annual average of 375 persons who formally adopt the citizenship of their host countries.

Significance of the Flow

The flow of high-level professionals from Turkey to other countries may constitute only a small portion of the global migratory movement. For example, 82 Turkish scientists and engineers who were admitted to the United States as immigrants in 1970 constituted only 0.6 percent of the world-wide immigration of 13,337. Similarly, 44 Turkish medical doctors admitted to the United States in the same year as immigrants were 1.4 percent of the total immigration of 3,155 for this category.[12] But the loss is substantial from the standpoint of Turkey. According to the figures given in the UN report, between the years 1962 and 1966, Turkey's loss of high-level professionals through emigration to the United States, France and Canada alone comprised 7 percent of the egineers produced at home during those years; the loss was 16 percent in the case of natural scientists and 15 percent in the case of medical doctors. As for the social scientists, the ratio dropped to 0.1 percent.[13] These ratios are indicative of the serious nature of the problem for Turkey.

There is also a qualitative aspect of the problem. It would certainly be an exaggeration to claim that those who choose to migrate from Turkey always represent the most outstanding individuals in their fields of specialization. But, there are many with outstanding records as scholars, researchers and professional leaders. In fact, a series of studies by İnönü and others using the Citation Index published annually by the Institute for Scientific Information in the United States indicates that some of the emigrants from Turkey have made significant contributions to research in mathematics, physics, chemistry and other fields.[14]

---

[12] *Ibid.* Calculated using the data given in p. 1.

[13] UN, *op. cit.*, pp. 60-65.

[14] The studies include one publication and several papers presented to the IV. Science Conference of the Turkish Scientific and Technical Research Council held in Ankara, November 5-8, 1973. The publication is by Erdal İnönü, *1923-1966 Döne-*

Studies on Migration

Systematic studies on the migration of talent from Turkey are limited. One of the earlier studies which was conducted by a team of researchers from John Hopkins University and Ankara School of Public Health dealt with the emigration of medical doctors. Ferguson and Dirican of this team reported on the findings of another survey which described selected characteristics of the Turkish medical school graduates in the United States. Franck reported the findings of a comprehensive survey of high-level emigration from Turkey as part of the Project of International Migration of Talent by Education and World Affairs (EWA); this study contains original materials on the emigration of Turkish engineers and a valuable analysis of major factors related to brain drain from Turkey. Oğuzkan studied Turkish Ph. D.'s working abroad. Üner investigated the cost of emigration of high-level professionals to the United States. In addition, there are references to high-level emigration from Turkey in some recent studies related mostly to the study-abroad program of the Turkish government. Some of the main findings of these studies are discussed below.

Medical Doctors Abroad

The John Hopkins-Ankara School of Public Health Study is a comprehensive survey of medical manpower problems in Turkey with a section devoted to Turkish doctors working abroad. [15]

minde Fizik Dalındaki Araştırmalara Türkiye'nin Katkısını Gösteren Bir Bibliyografya ve Bazı Gözlemler (A Bibliography Indicating the Contribution of Turkish Scientists to Research in Physics Between 1923-1966 and Some Observations), Ankara: Orta Doğu Teknik Üniversitesi, 1971. The papers are: Erdal İnönü, "1923-1966 Döneminde Türkiye'nin Matematik ve Mekanik Araştırmalarına Katkısını Gösteren Bir Bibliyografya ve Bazı Gözlemler" (A Bibliography Indicating the Contribution of Turkish Scientists to Research in Mathematics and Mechanics between 1923-1966 and Some Observations); M. Dizer and E. İnönü, "1923-1966 Döneminde Astronomi Dalındaki Araştırmalara Türkiye'nin Katkısını Gösteren Bir Bibliyografya ve Bazı Gözlemler" (A Bibliography Indicating the Contribution of Turkish Scientists to Research in Astronomy Between 1923-1966 and Some Observations); O. Birgül, S. Gürsey and E. İnönü, "Türkiye Kökenli Araştırıcıların Matematik, Mekanik, Astronomi, Fizik, Jeofizik ve Kimya Dallarındaki Makaleleri İçinde 1961 ve 1963-71 Citation Index Yıllıklarına Göre 9 veya Daha Fazla Referans Almış Olanların Listesi" (A List of Papers by Turkish Scientists in Mathematics-Mechanics, Astronomy, Physics, Geophysics and Chemistry Having 9 or More References in the Citation Index for the Years 1961 and 1963-71).

[15] C. E. Taylor, R. Dirican and K. W. Deuschle, Health Manpower Planning in Turkey, Baltimore: John Hopkins Press, 1968.

The data were based on a questionnaire sent to 10 percent random sample of 1,257 doctors out of a total population of 12,275 for the year 1964. It was estimated on the basis of this data that 2,284 or 18 percent of the living graduates of Turkish medical schools were working abroad. Germany attracted the highest number of Turkish doctors with 832, followed by the United States with 607. The rest were mostly in Great Britain, France, Switzerland and Scandinavian countries.

In reply to a question as to the main reason for the emigration of Turkish doctors, 68 percent of the sample mentioned unsatisfactory professional income at home. The need for professional advancement was indicated as the main cause by 12 percent. About 6 percent referred to lack of solidarity in the Turkish medical profession. Approximately 6 percent stated that the living conditions were more comfortable abroad. Finally, 5 percent attributed the migratory movement to inefficiency of the health organizations in Turkey.

The study showed that 4 percent of the general practitioners and 25 percent of the specialists in Turkey at the time of survey had had some previous work experience abroad. Half of this particular group stated that they were hoping to go out again. As for the entire group working in Turkey, 20 percent of the general practitioners and 22 percent of the specialists or residents expressed a desire to go abroad.

The survey of selected characteristics of the Turkish medical school graduates in the United States by Ferguson and Dirican was an outgrowth of the John Hopkins-Ankara School of Public Health Study.[16] The survey was based on the records of the American Medical Association as of May 1965. According to this source, the number of Turkish doctors residing in the United States at that time was 538, of whom 165 or 30 percent were engaged in specialized training mostly working as interns or residents, while the remaining 373 or 70 percent were employed by medical institutions or engaged in private practice. In examining graduation dates, it was discovered that comparatively few newly graduates go to the United States, while their number increases sharply five years after graduation.

---

[16] Donald C. Ferguson and Rahmi Dirican, "The Turkish Medical Graduate in America, 1965: A Survey of Selected Characteristics," *The Turkish Journal of Pediatrics*, July 1966, 8:3, pp. 176-190.

Ferguson and Dirican also analyzed the sources of income of Turkish medical school graduates in the United States, exclusive of those in training. They found that the largest proportion (58 percent) were working in hospitals or medical schools on full-time basis. The proportion of those whose incomes were derived primarily from fee-for-service activities was somewhat less (34.6 percent) but still substantial. An interesting fact was that 3.5 percent of practicing Turkish doctors held the rank of assistant professorship or a higher rank in the US medical schools, indicating rather a noteworthy achievement in view of the keen competition for such positions of high prestige.

No doubt, many Turkish doctors who go abroad for training or practicing purposes return home. The fact that more than one fourth of the doctors working in Turkey at the time of the John Hopkins-Ankara School of Public Health Study indicated to have had previous work experience abroad confirms this view. The extent of this turnover, however, is not entirely clear. Hence, the data in the Ferguson and Dirican report as to the citizenship and visa status of the Turkish doctors in the United States may be illuminating. The information on this aspect, however, was not as complete as for some other characteristics due to great many whose resident status were not known. No information was available in the case of 24 percent of trainees and 35 percent of the practicing doctors. Nevertheless, the data showed that more than half of the entire group of Turkish medical trainees held exchange visas which required the person to leave the United States at the end of his training for a minimum period of two years. Most of the practicing Turkish doctors, on the other hand, had either permanent visas or had already acquired immigrant status.

Engineers and Architects Abroad

Most detailed information on the emigration of Turkish engineers and architects is found in a recent study of Turkish brain drain reported by Franck. [17] The data were collected by using the records of Turkish Chamber of Engineers and Chamber of Architects. Although these records were far from perfect, they nevertheless provided a basis for fairly reliable estimates.

The records of the Chamber of Engineers and the Chamber of

---

[17]   See the citation 7 above, pp. 299-373.

Architects showed that there were 975 Turkish engineers and
architects working abroad out of a total of 17,233 registered
members as of April, 1968. The emigrant group constituted
5.6 percent of the total membership in both Chambers. The actual size of emigration, however, should be larger for at least two
reasons: First, members do not always inform their Chamber
when they leave Turkey in order to work abroad; second, the
Chamber does not keep a record of engineers or architects who
study abroad and remain there permanently. Franck was willing
to use a correction rate of 50 percent for underestimation. Table 2 shows in the first column the actual registered membership
of Turkish engineers and architects, and the following two columns list the number and percentage of those working abroad,
based on the information provided by the Chamber of Engineers
and the Chamber of Architects. The last two columns list figures
as adjusted by this writer according to 50 percent correction rate.
As it will be seen, adjusted number of Turkish engineers and
architects working abroad in 1968 consisted of 1,462 persons,
comprising 9.6 percent of all the registered members.

Table 2

Turkish Engineers and Architects Working Abroad 1968

Category	Total Number Registered	Working Abroad			
		Unadjusted		Adjusted*	
		Number	Percent	Number	Percent
Civil Engineers	5,257	187	3.6	280	5.3
Mining	1,264	11	0.9	16	1.3
Chemical	1,708	43	2.5	64	3.7
Electrical	2,356	231	9.8	347	14.7
Mechanical	3,527	176	5.0	264	7.5
Architects	3,121	327	10.6	491	15.7
Total	17,233	975	5.6	1,462	9.6

* After correcting for 50 percent underestimation'

Source: Adapted from Table 12.3 in the Committee on the International Migration
of Talent. *The International Migration of High-Level Manpower: Its Impact On the
Development Process. New York:* Praeger Publishers, 1970. p. 308.

Table 2 reveals also the variations in the rate of emigration according to fields of specialization. The architects and electrical engineers are affected the most by the movement, while the rate is lowest among the mining engineers.

The study reported by Franck also provided information as to the geographical distribution of Turkish engineers and architects working abroad. Of those whose locations were known, over one-fourth resided in the United States and England, while an equal proportion worked in Germany, Holland, and Switzerland. Only 4 percent were reported to reside in France. If the number of unknowns were to be distributed in the various countries based on the known residences, the Anglo-American share would be 38 percent, the German-Swiss 35 percent, the French 6 percent, leaving the rest for the other countries.

The study by Franck included a section on the possible causes of emigration of Turkish engineers. They were largely based on the impressions of Cevdet Kösemen, head of an engineering consulting firm in Ankara, who conducted a fact-finding survey for the Project. According to Kösemen, the main causes for the emigration of Turkish engineers were the lack of opportunity at home for professional advancement, administrative-political insecurity, lack of appreciation of work, and dissatisfaction with the slow rate of progress in managerial efficiency.

Turkish Ph.D.'s Abroad

The study by Oğuzkan dealt with the Turkish Ph. D.'s working abroad in 1968. Based on 150 replies to a questionnaire out of an estimated total of 217, the study analyzed the direction, nature and causes of the brain drain movement for this particular group. [18]

The analysis of the geographical distribution of the group indicated 71 percent of the respondents residing in the United States,

---

[18] Turhan Oğuzkan, *Yurt Dışında Çalışan Doktoralı Türkler: Türkiye'den Başka Ülkelere Yüksek Seviyede Eleman Göçü Üzerinde Bir Araştırma* (Turkish Ph. D's Working Abroad: A Study of High-Level Emigration From Turkey to Other Countries), Ankara: Orta Doğu Teknik Üniversitesi, 1971. For a comprehensive report of the main findings of this study in English, see Turhan Oğuzkan, "The Turkish Brain-Drain: Migration Tendencies Among Doctoral Level Manpower," in R.E. Krane (ed.), *Manpower Mobility Across Cultural Boundaries: Social, Economic and Legal Aspects*, Leiden: Brill Publishing Company, 1975.

followed by 10 percent in Canada, 8 percent in Germany, and the rest in France, England and other countries.

Natural scientists and engineers made up more than three-fourths of the respondents as Table 3 indicates. Most of them worked in universities, devoting their time mainly to research activities, followed by teaching. A partial comparison of professional earnings of the group working in the United States showed that on the average they did as well as their American colleagues.

An analysis of the forces pushing the emigrant Ph. D.'s out of Turkey and the ones attracting them to the countries of their residence indicated that the professional reasons ranked highest, followed by economic reasons and others such as social, cultural, political, personal or family reasons.

The questionnaire also inquired about the intention of Ph. D.'s working abroad to return to Turkey in the not too distant future. One-third of the group stated a definite or a probable intention to return. Another one-third was undecided. The rest expressed a probable or a definite decision not to return to Turkey, with some unknowns. Although two-thirds of the respondents had

Table 3

Fields of Specialization of Turkish Ph.D.'s
Working Abroad
1968

Field	Number	Percent
Natural Sciences	57	38.0
Social Sciences	20	13.3
Humanities	5	3.3
Engineering	58	38.7
Agriculture	8	5.3
Others	2	1.4
Total	150	100.0

Source: Turhan Oğuzkan, *Yurt Dışında Çalışan Doktoralı Türkler: Türkiye'den Başka Ülkelere Yüksek Seviyede Eleman Göçü Üzerinde Bir Araştırma* (Turkish Ph.D.'s Working Abroad: A Study of High-Level Emigration From Turkey to Other Countries). Ankara: Orta Doğu Teknik Üniversitesi, 1971. p. 70, Table 10.

been employed full-time abroad for more than three years, the great majority (79 percent) retained their Turkish citizenship.

Analyses on the basis of current need for Ph. D.'s in Turkey especially in sciences and technical fields suggest that the outflow of talent from Turkey at this level is substantial. It is estimated that the total of 217 Ph. D.'s working abroad at the time of the survey were equivalent to about 18 percent of the total number produced in Turkey between the years 1933 and 1968.

Cost of Migration

A variety of approaches could be used for estimating the cost of high-level emigration. On the one hand, only those who adopt foreign citizenship may be considered as permanent losses. On the other hand, one may include in his estimate the entire high-level professionals working full-time abroad, regardless their resident status. There may be other ways of interpreting the outflow such as by duration of stay in a particular foreign country or by the intention to stay abroad.

Another consideration in this regard is whether one limits his estimation of cost to the original investment on the person, or one adds the total value of future earnings during the productive years. While the first item involves living costs, spending on education and earning foregone while in school, the second item includes the value of estimated earnings throughout the professional life.

One of the studies on the cost of high-level emigration from Turkey was conducted by Üner. This particular study took into consideration scientists, engineers and medical doctors admitted to the United States with immigrant status in 1967. The cost per immigrant included both the original investment embodied in the person and the estimated value of future earnings lost to Turkey. It was estimated that the total cost per immigrant was approximately $ 90,000 on the basis of 1965 value of dollar. This unit cost was applied to 203 immigrants in the year selected, and the loss to Turkey in that year due to emigration to the United States alone was calculated as $ 18,270,000. [19]

---

[19] Hasan Üner, *The Economic Impact of the Outflow of High-Level Manpower From Turkey to the United States*, Unpublished master thesis, The George Washington University, 1968.

According to Franck the loss to Turkey per high-level emigrant is considerably higher -estimated to be $ 175,000 per person at 1965 value of dollar. If this is applied to 375 Turkish high-level professionals admitted annually as immigrants to various foreign countries, the yearly loss to Turkey would be over $ 65,000,000. Some $ 11,500,000 of this amount is attributed to the loss of original investment on emigrants, and the remaining $ 54,000,000 is an entry due to estimated output lost to Turkey during the professional life. When the $ 11 million loss in investment was compared with the total amount of capital-formation in the educational system each year, it was found to be around 2-3 percent. On the other hand, the $ 54 million which was estimated as the earning capacity embodied in the emigrants was equivalent to one month of commodity exports in foreign exchange in the mid 1960's. [20]

The fact should be underlined that both of the estimates given above take into consideration only those Turkish emigrants who have adopted the citizenship of another country. They do not include those who work abroad with non-immigrant status. It was pointed out earlier that there is a large body of Turkish professionals who work full-time abroad without changing their citizenship status. Some of them wait for their turn to be admitted as immigrants in the host country, while others prefer to keep their original citizenship although they are settled abroad for an indefinite period of time. Therefore, the loss of Turkey due to high-level emigration should be much higher than the estimates found in the literature.

Other Studies

The Turkish Scientific and Technical Research Council and the State Planning Organization have recently been active in sponsoring a number of studies on various scholarship programs for Turkish students in higher education. These studies provide valuable information as to the policies and the implementation of scholarship programs at the undergraduate and graduate levels abroad as well as at home. Among them are a comprehensive study of the government-sponsored Turkish students abroad by Uysal; two papers on the training of scientists and high-level

---

[20] Committee on the International Migration of Talent, *op. cit.*, pp. 342-344.

technical personnel by Türkeli; a survey of scholarships at home and abroad by Soy; another survey focusing on scholarship programs of the State Economic Enterprise System by Güven; and a description of NATO Science Fellowship programs in Turkey by Özoğlu. [21] There is an agreement in these studies that the existing policies of scholarship and the study-abroad program of the Turkish government should be adjusted to new needs and conditions which have emerged. The relationship between the study-abroad program and the migration of talent out of Turkey will be examined in the next section.

Migration In Broader Perspective

A complete analysis of the brain drain movement needs to take into account all the relevant socio-economic factors both in the country of emigration and in the countries of destination as well as the way these factors are perceived by the individual who is a potential emigré. Such a comprehensive treatment requires the development of a better theoretical basis for research in the area. Here, the discussion will be confined to two selected socio-economic factors in Turkey which can safely be assumed to be related to the movement, namely higher education as the agent producing high-level manpower, and the absorptive capacity of the local market to utilize this manpower.

Although the balance between the supply and demand of high-level manpower is basic in explaining the brain drain movement,

---

[21] Şefik Uysal, *Yurt Dışında Yetişen İhtisas Gücü: 1416 Sayılı Kanunun Resmi Öğrencilerle İlgili Uygulamasına Ait Bir Araştırma* (High-Level Manpower Trained Abroad: A Study of Public Law No. 1416 As Applied to Government-Sponsored Students), Ankara: TUBITAK, 1973; Arif Türkeli, *Planlı Dönemde Yüksek Seviyeli Bilim Adamı ve Teknisyen Yetiştirme Politikası* (The Policy of Training Scientists and High-Level Technical Personnel During the Planned Period), Mimeographed, Ankara: TUBI-TAK, 1971; Arif Türkeli, *Planlı Dönemde Yüksek Seviyeli Bilim Adamı ve Teknisyen Yetiştirme Politikası: 1416 Sayılı Kanun İçindeki Doktora Faaliyetleri* (The Policy of Training Scientists and High-Level Technical Personnel During the Planned Period: Training Ph. D's Through the Use of Public Law No. 1416), Mimeographed, Ankara: TUBITAK, 1972; Muzaffer Soy, *Yurt-İçi ve Yurt-Dışı Akademik Eğitim Bursları Üzerine Bir İnceleme* (A Study of Scholarships For Academic Training At Home and Abroad), Mimeographed, Ankara: Devlet Planlama Teşkilatı, 1971; Nuray Güven, *İktisadî Devlet Teşekküllerinin Burs Programları Uygulaması İle İlgili Bir Arastırma* (A Study of Scholarship Programs of State Economic Enterprise System), Mimeographed, Ankara: TUBITAK, 1970; S. Çetin Özoğlu, *Nato Science Fellowship Programmes in Turkey*, Mimeographed, Ankara: Turkish Scientific and Technical Research Council, 1971.

it certainly does not depend on that alone. There are a number of other factors influencing the movement such as cultural, political, or personal considerations. This particular aspect of the movement will be brought to attention at the end of this section.

Production of High-Level Manpower at Home

High-level manpower for Turkish economy is produced in domestic institutions of higher learning as well as through the long-standing study-abroad program.

Domestic institutions of higher education in Turkey can be grouped into three major categories: (1) autonomous universities; (2) semi-autonomous academies; (3) colleges under the sponsorship of various government organizations. There were 9 universities, 12 commercial or technical academies, and around 40 colleges in 1973. The existing institutions of higher learning are expanding, and the new ones are being added each year.

The total number of students in all higher learning institutions was around 70,000 during the academic year 1962-63; this number grew to more than 175,000 in 1972-73, representing an increase of two and half times within a period of one decade. The percentage of the age group attending higher educational institutions is also rising fast. While 3.3 percent of the group between the ages 19-22 attended these institutions during the academic year of 1960-61, the percentage rose to 6.8 in 1970-71. It is expected that 9 percent of this age group will attend the institutions of higher education in the academic year 1977-78.

In spite of these developments, institutions of higher education are far from being able to accomodate the increasing number of high school graduates who apply for entrance. From nearly 140,000 applicants who took the entrance examinations to universities and other institutions of higher learning in 1973, only about 37,000 were admitted. [22] Although many of these applicants were already university students taking the entrance examination for the second time for the purpose of changing their fields of study, it is estimated that only one out of two or three applicants find their way into institutions of higher learning. The pressure is mounting with each passing year in such a way that

---

[22] Milli Eğitim Bakanlığı, *Yüksek Öğretim Kuruluşları İle İlgili İstatistikler* (Statistical Data on Higher Educational Institutions), Mimeographed, Ankara: Bakanlık, 1973, p. 33.

access to higher education has become one of the political issues of recent years. The present trend favors the realization of a fast increase in the capacity of higher education by expanding existing institutions, setting up new ones, and experimenting with innovative approaches such as two-year degree programs and televized teaching. At the same time, there are attempts to guide more students into terminal programs at the secondary school level.

A continuing problem of Turkish higher education is the ineffective distribution of students in various major fields of study. While the greatest need of manpower lies in the areas of pure and applied sciences, the majority of students (about 60 percent) are enrolled in social sciences and humanities. It is noteworthy that the brain drain movement affects the scientific, technical and medical fields the most where student concentration is relatively low.

Aside from quantitative problems, another issue that has been raised is whether the instructional programs in higher education are in tune with the requirements of work in the economy. The feeling is that the universities and other institutions of higher education generally follow a rigid academic program. State Planning Organization complains that the graduates cannot find employment easily because of their highly theoretical orientation. As a result, when the labor market fails to absorb them or when it is unable to achieve maximum utilization of their talent, they seek employment abroad. [23] There is a growing tendency now to develop more flexible programs so that the need of the industry at various levels can be met.

The Study-Abroad Program

Turkish students planning higher education abroad may qualify for certain programs of grants and aids such as scholarship programs of Turkish Scientific and Technical Research Council and other research institutes; scholarships granted by domestic and foreign universities; grants by foundations; bilateral exchange programs such as those of Fulbright and AID; sponsorship of international organizations like the UN, NATO, CENTO, and other sources. Although the full extent of these various scholar-

---

[23] Devlet Plânlama Teşkilatı, *op. cit.*, p. 768.

ship programs has not been examined, they may all together constitute a sizeable operation. [24] The most extensive of these programs, however, is the study-abroad program of the Turkish government.

The study-abroad program which has been in operation for a long time, is administered by the Ministry of Education. The program has a dual purpose: To supplement the programs of domestic universities, and to keep abreast with the latest developments in sciences and technology. Students in the study-abroad program fall into three categories: (1) those financed by the government; (2) those under private sponsorship with permit to use official foreign exchange reserves; and (3) those without foreign exchange permit depending on private support abroad. In general, the private students with or without foreign exchange permit far exceed the government students in number. Both government and private students are controlled by inspectors attached to the Ministry of Education and stationed in various centers abroad. The official control is much tighter on government students.

There has been in recent years a sharp increase in the number of private students without foreign exchange permit. Basically due to the increase in this particular category, the total number

Table 4

Turkish Students Abroad By Type of Sponsorship
April, 1971

Sponsorship	Number	Percent
Government Sponsored	1,424	17.0
Private Students With Permit	1,603	19.2
Private Students Without Permit	5,309	63.8
Total	8,336	100.0

Source: Based on figures given in Milli Eğitim Bakanlığı. *Yurt Dışı Devlet Öğrencileri Bilgi ve İstatistiği, 1971* (Information and Statistical Data on Study-Abroad Program, 1971). Mimeographed. Ankara: Bakanlık, 1971, p. 69.

---

[24] For example, during the years 1959-1971, a total of 251 post-graduate and 163 post-doctoral fellowships were awarded in sciences and technical fields under NATO Science Fellowship Programs. See S. Çetin Özoğlu, *op. cit.*

of students in the study-abroad program rose from 4,622 in June 1968 to 8,336 in April 1971, and to 13,668 in 1972.[25] Table 4 shows that approximately 64 percent of the Turkish students in the study-abroad program in 1971 were private students without foreign exchange permit, while the rest were divided almost equally between the government-sponsored students and private students with foreign exchange permit.

The geographical distribution of the students studying in different countries under the study-abroad program as of April, 1971 is given in Table 5. The country which attracts the highest number of Turkish students is Germany, followed by the United States, England, France, Switzerland and other countries.

Table 5

*Geographical Distribution of Turkish
Students Abroad
April, 1971*

Country	Number	Percent
Germany	3,772	45.3
U.S.A.	1,576	18.9
England	918	11.0
France	625	7.5
Switzerland	317	3.8
Other	1,128	13.5
Total	8,336	100.0

Source: Same as that of Table 4.

A breakdown of Turkish students abroad by fields of study indicates that roughly two-thirds are enrolled in sciences and engineering.[26] In contrast to ineffective distribution of students at home among the major fields of study from the stand point of manpower needs, here the pattern tends to be dominated by labor market forces.

The division of Turkish students abroad between undergrad-

---

[25] The figure for 1968 is taken from Committee on the International Migration of Talent, *op. cit.*, p. 313. Figures for later years are obtained from the Turkish Ministry of Education.

[26] Committee on the International Migration of Talent, *op. cit.*, p. 319, Table 12.7; Arif Türkeli, *op. cit.*, (1972), p. 5, Table 2.

uate and graduate studies can be seen in Table 6. While 39 percent of the government-sponsored students were doing undergraduate work in 1971, this proportion rose to 61 percent among
the private students with official exchange permit and to 89 percent among the private students without official exchange. If the
entire student body abroad is considered as a whole, those who
were at the undergraduate level made up 72 percent of the total.

Table 6

Turkish Students Abroad By Level of Education
April, 1971

Level	Government Sponsored		Private Students With Permit		Private Students Without Permit		Total	
	No.	*Percent*	*No.*	*Percent*	*No.*	*Percent*	*No.*	*Percent*
Undergraduate	564	39.6	983	61.3	4,453	89.7	6,000	72.0
Graduate	860	60.4	620	38.7	856	10.3	2,336	28.0
Total	1,424	100.0	1,603	100.0	5,309	100.0	8,336	100.0

Source: Same as that of Table 4.

Since most of the undergraduate studies can be pursued in
Turkey, the large number of Turkish students doing undergraduate work in foreign universities may largely due to bottleneck
for entrance to the most popular fields at home. The practice is
not entirely in line with the purposes of the study-abroad program. It is especially open to criticism in view of the fact that the
monetary value of the whole operation was estimated to be as
high as TL 375 million, or approximately $ 27 million for the
academic year 1970-71. That was three times the total investment value spent in that year for creating additional space in
Turkish universities, or equal to 81 percent of the current expenditures allocated to all universities of Turkey. [27]

To what extent is the study-abroad program of the Turkish
government a source of drain on Turkish talent? Referring to
official sources, Franck estimated the loss to be around 5 percent. [28] This is rather a conservative estimate. A recent study by

---

[27]   Arif Türkeli, *op. cit.*, (1972), p. 3.
[28]   Committee on the International Migration of Talent, *op. cit.*, p. 313.

Uysal indicated that over a period of more than 40 years between 1929 and 1972, the rate of non-returnees among students sponsored by the government was as high as 8.2 percent or even higher. [29] Since students in this category are under contractual agreement to return to Turkey and to serve for an obligatory period of time, one may reasonably guess that the rate of non-returnees would be much higher among the privately supported students with or without foreign exchange permit. Furthermore, some of the students who return home after the completion of their studies abroad leave Turkey following a few years of work experience.

There is another type of evidence indicating a close relationship between study abroad and high-level emigration from Turkey. That is the rate of emigration tends to be much higher among those who study abroad compared with those who study at home. For example, the rate of emigration among the Turkish engineers who studied abroad was 15.8 percent as of 1968, whereas it was 3.9 percent among those who studied in Turkey. [30]

There is little doubt that whatever other benefits it may bring, the study-abroad program of the Turkish government is a major source of brain drain. Almost all those who have studied the program advise major policy changes such as the restriction of opportunity for undergraduate study and a more selective approach in sending the students for graduate study abroad.

Labor Market For High-Level Manpower

A crucial question to be asked is the extent to which the local labor market has the capacity to absorb highly trained manpower produced at home and abroad. Although there are important variations from one particular field of specialization to another, the over-all analysis on the basis of 1965 population census and the absorption rate over the years 1960-1965 indicated that the local labor market had the capacity to absorb almost all the graduates. [31] Recently, however, an oversupply of graduates has begun to pile up in such fields as architecture, civil engineering,

---

[29] Şefik Uysal, *op. cit.*, p. 71, Table 20.
[30] Committee on the International Migration of Talent, *op. cit.*, p. 312, Table 12.5.
[31] *Ibid.*, pp. 324-326.

chemical engineering, agriculture, forestry, dentistry, and phar-
macology, while the shortage continues to be most evident in
natural sciences, mechanical engineering, electrical engineering,
mining engineering, and teaching profession at the secondary
school level. [32]

What does the future hold? What kind of a balance is to be
expected between supply and demand of high-level manpower as
the economy continues to develop? State Planning Organization
estimates that the present shortages will continue in many fields
mentioned above through the year 1992; in addition, shortages
are expected starting from the mid 1970's in technical fields
where there is an oversupply at present. [33] This estimate, of
course, assumes a certain rate of supply of graduates and a particular pattern in economic growth. New conditions may arise due
to a number of possible developments, including a substantial
increase in the number of graduates as a result of a more liberal
admission policy to higher education, major changes in social and
economic policies, or simply failure to reach the targets of various economic projects. In the event of such changes, adjustments
will have to be made to restore a balance between supply and
demand for high-level manpower.

Certain inherent weaknesses of the present Turkish labor market for highly trained professionals constitute perhaps a more
serious problem than the problem of balance between supply and
demand. These weaknesses may be summed up as structural, re-

Table 7

Ratio of Technicians Per Engineer in Turkey

Category	1960	1965	1970
Construction Tech./Architect + Civil Eng.	1.5	1.0	0.7
Mechanical Tech./Mechanical Eng.	2.5	1.6	1.9
Electrical Tech./Electrical Eng.	3.5	3.5	2.5
Mining Tech./Mining Eng.	0.3	0.4	0.5
Chem.Tech.-Lab. Aid/Chem. Eng.	5.3	5.8	4.7
Agric. and Forestry Tech./Agric. and Forestry Eng.	0.6	0.5	0.5

Source: Devlet Planlama Teşkilâtı. *Yeni Strateji ve Kalkınma Planı: Ücüncü Beş Yıl
1973-1977.* (New Strategy and Third Five-Year Plan of Development, 1973-1977).
Ankara: Teşkilât, 1973. p. 697, Table 538.

---

[32] Devlet Planlama Teşkilatı, *op. cit.*, p. 81.

[33] *Ibid.*, pp. 704-707, Table 546 and 547.

gional and sectorial imbalances. They deserve special attention because of their relevance to the brain drain movement. In fact, they all limit, or affect the absorptive power of the local labor market for talent in unique ways.

Structural imbalance means lack of proper skill ratio in terms of supporting personnel per professional. Table 7 shows the ratio of technicians per various types of engineers. The situation has been far from satisfactory, and it grew worse in most fields between 1960 and 1970.

The problem is even more serious in medical profession. Table 8 shows the ratio of supporting medical personnel per doctor. The improvement was slow between the years 1962 and 1971. The nurse/doctor ratio in Turkey is four times lower than most of the developed countries.

Table 8

*Ratio of Supporting Health Personnel
Per Doctor in Turkey*

Category	1962	1967	1971
Nurse/Doctor	0.17	0.52	0.55
Midwife/Doctor	0.41	0.47	0.71
Health Officer/Doctor	0.37	0.49	0.63

Source: Same as that of Table 7. p. 698, Table 539.

There are similar structural imbalances in terms of junior instructional staff per professor in the universities, and secreterial or managerial help for the administrators.

The problem of structural imbalance forces high-level professionals to perform sub-professional duties, leading to lower efficiency and to lower morale. It is one of the major reasons for widespread dissatisfaction with their work.

The second weakness of the labor market for highly trained professionals in Turkey is the regional imbalances in living conditions and professional opportunities. The difference is even greater between the urban and rural areas, which naturally forces the educated people to establish themselves in larger urban centres.

The John Hopkins-Ankara School of Public Health Study provided interesting evidence concerning ineffective distribution of medical doctors, based on the doctor/population ratios in eight

different regions of Turkey as of 1964. As Table 9 indicates, the
Black Sea coast and Southern and Eastern Anatolia had the few-
est doctors, and the European and Central Anatolian regions had
the most. Further analysis by the research team showed that

Table 9

Distribution of Turkish Doctors and Population
By Region

Region	Estimated 1964 Population	Number of Doctor	Number of Persons Per Doctor
Turkey in Europe	3,006,000	3,948	761
Black Sea Coast	4,907,000	555	8,841
Marmara and Aegean Coast	4,933,000	1,462	3,373
Mediterrenean Sea Coast	2,336,000	473	4,938
West Anatolia	2,590,000	391	6,623
Central Anatolia	7,594,000	2,561	2,965
Southeast Anatolia	1,317,000	159	8,284
East Anatolia	3,946,000	451	8,749
Total	30,629,000	10,000	3,063

Source: C.E. Taylor, R. Dirican and K.W. Deuschle, *Health Manpower Planning in Turkey.* Baltimore: John Hopkins Press, 1968. p. 38, Table 3-3.

whereas 6,450 doctors out of a total of 10,000 (64,5 percent)
worked in three provinces, namely Ankara, Istanbul and Izmir
which represent 15.8 percent of the total population, 2,948 doctors or 29.5 percent were serving the 56 percent of the total
population in thirty-nine provinces, and 603 doctors or 6 percent were practicing in twenty-five provinces with 28 percent of
the total population.

An analysis by the State Planning Organization in 1970 indicates that this pattern has not been changing. It is reported that
65 percent of medical doctors were working in Ankara, Istanbul
and Izmir provinces where only 17 percent of the population
lived. [34]

Other professional groups also have a tendency to settle in
bigger urban centers. It is estimated that more than half (53 percent) of all technical and professional people of Turkey live in
three largest cities, namely Ankara, Istanbul and Izmir. [35]

---

[34] *Ibid.*, p. 699.
[35] Committee on the International Migration of Talent, *op. cit.*, p. 331.

Finally, a third weakness of the labor market for high-level manpower in Turkey is sectorial imbalances. Table 10 shows that 45 percent of engineers were working in the service sector in 1965 in contrast to 30 percent in construction enterprises and 23 percent in industry. Similarly, 67 percent of professionals in agriculture were employed in services, and only 22 percent in agriculture. In the case of professionals in chemistry and physics, the proportion working in the service sector stood at a very high 74 percent. The data are indicative of the traditional inclination of the Turkish educated classes to work in offices rather than out in the field.

Table 10

Sectorial Distribution of Manpower in Turkey 1965

Category	Agriculture	Industry	Construction	Services	Total
Engineers	0.8	23.3	30.0	45.9	100.0
Occupations Related to Agriculture	22.8	5.1	5.7	67.0	100.0
Occupations Related to Chemistry and Physics	0.5	22.4	3.0	74.1	100.0
Technicians	0.6	25.3	28.6	45.5	100.0
Skilled Workers	0.2	81.9	14.1	3.8	100.0

Source: Same as that Table 7. p. 699, Table 541.

In addition to structural, regional and sectorial imbalances, an important aspect of the labor market relevant to high-level emigration is the salary structure. Turkish medical doctors in the government service have always had the problem of low salaries unless they supplement their incomes by private practice. University staff and research workers are paid modestly. As for the technical personnel working in public sector, they are now paid according to a salary schedule common to all government employees while they were accorded a special renumeration between the years 1958 and 1970.[36] In addition, living standards

---

[36] Engineers and other technical personnel used to receive higher salaries compared with other categories of civil servants by use of a contractual arrangement on per diem basis. The recent law for government employees brought an end to this special renumeration.

of the civil servants haven been affected by spiraling inflation. Although the private sector generally pays better and adjusts salaries to rising prices more satisfactorily, the available positions in that sector are limited.

These adverse conditions are aggravated still further by poor organization and administration, lack of facilities for productive work, lack of recognition of the value of professional skill, seniority rule, and sometimes unsatisfactory human relations. Studies indicate that these and similar non-monetary factors related to working conditions often act as strong forces leading to high-level emigration from Turkey.

Other Factors Relevant to Migration

Even if the local labor market were to function satisfactorily, there would still be some highly trained professionals who would prefer to work abroad for a variety of reasons. These reasons include search for novelty, curiosity about a particular foreign culture, desire to master a foreign language, and desire to live in a more satisfying cultural milieu. Family reasons may play a part such as marriage with a foreign spouse. Political reasons may lead to migration. The study by Oğuzkan showed that although the great bulk of Turkish Ph. D.'s working abroad migrated for professional and economic reasons, push-forces from Turkey included social and cultural reasons for 8 percent, political reasons for another 8 percent, and personal or family reasons for 11 percent. [37]

Policies and Action to Deal With Migration

There has been a growing awareness of brain drain as a problem in Turkey within the past decade. The press has been instrumental in bringing the loss of Turkish talent through migration to public attention. Government circles have been stressing for some time the need for controlling the movement. Although limited in number and scope, studies have been sponsored by the Turkish Scientific and Technical Research Council and the State Planning Organization. Other organizations including the Ministry of Health and Public Welfare, the Chamber of Engineers, the Cham-

---

[37]   Turhan Oğuzkan, *op. cit.*, p., 86, Table 23.

ber of Architects, and medical associations have shown an active interest.

The State Planning Organization is the main body for developing policies and proposing specific measures to control, or at least to regulate the brain drain movement out of Turkey. The need for a policy to deal with the problem has been repeatedly expressed in the First, Second and Third Five-Year Plans since 1962. Specific measures have been stated both in the plan and annual programs. They range from measures of a forcing nature, to improvements of the local labor market and the encouragement of talent to work at home. Examples of proposed measures of a forcing nature are the establishment of obligatory work for university graduates in Turkey for a fixed period of time, passport restrictions, and avoidance of granting permission for work to students abroad after graduation. Proposed measures which aim at encouragement of high-level professionals to work at home include care in the use of scarce talent in most appropriate positions, dissemination of information about employment opportunities, salary adjustments, and recognition of professional experience gained abroad. [38]

It is clear from the nature of proposed measures that there has not been any consistent policy to approach the problem during the past years. In fact, none of the measures specified by the State Planning Organization has been put into operation in any effective way. In the meanwhile, a few institutions have been trying on their own initiatives to attract high-level Turkish professionals working abroad. Among them are the Turkish Scientific and Technical Research Council, and some of the newly established universities such as Boğaziçi University, Hacettepe University, and the Middle East Technical University.

Concluding Remarks

The evidence reviewed in this paper provides sufficient ground to conclude that the international brain drain movement affects

---

[38]   The specific measures proposed by the State Planning Organization up to 1971 to control brain drain are summarized by Parla Kişmir. "Outflow of High-Level Manpower From Turkey," in State Organization for Administration and Employment Affairs, *R.C.D. Seminar on Brain Drain, Tehran, Nov. 15-18, 1970*, Teheran: SOAE, 1971.

Turkey in several important ways. The loss of talent due to migration is substantial and continuous. The magnitude of the problem can be understood better when comparisions are made between the rate of outflow and the rate of production or the total stock of high-level professionals to meet the domestic needs. The movement costs Turkey millions of dollars each year in terms of monetary value of the human capital lost. But the greatest loss perhaps lies in the potential contribution that these people could have made to the economic and social progress of their native country.

The movement affects certain professional groups more than the others, namely medical doctors, engineers and scientists. These are the professionals relatively costly to train, generally more scarce, and invaluable in the process of development. The evidence suggests that there are several outstanding Turkish researchers and professional leaders working abroad. Data on geographical distribution shows that Turkish talent is particularly attracted to Germany in Western Europe and to the United States in North America. Other countries which attract Turkish talent in sizeable number include England, France, Switzerland, Scandinavian countries and Canada.

There may be several explanation of high-level emigration. Large demand for scarce resources of talent in the free international labor market is one explanation. The theory of supply and demand is certainly a most valid explanation, but it needs at least one qualification. That is the resultant balance at a given time is only partially controlled by the free play of market conditions. A considerable degree of control comes from the immigration policies of some of the advanced countries which try to use the brain drain movement to serve their own best interests.

Another explanation is the existence of a wide socio-economic gap among the regions of the world, creating centers of magnetic pull for high-level professionals from the less developed areas. The strength of the pull, however, seems to depend on factors existing in the countries supplying the talent.

What we may reasonably conclude at this stage of theorizing and research is that the international migration of talent is a highly complex phenomenon. It has at least three distinct dimensions: Pull-forces in the country of destination; push-forces in the country of origin; and the perception of these forces by the potential emigrant. This three-dimensional model implies also an interplay of a whole series of relevant socio-economic factors as well as psychological forces leading to migratory behavior.

Here in this paper, certain factors which seem to be most relevant to the outflow of talent from Turkey are examined. The higher educational system and the capacity of the local labor market to absorb or to satisfy the graduates are analyzed. Certain weaknesses of the higher educational system and of the labor market at home combined with favorable working and living conditions abroad act as strong forces pushing many high-level professionals out of Turkey.

Prospects For the Future

What are the prospects concerning Turkish brain drain during the immediate years ahead? Is the movement going to continue at an accelerating rate, or become stabilized at a certain level, or loose its strength? The answer depends on what relevant socio-economic developments may take place at home and in countries which attract talent from Turkey.

Present conditions and trends in Turkey seem to be conducive to an acceleration in the rate of high-level emigration. Among these are oversupply of graduates in certain fields, the phenomenal growth of the study-abroad program in recent years, plans for more liberal admission to higher education, structural and functional weaknesses of the local labor market for full utilization of high-level manpower, and the failure to implement effective measures to control the outflow. It seems that Turkey is very much at the mercy of developments abroad as far as the outflow of talent is concerned. Unless advanced countries attracting talent reach a saturation point and, as a result, change their present liberal immigration policies, brain drain will most likely continue to be a source of grave concern for Turkey in its efforts to make full use of her human resources for economic and social progress.

MANPOWER AND EMPLOYMENT POLICIES UNDER THE FIVE-YEARS PLANS AND EMIGRATION

İSMAIL HAKKI AYDINOĞLU

I. *Introduction*

It is required that a country willing to realize its economic development and achieve its foreseen growth targets, must consider and develop manpower, as well as the other factors, to a sufficient level and qualification so as to reach the desired production goals. Before taking any decision on an investment project, for instance, manpower requirements needed for the project are to be considered and planned.

The realisation of economic development consistent with the determined growth targets, will only be possible by taking into account the changes in manpower composition. Particularly in underdeveloped countries, skilled manpower is either insufficient or non-existent. Therefore, as development plans are prepared, the critical factor that needs to be determined is to increase the efficiency of manpower. However, the efficiency of the labour force in a branch of activity is determined by the present levels of technology and manpower composition. In reality, development in any country can be maintained by, in addition to all other growth factors, the efficient utilisation of existing manpower. But, optimum utilisation and mobilisation of manpower can bring a solution to the problem in the short run.

A real development plan implies that utilisation of all resources needed to achieve economic and social growth should be in balance. The rôle of manpower policy in such a plan is to greate a qualified labour force required in all stages of economic activity, utilize this according to its ability and skill, prevent imbalances in occupational distribution of active population, and improve its geographical distribution within the country.

II. *Concepts*

In reality, manpower, on which more emphasis should be placed, is the most important production factor used in development. However, this point has not been given sufficient importance.

Before going into manpower planning, it will be useful to distinguish some critical concepts which are usually confused by most of us and specify differences among them.

1. *Economically active population (Gainful Worker or Gainfully Occupied)*

In an economy, the economically active population is that part of the total population which is employed, active or fulfilling a function. The criterion here is the fulfillment of a specific function or having an occupation. It does not take into account whether an individual works during a short period of time or not.

2. *Labour Force*

The concept of labour force takes the activity of a person during the specified period as a basis. In other words, it considers the person's contact with the labour market during this specified period.

3. *Manpower*

Manpower expresses the potential or maximum employable portion which should be drawn from the total population. It is that portion of the total population which has knowledge and skill towards the production of goods and services.

The concern of an economically-active population, unlike the concept of labour force, is not the short run: it approaches the concept of manpower and covers all the persons having an occupation. What separates economically an active population from manpower is that it excludes first job seekers that is, those having no job experience before. Thus, an economically active population gives the inventory of present human resources in a more narrow sense than manpower.

Therefore, the concept of labour force has been proposed for evaluating the short-term changes which are impossible to evaluate by using the concept of an economically active population.

The common point that we faced in the definitions of both

economically active population and manpower concepts is the condition of having a gainful job. In principle, those satisfying this condition are included in the employed and those seeking a job are included in the unemployed. The sum of employed and unemployed gives the civilian labour force. Similarly, the sum of the civilian labour force and armed forces makes up the total labour force. The rest is the economically inactive population. Children, old people, students, housewives, permanent disabled pensioners, rentiers, beggars, etc. are included in this group.

III. *Manpower Planning*

Manpower planning is the formulation and determination of ways which will ensure the best and most rational utilisation of economically-scarce manpower resources in order to reach certain specified goals. The achievement of a socio-economic development plan largely depends on the effort which aims to provide the participation of manpower in sufficient quantity and quality in development efforts on time. Manpower planning should, therefore, consider a manpower inventory which easily follows the changes in economic and social structure. For this reason, a developing and growing economy should estimate, like other factors, manpower requirements both quantitatively and qualitatively in the development process.

Therefore, in order to achieve pre-determined targets, manpower requirements and their quality have to be estimated in the preparation of the development plans and the occupational breakdown thereof must also be determined. Otherwise, it could create manpower surplus or such a manpower inventory that is out of the desired skill level. As it is seen there is a close relationship between manpower and educational planning; in fact they go side by side. In other words, if education, in addition to its own educational goals, takes the training of manpower as a means to educate the labour force in both sufficient number and skill levels, it has to be studied together with manpower policy. Training-within-industry and on-the-job training, in addition to educational plans, play an important rôle in changing manpower structure and raising it to a desired skill level.

After deciding whether labour intensive or capital intensive methods should be adopted in production, future volume of work and manpower requirements must be estimated. The age composition of the active population is also one of the important points that need to be considered in this process. Furthermore, the removal of the organisational rigidities must be taken into account.

Manpower planning is not only related to the quantitative and qualitative aspects of manpower, but also to the distribution of manpower in the country level and the efficiency of this distribution.

IV. *Manpower in the Development Plans*

The attainment of a sufficient growth target in Turkey depends on the efficient utilisation of all economic production factors which are composed of natural and human resources and capital. Since capital is a relatively scarce factor, more emphasis should be placed on the optimum utilisation of capital and best distribution of manpower resources so as to meet the needs of the economy.

Prior to the First Five Year Development Plan period, no study had been carried out in Turkey on manpower and its distribution. The manpower situation of the pre-Plan period can only be drawn from the age composition of the population and the sectoral and occupational distribution of labour force from one population census to another. In a study carried out by the State Planning Organisation (SPO) in 1967, covering the years between 1955-60, it was seen that the proportion of engineers had increased by 58%, technicians by 21% and skilled workers by 23%. Although the number of health personnel has increased gradually within the same period, this rate of increase is insufficient.

Both the First and Second Five Year Plans linked the social and economic development of Turkey to industrialisation. In the 1960s, it was believed that the realisation of development could only be possible if surplus labour in agriculture were transferred into non-agricultural sectors by increasing investments in industry.

In the First Five Year Plan, manpower estimates were the assessment of required personnel and the measures that should be taken for the attainment of this volume. The then-present manpower situation in various sectors was determined first, then on

the basis of this data and in connection with the rate of increase
in production, future requirements in the subsequent 15 years
were projected. In addition to production and investments that
were used in the assessment of manpower requirements, these
estimates have also given weight to other factors such as population growth, rate of increase in per capita income, international
comparisons, and social standards of Turkey. Later there had
been established a relation between the labour force needed in
various sectors and the training institutions, and the necessary
re-orientation and direction that should be given to these institutions in order to attain manpower goals. Plan estimates and results in some occupations are shown in Table 1.

Table 1

First Five Year Plan, 1965 Estimates and Realisations

Occupation	1965 Plan Estimates	Realised	% Difference
Engineers	15,000	26,900	+80
Health Personnel	11,000	14,600	+33
Teachers	30,000	21,000	−30
Technicians	27,000	33,600	+25
Supporting Health Personnel	11,000	14,900	+35
Primary School Teachers	63,000	85,100	+33

The increase in achievements is not due to the measures
adopted, but it should be attributed rather to the low estimates
and inexperience in the field.

In the Second Five Year Development Plan, projections were
made by taking manpower needs in all sectors of the economy
into consideration. However, these projections were not carried
out for all occupational groups in sectors, but only those categories that were seen significant for economic development, such
as technical and health personnel, and the other related occupational groups. Estimates concerning manpower composition
were based on the elasticity coefficients between sectoral employment by occupations and sectoral production or income.

Since health personnel requirements are based on economic

factors rather than social factors, these requirements, in the Second Plan period, were estimated on the basis of population growth, national level of welfare and international standards. The international ratio of health personnel per doctor was taken as one of the determining criteria in the calculation of supporting health personnel requirements (dentist, chemist, nurse, midwife, and medical staff). Demand for managerial and administrative personnel was also determined by considering international standards. These projections were revised in the light of estimates and surveys made by employers, related institutions and ministries.

Problems concerning manpower in Turkey are twofold: first, the shortage of skilled, especially technical, manpower to achieve development targets; second, imbalanced distribution of available skilled manpower among various sectors and its inefficient utilisation. Although the First and Second Five Year Development Plans have proposed some measures and recommendations concerning the solution of these problems both for the short and the long-run, quantitatively and qualitatively, the result did not reach expectations—some of the measures remained in theory only. A great number of proposed measures were not put into force during the last ten years.

Existing manpower resources and gaps in the Second Five Year Plan period are given in Table 2.

As it is seen in the following table, manpower gaps are growing. Closing these gaps and establishing an effective management, the most productive utilisation of existing manpower resources, prevention of surplus in some sectors and increasing the mobility are required.

V. *Developments in the Planned Period and Manpower Problems of Turkey*

Although there have been significant increases in the number of skilled personnel in the planned period, bottlenecks and rigidities have continued to maintain their existence in satisfying manpower requirements on time both quantitatively and qualitatively, and their efficient utilisation. Within the technical branches, however the supply of technicians and some skilled personnel has fallen short of the requirements. A similar situation

Table 2

Second Five Year Development Plan—Existing Manpower and 1970-72 Gaps

Occupations	Present Manpower 1965	Manpower Gaps		
		1970	1975	1980
1. Engineers	20,132	12,418	23,912	44,635
2. Supporting Scientific Personnel	33,627	20,072	62,075	141,365
3. Agriculture and Forest	8,831	5,701	9,043	17,091
4. Physics and Chemistry related manpower	4,317	308	621	1,124
5. Skilled Workers	1,235,062	337,320	884,563	1,575,682
6. Doctors	10,895	16	2,775	9,605
7. Supporting Medical Staff	18,636	8,363	25,063	47,770

Source: Second Five Year Development Plan Studies for 1965, April 1967, Manpower, p. 15, Table 7, and p. 16, Table 8.

was also observed in the health personnel category. (Tables 3, 4 and 5)

In addition to these, imbalanced distribution of manpower both at country and sectoral level is apparent, and this point is particularly important concerning teachers, medical staff and technical manpower. The brain-drain also causes the existing gap to be enlarged. It was determined that, until 1970, 7% of architects, 5.3% of mechanical engineers, 8.2% of doctors and 21.4% of medical practitioners emigrated to foreign countries to work. Similarly the emigration of skilled workers increases this gap considerably. The emigration of 88,000 skilled workers in the 1965-70 period increased the requirements in this field by 26%. It will be recalled that the number of Turkish workers employed abroad at the end of 1971 reached 570,000, and it is estimated to be approximately 800,000 at the end of 1973. The Third Five Year Plan assumes that this rate of increases will not change and estimates the number of workers going abroad at approximately 350,000. This means a yearly outflow of 70,000. Although, during 1973, 134,000 workers went abroad, the 1974 picture is

Table 3

Quantitative Improvement of Technical Manpower

Occupation Groups	1960	1965	1970
Engineers	15,461	17,692	31,401
Construction Engineers and Architects	4,168	5,552	12,469
Mechanical Engineers	1,866	2,550	5,101
Electrical and Electronics Engineers	907	1,415	2,494
Metallurgists	660	773	1,474
Chemical Engineers	984	914	3,174
Map Makers, Cartographers, Topographers	1,023	1,386	2,721
Other Engineers	5,853	5,102	3,968
Technicians	27,056	37,417	54,753
Construction Technicians	6,336	5,505	8,162
Mechanical Technicians, Assembly Workers	4,263	4,179	9,522
Electricial and Electronics Technicians	3,205	4,904	6,348
Metallurgical Technicians	205	316	794
Technical Painters, etc.	1,925	5,572	8,502
Chemical Technicians	106	315	907
Laboratory Assistants and Pharmaceutical Laboratory Assistents	5,373	7,382	11,223
Other Technicians	5,643	9,244	9,295
Agricultural Staff	5,555	8,957	17,923
Agricultural Engineers	1,504	3,034	
Forestry Engineers	922	1,539	10,316
Veterinarians	1,398	1,574	1,927
Agricultural Technicians and Biologists	1,376	1,964	
Forestry Technicians	88	444	5,567
Animal Health Workers	246	345	113
Others	21	57	—
Skilled Workers	998,902	1,235,391	1,831,110
Furnace, Rolling mill and foundry workers	13,759	19,379	10,948
Machine, Equipment and Metal Products	182,874	235,981	291,231
Electricians and related Workers	24,924	39,393	59,184
Construction and related jobs	100,983	119,755	407,752
Other Skilled Workers	676,362	820,883	1,041,995

Source: State Institute of Statistics.

Table 4

Quantitative Improvement of Manpower in Health Services
(In thousands)

	1962	1967	1971
Doctors	9.0	11.9	15.8
Dentists	1.6	2.2	3.2
Pharmacists	1.5	2.2	3.0
Nurses	1.6	6.2	8.8
Medical Staff	3.4	5.9	9.9
Midwives	3.7	5.6	11.3

Source: Ministry of Health and Social Welfare

Table 5

Number of Teachers by Educational Levels

	1960-61	1966-67	1970-71
Primary Education	61,230	95,417	134,624
Secondary Education (General)	7,469	13,876	20,459
Secondary Education (Vocational and Technical)	5,123	8,688	10,895
University and Higher Education	4,071	5,517	8,499

Source: Ministry of Education.

clouded by the threat of a major recession aggravated by the oil crisis. If a serious recession occurs in 1974, not only will the outflow of workers cease, but people employed abroad cannot hope to remain in their host country. This particular aspect of the subject will be analysed in a later section of this article.

In the light of the results derived from the implementations of the First and Second Five Year Development Plans, the critical problems which must be solved immediately in the training of manpower in sufficient number and quality can be listed as follows:

1. *Quantity and Quality Problems*

a) The sectoral distribution of manpower in Turkey is not proportional to requirements. It is estimated that there was 1.6 million surplus labour in the economy at the end of 1972.

However, some branches of non-agricultural sectors suffer from certain manpower shortages.

b) A suitably comprehensive training system has not been designed to meet the requirements of the economy.

c) In 1972, the manpower requirements of the economy in such fields as architecture, construction, chemistry, agriculture and forestry were exceeded by increases in the availability of highly qualified manpower. An increasing number of Private Engineering Schools created this imbalanced situation.

d) Due regard has not been given to increasing the numbers of skilled and semi-skilled workers in order to keep pace with the evegrowing availability of highly qualified manpower. Thus, the numbers of technicians and skilled workers have not met the economy's requirements.

e) The number of students in technical and vocational training schools is less than the number in general education. For this reason the ratio of students per teacher in general education increased and the number of techers became insufficient to meet the increase.

f) Since in higher technical education necessary importance has not been given to scientific and technical research, this has caused scientific research to lag behind imported advanced technology.

g) The number of technicians per engineer is very low and gradually decreasing, causing manpower to be misused, so that the desired level of production falls behind predicted levels.

h) A similar situation is also seen in the health services: insufficiency of the ratio of supporting health personnel per doctor decreases the efficiency of medical services.

i) Although there are sufficient numbers of managerial and administrative personnel, their quality cannot be said to be high enough to meet the requirements of modern management.

2. *The Problem of Regional and Sectoral Allocation of Manpower*

In Turkey the regional and sectoral distribution of manpower is imbalanced. During the two planned periods this distribution has not been changed, and particularly in the service sector the surplus has increased. Despite the measures taken, this uneven distribution is more apparent in the allocation of teachers and medical staff than in other fields.

3. *Emigration of Skilled Workers*

For various reasons, trained manpower is seeking employment opportunities in foreign countries and the problem of the brain-drain is becoming exceedingly important. At the time of writing, one-tenth of existing skilled manpower is employed abroad. In addition to the emigration of professional manpower, skilled workers are also leaving the country at an ever-increasing rate. Between 1965 and 1972 the average skill mix of the emigrated labour force was between 30 and 35 per cent: in 1973 it reached the striking proportion of 45.7%, severely aggravating the situation in some already hard-hit branches.

4. *The Problems of Manpower Supply*

The main problems encountered in manpower supply are the insufficiency of resources allocated to training, imbalanced distribution of scarce resources among technical, vocational and general training, long gestation periods of investment in the field of training, and lack of adjustment of the training system to an expanding economy. In the field of higher education scarce resources were diverted from the technical branches requiring high cost and long-maturity periods that the economy demands to those in which there were already surpluses that the economy cannot use such as literature, philosophy, languages, etc.

The high tendency of supporting personnel in various fields to go on to higher education caused a sharp decline in filling their places.

5. *Wage Problem*

Imbalanced and insufficient wages have caused the already existing wage differentials between private and public sectors to increase. Thus, there have been technical manpower movements from the public to the private sector and from the private sector to foreign countries.

VI. *Manpower in the Third Plan*

The Third Five Year Plan stipulates that in the manpower policy of the years ahead due account will be taken of the inter-dependencies between training, industrialisation and employment and prime emphasis will be put on supplying the necessary manpower required by an expanding economy. Skilled manpower trained in past plan periods will be used for the new requirements of industrialisation and growing manpower needs precipitated by the new technology will be trained.

From the end of 1976 Turkey will be affected by the free circulation of labour within the Common Market in accordance with the provisions of the Additional Protocol which states the conditions of full association between Turkey and the European Economic Community.

Manpower requirements in the Third Five Year Plan were estimated by the SPO by taking into account production, value-added, investment, employment and improvements in productivity and international comparisons. It was assumed that the volume of emigration will not be different from previous years. Sectoral breakdown of manpower structure in the years 1970 and 1992 is given in the Table 6.

In addition to the policies which will be followed in the field of education, it will be necessary to develop policies concerning the efficient utilisation of manpower, wages, working conditions and social status in order to attain targets in the manpower field. It was assumed that, in the Third Plan period, manpower demands would be met by the working of the present training institutions at full capacity. Since the results of the investments in the field of education and the new training system can be achieved solely in the long run, manpower gaps can only be closed in the Fifth Plan Period.

Manpower needs in health services have been estimated by assuming no change in physical units and manpower utilisation standards. Since health service standards will be increased after 1982, there will be a significant increase in manpower requirements depending on these targets. The supply of managerial and administrative personnel will rise so as to meet the demand in 1977.

Table 6

Sectoral Breakdown of Manpower Structure in 1970 and 1992 (Per cent)

Occu-pational Groups	1970				1992			
	Agri-cul-ture	Ind-ustry	Ser-vices	Total	Agri-cul-ture	In-dustry	Ser-vices	Total
Engineers	1.0	54.0	45.0	100	0.6	64.4	39.0	100
Agricul-tural per-sonnel	22.0	11.0	67.0	100	45.0	12.0	43.0	100
Natural Science personnel	1.0	24.0	75.0	100	1.2	46.8	52.0	100
Technic-ians	1.0	57.0	42.0	100	0.8	65.2	34.0	100
Entre-preneurs and manage-ment class	2.0	20.0	78.0	100	1.0	32.0	67.0	100
Skilled workers and arti-sans	4.0	54.0	42.0	100	2.0	87.0	11.0	100

The solution of the above-mentioned problems, in addition to meeting growing demands rationally and the utilisation of manpower in accordance with rational priorities will be the keystones of the Third Five Year Plan. This of course requires national manpower planning.

Manpower mobility between sectors and regions is affected by wage and employment policies. If the necessary measures are taken, the drain of skilled workers from the public to the private sector will be discouraged.

The existing educational system is not considered adequate for the training of skilled manpower and therefore the emphasis will be given to on-the-job training and the necessary programmes will be prepared. Surplus labour in agriculture will be trained and transferred to industry in order to increase labour mobility. As soon as the "Industrial Training Bill", which was prepared by the

Employment Service, becomes law it will bring major improvements in the fields of pre-employment and on-the-job training. This bill encompasses work sites employing more than 15 employees in order to transform unskilled workers into skilled ones. Thus the requirements of an expanded economy for skilled manpower will be satisfied this way.

VI. *Employment—Domestic and External*

In the First and Second Five Year Development Plans, it was expected that the employment problem would take care of itself as a result of rapid economic growth. It was thought that rapid economic development would generate ample employment opportunities.

Although the First Five Year Plan adopted employment as an independent goal *per se* this was only a qualitative objective and was not integrated into the macro model as an independent variable. In the Second Development Plan employment was considered a dependent variable and employment targets were derived as a result of income growth.

In the Third Five Year Plan strategy, long-term development targets are broken down in a systematized manner. These ultimate targets are industrialisation, decreasing dependence on external sources, amelioration of the employment problem and equitable income distribution. Therefore the solution of the employment crisis was considered as one of the most important ultimate aims of the 25-year Perspective Plan. It was assumed that employment and income distribution problems would resolve themselves during the process of industrialisation, so they are not considered among the short-term goals of the Third Five Year Plan. In summary it can be stated that full employment will be reached by the end of the Perspective Plan period (1995) but no policy action was proposed as a means of reaching the target.

1. *Progress in the Employment Situation during the First two Development Plans (1962-1972)*

Improvements in employment during the First and Second Five Year Plan periods are given in Table 7.

Table 7

Improvements in Employment (1962-1972)
(in thousands)

Year	15-64 Population Age Group (1)	No. Employed (2)	15-64 Population Age Group not in the active Labour Force (3)
1962	15,970	12,520	3,450
1967	17,920	13,270	4,650
1972	20,350	14,110	6,240

Source: Third Five Year Development Plan p. 76.
Turkish workers abroad were not taken into account.

Employment in the 15-64 age group during the planned period rose from 12.5 million in 1962 to 14.1 million in 1972 at an increase of 12.7%. However, the rate of increase of the same section of the population was 27.3%. As this situation shows, employment opportunities increased less than the population growth.

The analysis of the sectoral breakdown of employment in the past two Plan periods leads to important observations. Table 8 shows the sectoral distribution of civilian employment in the last ten years.

Table 8

Sectoral Distribution of Civilian Employment (1962-1972)

Sectors	1962 (1)	1967 (2)	1972 (3)	1962 (4)	1967 (5)	1972 (6)
Agriculture	9,220	9,070	8,770	77.1%	71.3%	65.0%
Industry	995	1,175	1,520	8.3%	9.2%	11.3%
Services	1,660	2,150	3,070	13.9%	16.8%	22.7%
Other	80	340	130	0.7%	2.7%	1.0%
Total Employment	11,955	12,735	13,480	100.0%	100.0%	100.0%

Source: Third Five Year Development Plan, p. 78.

Analysis of the Table shows that there is a marked decline in the share of agriculture in employment. This is the usual pattern observed in an expanding economy. The second conclusion derived from the Table is that employment opportunities generated during this ten-year period have been mostly in the service sector. This is an indication of an uneven development strategy.

2. *Employment in the Third Five Year Plan*

In the Third Five Year Plan, the realisation of full employment and the attainment of just income distribution have been adopted as the long-term perspective goals. Also it was accepted in the perspective Plan that in 1995 full employment will be attained with one-quarter of the working population being employed in agriculture, one-quarter in industry and the remaining portion in services.

The policies to be implemented in the Perspective Plan period to increase employment possibilities and ameliorate income distribution will be put into effect in such a way that the pace of industrialisation will not be slowed down. In other words, the solution of the employment problem in the short-run will not be found by adopting labour intensive technology and setting up an unemployment insurance system system at the expense of industrialisation. The contrast between rapid industrialisation and full employment in the short run will be gradually eliminated at the end of the Perspective Plan period. In fields such as chemicals, petro-chemicals, machinery, iron and steel and metal working industries the most advanced and capital-intensive technologies will be used. However, in the construction, ship-building, electronics, forest products and earthenware industries labour-intensive technologies will be adopted. These industries require intensive labour and do not suffer from international competition.

During the Third Five Year Plan period, emphasis will also be given to the collection of more accurate employment data.

Long-term projections in the labour supply and demand situation are given in Table 9.

Table 10 gives the sectoral breakdown of employment in percentage terms.

This table shows the sectoral distribution of employment in the Perspective Plan period.

Of course the employment opportunities foreseen to be created in the non-agricultural sectors will depend on the attainment of production targets. On the assumption that these targets will be achieved total demand for labour will reach 14,980,000. (See Table 11).

Table 9

Supply of and demand for Civilian Labour Force

	1972	1977	1987	1995
Supply of Civilian Labour Force	14.3	16.0	21.0	26.0
Agriculture	8.8	8.6	8.0	6.2
Non-Agriculture	5.5	7.4	13.0	19.8
Demand for Labour force	13.5	14.9	19.0	25.2
Employment in Agric.	8.8	8.6	8.0	6.2
Employment in Non-Agric.	4.7	6.3	11.0	19.0
Industry	1.5	2.1	3.4	5.6
Services	3.2	4.2	7.6	13.4
Total unemployment	1.0	1.8	2.5	0.8
In Agricultural Sector	0.9	0.7	0.5	—
In Non-Agricultural Sector	0.8	1.1	2.0	0.8

Table 10

Sectoral Breakdown of Employment (%)

Sectors	1972	1977	1987	1995
Agriculture	65	58	42	25
Non-Agriculture	35	42	58	75
Industry	11	14	18	22
Services	24	28	40	53
Total	100	100	100	100

Table 11

Total Civilian Employment Projections in the Third Five Year Plan Period (15-64 age group)
(in thousands)

Male + Female	1972	1977
Agriculture	8,763	8,600
Non-Agriculture	4,586	6,197
Other	133	133
Total Demand for Labour Force	13,482	14,930
Labour Force Emigration	85	50
	13,567	14,980

Source: Third Five Year Plan, p. 662.

The supply of labour force in the Third Five Year Plan period is shown in Table 12.

Table 12

Projections of Labour Force Supply in the Third Plan Period
(15-64 age group)

| | *(in thousands)* | |
	1972 *(1)*	1977 *(2)*
Total Population	37.536	42.630
(15-64 age group)	20.350	23.371
Labour Force Supply	14.317	16.080

Source: State Planning Organisation.

Even if the production targets foreseen in the Third Five Year Plan period are attained it is expected that there will be no significant change in total labour surplus. As it was 11.2% in 1972, it will be the same in 1977. The problems of low working hours, low productivity and low wage levels will remain.

As it is seen, the Third Five Year Plan, unlike the preceding two, foresees keeping the surplus ratio constant and perpetuates the unemployment problem.

VIII. *Critical Appraisal of the Third Five Year Plan*

It is obvious that the closing of manpower gaps can only be achieved if it can be combined with a training programme and a purposeful educational system. Developing countries have to put more emphasis on the problem of satisfying manpower needs which are created in the process of economic development. The problem is not only training, but at the same time the optimum use of already-trained manpower.

The choice of training systems determines the skill mix of manpower and selected production techniques affect employment generation. Therefore, manpower planning and employment policies have a direct and indirect bearing on every sector of the economy.

The focal point of economic development is not the search for a factor or factors that have to be stressed to accelerate the rates of growth to pre-conceived levels, but the discovery of the right relationships or proportions among the various factors of development which, if observed, would ensure an organic and vigorous development of the economy. Perhaps the most important method of discovering these relationships is to proceed on the assumption that the process of economic development is essentially an organic process and the proportion observed in the early stages of development in the advanced countries are relevant for other countries also. This thought is developed and illustrated by tracing Japan's educational development in the early stages and comparing it with the conditions and targets of the Turkish Third Five Year Plan.

In developing countries the capital-output ratio in training is high. This ratio decreases after the required expenditures are made on infrastructures. The relationship between manpower and national income is shown in Table 13.

Table 13

Relationship Between Manpower Needs and National Income

Year	Rate of Growth of Manpower	Rate of Growth of National Income	Ratio of Manpower to National Income
1960	—	—	—
1965	15.6%	13.2%	1.18%
1970	16.7%	18.5%	0.94%

In Japan this ratio was 1.7% between 1896 and 1900, 3.3% between 1901 and 1905, and 3.5% between 1906 and 1910. Questions about the quality of graduates and the possibilities of disguised or open unemployment present some difficulties in applying this ratio to the situation currently prevailing in a developing country like Turkey. However, this does not minimize the basic significance of this relationship to any considerable extent. Table 14 and Table 17 showing training expenditure and growth of national income show the relative position of Turkey in this context with respect to other countries. That Japan's expenditure on education and training was less than 2 per cent of its national income during the first three decades of its development and that it was less than 3 per cent during the take-off period, is of considerable importance. Many developing countries are currently spending more than that without any appreciable increase in the rate of growth. This raises the question whether they are right in spending that much from the point of view of ensuring co-ordinated development, and optimum resource allocation. The educational structure of manpower is given in the following table:

Table 14

Educational Structure of Manpower   *(in thousands)*

Level of Education Graduated	1960		1965		1970	
	No.	%	No.	%	No.	%
University and Higher Education	99.4	0.8	146.5	1.1	230.9	1.7
Vocational School	127.6	1.0	193.2	1.5	315.1	2.3
High School	100.7	0.8	135.4	1.0	216.4	1.6
Middle School	255.9	2.1	297.5	2.3	435.5	3.2
Primary School	2,829.8	23.0	3,724.6	28.6	4,933.7	36.1
Literate, not graduate	–	–	1,684.5	12.9	1,372.7	10.0
Illiterate	8,872.9	72.3	6,824.9	52.6	6,170.1	45.1
Total	12,286.3	100.0	13,006.6	100.0	13,674.4	100.0

Source: State Institute of Statistics.

The following table shows the comparative educational standard of the emigrated labour force and the domestic labour force.

Table 15

Educational Attainment of Migrants and Domestic Labour Force

Graduates of:	Migrants		Domestic 1965 Economically Active Population — Males
	TES	SPO	
Primary	60.5	55.7	39.1
Secondary	2.5	4.2	3.4
Vocational	1.4	6.7	2.0
High School	0.6	1.1	1.4
Higher	n.a	2.8	1.6

Source: Turkish Employment Service — 1969, (10, p. 11). SPO, Table 10.

Those emigrating are from the most dynamic, younger section of the population and, as the table shows, are also the most educated and highly trained workers. If Turkey continues to meet the ever-increasing demand for skilled workers from abroad she can do so only at increasing costs to her own industrial growth. Undoubtedly, Turkish industrialists are already incurring higher costs and lower marginal productivity because of the increased labour turnover and skilled labour losses emanating from emigration. If Turkey, in order to alleviate the domestic unemployment problem, continues to send workers abroad, a drastic review of her emigration policy will be necessary bearing in mind her future partnership in the Common Market. Turkey now faces severe shortages of semi-skilled and skilled labour as identified in the Third Five Year Development Plan.

In Turkey, training expenditures within the national income in the 1950-1965 period were 4.37%, and the annual rate of increase was 9.5% the same period. Table 17 indicates that although the annual rate of increase in training expenditure is less than the averages of other countries, there is however an increase in the ratio of it to Gross National Product and National Income. Table 18 shows the biased composition of the Turkish educational system compared with other countries.

The ratio of technical training within higher and middle education is very important, particularly so in a developing country like Turkey. The ratio of technical training to general education in Turkey is 20.2%, whereas the same ratio is 54.0% in Germany, 73.5% in Yugoslavia and 32.3% in Italy.

As mentioned above, the problem of Turkey's development is not only the problem of creating the manpower required for industrialisation, but also its efficient utilisation. The rate of growth of the active labour force (15-64 age group) is much higher than the employment opportunities created and this has caused the significant unemployment problem to deteriorate.

It is estimated that the participation rate to the labour force will reach 39-40% in 1990 in accordance with the estimated development. It is also estimated that the labour force supply will increase from 14.3 million in 1972 to 26.0 million in 1995. Thus, Turkey is confronted with the creation of 12 million jobs until 1995. This will become the major problem of subsequent Plan periods.

Out of 14.3 million in 1972 only 12.7 million are fully employed, leaving 1.6 million of which 850,000 are under-employed in agriculture and 750,000 are either employed in marginal activities or are urban unemployed.

External Employment—Emigration

The Position of Turkey as a Supplier of Labour

Turkey is a late-comer to the migratory labour movement. Labour movement from Turkey to western European countries started in 1961 on a small scale and reached important proportions depending on the development trends of the manpower demanding countries. Turkish workers went mainly to central European countries at the start; when the idea spread migrant workers began to go to Australia, Canada, the United States and the oil-producing Arab countries but the numbers going to these countries are still small compared with those going to Europe. Although the migratory flows from Turkey extend to all the developed countries of western Europe, West Germany occupies by far the most prominent position among countries receiving Turkish workers.

The impact of the manpower export on the domestic employment situation

In neither the First nor the Second Five Year Plans did the macro models incorporate employment as an independent variable but rather considered it a problem which would be solved automatically as a result of the industrial growth and rapid implementation of industrialisation objectives. In actual fact although the volume of employment increased in both Plan periods, the rise has not been sufficient to prevent steadily increasing unemployment year by year. The surplus labour increased from 985,000 in 1962 to 1.6m in 1972 and to almost 1.7m in 1973; in percentage terms it increased from 8.8 per cent in 1962 to 11 per cent in 1973.

The Perspective Plan covering the next 22 years has as one of its greatest targets full employment in 1995. Between now and that date the prime target will continue to be rapid industrialisa-

tion unhampered by employment considerations. This situation
makes the choice of technology an important factor. It was stipu-
lated in the Third Five Year Plan that Turkey should adopt the
most sophisticated technologies in the production of basic and
intermediate goods producing industries which are subject to international competition without worrying about the employment
objective; but she should adopt labour-intensive technologies in
the production of domestically traded goods, and infrastructure
projects. In addition it was foreseen that labour-intensive industries such as electronics and metal-working branches should be
encouraged in order to increase employment creation. It is obvious that, like the two preceding Five Year Plans, employment
creation has not been considered the prime mover in the Third
Five Year Plan either. There is no need to explain the basic
fallacy inherent in this kind of philosophy, which does not take
the resource endowment of the country into proper account. Of
course, as might be guessed, the natural corollary of such a policy
is an even deteriorating employment situation which renders the
export of manpower an unavoidable alternative.

In the First Plan period 240,000 workers were sent abroad; in
the Second Plan period 450,000 emigrated in the same way. If it
is assumed that the number of workers who return permanently
to Turkey each year equals the number who go abroad illegally
to find work the ratio of the external employment to the surplus
domestic labour force can be determined. This ratio was 16.6 in
1967 and it reached 43.6 in 1972. Moreover the ratio of the
external employment during the first two Plan periods (approximately 690,000) constituted 43 per cent of the domestic employment generation in the same period (which was approximately 1.6m).

The Perspective Plan predicts that an additional 1 million will
be sent abroad from 1972 to 1987 and from then on inflow and
outflow will cancel each other out, and the level of the external
employment in 1995 will continue to maintain the level at the
end of 1987. That is to say the attainment of full employment in
1995 will only be achieved under these conditions. This explanation clearly indicates that emigration will play an important role
in fulfilling the targets set down in the Perspective Plan period.

Although long-run trends in the main European worker-receiving countries show immigration as a permanent feature of those

economies as shown in the Table 16, the conjunctural fluctuations will of course influence these migratory flows.

Table 16

Labour Surpluses and Shortages in Europe in 1980

		Variants for Scarcities (−) or labour demand redundancies (+) (million)
Group I (industrialised market countries)	Low	− 4.7
	Central	−11.2
	High	−12.8
Group II (countries of emigration)	High	+ 7.6
	Low	+ 10.5
Group III (centrally-planned countries), (incl. Soviet Union)	High	+ 15.9
	Low	+ 24.5
Group III excl. Soviet Union	High	+ 4.1
	Low	+ 6.8

Source: Luisa Danieli, "Labour Scarcities and Labour Redundancies in Europe by 1980: An Experimental Study," in *The Demographic and Social Pattern of Emigration from the Southern European Countries,* Florence: Dipartimento Statistico Matematico, 1971

What emerges from this table is that large scale immigration of workers to European labour markets is likely to continue for the foreseeable future. But the fact that countries of immigration asked for workers and got families and human beings created severe problems concerning the absorbtive capacity of the host countries. Furthermore officials in some recipient countries are concerned about the heavy concentration of foreign workers in certain regions and key metropolitan areas. For instance the regional concentration of foreign workers is indicated by the fact that over 50 per cent of foreign labour live on less than 4 per cent of German soil. In addition to these mounting social problems caused by lack of the necessary infrastructure it should be borne in mind that there is a widespread belief in the most industrially-advanced countries of the West that economic growth will soon reach limits beyond which further growth might become self-defeating and will undermine the environment. Therefore we do not know for the time being how long this growth race will continue. These are long-run considerations working against large-scale worker immigration.

Since some of these current problems strike at the very foundations of the social fabric of a country, the current topic under discussion in some of these host countries is the idea of exporting capital rather than importing labour. This in essence becomes the reversal of labour migration. But there is a dichotomy here: for-

Table 17

Training Expenditures and Growth of National Income

Country	Annual Percentage Growth in Training Expenditure	Annual Rate of Growth in GNP (1955-1957)	Training Expenditure			
			% of of GNP		% of National Income	
			1955	1965	1955	1965
W. Germany	9.3 (1950-1966)	5.1	2.17	2.93	2.80	3.48
Belgium	9.3	4.4	3.11	3.68	3.98	4.79
Spain	10.4 (1950-1966)	7.0	1.08	1.96	1.24	2.27
France	11.0 (1952-1967)	4.9	2.83	4.55	3.73	6.05
Greece	12.2 (1950-1966)	6.3	1.50	2.10	1.78	2.55
Italy	13.7 (1957-1965)	5.3	2.98	5.19	3.79	6.48
Japan	9.8 (1950-1965)	9.6	4.56	4.55	5.70	5.64
Netherlands	11.4 (1950-1967)	4.4	3.57	6.19	4.41	7.53
Portugal	6.5 (1950-1965)	5.4	1.58	1.44	1.85	1.66
United Kingdom	7.8 (1953-1965	3.0	2.77	4.17	3.32	5.21
Yugoslavia	17.5 (1952-1967)	8.5	2.22	4.33	2.47	4.68 ·
Turkey	9.5 (1950-1967)	4.6	2.17	3.76	2.50	4.37

Source: OECD.

eign workers are heavily concentrated in branches of industry which cannot be exported, namely mining, construction, and services. On the other hand, private foreign capital most often takes the form of simple assembly operations, the value of which is questioned by many planners in Turkey.

Although a relatively latecomer into the recent migration phenomenon, Turkey is one of the major suppliers of workers for western Europe, especially so for Germany. Almost 45 per cent of the immigration to Germany in 1973 was from Turkey. Over 80 per cent of the Turkish migration in the past was to Germany. It is not necessary to point out the danger of vulnerability stemming from this situation as was clearly demonstrated by the German decision to impose a temporary halt on further immigration as a result of the oil crisis. There is no doubt that Germany needed an opportunity to put long thought-out measures concerning immigration into effect and the oil crisis came at a very convenient time in that respect. There were already visible signs of uneasiness in German society when the number of foreign

Table 18

Rate of Professional and Technical Manpower in the Working Population*

Country	Active Population (in thousands)	Professional and Technical manpower (in thousands)	Ratio of professional and Technical Manpower to Active Population (%)
Belgium	3.375	281	8.3
Canada	6.472	627	9.7
Denmark	2.094	158	7.5
France	18.955	1.882	9.9
Germany	26.527	2.037	7.7
United Kingdom	23.100	1.994	8.6
Greece	3.663	156	4.2
Japan	43.690	2.137	4.9
Netherlands	4.168	380	9.1
Norway	1.406	113	8.0
Portugal	3.316	92	2.8
Sweden	3.244	374	11.5
Yugoslavia	1.256	362	28.9
TURKEY (1960)	11.999	205	1.7
TURKEY (1965)	13.590	289	2.1

Source: OECD, 1969 Statistics.

* Statistics given for above countries cover the years 1960-1962, except Turkey.

workers reached the 2 million mark. The same crisis has also provided a good example to Turkey of the danger of relying heavily on labour migration as a means of solving the employment problem. The recent crisis flagrantly demonstrated that the host countries still continue to see the foreign labour in their economies as a kind of conjunctural shock-absorber, to be ma-

Table 19

Percentage Distribution of Students in Secondary Education
Between General and Vocational Training (1968)

Country		Number	Percent
Turkey	General	849,533	79.8
	Vocational-Technical	214,013	20.2
	Total	1,063,546	100.0
Italy	General	2,365,059	67.7
	Vocational-Technical	1,124,556	32.3
	Total	3,468,915	100.0
W. Germany	General	2,038,948	46.0
	Vocational-Technical	2,616,093	54.0
	Total	4,424,737	100.0
France	General	2,879,264	74.3
	Vocational-Technical	991,069	25.7
	Total	3,870,333	100.0
USSR	General	4,440,000	51.0
	Vocational-Technical	4,261,500	49.0
	Total	8,701,500	100.0
Yugoslavia	General	183,193	26.5
	Vocational-Technical	505,629	73.5
	Total	688,822	100.0
Mexico	General	1,085,829	82.5
	Vocational-Technical	229,519	17.5
	Total	1,315,348	100.0
Persia	General	781,507	96.8
	Vocational-Technical	25,118	3.2
	Total	806,625	100.0
Luxembourg	General	9,946	58.0
	Vocational-Technical	7,179	42.0
	Total	17,125	100.0
Bulgaria	General	107,915	28.7
	Vocational-Technical	266,807	71,3
	Total	374,722	100.0

Source: UN "Statistical Yearbook" 1970.

nipulated according to the vagaries and the dictates of the current situation.

IX. *Conclusion*

The preceding pages clearly show that Turkey suffers from an employment crisis like many similar developing countries. Economic science so far has not discovered the law of motion of employment creation. It is the most difficult economic problem to tackle; the economic philosophy of the post-war world carries a share of the blame for this. None of the Five-Year plans have proposed a viable solution so far to this problem of employment. Underlying all the three Five-Year plans is a basic assumption that economic development is a push-button process in which capital is considered the master switch which could set the process in motion and lead the country to an advanced stage of development. The focal point of development is not putting so much emphasis on capital but the finding of the right relationships or proportions among the various factors of development which would ensure an organic and vigorous development of the economy. The emphasis of the 1950s and '60s shows clearly that economic development cannot be achieved unless the right emphasis is given to the resource endowment of the country involved. Turkey has an abundant supply of labour and any economic development philosophy has to take this fact into proper account. The neglect of this important point has been at the expense of the deteriorating employment situation. It would be a natural corollary of the experience of the last two decades to formulate a different policy approach in the Perspective and Third Five Year plans. Unfortunately the Third Five Year plan repeats the mistakes of the preceding two and elevates the emigration of workers to an unavoidable alternative. It cannot be claimed that the Third Five Year plan is realistic in this respect either because it does not take the emerging conjunctural tendencies into consideration. It seems that the highest Turkish labour-absorbing western European country—Germany—has reached a saturation point as far as labour immigration is concerned. Many surveys have been conducted on this theme and generally speaking they can be reduced to the following common denominators:

a. Employing foreign workers increases economic growth but
    slows down the growth of living standards because the essen-
    tial extra investment on the factory floor and in infrastruc-
    ture cuts down the amount of consumer goods available for
    per capita consumption.
b. The extension of the potential foreign labour force slows
    down the drive towards streamlining and rationalisation and
    hampers technological progress.
c. Although national income increases by using foreign labour,
    the national product per capita does not increase. This is the
    current thinking in Germany, where over 80 per cent of the
    emigrating Turkish labour force has been going up to now.

Moreover the Third Five Year plan did not take the emerging
policy conflicts between Turkish worker-receiving countries and
Turkey into proper account. The first policy conflict is the ever-
increasing percentage of skilled worker immigration creating
shortages of skilled workers in many branches of domestic industry as identified in the Third Five Year Plan. The turnover rate of
labour in some Turkish industries has already reached over 40 per
cent.

Turkey's long-run interest is to advocate a mandatory rotation
system in order to bring back her skilled labour from abroad.

The most serious conflict centres around the free labour mobility between Turkey and the European Common Market between 1976 and 1986. Germany is concerned about it and is
approaching very cautiously any further negotiations concerning
Turkey's entry into the Common Market. The future of emigration is frought with difficulties and uncertainties: scarcities of
space, raw materials and labour might reverse the present flow
from developing countries to developed ones.

ECONOMIC IMPACT OF THE MIGRATION

"Give up eating, Ahmets; give up eating, Jales. Load your stuff on trains, Osman and Ayshes ... Fly to Turkey. your marks weigh little, but their value goes a long way. Fly home with your marks. Buy plots in our big cities. Even the cemeteries have been uprooted in recent years. These days, second-rate and third-rate cemeteries for those who had died of hunger are going for a song ... For those who don't care for farming, there are some other fields of investment. Buy stocks and shares, buy into new industries. When you return to your country, you could become industrialists, no less. What's wrong with that? Haven't you worked long enough? In this mortal life, it should now be your turn to hire others, to put others to work."

Bekir Yildiz
Alman Ekmeği (German Bread)
İstanbul, Cem Kitabevi, 1974
Translated by Talât Sait Halman

Analysing the economic impact of migration requires a sharp distinction between the micro and macro effects of large-scale human displacements. Almost all experts and scholars investigating the overall economic impact of migration have focused their attention so far first on the question of remittances, particularly on the closing of the payments deficit and the use of foreign currency so acquired for investment. Indeed, in 1973, "the current annual flow of remittances from all migrants in Europe to their home countries was over $ 2.5 billion, which is a comparison, well in excess of the total value of actual lending disbursed worldwide by the World Bank Group each year" (İ.M. Hume).

However, as indicated by major international specialised agencies such as ILO (January 1974) mechanically adding remittances to the payments deficit makes even less sense than mechanically subtracting emigrants from the number of unemployed. Remittances are used to meet daily needs, close up old debts buy consumer goods and none of this expenditure is more than marginally productive. In macro-economic terms, foreign currency tends to be used, wherever there is no strict control of imports, to pay for imports of foreign consumer goods by the non-migrant population and by recipients of remittances. Thus there occurs an increasing familiarisation with foreign consumer goods, leading to a widespread disdain for domestic products.

Similarly the hope that temporary migration to Europe might

help the sending countries to acquire much needed skills for industrialization appears not to be confirmed. The screening process functions almost inevitably in favour of the recipient country: it is principally the better qualified workers who tend to stay on. Those who return by their own decision actually represent a negative selection and can hardly be expected to be the type most needed in their homecountry. The latter mainly need highly skilled and versatile manual workers, foremen, not people who have emptied dustbins, turned screws or washed dishes. (M. Trebous)

A further worry is that, of the few who return permanently, too few envisage working in industrial jobs. Many prefer rather marginal jobs in service activities. In spite of strong recommendations of some ILO experts, the character of the informal sector-composed of activities characterised by ease of entry, reliance on indigenous resources, family ownership of enterprises, small-scale of operation, labour intensive and adapted technology, skills acquired outside the formal school system, unregulated and competitive markets—seems unfit to become a powerful vehicle for national development. This tendency appears indeed to be a cultural phenomenon which requires a massive and sustained campaign by governments to popularize industrial employment and to encourage investment and participation in agro-industrial cooperatives. Upon adding the loss of expenditure invested in the upbringing of the migrant, the main economic benefits of emigration become far less certain than has been maintained hitherto.

The three papers in this section may help the reader to understand better the unintended, dysfunctional effects of migration, both on the micro and macro level. In her stimulating paper Tufan Kölan, a young Turkish economist, has analysed the individual earnings of migrants in terms of economic costs and benefits and gains and disadvantages by using extensively the findings of the State Planning survey on returning migrants. Her study indicates that migrated or potential migrants from Turkey have, on the average, well-founded expectations of financial success. For migrants with an assured uninterrupted employment of over ten years, the gain for those with rural background is at least 170%, for urban workers about 20%. However, the author warns Turkish policy makers on an important point: urban workers who have higher domestic productivity and hence earnings, ap-

parently earn less after returning from abroad than they would
have earned had they not migrated. The major reason seems to be
that these workers, once returned, are turning away from "wage
work" to self-employment. Due to this option, in the short run,
it seems that not only do they earn less than they could by
working for some one else, but that they also get negative returns
on their invested capital. Thus not only then labour, but also
their capital is being inefficiently used.

A second important point seems to be the fact that because a
number of migrants are not motivated or are barred from the
advantage of acquiring new skills, an important gain from a migration policy is being wasted. Finally, T. Kölan indicates that
since an important part of the gains from migration are being
taken largely in the form of increased leisure, this might definitely be a gain to the individual migrant, but that it does hinder
economic development and from the standpoint of the national
economy it should be considered a cost.

The second paper of Duncan R. Miller concentrates on the
relationship between the exportation of labour and its implica-
tion for Turkish wage and education policy formulation. His
findings openly show that in essence, unskilled workers are sub-
sidizing the education of skilled workers. At the micro level, in
the absence of adequate replacement workers, Turkish employers
suffering a loss of skilled workers must either cope with a loss in
output or with the increased cost of training new workers. The
author foresees in the long run major conflicts in terms of Turkey's forecoming membership in the EEC, Germany's inconsis-
tent migratory policy and its repercussion on Turkey's economic
structure. The abrupt stop of all recruitment since the last
months of 1973 seems to confirm the fears of the author, leaving
Turkey with a substantial loss in terms of skilled labour force.

In the third paper, Ruşen Keleş, an expert in urban affairs,
attempts to evaluate the migrants' investment practice in terms
of urbanization and the realisation of Turkey's Third Five Year
Plan targets. According to his assessment, one of the less com-
mented aspects of Turkey's recent external migration lies in the
fact that this exodus serves in the long run to speed urbanization.
Almost 50% of the returning workers—even in cases of rural
background—are settling in urban environments. This pronounced trend has caused an "inflated demand" in the housing

sector. According to R. Keleş's observation, the originally pertinently designed bankcredit scheme for the construction of social dwellings turned into a failure because of unrealistic conditions demanded in the terms of participation. This has led to a
quasi-monopolistic position of private entrepreneurs or housing
companies, who regardless of the targets of the Third Five Year
Plan are successfully attracting the savings of returned or presently migrated workers.

Summing up, while receiving countries suddenly are becoming
aware that migration actually creates the subproletariat of tomorrow, with explosive implications in terms of class and ethnic
strife and seriously attempt to slow down the move toward center nations, the asymetric dependency of sending countries and
their incapacity to implement rational national development
plans leads to a serious deficit in terms of economic gains.

AN ANALYSIS OF INDIVIDUAL EARNINGS EFFECTS DUE TO EXTERNAL MIGRATION*

TUFAN KÖLAN

This study approaches migration issue from the viewpoint of the effects on the Turkish migrant's earnings. Migration is an activity undertaken to achieve certain objectives, and the underlying assumption is that the worker would not make the decision to migrate if his decision would end up making him any worse off than he otherwise would be. It is further assumed that, whatever his specific objectives, the decision to migrate represents the best way for him to achieve them.

Migration for the Turkish worker involves both costs and benefits. In general, the benefits are quite well known, at least in the very short run: Most evidence indicates that wage levels in the labor-scarce European countries are at least three, and often many more, times earnings rates in Turkey. For a person wishing to better his economic position, either by a permanent move or through accumulation of capital over a limited time span, this represents an attractive opportunity. In addition, the work abroad may, if he wishes, involve on-the-job or more formal kinds of training which should increase his future earning power. Living in Europe, working in advanced industries, and acquiring durable goods may also figure in the thinking of some migrants.

On the other hand, migration involves both economic and psychic costs, which, like the benefits, may not manifest themselves until he returns or long after. In making the migration decision, the long-term costs and benefits must be appreciated to the extent of his time horizon. Not only must the "instantaneous" benefits during time abroad be considered, but also the effects which migration will have on his future earnings path. Because the overall effects of migration are to a large extent unknown, and also stretch forward into time, the migration decision involves risk and uncertainty. The number of Turks abroad

* The author wishes to express her appreciation to Dr. Burman Skrable for his very competent methodological and statistical assistance.

and on waiting lists to migrate indicates that they consider the benefits on balance to be worth the risks.

Theoretical Considerations on Individual Earnings Effects due to External Migration

The conceptual framework taken in this study for determining the earnings effects of migration is closely akin to the "human capital" approach to the analysis of many facets of labor market behavior.[1] The effects of migration on earnings are illustrated schematically in the chart. It portrays the case of a worker who migrates for a limited time (in this case, three years) and then returns; this is the relevant case for most Turkish considerations. Line aa' portrays the path of his annual earnings if he does not migrate. It is presumed that earnings will rise year by year under the stimulus of inflation or productivity, or both. If he should suffer intermittent unemployment, aa' would have dips or blank spots in it; the line could fall all the way to zero earnings.

It is then assumed that, at the end of year 3, the worker migrates. The earnings illustrated imply that he makes the transition from work in Turkey to work in the host country with no intermittent unemployment and with no out-of-pocket costs of mov-

---

[1] This approach was pioneered by Theodore Schultz and received its most complete formal statement at the hands of Gary Becker. Essentially, it involves an investment approach to decisions regarding training (on-the-job or formal), migration, and health. Resources expended on training or migration or health involve a reduction in present levels of consumption for the sake of future gains; in short, they change the long-term earnings path of the person making them. If done wisely, they result in long-term improvements.

This human capital method was applied directly to the analysis of migration decision by Larry Sjastaad, although he considers the problem in the context of a permanent move. His analysis was given some empirical content by Samuel Bowles in a paper quantifying the net benefits from migration out of the South of the United States. Bowles concluded that the human capital model was supported by migration data from the 1960 U.S. Census of Population data. See Theodore W. Schultz, "Investment in Human Capital," *American Economic Review*, Vol. LI (March, 1961), pp. 1-13; Gary S. Becker, "Investment in Human Capital: A Theoretical Analysis," *Journal of Political Economy*, Supplement, Vol. LXX, No. 5, pt. 2 (October, 1962), pp. 9-49; Larry A. Sjaastad, "The Costs and Returns of Human Migration," *Journal of Political Economy*, Supplement, Vol. LXX, No. 5, pt. 2 (October, 1962), pp. 80-93; Samuel Bowles, "Migration as Investment: Empirical Tests of the Human Investment Approach to Geographical Mobility," Harvard University Program on Regional and Urban Economics, Discussion Paper 51 (July, 1969).

Chart

Hypothetical Earnings Paths Before, During, and After Migration

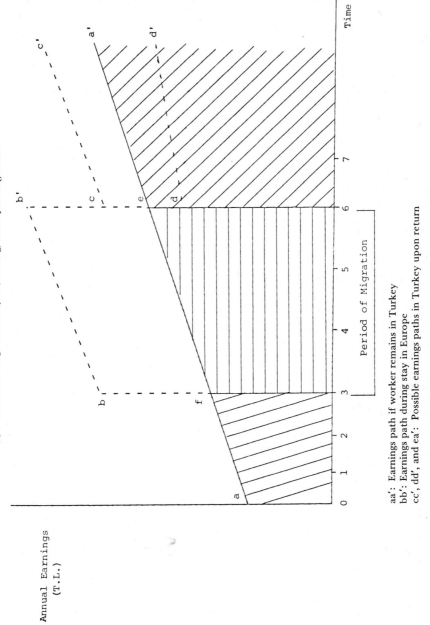

aa': Earnings path if worker remains in Turkey
bb': Earnings path during stay in Europe
cc', dd', and ea': Possible earnings paths in Turkey upon return

ing. For some workers—in fact, apparently, the majority—this is not an unrealistic assumption. For others, however, the process of preparing to migrate may entail both considerable out-of-pocket expenditures and the loss of time, or even induce him to cease his regular employment. If this is the case, there would be an extension of bb' to the left of point f which would dip below aa' or show a blank spot to represent the decline in his net earnings during that time. If he suffered some unemployment in the country of migration before becoming settled in his new job, this would reduce the earnings during the first part of year 4 and hence cause bb' to be lower than otherwise. Over the entire period of his stay abroad, his annual rate of earnings is described by bb'.

Upon return to Turkey at the end of his sixth year and resumption of work, three earnings paths are possible: (1) He could earn what he would have been earning had he never left (continuation of aa'); this would imply the acquisition during his period of migration of no skills (beyond what he would have acquired in Turkey) which raised his productivity, or else his inability to find work in Turkey which would allow him to use his newly acquired skills in such a way as to raise his productivity (and earnings); 2) he could be successful in acquiring skills and putting them to work, and earn more upon return than he would have had he not migrated (line cc'), or 3) he could encounter discrimination against those who have migrated or have other difficulties and earn less (dd').

The chart shows very clearly that the standard of comparison or of success is what the migrant's earnings (or more properly, from the standpoint of his decision making, his total income) experience would have been had he never migrated. Thus the line aa', delineating this hypothetical experience, represents the opportunity cost of migrating. The gains from migrating—before,[2] during, and after the actual migration takes place—must be net of aa', and shown in the chart as the shaded area. Thus the area between bb' and the shaded portion under aa' would represent the net gain during the period of migration. Should, as a result of his migration experience, the migrant earn more in Turkey upon

---

[2] Some prospective migrants may leave their jobs early to get ready to migrate or may not be as efficient since they know they will not be staying at their present employments for long.

his return (e.g., along the schedule cc′), then the area between the lines cc′ and the relevant portion of aa′ represents a further gain due to migration. However, should his earnings decline below aa′, the resulting loss (e.g., the area between aa′ and dd′) must be offset against the earnings gains he experienced while abroad.

Direct or out-of-pocket costs should be treated as reducing his actual earnings during migration (i.e., lowering his net income, line bb′). Strictly speaking, these are only incremental costs, just as the relevant earnings measure is the incremental earnings. It costs a person money to eat, to clothe himself, and to have housing no matter where he lives. Therefore, the costs considered here are only the extra ones entailed as a result of the migration decision.[3] However, other costs, such as transportation and visas, would not be incurred in the absence of migrating and hence are automatically net costs. In addition, should the worker have property which he is in danger of losing or forfeiting in his absence, or upon which the returns decline due to his absence and lack of attention, these costs must likewise be taken into account.[4]

Since a decision must be made on the basis of commensurate magnitudes, it is necessary to be able to compare the net result of migrating with the net result of remaining in Turkey. The usual

---

[3] In the case of the temporary migrant, these may be extremely difficult to measure in the abstract as well as empirically. The reason for this is the fact that a migrant with short-term work ambitions is generally intent upon maximizing his rate of saving. Consequently, he will live in extremely poor surroundings, often in the same apartment with many of his countrymen to further defray costs; eat modestly; and buy no more clothes or other consumer items than absolutely necessary. He certainly would not live this way in Turkey unless forced to do so by abject poverty. Since the "incremental costs" actually presume comparability of intentions and living conditions, the comparison of his living costs in Turkey and in Europe is not valid without some modifications. To accurately specify the incremental cost, therefore, it would be necessary to price the expense of living in the same condition in Turkey, and applying the difference (positive or negative) to the worker's realized gross earnings. See Larry Sjastaad, "The Costs and Returns of Human Migration," pp. 83-84.

[4] A discussion of these costs may be found in Solomon Barkin, "The Economic Costs and Benefits and Human Gains and Disadvantages of International Migration," *The Journal of Human Resources*, Vol. II, No. 4 (Fall, 1967), pp. 502-03. One cost listed by Barkin there, however, is not correctly specified; he speaks of "the funds required for sustaining him until earnings begin" (p. 503). These expenditures would have to be made anyway, and only the increment occasioned by being in a foreign country is a cost of migration; the only cost occasioned by using "funds" for this purpose is the forgone interest or other earnings accruing to these funds if kept in Turkey.

way of doing this is to reduce all the earnings figures, over the worker's time horizon, to present values. In this way, all magnitudes are reduced to the same time dimension by the application of an appropriate discount factor. Future earnings are discounted to reflect the fact that earnings yet to be received have less value to the recipient, both physically and because of interest earnings on invested funds.[5] In effect, each present value will represent the earnings under each of the schedules in the chart, discounted for the year in which they are to be received, with the year in which the migration decision is made (assumed to be the year before the migrant leaves) treated as year 0. The present value of earnings under the assumption of migration (the discounted sum of all earnings under schedule aa' to point f, then bb', and the area under cc', ea', or dd', whichever is the appropriate earnings path) for the relevant time horizon is therefore compared with that under aa'. The following formula is used:

$$PV = Y_0 + \frac{Y_1}{(1+r)^1} + \ldots + \frac{Y_n}{(1+r)^n}.^6$$

The appropriate discount rate, (r), is a matter of some dispute, although the argument revolves chiefly in the area of the appropriate discount rate for evaluating social programs or public expenditure projects. For the individual worker, the appropriate rate is his rate of time preference, i.e., how much he is willing to pay in a year so that he might have one Turkish Lira today, the rate at which he will borrow money to enjoy present instead of future consumption. An expression of this is the rate at which he is able to borrow money. Alternatively, one could use the rate which he can earn on invested money, although this will be lower, generally, than the rate to him as a borrower (if he is an ordinary wage earner).

It is clear from the formula that the higher the rate of discount, the smaller the weight given to future earnings. This is perhaps best understood from the standpoint of the individual

---

[5] This is the method employed by Samuel Bowles, "Migration as Investment: Empirical Tests of the Human Investment Approach to Geographical Mobility."

[6] Alternatively, one could subtract from the gross earnings due to migration during each year the relevant costs during that year, and take the present value of the difference. In this case, a positive present value indicates that the decision is justified on earnings grounds. Whether the resultant present value is sufficient to overcome the psychic costs of migrating can only be known to the migrant himself.

decision maker; if he has a high rate of time preference, i.e., a high preference for present over future consumption, he will "discount" all future amounts heavily and make his decision primarily on the basis of present magnitudes. Thus a course of action which promises a high payoff in the short run but a lower return after a certain number of future years (e.g., as typified by the migration case in which the post-migration earnings stream is dd'), will be attractive to a present-oriented person (one who applies a high rate of personal discount) but not to a person who is able to defer gratification and who can take the long range view of his earnings prospects.

Methodology and Data Requirements for the Model

The ideal method of isolating the effects of migration on a worker's earnings and being able to generalize the results to the entire migrant population would be to determine the universe of potential migrants. Since not all can go at once, a random sample of migrants sufficiently large to be representative would be selected. At the same time, a control group would be chosen randomly from the same population, or a study group would be identified and the migrants randomly selected from that group with the others remaining as controls. If the group selected is large enough, the random selection process would control the differences in the workers' personal characteristics, occupations, and sectors of employment—all the factors which could obscure the effects of migration per se.

Both migrants and controls would be followed longitudinally to obtain records of their earnings, year by year, over the entire period of the study. After a sufficient number of years had passed to enable a clear establishment of earnings trends during the migration and post-migration periods, the earnings experience of the two groups would be compared. Simple statistical tests can be used to determine whether any earnings differences between the two groups are large enough to ascribe to the migration experience. If so, it can be inferred for the entire population that migration would have a measurable impact on earnings.[7]

---

[7] This is the simplest kind of effectiveness test, and relies on a very clear statistical design. A description of this method is contained in the excellent article by Tom R. Houston, Jr., "The Behavioral Sciences Impact-Effectiveness Model," in Peter

Since one is rarely, if ever, able to establish the kind of statistical design in advance which will enable the clear identification of program effects, more complex statistical tools are usually required to approximate the same result.[8] The common methodology involves drawing a sample of participants in the program and following them for a certain length of time after their completion or withdrawal from the program (whether it be a training program, migration, education or other human capital investment experience). Regression analysis is used to hold constant for individual characteristics and allow for an "other things being equal" measurement of the effects of the program being studied. The chief problem becomes choosing either a control group or other means of estimating what would have happened to participants had they not been in the program.[9] A further problem common to most evaluations is that funds for a long follow-up period are rarely available; consequently, when long-term present values are calculated, assumptions must be made about the path of earnings beyond the period of observation. These assumptions can be critical to the determination of success or failure of the program being evaluated. For example, a program can produce earnings increases but these may or may not persist over time. But if measurements end shortly after completion of the program, it may be easy to assume that the increases will persist; such may not be the case in fact, and a longer follow-up period would show it. As indicated above, this is a crucial consideration for the analysis of migration programs since it is important to know

---

H. Rossi and Walter Williams (eds.), *Evaluating Social Programs: Theory, Practice, and Politics* (New York: Seminar Press, 1972), pp. 51-65. The emphasis is on program impact evaluation. However, the principles involved are identical.

[8] The only manpower evaluation study employing random assignment to control and test groups in manpower programs is the one done by Gerald Robin, *An Assessment of the In-School Neighborhood Projects in Cincinnati and Detroit, with Special Reference to Summer-Only and Year-Round Enrollees*, Prepared for the Manpower Administration; U.S. Department of Labor (Washington, D.C., 1969).

[9] Good discussions of this problem are to be found in D.O. Sewell, *Training the Poor: A Benefit-Cost Analysis of Manpower Programs in the U.S. Antipoverty Program*, Industrial Relations Centre, Research Series No. 12 (Kingston, Ontario: Queen's University, 1971), pp. 23-26; and the book by G.G. Somers and W.D. Wood (eds.), *Cost-Benefit Analysis of Manpower Policies, Proceedings of a North American Conference* (Kingston, Ontario: Queen's University Industrial Relations Centre, 1969), especially the articles by Richard W. Judy, "Costs: Theoretical and Methodological Issues," pp. 16-29, and Glen G. Cain and Robinson G. Hollister, "Evaluating Manpower Programs for the Disadvantaged," pp. 119-51.

what the post-migration earnings experience is likely to be.

As in the case with most evaluations, the ideal or very often even much less than the ideal is never realized in practice. This is true of this study as well. The assessment of the gains to migration for Turkish workers is severely limited by available data, and many assumptions—several of them the same ones mentioned critically above—will be required to give some empirical content to this issue. Consequently, the results given below are more illustrative than definitive, even though they probably represent the best information available on the subject.

Available Data on Turkish Migrants' Earnings

The basic data bearing on the earnings of migrants from Turkey come from a 1970 survey done by the Turkish State Planning Organization (SPO).[10] The sample was gleaned from an interview survey of returnees from a spell of work in Europe. Names of 4,400 returnees who had worked abroad at some time between the beginning of migration in 1961 to 1969 were obtained and a 10 percent sample drawn. Due to problems of locating some, the sample was reduced to 370 of which 340 provided responses usable for the purposes of this study. It is clear that there has been substantial erosion of the sample and, since also the randomness of the original sample is questionable, one cannot be clear about the degree to which the persons reported on are representative of Turkish migrants in general.[11]

For the purposes of this paper, the SPO survey provides the following information. Earnings of migrants before, during, and after migration (i.e., 1970 earnings) are reported in distribution form for urban, rural, and total workers. Earnings in Europe are shown for different occupations although there is no comparable pre- or post-migration earnings distribution for these workers. Earnings for the entire group, and for rural and urban workers are shown year-by-year. The counts of persons involved indicate that most of the workers were abroad during 1963-67. Summary

---

[10] T.C. Başbakanlık Devlet Plânlama Teşkilâtı, *Yurt Dışından Dönen İşçilerin Sosyo-Ekonomik Eğilimleri Üzerinde Bir Çalışma* (Ankara, 1974).

[11] A broader question concerns the extent to which returnees might differ from migrants who remain abroad. This question has broad policy implications and requires further surveys.

data show that urban workers stayed abroad an average 2.9 years, while rural workers spent 2.4 years.

Because of the way the survey has been tabulated, it is not possible to relate directly earnings to time in which received. For proper analysis, it is necessary to be able to relate the individual's earnings while in Europe to his pre- and post-migration earnings. The survey, however, gives only a distribution of pre-migration earnings (which were probably earned somewhere between 1960 and 1967); this would not be so important except that due to inflation particularly, earnings in Turkey were rising at the rate of 10 percent [12] per year in covered employment in the urban and 5.3 percent [13] per year in the rural sector between 1963 and 1970. Consequently, simplifying assumptions will be needed to use these earnings for estimating purposes. It will be assumed that the "average" migrant, both urban and rural, spent three years abroad, specifically the years 1964-66. Therefore, by assumption, pre-migration earnings refer to the year 1963; and present earnings, as is clear from the year of the survey, refer to the rate of earnings during 1970.

For calculation purposes, benefits and costs of migration have been defined as follows:

Benefits: Based on the SPO survey, benefits are determined to be wage earnings only. Data on supplementary earnings are given also, but since these can be influenced largely by decisions as to the distribution of wage earnings between savings and consumption or transfer payments, they were not used in order to avoid additional assumptions where assumptions already abound. For both urban and rural workers, earnings in Europe are taken to be median earnings for the entire distribution of urban and rural workers in 1965. The survey presented some rates of earnings growth for workers in similar occupations. An unweighted average of these rates of growth indicated that earnings would grow at about 8.9 percent during the first to second year, and 8.6 per-

---

[12] Calculated from T. C. Devlet İstatistik Enstitüsü, *Türkiye İstatistik Yıllığı, 1968*, Yayın No. 580 (Ankara: Devlet İstatistik Enstitüsü Matbaası, 1969), p. 159, Table 141, and Sosyal Sigortalar Kurumu Genel Müdürlüğü, *Sosyal Sigortalar Kurumu İstatistik Yıllığı, 1969*, Yayın No. 172 (Ankara: Başnur Matbaası, 1970), p. 39, Table 8.

[13] T.C. Başbakanlık Devlet Plânlama Teşkilâtı, SPD Araştırma Şubesi İstihdam-İnsangücü Grubu, Ahmet M. Gökçen, *Kırdan Şehire İşgücü Göçleri (1965-1982'ye ait Tahminler)* DPT: 1107-SPD: 240, Ankara, 1971, p. 28, Table 17, p. 34, Table 23.

cent from the second to third years. Using these data, 1964 earnings for both individual urban and rural workers were estimated by reducing measured 1965 earnings by 8.9 percent, and 1966 earnings by increasing 1965 earnings by 8.6 percent. [14]

Post-migration earnings were given in the survey for 1970. Earnings for 1967 through 1969 were estimated by reducing the 1970 figure by 10 percent per year for urban and 5.3 percent per year for rural workers. [15] The 1970-72 earnings were projected forward at the same rates.

Costs: The largest cost facing the prospective migrant is the wages he could have earned in Turkey had he not migrated. [16] As noted above, this is preferably measured by observing the earnings of a control group of non-migrating workers with characteristics as closely as possible paralleling those of the migrants. Since no control group was selected as a part of this survey, another method was chosen. This is a variant of the "before-after comparison methods" in which the migrants themselves essentially become the control group. [17] This variant assumed that, starting with the measured pre-migration earnings figure from the survey, the migrant would have earned at the rate of growth of average earnings in Turkey: 10 percent in urban and 5.3 percent in rural employment.

Other Costs: The potential direct costs associated with migration have already been identified. These are basically the increased living costs and the costs of transportation, medical examinations, and visas. It is difficult to price the increase in living costs because the Turkish migrant generally lives differently abroad than at home, and no studies have attempted to

---

[14] Since the survey gives earnings abroad by year, the medians for 1964 and 1966 are available. However, these represent a composite of first-through-fifth year earnings, which is not the measure desired here.

[15] This may overstate the rate of urban workers' earnings growth, since nearly half (47 percent) were self-employed in 1970. This is offset, therefore, by the possibility that a substantial portion of their earnings represented not true wages but a return to their own capital—a distinction the typical wage-earner would not be able to make.

[16] Aker survey shows that at least 81 percent of the migrants were employed before migrating. See Ahmet Aker, *İşçi Göçü: Nisan 1970 ile Nisan 1971 Arasında Almanya'ya Giden Türk İşçileri Üzerinde Sosyo-Ekonomik Bir Örnekleme Araştırması* (İstanbul: Hilâl Matbaacılık Koll. Şti., 1972), p. 96, Table XXXII.

[17] See D.O. Sewell, "Training the Poor: A Benefit-Cost Analysis of Manpower Programs in the U.S. Antipoverty Program" for a discussion of before-after comparisons with reference to manpower training programs.

make calculations of living costs under identical conditions in
Turkey and countries where he is employed. However, since,
according to the SPO survey, housing and other living expenses
constitute only about 40 percent of the worker's budget, even a
25 percent increase in costs does not represent a major error.

As another consideration, many of these costs are absorbed by
the employer, especially when the worker comes over under contract; often the contracts cover medical examinations, visas,
transportation, and initial housing allowances.[18] Actually, although these may represent costs to the employer (along with a
"migrant tax" on employers) or to the host country at large,
these costs are either passed forward to the consumer in the form
of higher prices or backward on the migrant worker in a form he
would not recognize, i.e., as wage rates lower than they otherwise would be. For these reasons, direct costs will be ignored in
computing present values of migrant earnings.

Paths and Present Values of Turkish Migrants' Earnings

Estimated 10-year earnings paths and present values are presented in the table. The urban migrants receive a very large increase in earnings by migrating, but their earnings return to a
level in Turkey below that of what they would have earned had
they never migrated. This drop, if verified by a survey which
accurately records earnings by year, should be of considerable
concern for Turkish policy-makers.

Rural workers experience a greater increase upon migrating
and their post-migration earnings exceed slightly the "control
group" earnings.

The post-migration earnings decline would only be of concern
to workers, however, if their total long-run prospects are wor-
sened over not migrating. To see if this is the case, 10-year present values were calculated using discount rates of 5, 8, and
12 percent. These indicate that after 10 years, the migrants are
better off even in the "worst case," i.e., that of the urban
worker. With a discount rate of 5 percent, the urban worker who
migrates is approximately 20 percent better off than if he does

---

[18]   It is estimated that moving a migrant worker from one country to another costs,
on the average, between $ 3,000 and $ 4,000. *Washington Post*, "Tax Industries Using
Migrants EEC Urged" (April 13, 1974).

Table

Ten-Year Annual Earnings Paths and Present Values:
Turkish Urban and Rural Migrants and Controls (Current T.L.)

Don't include

Year	Annual Earnings										10-Year Present Values Discount Rate of		
	(1963) 1	(1964) 2	(1965) 3	(1966) 4	(1967) 5	(1968) 6	(1969) 7	(1970) 8	(1971) 9	(1972) 10	5%	8%	12%
Urban Migrants	7,661[1]	20,607	22,620[2]	24,565	8,201	9,113	10,125	11,250[3]	12,375	13,613	115,613	104,306	92,086
Urban Controls[4]	7,661[1]	8,427	9,270	10,197	11,216	12,338	13,572	14,929	16,422	18,064	95,390	83,320	70,738
Rural Migrants Returning to Urban Areas	3,132[1]	20,552	22,560[2]	24,500	3,902	4,335	4,817	5,352[3]	5,887	6,476	86,496	79,347	70,905
Rural Migrants Returning to Rural Areas	3,132[1]	20,552	22,560[2]	24,500	4,545	4,799	5,068	5,352	5,636	5,934	87,057	79,889	71,922
Rural Controls[5]	3,132[1]	3,298	3,473	3,657	3,851	4,055	4,270	4,496	4,734	4,985	31,727	28,022	24,103

[1] Median pre-migration earnings, set at 1963.
[2] Median earnings abroad, for 1965.
[3] Median present earnings of returned migrants (1970).
[4] Assumed to increase 10% per year after year 1.
[5] Assumed to increase 5.3% per year after year 1.

Source: Calculated from data in T.C. Başbakanlık Devlet Plânlama Teşkilâtı, Yurt Dışından Dönen İşçilerin Sosyo-Ekonomik Eğilimleri Üzerinde Bir Çalışma (Ankara, 1974).

not migrate. At 15 years (not shown) the advantage is still about 2 percent. For rural migrants, the advantage is extremely large. As discount rates are increased, the relative advantages likewise increase, because emphasis is put on the early years, i.e., the migration years.

Conclusion

This study strongly implies that the massive numbers of Turks who have migrated or who are striving to migrate have, on the average, well-founded expectations of financial success if nothing else. The shorter their time horizons and the greater their rates of time preference, the better is the decision to migrate. For the rural workers, who can anticipate a gain of at least 170 percent over 10 years, this is especially true. However, even for the urban worker, the gain is on the order of 20 percent over 10 years with the relatively low discount rate of 5 percent. [19]

Although the individual returns are clear, policy-makers in Turkey should be concerned by the finding that urban workers—who have the higher domestic productivity and hence earnings—apparently earn less after returning from abroad than they would have earned had they not migrated. If this is borne out by subsequent, better-designed research than the survey used here, it could indicate one or more of a number of things. From a national perspective, none of them are particularly welcome. On one hand, it could mean that workers are turning away from "wage work" to self-employment (as nearly half of the urban respondents to the SPO survey did). Although they might increase their business earnings in the long run, in the short run it seems that not only are they earning less than they could by working for someone else, they are also making negative returns on their invested capital, which are probably acquired abroad and remitted or repatriated. Thus not only is labor but also capital being inefficiently used.

---

[19] To be weighed against these earnings effects are social, economic, and psychic costs. To name a few, the migrant may encounter treatment as a second-class citizen in the foreign country, employment in undesirable jobs, work exploitation, isolation accentuated by language difficulty and living in ghettos, problems in finding Turkish teachers for his clementary-school-age children, or, if some members of his family remain in Turkey, traumas of separation as well as risks of family dissolution.

Secondly, it could indicate that the opportunities for returning migrants to use their newly acquired skills do not exist, or that the migrants are being barred from taking advantage of them. If this is the case, it implies that the on-the-job training and experience, which are or should be an important part of the gains from a migration policy, are being wasted.

Thirdly, it could just mean that the gains from migration, chiefly in the form of accumulated capital, are being taken largely in the form of increase leisure. While this definitely represents a gain to the individual migrant, it does hinder economic development and from the standpoint of the national economy should be considered a cost.

It must be emphasized that the findings of this study do rest upon somewhat shaky empirical grounds. The way the SPO survey has been tabulated makes it very difficult to relate earnings to the time of earning. This is an important deficiency in the light of Turkish price and wage inflation, ranging from 5.3 to 10 percent per annum during the period in question. There is thus some chance that this may be largely responsible for the somewhat surprising finding regarding the earnings path of returning urban migrants.

However, the urban migrant finding is by itself serious enough to warrant a better effort to measure the gains and losses of migration, both from the standpoint of the individual migrant and from that of the country as a whole. Such a study could follow the "ideal model" outlined above and would represent a most important contribution to the furthering of our understanding of the effects of migration.

EXPORTATION OF LABOR AND ITS IMPLICATIONS FOR TURKISH WAGE AND EDUCATION POLICY FORMULATION

DUNCAN R. MILLER[1]

I. *Introduction*

Since its inception the recent international migration into and within the European community has given rise to socio-economic-political phenomena so large scale and multifacited as to almost preclude comprehensive investigation. The dimensions of this labor movement yield implications far beyond simple employer demands and individual propensities to migrate. As a recent Council of Europe study [5] indicates, labor force migration continues to have a dramatic impact on both supplier and recipient economies. For example, between 1950 and 1965, total net emigration of the major Mediterranean labor supplying countries (Turkey, Portugal, Spain, Italy, Greece, and Yugoslavia), Finland, and Ireland represented a population movement equivalent to approximately one-quarter of their corresponding natural population increase or, more importantly, in terms of economically active populations, an amount approaching one-half of their increase in labor force new entrants. On the other hand, the scale of emigration into recipient labor markets, as one impact indicator, can be gauged by the ratio of increase in foreign workers to domestic work force. As McLin [19] reports, this ratio has averaged from about 22 percent for Belgium to over 100 percent for West Germany.

For present purposes, the West German experience is particularly noteworthy since over 75 percent of Turkish emigrants reside there. The macro impact of emigration on the Turkish economy is most evident in two statistics, namely, (1) the ratio of emigrants to the increase of the economically active population, a measure of the impact on the Turkish labor market, and (2) the relationship of workers' remittances to other sources of foreign exchange, most notably exports.

[1] Dr. Miller is an Assistant Program Economist with the Agency for International Development, Ankara, Turkey. This paper is the personal effort of the author and views and opinions expressed are not necessarily those of the Agency.

Although 1970 Population Census data are not yet available, calculations based on preliminary estimates indicate that between 1965 and 1970, emigration from Turkey approached an amount equal to 40 percent of the increase in total economically active population; furthermore, given historical labor force participation ratios, emigration could easily represent amounts exceeding 50 percent of the change in the active labor force.

Remittances by emigrant workers have had an even more profound impact on the Turkish balance of payments. In fact, as Table 1 highlights by 1969 workers' remittances became the largest single foreign exchange earner for Turkey, and in 1972, remittances almost equalled all exports. Obviously, this recent migration phenomenon should be of great concern to Turkish manpower and financial planners.

Table 1

Balanced of Payments — Turkey Selected Current Account Items
($ Millions)

	1968	1969	1970	1971	1972
Total Imports	−763.7	−801.2	−947.6	−1170.8	−1562.7
Total Exports	496.4	536.8	588.5	676.6	885.0
Major Exports:					
Cotton	139.1	113.6	173.1	193.1	191.3
Tobacco	94.8	81.5	78.5	85.9	130.9
Nuts	84.0	115.2	95.6	92.3	125.3
Total Workers' Remittances	107.3	140.6	273.1	473.4	740.2
Net Tourism	− 9.0	− 5.0	− 3.8	20.7	44.4
Balance on Current Account	−224.0	−220.0	−171.0	−109.0	− 8.0
Remittances as % of:					
Exports	21.6	26.2	46.4	70.0	83.6
Imports	14.1	17.5	28.8	40.4	47.4

Source: Ministry of Finance, Monthly Economic Indicators.

The fact that Turkey has participated energetically in this labor transfer is well established. From 1961 through 1972, the Turkish Labor Placement Office (İş ve İşçi Bulma Kurumu) placed some 650 thousand workers abroad through official channels. The total number of Turks including family members abroad is, of course, much greater. For example, as of January 1973, there were over 1 million Turkish men, women and children in Germany alone. As the attached bibliography indicates, emigrant Turkish workers have been and continue to be the subject of a good deal of scholarly research. Unfortunately, too little investigation has been undertaken regarding the implications of this migration flow for Turkish domestic policy formulation. The aim of this paper is to fill this gap in policy—oriented research at least in as much as can be ventured in the area of education and the generation of skilled labor force.

Before proceeding to the main thesis of this paper. It may be instructive to clear up some misconceptions concerning emigrant workers. Although by definition emigrant workers relieve unemployment, it is misleading to regard this recent migration as a vent for surplus labor. Specifically, as reported by Miller and Çetin [22], the following mean values of emigrant workers' characteristics do not support the vent for surplus labor hypothesis: 1) the mean age of emigration was 29 years, 2) the proportion of unemployed emigrants was less than half of the national urban unemployment rate (around 7.2 percent in 1970), 3) the percentage of semi-skilled and skilled workers was 46.3 in 1971—by German standards—a proportion in the order of magnitude of two to three times greater than the domestic average, and 4) as shown below, educational attainment data also infer more of a brain drain than solely a brawn drain, especially in terms of these who might be upgraded by domestic training:

Educational Attainment of Migrants
and Domestic Labor Force

Graduates of:	(percent) Migrants[a]	Domestic[b]
Primary	63.7	39.1
Secondary	3.2	3.4
Vocational	4.7	2.0
Lycee	1.2	1.4
Higher	n.a.	1.6

Sources:

a [3, Table 2].

b Duncan Miller and Ihsan Çetin, 'Regional Variations in Educational Attainment in Turkey." United States Agency for International Development, *Economic Staff Paper* No. 12, 1973.

The purported net benefits of massive inflows of foreign exchange also are less than obvious. The foreign exchange has been allowed simply to stockpile in the Central Bank, a historical level of net convertible free reserves of 1.7 billion dollar equivalent as of 30 June 1973, without a significant liberalization of imports or relief of foreign debt burden. Clearly, the Turkish Lira (TL) counterpart has had some inflationary impact but examination of the magnitude and incidence are beyond the present scope. Existing data do indicate that, contrary to the commonly-held view, relatively few of the workers devote their savings to create new investments or industrial capacity; in fact, slightly over 26 percent of the returned urban migrants invested in work ventures and the mean amount declared was just over 25,000 TL.[2]

The domestic (Turkish) employment impact of migration, in terms of skill acquisition and increased mobility upon return, are the most difficult to access. Estimates of German and Turkey-based learning curves by Munson [23, p. 105], however, indicate that learning, especially experience generated on the job, was much more rapid in Germany than in Turkey, 59 and 334 days respectively, for similar Turkish laborers. In terms of skill utilization and mobility, Miller and Çetin [22, p. 4] report that only 11.6 percent of the workers stated employment in the same occupation before, during, and after migration, whereas 48.8 percent indicated the same occupational status before and after but not during migration.

II. *International Migration and Welfare Calculus*

Recently, economists and other social scientists have renewed their struggle to comprehend the continuous outflow of scarce talent from the developing to developed countries, a phenomenon usually referred to as the brain drain.[3] Unfortunately, investigations of the so-called brain drain either have yielded a few

---

[2] Utilization of workers' savings is explored in depth in Duncan Miller and Ihsan Çetin, "Workers, Wages and Labor Markets," unpublished paper. For a theoretical model which explains the individual worker's tendency to migrate, the manner and timing in which he allocates his earnings abroad, and his aspirations upon return to Turkey, see Miller [21].

[3] See, among others, S. Watanabe, "The Brain Drain from Developing Countries," *International Labour Review*, Vol. 99, April 1969, pp. 401-433.

generalized qualitative insights or, more often the case, suffered from the lack of a well articulated theoretical framework. R. Albert Berry and Ronald Soligo[4] have put forth a new model which attempts to establish a sound basis to formulate domestic wage and education policies under conditions of international migration of skilled labor. In the following sections, the Berry-Soligo model is summarized, the major policy conclusions are analyzed, and, finally, implications from the emigrant Turkish workers case are evaluated.

Given international migration of skilled labor, the Berry-Soligo model attempts to define, in theoretical terms, the optimum skilled to unskilled labor force ratio which should maximize the increase in per capita income of non-emigrants. The policy variable to be manipulated, ie. the decision variable, is that of the extent of subsidization of education. An alternate model investigates the same optimaliity criterion but utilizes a wage subsidization policy mechanism. The major import of the model may be seen in the simple case of no emigration.

Education Subsidization Without Emigration

If, as assumed in this model, policy makers are committed to maximizing the income of the domestic population at any given point in time, the government may be forced to subsidize education, at least in part, because, "(a) individuals are risk averse and lack information abour the returns to education and (b) capital markets are imperfect; hence, the amount of investment on education which would occur without government assistance would be less than the social optimum."[5]

Given the presumption that one of the major policy mechanisms of increasing the income level of the population is that of increasing the ratio of skilled to unskilled labor via education and training, the calculation of the optimum level of education subsidization is indicated in Figure 1. Here, the horizontal axis shows the ratio of skilled to unskilled labor and the vertical axis measures per capita costs and benefits of education. The line CC^1 exhibits the per capita cost of an incremental addition of one

---

[4] R. Albert Berry and Ronald Soligo, "Optimal Wage and Education Policies with International Migration," Rice University Program of Development Studies Paper No. 25, 1972.

[5] *Ibid.*, pp. 3-4.

Fig. 1

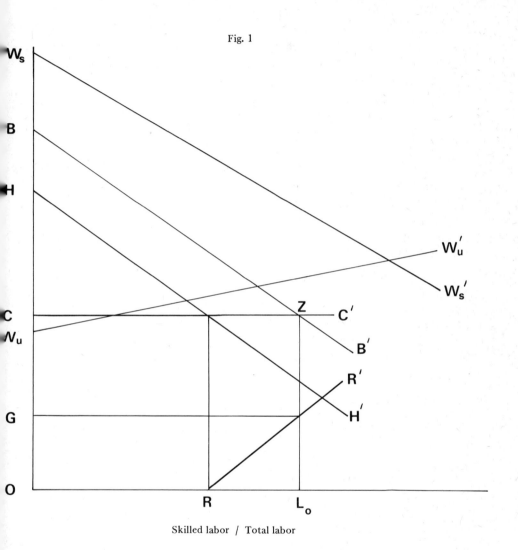

Skilled labor / Total labor

skilled labor to the total stock of skilled labor. The per capita benefit, in terms of marginal productivity gains, of this added skilled worker is given by BB^1. Simply put, CC^1 is the cost of producing a unit of skilled labor and BB^1 represents the difference between per capita discounted future earnings of a skilled worker $(W_s\ W^1{}_s)$ and an unskilled worker $(W_u\ W_u{}^1)$.[6] Note, as the stock of skilled workers increases, the wage rate for skilled workers falls and that of unskilled workers rises, both expressed in terms of the skilled to unskilled labor force ratio.

Experience indicates, however, that individuals often underestimate or simply do not realize the amount of benefits to be derived from additional education; hence, the amount individuals are willing to pay, herein indicated by HH^1, is less than benefits to be accrued, BB^1. Consequently, although perfect knowledge and perfect market conditions would dictate that individuals would pay the cost of attaining further education, the optimum ratio of skilled to unskilled labor $(O\ L_o)$ may require government subsidization of education. Thus, the level of education subsidization may be calculated as the difference of what individuals are willing to pay and the costs of the social optimum level of skilled labor. For example, at skilled labor force ratios less than OR, individuals are willing to pay (HH^1) an amount greater than the required costs (CC^1) of education and government subsidization is not necessary. Above OR, however, individuals are unwilling to pay the total costs of education and government subsidization is necessary. The amount of subsidization may be derived from the difference of CC^1, and HH^1. The curve ORR^1 represents the required levels of subsidization to attain the optimum level of skilled to unskilled labor, OL_o. Clearly, skilled labor ratios greater than OL_o would not be economically rational since social costs exceed social benefits.[7]

Conceptual Complexities Caused by Emigration

Even with a disaggregated three factor model (capital, skilled labor and unskilled labor), emigration causes severe difficulties

---

[6] BB^1 is thus the flow of educated laborers to maintain a given stock of skilled labor. Retirements, drop-outs, and non utilization of skills are herein treatled implicitly but could be refined.

[7] If, for some reason, the amount of government subsidy is severely constrained, the government could control or ration the supply of education offered.

for conceptualizing optimal levels of subsidization to education. An immediate problem is that of the emigration propensity of each type of labor and their relative propensities to hold wealth. As in most theoretical exercises, Berry and Soligo purport a pure case where only skilled labor emigrates and they assume that either the emigrants leave all their capital behind or have equal wealth holding propensities and take all of their capital with them. The type of labor emigrating and their wealth holding propensities have a significant impact on the concept of income to be maximized. It is assumed, however, that policy makers are concerned only with the maximization of domestic population at discrete points in time and, to the extent at all, discount future income streams of only those individuals who are present in both sets of time periods, ie. non-emigrants.

In order to be able to clearly separate cost and benefit between emigrant and non-emigrants, the authors assume independent welfare functions. Simply put, this means that non-emigrants will suffer a loss in welfare if they pay for the education of emigrants. This assumption makes the model conceptually easier but can be challenged since, inevitably, utility functions of many emigrants and non-emigrants are at least partially interdependent. For example, a father may directly or indirectly accrue benefits of a son's education and thus be willing to pay for the education even if he knows the son will emigrate.

Apart from the question of welfare, questions of the cost of educating skilled workers and external effects relating to skilled workers must be addressed. The authors assume constant costs to train skilled workers; however, as is probably more realistic, there are increasing costs in educating higher and higher proportions of skilled workers. Thus, emigration of skilled workers implies an income loss to non-migrants whereas unskilled worker migration yields a gain. Moreover, where there are positive external effects relating to the mere presence of skilled workers, emigration of skilled workers causes further income and welfare losses for non-migrants.[8],[9]

---

[8] Increasing costs in the education sector could be caused by either decreasing returns (total costs rise, after some point, faster than total numbers being educated) or declining quality of students as more and more are educated at any constant cost.

[9] For example, we can express the positive external benefits of skilled laborer on other workers quantitatively as follows:

Education Subsidization With Migration

For purposes of illustration let us assume that education is entirely subsidized by the government and that the emigrants are from the last group to be educated in the sense that the migrants would not have been trained if the flow of educational resources were diminished, what policy implications can be drawn from the model? [10] The right hand quadrant in Figure 2 is identical to that of Figure 1: CC^1 represents the cost of training one more skilled worker; BB^1 is the benefit accrued in terms of discounted earnings, $W_u W_u^1$ is the skilled wage function, and HH^1 the demand function for education. By allowing free mobility of skilled labor, the analysis becomes more complicated. First, the international skilled labor wage function must be included in the model. Here, $W_{sw} W_{sw}^1$ represents discounted earnings of skilled labor abroad. The difference between domestic skilled labor earnings ($W_s W_s^1$) and worldwide rates ($W_{sw} W_{sw}^1$) is given by the curve DD^1. DD^1 rises since $W_s W_s^1$ decreases at higher and higher ratios of skilled labor.

The left hand quadrant measures the relationship of working life span abroad to income differentials, ie. the greater the wage differentials, the greater the propensity to migrate and work abroad for a longer time; hence, the curve JJ^1 can be derived.

The curve TT^1 shows the relationshiip between time abroad and the average cost of educating a skilled worker. This relationship is so constructed that in the case of no migration (100 percent working life spent at home) the average cost JT equals OC, as in Figure 1. The implications of emigration can be traced as follows: For example, with a skilled labor force ratio of OL_1, the domestic to international skilled labor wage differential equals

---

$X(t) = f[K(t), h_1(t), h_2(t), e(t)]$
$X(t) =$ a worker's output in time t
$K(t) =$ physical capital combined with an inexperienced worker
$h_1(t) =$ number of skilled workers with whom an inexperienced worker is employed, ie. a human capital factor
$h_2(t) =$ experience level of co-workers
$e(t) =$ experience level of the worker

For further details, see Duncan Miller, "Toward a Human Resource Development Plan for Turkey," İş ve İşçi Bulma Kurumu, 1972.

[10] The authors also present a variant of the model in which the migrants are from a sub-set of the population which would have been educated even if the amount of education was less. Although this variant yields a slightly different welfare calculus, it does not appear to be germane to the emigrant Turkish worker case.

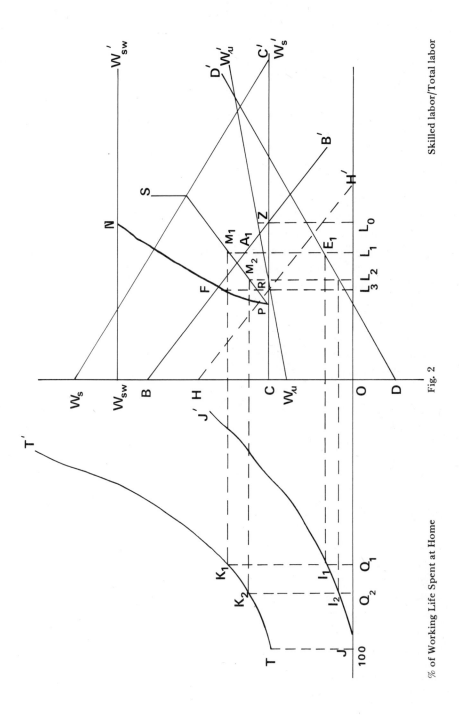

Fig. 2

L_1 E_1. Transposing L_1 E_1 to the left hand quadrant implies a period of work life abroad of $(100 - 0\ Q_1)$. Likewise, at OL_1 the average cost per skilled worker is Q_1 K_1, which corresponds to L_1 M_1 on the right hand quadrant. Similarly, a skilled labor force ratio of OL_2 implies L_2 M_2 average cost to train a skilled worker. Iterating this procedure yields an average cost curve function of CPS. [11]

The optimal skilled labor force can be determined by locating the intersection of the marginal cost curve (CPFN) and the benefit curve (BB^1). In the case of skilled labor emigration, the optimum skilled labor force would be OL_3. Two immediate implications are important. First, the optimum level skilled labor is less than would be the case without migration. In other words, emigration increases the marginal cost of "producing" a skilled worker thereby reducing the optimal supply, given a fixed education subsidy. Second, non-emigrants will not be able to benefit fully from the normal benefits of education due to two factors: one) due to the lower optimum level of skilled labor, the area FZR cannot be gained, and two) due to subsidies paid to migrants, the area PFR is lost.

In summary, "the emigration of skilled workers whose education has been paid for by non-emigrants will lower the welfare of the latter group unless the utility functions of non-emigrants include the welfare of the emigrants. [In other words] the emigration of recipients of subsidized education will harm non-emigrants; the optimal proportion of skilled to unskilled workers will be smaller than in the no-migration case." [12]

Wage Subsidy With Migration

Since, as seen above, emigration tends to reduce the benefits accruing to education subsidies, an alternative policy to attain an optimum skilled labor force might be a skilled wage subsidy. The government can directly or indirectly maintain an artificially high skilled wage rate in an attempt to discourage emigration. In essence, the policy implies that unskilled workers are forced to subsidize skilled workers. Apart from the fact that such a policy may be less appealing than the education subsidy to unskilled

---

[11] Since the intersection of the HH^1 curve and the horizontal axis represents the highest attainable voluntary skilled labor ratio, CPS becomes vertical at this point.

[12] Berry and Soligo, *loc. cit.* p. 29.

workers, the wage subsidy may have dysfunctional implications. The major impact of a wage subsidy should be to shift the DD^1 (Figure 2) curve downward and to the right. Although the domestic to international skilled wage differential would be smaller, the optimum skilled labor force ratio would be higher than under the policy of education subsidy. Consequently, the wage subsidy policy might encourage emigration of skilled workers rather than inhibit emigration as intended.

III. *Emigrant Turkish Workers: Policy Implications*

The aim of this paper is not to investigate the weaknesses of the model; rather, the implications for education and wage policy formulation are addressed. Indeed, adequate data are not available to test the model. After more than a decade of relatively rapid growth, albeit largely import substitution, Turkey now faces the triple tasks of: one) continue to achieve high levels of growth of the macro economy, two) at least partially relieve the pervasive regional imbalances and structural rigidities characteristic of an economy in transition to industrialization, and three) begin to adjust to the trauma of membership in the European Economic Community. Expansion of the required industrial labor force base is cardinal to each of these tasks. Indeed, the Third Five Year Development Plan acknowledges that a critical shortage of skilled labor is upon us already.

On the pessimistic side, continued emigration of skilled labor along with domestic shortages of skilled labor may very well have a perverse influence on current industrialization policies, not to mention a welfare loss to non-emigrants. At the micro level, in the absence of adequate replacement workers, Turkish employers suffering a loss of skilled workers must either cope with decreased productivity of workers (an output loss) or increased cost of training new workers. Moreover, at such a crucial stage in her economic development, Turkey is losing many of the potential positive external effects of a skilled labor force base. At the macro level, emigration of skilled labor largely vitiates the impact of an education policy aimed at fostering skill acquisition. Thus, with almost half of the present flow of emigrants either semi-skilled or skilled, Turkey must be prepared to bear an increasing cost along with increasing emigration of skilled labor.

On the more optimistic side, emigrant Turkish workers are acquiring valuable industrial experience and discipline. [13] Upon their returnn—if ever—these workers should have a tremendous impact on the Turkish industrial labor base; thus, it may be time to look beyond the gains from the flow of workers' remittances and attempt to internalize into Turkey's development the gains from the flow of returned, upgraded workers. One such attempt could be to establish a policy under which the period of emigration is part and parcel of a formal apprenticeship or master craftsmen program. Before or upon return, the government of Turkey could issue a formal certificate of skill accreditation, give the worker priority for—or better yet guarantee—a job placement through the Labor Placement Office, and assist the worker financially to relocate his family if necessary. In any case, the continued lack of a migrant worker policy has many implicit costs (benefits) which are not being calculated (exploited).

IV. Problems and Prospects of Turkish Workers in Germany

In the final analysis, the Federal Republic of Germany emerges as the centrum of any Turkish migration policy. Although a relatively latecomer into the recent migration complex, Turkey now represents the present and future major supplier of workers for Germany. As of January 1973, almost 23 percent of all male foreign workers in Germany were Turks; from January to April 1973, the flow of Turks as a percentage of total rose to over 43 percent. Turks are generally regarded as reliable and highly industrious workers; moreover, as of 1971, 46 percent of the new

---

[13] Miller and Çetin [22, Table 7] report the following survey results of skill acquisition from migration:

Skill Level	Before			Abroad (Fourth Year)		
	Total	Urban	Rural	Total	Urban	Rural
Unskilled	50.7	32.4	75.3	30.1	13.2	51.9
Semi Skilled	2.2	2.4	2.0	15.6	5.9	17.0
Skilled-General	6.9	9.6	3.3	30.0	36.8	7.4
Skilled-Master Workman	23.6	29.0	16.3	17.8	22.1	3.7
Skilled Technician	4.7	7.7	0.7	n.r.	n.r.	n.r.

Turkish emigrants were skilled workers, the highest proportion of all labor supplying countries. The future of Turkish-German relations concerning migrant workers is, however, froth with difficulties.

German economic dependency on foreign labor has assumed an almost structural relationship; assuming further economic growth, the following factors indicate a continued, if not expanded, reliance on foreign labor: 1) longer periods of training and skill upgrading, 2) continued decrease in normal working hours, 3) prolongation of holidays and other periods of time off, 4) pensions at less than 60 years of age and wider coverage of disability pensions, and 5) continued low population growth. The dramatic increase in foreign workers some 700 thousand in 1963 to over 2.4 million in 1973 exhibits the capacity of Germany's economy to absorb migrants; however, serious concern is now evident about the German society's capacity to absorb more labor. In fact, without fanfare German policy-makers are now struggling with attempts to align labor market demands with the more elusive concept of social infrastructure capacity, including adequate housing, schools and health facilities. Whatever the outcome, Germany is now embarking on an effort to grant foreign workers greater economic security and greater access to the high level of German social services. Thus, the earlier debate concerning possible extreme policies of a rigid, mandatory rotation system versus full integration appear to have struck a compromise in a more moderate policy of assimilation. In the medium and long run, German officials want to force employers of foreign workers to assume a greater burden for social infrastructure investments and begin to export capital rather than import labor. Apart from some obvious internal inconsistencies of the most-likely German policies, the following areas of policy conflict between Turkey and Germany appear noteworthy.

The most immediate conflict of interest continues to be the trade off of skilled versus unskilled workers. German officials have repeatedly warned Turkey that unskilled workers are no longer in much demand. The implications of this trade off are the main theme addressed in the sections above. The long run conflicts are ever more substantial. With over one million people on the official waiting list to go to Germany, it would appear to be in Turkey's best interest to advocate a rigid, mandatory rotation system. German attempts at assimilation may, therefore, destroy the chance for many to go but also, as will be articulated below, decrease the incentive for the over one million Turks in Germany to return to their homeland. The greatest conflict centers around Turkey's ambition to be a full member of the European Economic Community (EEC). The present Turkish-EEC protocol advocates a gradual relaxation of labor mobility restrictions with the aim of creating free labor mobility sometime between 1976 and 1986. Quite obviously, the Germans are concerned, indeed frightened, about the prospects of a horde of millions of Turkish migrants suddenly invading their country. Consequently, the Germans are cautiously approaching any further negotiations of Turkey's entry into the EEC. The prospects for Turkey likewise may be somewhat catastrophic. If over one million Turkish emigrants wake up to a European labor market guaranteeing greater economic security and vastly superior social benefits, they may withdraw their families from Turkey, never return, and cease to remit.

INVESTMENT BY TURKISH MIGRANTS IN REAL ESTATE

RUŞEN KELEŞ

Urbanization, Housing and the Plan

In Turkey only 35.8% of the population live in urban areas. Inspite of this Turkey is among the developing nations one of the most rapidly urbanizing countries. During the last twenty years, the annual average urbanization rate has varied between 5% and 6.5%. The number of cities is also increasing continuously. There were 66 cities in 1927, 106 in 1950, 149 in 1960 and finally 264 in 1970. With the influence of the land speculators, the housing demand, inflated in cities by the rapid urbanization, has pushed upward the prices of dwelling units to very high levels. In addition, the general structure of the economy and the inflation have kept alive the attraction of investing in real estate. In fact, until 1960, the share of housing investments in total investments changed between 25% and 35%. But during the last ten years the Development Plan have tried to keep this ratio below 23% and to direct the resources into more productive sectors. The main principle in the three Five-Year Development Plans is to meet the housing demand without increasing the share of housing investment in total investment and to decrease this ratio as far as possible. Under these conditions, it is obvious that the amount of workers remittances that goes to housing can be considered as meaningful only if it is below the ratio set by the Plans as a ceiling.

Workers Migration

The phenomenon of workers emigration from Turkey stems from economic necessities. It is a part of the international population movements that are created by economic underdevelopment. The Turkish economy could no longer bear the burden of the underemployed or unemployed population and has pushed them away into the international labor market, starting from 1960. There is a close similarity between this movement and the movement of the population from the rural to urban areas.

The labor demand of the Western European countries that have undertaken large scale reconstruction programs following the Second World War, has been a source of attraction for the Turkish workers. Both the host countries and the home countries have advantages and problems that are associated with this movement. The migrant workers undergo a rapid social transformation and the workers remittances contribute to a great extent to the solution of the balance of payments problem. In the last five years, The Turkish planners have witnessed a new developmental problem in addition to the problem of the shortage of foreign currency: it is that of finding the ways of using the foreign currency saved by the workers abroad.

Between 1961 and 1973 the number of workers sent abroad through official channels is 656,401. When 137,000 students and 84,000 professionals and another 70,000 which is the number of workers working abroad outside from the manpower agreements is added to this figure, it reaches 950,000.[1] 80% of this population lives in Germany, 13% is in Holland, Austria and France and the rest is working in other West European countries. The findings of a Turkish survey[2] carried out in 1971 on workers going abroad, show that 66.2% of these are industrial workers. According to the official statistics 71.3% of the workers abroad are employed in manufacturing industries, 15.5% in construction and 11.1% in services.[3] Undoubtedly, this sectoral distribution with a definite preference for the manufacturing industries, will have a positive effect both on the income and savings and on the employment opportunities of the workers when they come back to Turkey. The ratio of qualified workers has changed over the years between 31% (1966) and 46% (1971), thus occupying the first place among all national contingents in terms of skilled manpower.[4]

It has been observed that the workers going abroad mainly come from developed regions and urban areas. The provinces of the Aegean, Marmara and Thrace regions occupy the first rank on

---

[1] T.C. Disisleri Bakanligi, Ekonomik ve Sosyal İşler Genel Müdürlügü, *Yurt Dişi Göç Hareketleri ve Vatandaş Sorunlari*, Ankara, 1973, p. 22.

[2] Ahmet Aker, *İş Göçü*, Istanbul, 1972, p. 43.

[3] *Yurt Disi Göc Hareketleri* ..., p. 24.

[4] Bundesanstalt für Arbeit, *Ausländische Arbeitnehmer*, Beschäftigung, Anwerbung, Vermittlung Erfahrungsbericht 1970, 27. August 1971, p. 35.

a list indicating the geographical distribution of the workers abroad. The one who go to West Europe from these regions are mainly urban workers or small shop owners, craftsmen. On the other hand, relatively underprivileged regions such as the Black Sea region or Eastern, South-East Anatolia send abroad workers of rural origin; their number is usually relatively small. During the recent years, there is an increase in the number of workers that go abroad from Central Anatolia and the Eastern regions. According to a recent survey,[5] carried out by the State Planning Organization, the ratios of urban and rural migrant workers are almost equal; they split up around 50% each. It should also be emphasized that this migration contributes in the long effect to the urbanization of the total population at a ratio of almost 50% since the migrant workers who do return to their home country usually settle in urban areas, even if originally they are coming from a rural setting. The remaining 50% are returning again to one of Turkey's major cities; they were already settled in a large city before they departed from their home country. Regardless of their place of origin, it seems interesting to note that the industrial atmosphere of the host countries does exercize a decisive impact on their way of thinking, frame of reference, attitudes. This again determines to a great extent their decisions concerning investment of their savings.

Workers Remittances

Workers remittances have increased from 0.5 million $ in 1965 to 2 billion $ in 1972.[6] The share of workers remittances in the amount of foreign currency earned through exports has increased from 15% in 1965 to 84% in 1973.

Today, it is widely accepted that workers remittances are not used in the development satisfactorily.[7] The Third Five Year

---

[5] D.P.T., *Yurt Disindan Dönen İşçilerin Sosyo-Ekonomik Eğilimleri Üzerinde bir Çalışma* Ankara, 1974, p. 8.

[6] The total sum of workers remittances in 1965 covering Federal Republic of Germany, Belgium, Holland, Austria, Switzerland was 69.7 million $. This sum raised in 1966 to 115.3 million $, in 1967 to 93.0 million $, in 1968 to 107.3 million $, in 1969 to 140.6 million $, in 1970 to 273 million $, in 1971 to 471.3 million $ and in 1972 to 740.1 million $.

[7] Türkiye Ticaret Odalari, Sanayi Odalari ve Ticaret Borsalari Birligi, *Yurt Dişindaki Isçilerimizin Tasarruflarinin Degerlendirilmesi Semineri*, Ankara, 1972.

Plan points out to the fact that there is a tendency that channel workers remittances into small, uneconomic investments and that they create an "inflated demand" in the housing sector.[8] The Third Five-Year Plan foresees the direction of workers remittances toward more productive investments on one side and on the other side it points out that in order to meet the demand of the workers abroad for social dwelling units of certain minimum acceptable standards, encouragement of the large social housing projects, allocation of cheaper urban land to them and the control of their saving plans and standards will be taken into consideration as a whole.[9]

The distribution of workers remittances among economic sectors is not known but the tendency of workers remittances to be invested in real estate instead of manufacturing industry and other industrial sectors is fairly clear. For this, one has to depend on the data furnished by the State Real Estate Bank (Emlak Kredi Bankasi) that provides housing credit to homeless families and on the data of several field surveys.

According to these surveys an important part of the workers—actually more than 90%—state that they have been saving some part of their income. According to the findings of Ursula Mehrlander, author of a large scale five nation survey carried out with the help of the Friedrich Ebert Foundation in 1971, 6% of the Turkish workers are saving less than 100 DM per month. 31% are saving between 100 and 200 DM, 30% between 200-300 DM, 12% between 300-400 DM, 4% between 400-500 DM, 10% between 500-600 DM, 1% between 600-700 DM, 3% between 700-900 DM. [10] Estimates are also showing that the saving propensity is much higher than the amount they sent home. Therefore, it can be assumed that workers savings are much higher than the workers remittances and that the difference between the two is either kept abroad in form of savings or spent on consumer goods.

---

[8] D.P.T. *Kalkinma Plani*, Üçüncü Beş Yil (1972-1977), p. 676.
[9] D.P.T., *Ibid.*
[10] Ursula Mehrlander, *Soziale Aspekte der Ausländer-beschäftigung*, Verlag Neue Gesellschaft Bonn-Bad Godesberg 1974, p. 235, Table 149.

Ways of Meeting the Housing Demand

Migrant workers have three major alternatives to satisfy their housing demands.

A. To acquire a dwelling unit by using the housing credit the government is providing. In 1964, the Turkish Government has tried to attract workers savings by adopting the Law No. 499. Accordingly a fund has been established at the Turkish Real Estate Bank to support the workers both by extending small industry credits with the purpose of helping them setting up individual business and by furnishing housing credits to meet their housing demands. According to the above cited law, housing credits are given out of this fund to those workers who have already opened a housing account in the Bank. The assumption is that the workers will send some part of their savings in form of foreign currency, which then will be converted in Turkish currency and represent the nucleus of their new savings account. Workers with such a savings account are entitled to obtain a housing credit, which varies between 30 and 75,000 TL, depending on the preference of the worker. Until 1973, the maximum amount that could be allocated to each worker, was only 40,000 TL. Considering the rapid increase in the cost of construction and the dwindling purchasing power of the Turkish currency, this amount was recently increased with a ceiling of 75,000 TL. According to present regulations, a worker with a savings account, can dispose over a sum between 50,000-125,000 TL; this would include both his savings and the credit accorded. Workers indicating a preference for the highest amount of available credit, will have to pay a monthly installment of 731.- TL (139.24 DM)

Housing Credit	Workers Savings	Total Amount (TL)
30,000	20,000	50,000
45,000	30,000	75,000
60,000	40,000	100,000
75,000	50,000	125,000

As it is seen on the table above, the workers will have to send at least 40% of the total amount they want in form of foreign exchange to the bank account they opened in Turkey. The Bank is paying an interest of 2.5% to this amount. Housing credits have to be paid back within 15 years at an interest rate of 9%. These credits can only be used for social housing. According to the Turkish standards, set up by the Ministry of Reconstruction and Resettlement, social dwellings are the one, which dispose over a habitable space less than 100 square meters.

The workers benefiting from these credits or their wives are not entitled to own a house or a flat elsewhere in Turkey. The housing credit offered has to be used for the first time by the applicant. Until recently the major precondition in order to benefit from this credit source was the decision to return definitely home to Turkey. This precondition is abolished since the beginning of 1974 and the cited facilities are kept open also for workers who continue to work abroad.

It should be pointed out, that the number of workers, applying to the Turkish Real Estate Bank to open a housing savings account, is quite limited. The number of newly opened accounts is 2,986 for the whole period of ten years, namely between 1964 and 1974. The ratio of workers who have tried this alternative to the total number of migrant workers is just 0.3%. Out of these, only 0.2% have actually constructed a flat using this credit. The amount of foreign currency sent to Turkey through housing savings accounts is just 20 million TL so far. This is even less than 1 : 1,000 of the workers remittances.

There are mainly two reasons for this lack of interest. One is the low amount of housing credit, which was never sufficient to meet the actual building costs of a decent dwelling unit, the other is the precondition of returning to Turkey. These two shortcomings have been partly modified today. Time will show how effective it will be on the demand for housing credits.

B. The second alternative for migrant workers in Turkey to channel their savings into housing, is the formula of financial participation with private companies in Turkey. The number of these companies ranges around ninety; they all pursue the aim to invest in industry and commerce. Recently some larger companies such as TURKSAN, attempted to build homes for their shareholders. However only a very small amount of the workers' savings does go into these companies.

C. The third alternative is to invest directly in housing or land acquisition without neither using the help of the Turkish Real Estate Bank nor the assistance of any business group of the private sector. Investments of this type are either realized during the holidays or with the assistance of relatives living in Turkey. It is generally believed that the major part of the workers' remittances are used for this type of investment. The various surveys carried out in Turkey and Federal Germany confirm the observation that the great bulk of workers' remittances are mainly used to buy flats (condominium), land and other real estate properties that do not carry any risk. [11] Workers just about to leave their native country indicated within the framework of a survey that 45.7% had taken the decision to invest their future savings in housing and land within city boundaries. [12]

Findings from empirical data

The relative limitedness of the workers' tendencies about housing investment and urban landownership led us too to carry out a small sized empirical research. The method of this small scale survey may seem unsatisfactory to social scientists. But our aim here is not to make contributions to the theory of social science research, but to find out within the framework of certain reliability limits some tendencies with respect to the investment patterns. Therefore the sample size and the way the samples are chosen are not in conformity with the international standards.

A questionnaire has been used in this study. The Turkish Labor Attache in Hamburg selected 76 workers, representing the characteristics of the total workers of the area; of course he used his personal discretion and asked them to fill the questionnaire we had sent. According to the answers, 55% of the respondents indicated that they have bought flats in Turkey. Their purchase was done through the savings they managed to accumulate abroad. The duration of their stay abroad changes between two to thirteen years. The average period of these buyers of flats or parcels of urban land, was around six years. On the other hand, the workers who did not buy either flats or land, have stayed in F. Germany between one and seven and a half years. For this second group the average period of stay is 4 years. It should not

---

[11] Ihsan Çetin, *Migrant Workers, Wages and Labor Markets*, USAID, Discussion Paper, No. 18, Ankara 1974, p. 13.

[12] Ahmet Aker, *Ibid.*

be assumed that this second group was not interested to invest in
real estate. They should rather be considered as members of a
group who could not save enough for housing during their stay.

The majority of the workers have invested in housing rather
than in rural and urban land. The rural and urban land, which is
bought by these workers is usually near or just out of the municipal boundaries. Sometimes, they buy also agricultural land in
the villages.

The workers who participated in this small scale survey, have
paid between 20,000 to 240,000 TL for the houses they bought.
The average amount paid per flat is around 100,000 TL (20,000
DM). If we assume that half of the workers abroad invest in real
estate and that they pay 100,000 TL in average, we may reach the
conclusion that investment in housing by migrant workers does
reach a total sum of 40 billion TL so far. This amount is very
close to the investment projection foreseen for the whole housing
sector in Turkey, namely 44 billion TL in the Third Five Year
Plan.

The sizes and other standards of the houses bought by migrant
workers or by their relatives for the workers, show that these
flats do not conform with the social housing standards of the dwellings and that most of them are built by private contractors. Only
40% of the flat bought by the group under study have a surface
below 100 square meters, which is a well established standard of
social housing. This shows that the migrant workers prefer to
invest in relatively luxurious flats, even if they do not plan to live
in them. The number of rooms these flats dispose, also support
this observation. As the provision in the Turkish Constitution of
1961 concerning the satisfaction of housing needs of poor and
low income families as a public service is not properly implemented, the migrant workers both solve their future housing
problems and protect their savings from inflation by investing in
a sector that does not feel the inflationary pressures so much. [13]

The sizes of rural or agricultural lands that these workers are
buying vary between 2,000 and 5,000 square meters. The location of the flats and land parcels gives an idea about the places
where migrant workers plan to settle and points out the cities
and regions where real estate is considered most valuable invest-

---

[13]   The Turkish Constitution, Art. 49: "The State shall take measures to provide
the poor and low income families with dwellings that meet sanitary requirements."

ment field. 30% of the workers investing in real estate have invested their savings in Istanbul. This figure reaches up to 50% if we take Istanbul metropolitan area together with some cities in the Agean Regions. But the most striking point is the fact that three fourth of the investment of the migrant workers is located in cities that have populations over 100.000. The less developed eastern regions of the country do not exercize any attraction in regard of housing investment. Only two of the workers who did invest in housing, have bought flats in Eastern and South-Eastern Anatolian cities such as Malatya and Maras.

In general, the workers who have bought flats and land have not used sources other than their own savings. The ratio of workers that have used mortgage credit from the Turkish Real Estate Bank and from the Social Security Agency is around 4%. The great majority pays the price of their flats in advance and in cash. The ratio of these is 45%. Seventy percent of the remainder have paid between 20 to 50% of the price in advance. The ratio of the ones that pay less than 20% or more than 50% are the same.

Conclusions

1. There is relatively few empirical data concerning the real estate investments of the migrant workers. Some empirical studies show that these sectors are given priority in the investment preferences of the workers. Their desire to invest in such fields as manufacturing industry or in commercial activities comes later on their list of priorities. The workers who have already bought a flat, are mentioning an independent economic activity as a possible field of investment, when they are consulted about their preferences. This shows that there is a positive change in the way of thinking of the migrant workers. The migrants that do not own flats either mention housing as a first choice or they mention industrial and commercial enterprises along with the housing. To import manufactured goods, cars and to keep their savings in banks abroad do not seem to have priority.

2. The official policy of the Government as expressed in the Third Five Year Plan is to encourage the use of workers remittances especially in the manufacturing sector. Since existing companies, cooperatives and other establishments set up by individuals, groups and the state, seems to be not sufficiently attractive

and safe for the use of their savings, the migrant workers find today real estate as the most profitable, dependable and preferable field of investment.

3. The housing investments of the migrant workers show the tendency both to surpass the ceiling set for the housing investment in the Five Year Plan and to direct investments in dwelling units that do not fit well to the social housing standards supported by the State. Therefore it is not possible to maintain that these savings are used in a rational way. The Ministry of Reconstruction and Resettlement should cooperate with the Ministry of Labor in order to render the funds going to the housing sector more productive by encouraging the creation of large scale housing cooperatives or other non-profit housing institutions or directly through a State Housing Bank like the Turkish Real Estate Bank. There is no doubt that the ideal solution would be to take the necessary economic measures to channel the available funds into other sectors than housing.

4. The way workers remittances are used is closely related with the general conditions of the Turkish economy. So long as the private entrepreneurs supply the market with luxurious flats and apartments more rapidly and more easily for their own profit, and as long as the operation of the economic system favors such imperfections, preconditions for asking state guidance for the migrant workers would be the elimination of the present market conditions.

SOCIAL ISSUES RELATED TO MIGRATION

"When you are in exile as a migrant worker, your wife is like a widow"

KEMAL TAHIR

"City shock is what I have
I came from another age, that's why
This dizzy spell will go away
I'll get used to your air and water
One evening by the seashore
I'll light my cigarette from yours
We'll sit down to talk about villages and civilizations
Since we live in the same country
This is no way
We must think together
How we are going to close the huge gulf?

M. BAŞARAN
Translation by Talât Sait Halman

All countries subject to large scale external migration are confronted with two major juxtaposed processes; the resulting dichotomy reveals on the economic end extensive foreign currency gains, while the social end indicates a variety of deprivations ranging from insufficient orientation and information to fragmentation of family life and blatant segregation. The major reason for such negative consequences lies in the fact that migrants, like other special classes, are liable to suffer the consequences of inequality of opportunity and discriminatory practices, whether these result from prejudices or from other defects in attitude or simply from their ignorance or feeling of intimidation. Among the difficulties most often mentioned are the following: open or more commonly concealed dislikes that affect their chances of obtaining or keeping a job, gaining access to vocational training or being promoted; systematic practices regarding the type of engagement or contract accorded that deprive them of certain forms of protection and of certain advantages; inequality of pay for identical or similar jobs. Sharp discrepancy between the cultural values of the sending and receiving countries may also aggravate these inequalities.

Other situations of factual discrimination may also exercise an impact on the living conditions of foreign workers in a more

general way. This happens in the field of housing, where apart
from the problems of law or official policy, the practices of
individuals may bring these workers face to face with refusals or
imposition of discriminatory conditions. Similarly, the problem
of uniting families represents also one of the major obstacles towards equality. The situation of large numbers of migrant workers, cut off from social relations and living on the fringe of the
receiving community, creates many well-known social and
psychological problems that largely determine community attitudes towards migrant workers.

The inability of the governments of sending countries to elaborate comprehensive coordinating organizations, especially created
to promote better placement, training and reintegration of the
workers, also affects the migrants. Finally, a shortsighted educational policy in regard to migrant children and an insufficient
mobilization of available national teaching staff leads toward the
emergence of "bilingual, half-educated, uprooted" youngsters, a
prematurely lost generation.

The four papers presented in this section reflect the major
features of the above sketched rather negative social effects of
migration. J. Akre deplores the fact that the Turkish government
has so far adopted a rather narrow view in regard to migration,
which culminates in the view that labour exportation is a welcome complementary element of national development. The author justifiably insists that the Turkish government should focus
its attention on future manpower and development strategy. He
points out that migrant workers are victims of lack of information resulting from inadequate briefing prior to leaving home and
are very often ill-prepared to face the reality of their overseas
experience. This fact deserves even more importance nowadays
when large numbers of Turkish workers are about to leave France
for instance, in order to take up jobs in Lybia, a country with
which so far no manpower exchange agreement has been signed
and which in terms of social security, social assistance, equality
in job opportunities is very far from the European labour employing countries.

Indeed, it is to be regretted that in spite of the accumulated
experiences of the past decade, no effective organizational set-up
for coordination has been created so far. In spite of the officially
declared goals of the three Five Year Plans, no centralised organ

has been capable to put into action the aspiration of Turkish workers abroad, be it in terms of enlarging Turkey's industrialization or grouping them in viable individual enterprises. Akre also insists with good reason that the provision of a fair distribution of available jobs abroad certainly is not sufficient to achieve a harmonious cooperation in the administrative mechanism. Indeed, the policy of fragmented national policy has so far fallen completely short of bringing about any noticeable regional or local development. On the contrary, this immobility has only encouraged the prevailing tendency to invest heavily in real estate—a solution deprived of any imagination and enterprising spirit. Akre argues rightly that comprehensive measures have to be taken in order to enable Turkey to survive the post-migration era. Although restrictive measures adopted in 1973 by the major labour importing countries partly eliminates the necessity to introduce a comprehensive governmental, pre-migration orientation programme, there is no doubt that the Turkish government has to concentrate more than ever on the problems of skill acquisition, unemployment relief, placement of foreign exchange earnings. The asymetric dependency relationship of almost all Mediterranean countries with the Central European centres of heavy industry obliges the governments of all these countries to devise an effective policy of re-integration. As long as new employment opportunities are not created, the experience gained by Turkish migrant workers is wasted in terms of Turkey's development and modernization.

The second paper by M. Kiray, attempts to delineate the most important consequences of migration in terms of family life— both at home and abroad, living styles and the structural changes which accompany fast de-peasantization. Indeed, we are confronted not only with "marginal men" representing second rate citizens in the receiving countries but new family patterns are also developing, which no doubt deserves special attention. The major phenomenon to be studied carefully is the fact that almost all European receiving countries are, rather than assisting the movement of the spouse, more or less encouraging disintegration. Thus, family integration among Turkish workers abroad is the exception while disintegration or fragmentation is the predominant mode. Another noticeable change to be observed among Turkish families abroad is the increasingly temporal character of the household residence pattern. As A. Kudat-Sertel states the high turnover workers of the Turkish migrant population abroad, the presence of large number of illegal workers who must be roomed in private apartments by relatives or acquaintances, the functionality of extended solidarities, all contribute to the particularities and diversity of residential configurations observed among migrant households abroad. Another significant change attributable to massive international labour migration is observed in the division of labour amongst the family. The effects of this drastic new development in the economic bases of sex role differentiation will no doubt diffuse more widely into Turkish society.

However the most accentuated human tragedy in terms of alienation and unsuccessful acculturation doubtlessly touches mostly the children of immigrant workers. The problem represents a two-fold aspect: on the individual level, traumatic experiences caused by repeated trips, life with grandparents, foster-homes, nonadjustement in foreign schools, loneliness leads to serious psychic dysfunctions. These "bilingual illiterates" are candidates to become the loafing, jobless "lost generation" of tomorrow. Together with the growth in the number of these uprooted youngsters, so far unidentified secondary institutions are also emerging. With the increase of immigrants with young children and the discontinuance of the help of extended family kin, new anonymous commercial "houses", "nurseries" to take care of workers children have been established. It is interesting to note, that because of the discriminatory schooling practice in some European countries, such as in the socalled "mother tongue" classes in Bavaria, the only remedy advocated by Turkish educators lies in the direction of establishing special governmental boarding schools.

The paper of S. Bilmen on the subject of educating migrant children may serve as an eloquent case study illustrating how relatively little binding effect supranational organizations may have in translating abstract targets such as equality of opportunity in education into palpable facts. Actually the failure to secure better schooling opportunities for the growing generations stems from two major groups of reasons: The first are related directly to the outlook of migrated parents: permanent uncertainty about employment abroad, hinders planning logically for the kind of education to be given to the children. In addition, ignorance of complicated, sophisticated school systems, lack of command over the dominant language of the country, inability to help the children with their homework, split loyalties, all these factors constitute heavy barriers for intelligent choice in terms of preparing children for a successful integration. However, the most important handicap seems to lie in the clashing interests between sending and receiving countries.

Turkey, similar to all other sending countries, would like to assure its children abroad a free access to all educational institutions. However, the introduction of "special, introductory, transitional, preparatory classes, *de facto* retains Turkish children in much lower classes than their peer groups. These classes serve rather as a kind of caretaker arrangement instead of contributing to the enlargement of the mind and the training for independent thinking. Furthermore, the popularity of the "Bavarian" model—instruction only in the mother tongue without possibilities of transferring to regular classes—provides the discriminated children with an emotional shelter, but reinforces even further the socially existing segregation. It certainly is not exaggerated to predict that especially because of the failure to integrate the great majority of foreign children, an alarming spreading of the xenophobic stereotype will contribute to the widening gap between migrant workers and indigenous population. Actually the insoluble root of the problem lies—as Bilmen points out—in the aspirations of the receiving countries, who want to assimilate certain select groups, while exerting efforts to keep the bulk of foreign workers away.

The fourth paper touches upon the problem of residential segregation in the Netherlands. The authors, Mik and Verkooren-Hemelaar, have successfully developed the major concepts related to the process of segregation, namely the phases of infiltration, invasion and succession, while comparing the same phenomenon in the context of recent American and European experiences. Their excellently illustrated empirical research on segregation in Rotterdam and Utrecht, shows that the major causes for segregation such as preference of low-cost rent houses, chain processes, resulting prejudices are primarily economic.

Looked upon this way, segregation cannot be treated as a unique development which pertains to the immigration of foreign labourers, but also accomodates Dutch people in the same socio-economic classes. What kind of deep-rooted changes will occur within the social stratification pattern of the Europe of tomorrow is at present hard to foresee. But it seems certain that the "tenth" unofficial member of the EEC—the 12 million migrant workers, constituting a kind of nation—will continue to exercise their impact on the receiving countries. This impact, once it is strengthened with political rights, might give way to new forms of co-existence or more probably to new forms of continuing contestations and clashes.

TURKISH ADMINISTRATIVE STRUCTURES
AND THE MIGRANT WORKER

Towards Greater Government Support and Participation

JAMES E. AKRE

Dimensions of the Problem

Large-scale Turkish labour migration is well into its second decade, and, for the present at least, shows no signs of decline either in terms of potential supply or potential demand. Official Turkish government policy in this regard has been an affirmation of the axiom that "more is better", and has correspondingly encouraged a steady increase in the numbers leaving for employment abroad. A glance at the balance of payments figures and their rapid rise from 1963 onwards goes far in explaining Government's preoccupation with labour migration as a central policy issue.

Unfortunately, the Turkish Central Government continues to focus on the relatively narrow economic dimensions of labour migration, while giving little consideration to the social aspects of The Problem. In so far as Turkish labour migration has shown itself a convenient safety valve for drawing off large numbers of unemployed and a steadily increasing source of hard currency in the form of workers' remittances, labour exportation has been officially welcomed as a boon to national development. Of major concern to Turkish authorities, not surprisingly given such a limited economic definition of the implications of this migration, has been an increase in both the number of workers going abroad and the amount of foreign exchange they remit.

Such a singular emphasis on unemployment rates and foreign exchange balances, however, is not a sufficiently broad view for so complex a problem. Although these are factors of understandable importance, they are not the only issues which deserve the attention of policy makers. They comprise, by themselves, an incomplete definition, more the result, albeit superficially positive, of a peculiar combination of circumstances in which Turkey's underdevelopment is engaged in yet another symbiotic relationship with the western European industrial bloc. The Problem, if it is to be fully defined in terms relevant to Turkish labour resources and Turkish development needs (and not Western manpower requirements or capitalist-expansionist values) requires that attention also be given to the all-important social dimension. The traditional sole emphasis on the economics of migration is inadequate to deal with the Problem.

The purpose of this chapter, then, is to argue the case for a re-orientation of Turkish labour emigration policy in a manner consistent with a broader set of national priorities and a unified approach to the exportation of labour to western Europe. Based on a re-definition and re-orientation of policy, a number of specific proposals are made for government action on behalf of migrant workers.

Any statement of priorities must contain provisions both for dealing with present realities (the short-term), and a potential for adapting to future exigencies (the long-term). The Problem, as defined here, is two-fold:

— It is at once necessary to maximise the short-term gain potentially accruing to the individual migrant worker and the country as a whole while minimising the short-term costs incurred. This is a matter of increasing the number of migrants, in labour surplus categories, going abroad; increasing social assistance, before, during and after migration, to facilitate individual adjustment; increasing foreign exchange remittances while encouraging investment in capital-formation and job-creating ventures; increasing benefits for the individual worker through skill acquisition; and increasing national developmental capacities through broader manpower-skill availability.

— It is necessary that, even as it attempts to fully exploit contemporary circumstances, the Central Government seek to identify the underlying structural imbalances in the Turkish economy and society—the origins of this migration—and set about to gradually reverse their influence on future manpower and developmental strategy. The long-term goal must be to put an end to economically forced manpower movement.

Turkish Labour Migration: Recognising the Negative Implications

Turkey has been formally participating in the exportation of labour to the manpower-short, capital-rich economies of western

Europe since 1961 when it signed its first bilateral agreement with the Federal Republic of Germany. The most visible result of this international movement of workers has been the startling effect on the country's balance of payments. Yet while workers' remittances are a highly positive contribution to the general health of the economy, they are by no means the only consequence, positive or negative, affecting the Turkish economy and society more than a decade after the inception of official migration policy.

The temporary expatriation of Turkish workers to western Europe appears to be highly beneficial. For example, it provides a degree of relief from high unemployment and underemployment, adds significantly to foreign exchange reserves, and permits a higher rate of capital investment and more favourable balance of payments than would otherwise be possible.

Beyond these obvious positive elements, however, lie the potential short- and long-term negative socio-economic effects of this policy, for the individual migrant and the nation as a whole, which have not been receiving sufficient consideration. The benefits of this migration, in their turn, have been accepted passively, as though they might be expected to continue unabated under their own momentum, rather than enhanced through positive exploitation so as to maximise their effectiveness within the framework, and in the best interests, of Turkey's economic and social development.

Migrating workers, victims of misinformation and simple ignorance resulting from inadequate briefing prior to leaving home, are very often ill-prepared to face the reality of their overseas experience. As individuals, they can be adversely affected by social isolation, personal adjustment and adaptational problems, substandard and often overcrowded housing conditions, educational difficulties for their children, etc.

As for effects on the larger economy and society, in a very real sense the migration of labour from Turkey has acted as a drain on valuable, scarce manpower resources. This is evidenced in the number of skilled artisans, trained professionals, and the overwhelmingly youthful make-up of the exiting work force. Since there is little qualitative control of departures, it is almost certainly the most enterprising who are the first to leave low paying jobs or unemployment, and low levels of production and consumption behind them. Further, the continued emphasis on migration over internal adjustment has activated a "temporary relief mechanism" which momentarily frees Turkey from coming to grips with the structural difficulties of an economy persistently incapable of dealing with a large proportion of its active population idle or unemployed. Continued reliance on such means and emphasis on migration in place of structural reform and re-organisation runs the risk of Turkey accepting migration as *the* solution to its economic development problems, and diverts the energies of politicians and planners from vital commitments in other, quite different directions.

In post-migration terms, instead of forming cadres and carefully integrating any skills acquired abroad with the economic and social patterns peculiar to Turkey, many former migrants prefer the less productive path of self-employment. Rather than utilising these workers as a partial base for creating and leading the conditions most favourable to development, the Government unfortunately fails to maintain contact with the majority of those who have returned.[1] It consequently has no way of assuring that the overseas experience and specialised training that they may have had are being put to optimal use in strengthening the Turkish economy and society.

A Need for Policy Co-Ordination

A major problem facing the Turkish government, as the only single authority capable of successfully dealing with the problems raised by this large-scale out-migration, is essentially administrative in nature. And while formulating a policy designed to maximise the benefits and minimise the costs of labour migration is a necessary first step, creating the effective machinery to carry out the proposed policy in a co-ordinated approach is far more complicated in that it requires the interest and simultaneous efforts of many government agencies over several time frames.

---

[1] In December, 1972, The Federal Republic of Germany and the Government of Turkey concluded an agreement on the "Promotion of Re-Integration of Migrant Workers in the Turkish Economy" whereby a restricted number of Turkish workers would receive practical middle-level management training in Germany and a theoretical course upon their return to Turkey. This is one very limited example of Government assistance to the re-integration of returning migrants and one means of keeping in contact.

Thus, the Ministries of Labour, Finance, Social Welfare, Information, Education, Planning, etc., each within its own sphere of activity but acting in concert with the others, must strive to make a significant contribution to a set of unified policy objectives of the Turkish State towards Turkish workers, before they go abroad, while they are at work abroad and after they have returned home. Here then lies a major difficulty: how to forge a unified national approach to labour migration that is adequate to both present and future needs, and that effectively co-ordinates the activities of the many different agencies which at present treat the myriad aspects of the problem from their own individual perspectives.

The Managing Board of the Turkish Central Government Organisation Research Project clearly recognised the difficulties inherent in any such efforts to secure co-ordination among different agencies when it stated in its 1965 report that

> it would be wrong to assume that the aim of harmonious co-operation in the administrative mechanism will be automatically realised by merely distributing functions ... A rational distribution ... would only achieve one of the basic conditions for harmonious operations. After that, the problem of taking the units which have been given definite functions in certain fields and leading them towards the desired objectives is still one of the most important administrative tasks to be confronted. After securing a rational distribution of functions among the agencies, it will be necessary to devise solutions which will enable them to operate in harmony and to perform functions with due considerations for the objectives.[2]

In matters of migration, the Ministry of Foreign Affairs negotiates the treaties and finalises arrangements with foreign governments for worker flows between Turkey and western Europe. The Ministry of Labour, through its Employment Agency (İş ve İşçi Bulma Kurumu), is the chief recruiter and generally determines who eventually leaves to work abroad. The Ministry of Finance collects taxes from the migrants, determines duty on foreign goods they bring back into Turkey, and exchanges their hard currency for Turkish lira. The children of workers are the interest of the Ministry of Education if they are with their parents in western Europe, or of the Ministry of Social Welfare for

---

[2] *Organisation and Functions of the Central Government of Turkey*, Report of the Managing Board of the Central Government Organisation Research Project (Ankara: 1965), p. 56.

the remittances due then for support if they remain in Turkey. Workers depend on the services of the Ministry of Communications, whose special short-wave broadcasts keep them in touch with what is happening in Turkey while they are abroad. The State Planning Organisation is directly concerned with migrant worker policy in its position as the body whose chief functions are "to assess the economic and social situation in detail ... ascertain the trends (and) ... assist the government in deciding ... policy to be pursued ..."[3]

The question remains of how all of these individual ministries, each responsible for only a small portion of the migration question, should be organised to provide maximum service and benefit to the individual worker and the country. Even more important is the question of which office will have the overall administrative authority and budgetary support, and how it will use these tools to co-ordinate the many different activities.

A Non-Policy through Fragmentation

Although bits and pieces of a national migration policy exist, for example, in general statements of intent in successive Five-Year Plans or the pronouncements of individual ministries as they deal with their particular concerns vis-a-vis migrant workers, this has clearly not been a sufficient response to so large a problem. The single greatest obstacle preventing any straightforward analysis and treatment of the problem of Turkish labour migration is the lack of a comprehensive, co-ordinated Central Government policy to deal with migration as a whole by providing a framework for inter-sectoral co-operation.

Yaşar Yaşer, as President of the Ministry of Labour's Research Board, underscored this situation at the CENTO Conference in Tehran, Iran, in February 1972 when he declared that

> ... no government policy has been determined to investigate the labour market in foreign countries, to send workers abroad, to find solutions to the problems they face there, to guarantee their future on their final return, to re-integrate them with the economic and social conditions of our country, and to enable them to lead the development of these conditions. On the other hand, within the Ministry of Labour, there is no section or department that plans, co-ordinates, controls

---

[3] *Ibid.*, p. 62.

and evaluates the work of the representative units in the foreign countries, and that also has the responsibility of reaching certain goals.[4]

Although a "co-ordination committee" was established and eighteen labour attaches were reported by State Planning Organisation sources as being assigned abroad to "deal with the Workers' problems", the results have not been encouraging.[5] For example, there were 110 personnel in 1968 whose job it was to assist migrant workers. By late 1971, with the number of workers exceeding 600,000 (more than twice that of 1968) the number of personnel had dropped to 66.[6]

In spite of the stated government policy to limit labour exportation to non-skilled categories and to emphasise areas of underemployment, especially agriculture, for migration purposes,[7] 46.3% of Turkish workers entering the Federal Republic of Germany in 1971 were classified by authorities there as "skilled".[8] Given the fragmentary nature of present policy and the corresponding implementation difficulties, it is quite likely that Turkey will continue to export a relatively large number of skilled workers in spite of occasional official statements to the contrary.

The Need for Further Government Involvement

The Turkish Central Government has begun to pursue a policy of supervision and control of migration activities through a central co-ordinating agency with the establishment, in April 1972, of a General Directorate for Workers Abroad. Attached to the Ministry of Labour, the new Directorate, according to Yaşer, is expected to follow closely the employment policies of the receiving countries for the purpose of strengthening Turkish participation; aid the Ministry of Labour in formulating strategy to deal with foreign employment problems; assist in determining and solving the social, cultural and economic problems of Turkish Workers; and support financial organisations and legal establish-

---

[4] Yaşar Yaşer, "The Turkish Workers Abroad and their Problems", Paper presented at the CENTO Conference, Tehran, Iran, February 1972.

[5] State Planning Organisation, *Second Five-Year Plan* (Ankara: State Planning Organisation), p. 157.

[6] Yaşer, *op. cit.*, p. 5.

[7] State Planning Organisation, *op. cit.*, p. 157.

[8] Bundesanstalt für Arbeit, *Ausländische Arbeitnehmer*, (Nürnberg, 1971), p. 40.

ments that will create investment opportunities in Turkey which gain the confidence of workers, as well as direct and inform workers of their availability.[9]

The announcement of the formation of this General Directorate is an encouraging development and a hopeful indication that Government is finally reacting and moving responsibly to deal with migrant problems and the enormous present and future economic and social implications they present for Turkish society. Yet such an organisation is unlikely to cause much change in what has been traditionally an essentially haphasard approach to the movement of workers abroad unless that organisation receives the full support of the highest national authority and the co-operation of its constituent parts in the formulation and implementation of a policy based on *both* economic and social development considerations.

Mr. Yaşer desires that this Directorate adopt the flexibility required to deal with a quickly changing labour picture and achieve a mobility necessary to find adequate, on-the-spot solutions to problems as they arise.[10] But such expectations are in vain in the absence of firm inter-sectoral co-operation from all relevant domestic institutions at every level of government activity. For although Directorate activities, on the surface, appear adequate to deal with the situation, it remains that

> a comprehensive emigrant worker policy has yet to be articulated. Unfortunately, even though Turkish emigrant workers have been the subject of numerous scholarly investigations, a paucity of adequate data on all stages of this labour force transfer (before, during and after emigration) persists. A few surveys have been conducted to assess certain key socio-economic factors of workers either before or after emigration, but *no comprehensive investigation has been undertaken throughout the whole time stream of the migration process* ...[11]

Taken at face value, the flow of workers to western Europe is an economic boon to Turkey. Remittances have grown steadily since migration began seriously a decade ago, and the number of persons unemployed is certainly less than without migration. Yet

---

[9] Yaşer, *op. cit.*, pp. 8-9.

[10] *Ibid.*, p. 8.

[11] Duncan Miller and Ihsan Çetin, "The International Demand for Brawn Power and Wealth Effect of Migration: A Turkish Case Study", Paper presented at Middle East Studies Association (MESA) Annual Conference, Binghamton, N.Y., November 2, 1972, p. 4 (emphasis added).

from the standpoint of public policy, given the lack of relevant data, it is not possible to fully assess these benefits vis-a-vis the costs incurred: in domestic productivity losses during the workers' absence; educational and skill drain; the inflationary impact on the domestic economy, the growing dependence on a relatively unstable and insecure means, in the long-term, of alleviating employment and foreign exchange difficulties; and the personal costs borne by the workers themselves. It is essential that much more thorough study and analysis be undertaken to determine what price Turkey must really pay for the out-migration of its workers.

An Active Migration Policy based on Socio-Economic Realism

What the Turkish Central Government has still failed to do by 1973 is formulate and implement a co-ordinated inter-sectoral migration policy. The Third Five-Year Plan (1973-1977) is perhaps most notable in this disappointing respect in its all but total failure to make any but decidedly oblique references to the serious present and near-future manpower problems facing the Turkish economy. It is all but a useless document when it comes to facing squarely The Problem of labour migration.

West European migration policies—and for Turkey this means essentially those of the Federal Republic of Germany—continue to evolve in the midst of heated debate in worker, employer and government circles. The extremes of proposed policy call for forced rotation on the one hand and full assimilation on the other. A sort of middle ground suggests that the number of foreign workers permitted in the country conform rigidly to the availability of social infra-structure, leaving the question of eventual settlement or return to the individual workers.

West Germany's policy continues to evolve while Turkey's appears to remain static. What is required in response is for the Central Government to begin actively asserting itself. This implies an added dimension to the traditional "action-reaction" formula with Turkey remaining the passive partner. Turkey must go on the offensive and begin to pursue a positive policy of *pro-action* whereby it looks ahead to determine the existence of problems *before* they attain crisis proportions and demand hasty solutions. Acting in advance of the need for crisis management demands a hard look at government priorities for labour migration, and a reversal of the traditional singular emphasis on increasing both the numbers of workers abroad and the amount of foreign exchange they remit.

Turkey, as one of the leading supplier countries to western Europe both quantitatively and qualitatively, has the labour receiving countries, in some respects, over an "economic barrel". While not negotiating from an overly impressive position of economic strength, it is still possible, given the potential future availability of Turkish manpower, for the Government to adopt a legitimate posture of firm advocacy on behalf of workers without damaging its bargaining position. Provisions which truly reflect Turkey's needs in both the short- and long-term and benefit Turkey both economically and socially should form the basis of any accords on the out-migration of labour.

Facing an Uncertain Future

There is still the question of how long the present situation will persist; the inter-related variables are too numerous and complex for any definitive answer to future Turkish migration trends. It appears that the manpower, in raw numbers, will be available in Turkey, but there can be no absolute certainty as to its continued exportability. Given the vagaries of European economic policies, the possibility of economic slow-downs, increased rationalisation of industrial plant, extremes of public opinion and prejudice and ensuing political pressure to limit further influx, etc., the Turkish government must look to the future when the migration safety valve may no longer be open to realistic exploitation. Policy formulators should begin *now* to consider what steps must be taken to ease withdrawal from a device that has become such an important component of Turkish growth and development strategy. There must be persistent efforts to strike at the root causes within the domestic economic and social order which continue to permit, even demand, this flow of emigrating manpower. And finally, Government must be prepared for, and actively seek, by degrees, the end of such massive manpower movement *even as it strives to take advantage of contemporary short-term circumstances* to assist in fabricating an enduring framework which will serve the Turkish economy and society well in a post-migration era.

Although official policy in the Federal Republic of Germany still clings to the notion that foreign workers are present in the economy on a "temporary" basis, it has become increasingly clear in recent years that many of these workers have adopted quite different intentions. The inclination to remain for longer periods and eventually settle abroad, not surprisingly, has replaced the intentions of many workers who had initially anticipated staying only a few years. The implications of this phenomenon for a continued Turkish policy based on the narrow considerations of increasing the number of migrating workers on the one hand and the amount of money they remit on the other are obvious: workers tend to remit the highest proportion of their salaries in their first years abroad, less in the later years, and presumably little or nothing at all if they have become established, together with their families, in the receiving country.

Repressive policy measures designed to restrict worker movement and length of sojurn abroad may appear to some as necessary and appropriate in the face of this tendency, but such a negative approach is likely to be met with strong and not altogether unsuccessful opposition from those already at work. A far more reasonable, positive course lies in making eventual return and re-integration into Turkish society the more attractive alternative by creating those conditions, throughout the migration experience, most favourable and most likely to foster this return.

If the Turkish Government hopes to insure the eventual return of the majority of its citizens at work overseas, and as well take full advantage of the short-term benefits to be derived from their temporary expatriation, it must take positive steps towards a reformulation of its traditional policies with respect to this special group. At the same time in order to avoid, as far as possible, any negative economic and social impact on domestic society calls for a careful re-examining and re-structuring of the government role as it pertains to labour migration. Government has begun to act positively with the formation of the General Directorate. While it is not the intention to presently attempt a critique of this agency, specific recommendations for further government action on behalf of migrant workers, based on a human resources development approach, remain in order.

Maximisation of Short-Term Benefits: Deepening Government's Commitment

Any suggestions made for a modification of existing arrangements or the addition of new activities in government supportive efforts to aid migrant workers concern the approximation of two primary objectives: the *maximisation* of the overall economic and social cost-effectiveness of Turkish labour migration, and the *minimisation* of the potentially negative economic and social aspects for Turkey and the migrants themselves. For purposes of discussion, the migration experience is divided under four headings : (1) recruitment, (2) the briefing period just prior to emigration, (3) the term of residence abroad, and (4) the point of final return, including a "follow-up" period of one or more years.

1. *Recruitment*

Currently in Turkey there are two principal agencies, one foreign, the other domestic, which channel workers into jobs abroad. These are the Bureau for Employment Insurance of the West German government (with its main office in Istanbul), and, of more immediate interest, the Employment Bureau of the Turkish Ministry of Labour. In general, the Employment Bureau serves to establish and carry our public employment services, gather information about jobs, correlate the supply and demand for labour, and prepare and publish lists of employers and employees in various categories of trades and crafts. It is the Placement Directorate within the Bureau which organises the sending of workers to foreign countries. [12]

The Federal Republic of Germany favours the continued importation of Turkish workers over other nationalities given Turkey's willingness to send relatively greater numbers of skilled workers than other supplier countries. [13] There is frequently a wide discrepancy between data on migrant flows as supplied by Turkish and West German authorities; but this is not the case with regard to statistics on skill categorisation. West German sources report that for 1970 the number of Turkish workers

---

[12]   Turkish Government Organisation Manual (Ankara: The Institute of Public Administration for Turkey and the Middle East Publishers, 1969), pp. 303-4.

[13]   This skill drain is in fact less the result of an active complicity with German labour demand and more the absence of a concerted Turkish Government effort to carefully screen and control the flow of exiting skilled workers.

entering the country who were classified "skilled" reached 34% of the total for that year. This compares closely with the Turkish Government's claim (in the second Five-Year-Plan) that 38% of the total workers abroad are skilled. Most startling is the information, already reported above, that in 1971 the proportion of skilled workers had attained an unprecedented 46.3% of the total admitted for the year.

However one reads the statistics, the situation is alarming in its potential negative impact on Turkey and Government plans to realise its long-term economic and social objectives. Turkey's efforts both at controlling the skill-mix of migrants and encouraging migration of the unemployed, by its own admission, have been notably unsuccessful. [14] The impression is that, given the educational and skill attainment of workers going abroad under present circumstances, labour migration from Turkey is in many respect a clear example of brain drain. [15]

This situation accurately reflects the general inadequacies of Government efforts to date to stem the outward flow of trained manpower. Specific steps must be taken to check this drain and the following is a partial list of potential means:

— institution of tighter controls in recruitment according to age and skill qualifications;

— co-operation with foreign governments and employers in order to encourage the hiring of Turkish nationals in job categories most useful to Turkey on the migrants' return;

— tabulation of skill category data which accurately reflects job availability, useable manpower resources, and future market elasticity both in Turkey and the European receiving countries;

— co-operation with receiving countries in the formulation of complementary manpower policies based on this information;

— institution of a precise system of job categorisation and skill classification comparable with, or easily translated into, the standards of the receiving countries;

— introduction of a positive quota system, based on the needs of domestic labour categories, which safeguards against overdrawing the available resources in any one category, while at the

---

[14] State Planning Organisation, *op. cit.*, p. 157.
[15] Duncan R. Miller, "Emigrant Turkish Workers: A Socio-Economic Analysis" in *Essays on Labour Force and Employment in Turkey*, Duncan R. Miller (ed.), (Ankara: USAID, 1971), p. 203.

same time attempting to assure adequate levels in all categories;

— maintenance of a system of "alternative means" for workers to upgrade personal skills and/or increase individual earning capacity within skilled, semi-skilled or unskilled categories, e.g., changing from a relatively common to a relatively scarce skill category domestically without necessarily having to consider migration in order to achieve this end;

— provision of a system of on-the-job training for unemployed, unskilled workers (possibly foreign government subsidised as a form of development aid) to learn the skills necessary both for work abroad as well as on their return;

— continuation of an active effort on the part of both the domestic and foreign employment agencies to promote the recruitment and training of predominantly unskilled and semi-skilled surplus agricultural workers;

— continuation of an effort at the highest government level to properly utilise foreign investment capital generated by workers abroad towards the creation of a greater number and variety of jobs in the domestic labour market.

2. *Pre-Migration Preparation*

At present, workers generally stand passive in the face of all that is happening about them as they prepare to travel abroad for the first time. They are more concerned with the imposing logistical implications of transporting themselves, their belongings and, possibly, their families for an uncertain period of residence abroad than with thoughts of what lies directly ahead. In most cases, the migrant has never before been outside of Turkey, or had to face an unfamiliar language, a distinctly different (i.e., Christian, western) cultural and value system, and an often inhospitably cold receiving-country public. For the first time in his life the migrant worker is physically and emotionally removed from the social and cultural supportive milieu of the familiar society he always took for granted.

It is the exceptional foreign worker who has had any realistic briefing prior to his departure from home or preparation as to what he might expect in the country of immigration. While abroad, he tends to seek out and remain with his own, thus reinforcing his "foreignness". There is minimal mixing with receiving-country nationals or, for that matter, with other migrant groups. Communication is hampered due to absence of formal language training and, in some cases, even the opportunity to learn.

The resultant pattern is growing increasingly familiar: worker segregation, if not outright ghetto formation, in the receiving countries; little direct contact with nationals of the countries in which they are working due to a cultural distance which is further re-inforced by lack of language proficiency; a rise of negative feelings on the part of Turks which directly affects their perceptions of personal gain while abroad; and occasional open conflict with European nationals based on mutual mistrust and misunderstanding.

As Clark has noted in his study of spatial relationships and settlement patterns among Turkish workers in Cologne,

> Turks in more segregated and substandard housing feel that they have learned fewer skills in Germany and hold a less positive view of Germans than those who are spatially integrated ... the segregation in housing is coupled with lack of social contact between Turks and Germans. The Turks come expecting Germans to be open and welcoming to strangers as they see themselves to be. Usually they are disappointed ... Turks come to Germany with the highest expectations of any group of workers of establishing friendly relations with the host country population but are the most unhappy about what they actually experience ...

> The effect of social isolation on the development dividends hoped for by Turkey from the creation of a European labour force cannot be good. Much of the learning that could take place through exposure of Turks to European industrial and social life does not appear to take place. Of the interview group, 52.9 per cent said that they had learned no new skills or had lost some since coming to Germany. Only 16.4 per cent had taken or planned to take vocational training courses. [16]

Turkish workers who are about to go abroad, as with any group soon to encounter sharp variations in "normally" expected behaviour patterns, must be duly prepared *in advance* for what they are likely to experience. They must be carefully briefed on the cultural orientation of West Europeans; their attitudes towards foreigners and especially foreign workers; religious beliefs;

---

[16] John R. Clark, "Residential Patterns and Social Integration of Turks in Cologne, West Germany", Paper delivered at MESA Conference, Binghamton, N.Y., November 2, 1972, p. 18 and Introduction.

interpersonal behavioural expectations (that it is "impolite" to stare, for instance, a favourite Turkish pastime, as it strongly violates the Western sense of propriety and individual spatial soverignty); sexual mores (that the Western penchant for "sex shops", a pre-occupation with sex in cinema, and certain female dress and behavioural patterns are not to be confused or equated with individual permissiveness).

Government organised briefings, if possible, in collaboration with the foreign employer, should include, *inter alia*:

— specific information on the rights and duties of migrant workers abroad;

— a realistic orientation effort designed to "walk" the migrant through his future experience, from the insular safety of Turkey, so that he may begin to adjust mentally to his new status prior to departure;

— some sort of psychological screening process;

— information on the availability of economic and social services for the migrant worker and his family while they are in western Europe;

— instructions on where the migrant may turn to air grievances and seek the resolution of personal and work-related problems;

— formal exposure and briefings conducted by knowledgeable returned workers;

— provision of some preparation and initiation into the language of the receiving country, with opportunity for continued study while abroad;

— an idea of western reactions and expectations vis-a-vis the migrant's specific cultural values;

— provision of a simplified "area handbook" and other educative materials which have been prepared by Turkish consular staff in co-operation with foreign governments and commercial firms which employ significant numbers of Turks, as one means of aiding and simplifying the physical and emotional transitional adjustment of new migrants;

— consciousness-raising techniques designed to instill a sense of national solidarity among the soon-to-depart workers, create and maintain an awareness among migrants of their country's concern for their welfare and the important role they play in national development, and increase devotion to the goal of strengthening Turkey's overall economic and social prosperity.

3. *Residence Overseas: Continuity of Government Interest*

Turkish government responsibility must not cease while its workers are abroad. Government concern should rather heighten given the potential substantial gain which may accrue to Turkey in terms of skill acquisition, unemployment relief, foreign exchange earnings, etc. *These benefits cannot be left to chance.*

Individual workers are not capable of meeting all of their personal and family needs, and it cannot be assumed to be in the direct interest of foreign governments or employers to minister to the larger economic and social needs of Turkey as a nation. It is only through the precise, calculated efforts of the Turkish Central Government that these benefits, both for the country and the individual worker-citizen, can be potentially realised in the short- and long-term.

It has been suggested that the major short-term and immediate function of the General Directorate for Workers Abroad should be a sort of "Problem Solvers, Inc.". This would be a practical orientation given the formidable obstacles which the migrant faces in his attempt to function successfully within the West European socio-cultural context.

Directorate responsibility for migrant workers involves both the economic and social aspects of living abroad and should include, *inter alia*:

— requiring the worker, as a necessary function of obtaining his work permit, to register with the area overseas Turkish Labour Office;

— welcoming workers in groups and, where possible, individually with a personal visit from a Directorate representative who informs workers of available services and assures them of the continuity of Government interest while they are abroad;

— maintaining regular contact with workers through a type of newsletter which would highlight news from home, provide hints on dealing with common problems experienced abroad, advise workers on their rights and obligations, and allow for a free transfer of information concerning specific employment opportunities in Turkey in an attempt to match the skills of those returning with available jobs at home;

— providing trained social workers who, in conjunction with Directorate representatives, can assist migrants with their special problems, e.g., providing for dependents remaining in Turkey, the status of women in a western cultural context, married workers abroad without their families, etc.;

— seeing to the educational needs of children;

— assisting occupational mobility by arranging training activities, acting as agent for foreign firms seeking particular types of skills, advertising openings in other fields and enterprises, etc.;

— continuing language training;

— providing financial advice with regard to tax refunds and tax returns made to foreign governments, remittances made to relations in Turkey, and the possibility of capital investment and equipment transfers back to Turkey;

— providing legal advice and assistance;

— continuing availability of representatives to assist migrant workers in handling their personal and job-related problems of whatever sort.

4. *The Returning Worker*

Constructing an adequate statistical framework—There are virtually no reliable data on the number of migrants who have returned permanently to Turkey. Statistics which would accurately reflect this return migration are lost in that, while Turkey does record citizens entering the country, there is no way at present of distinguishing between those who remain permanently and those who remain temporarily (e.g., on holiday) and soon exit the country again.

There is an obvious need for a more reliable system of counting. An essential basis of sound policy formulation and manpower planning is the availability of reasonably sound statistical data for use in projecting a society's future economic and social needs and growth potential. In the absence of such data, *meaningful planning is all but impossible*.

Government might consider the use of a system of positive incentives to spur returning migrants to register their final return with local authorities in Turkey. This might take place in the province where the migrant is to settle, or more likely, at the point of entry back into the country. The incentive could be financial, e.g., a percentage reduction in tax on in-coming goods, assistance offered in resettlement and job location, low interest loan availability, etc.

A new, streamlined approach to more effective data collection is necessary and a less rather than more complicated formula is needed to facilitate the administrative formalities within the Institute of Employment in order to better answer informational needs.[17] Yaşer suggests that "punch card methods" be introduced for *all* migrant workers to determine and keep track of the skill categories they represent. Such a system could be something as simple as an anonymous card, bearing relevant, up-to-date skill data, which each worker automatically carries in his passport. This information would enable government planning authorities to maintain contact with worker flows and skill availability as well as aid in projecting present and near-future domestic manpower supply.

Whatever the method, or, more likely, combination of methods employed for this purpose, it is certain that no accurate planning or projections can be carried out, nor eventual valid observations made on the short- and long-term effects of labour migration on the economic and social life of the country, until a systematic effort is underway.

Re-Integrating the Migrant Worker—For the worker who returns after four to six years of living and working abroad, the re-entry experience can be as traumatic in some respects and as difficult in terms of adjustment as when he first went abroad. The condition may be described in its social and economic manifestations. Although the migrant worker may have actually enjoyed a lesser standard of living (sometimes at near subsistence levels) *while* in western Europe than that experience prior to migration, or "lived on the margin of the host society and ended up forming a decidedly proletarian group,"[18] his re-entry into Turkish society is characterised by the decidedly strong influence of steadily rising expectations. Government efforts, through Employment Office activity, on behalf of migrant workers *before* they leave the country are relatively substantial when compared to the nearly complete absence of attention paid to the needs of returning workers. Jobs, especially those which would utilise, even mar-

---

[17] See the Council of Europe's Resolution (72) 18 on "Methods of Compiling Statistics on the International Migration of Workers" adopted by the Committee of Ministers on 30 May 1972.

[18] Organisation for Economic Cooperation and Development, *Report on the Progress of Research by the Working Party on Migration*, (Paris: OECD, 7 February 1972) p. 5.

ginally, the skills a worker may have acquired abroad, are still very scarce. Consequently many attempt to re-emigrate. According to a study conducted by Dr. Orhan Tuna (Istanbul University), even at the height of the West German economic downturn when 20,417 workers returned to Turkey, only 78 applied for a job through the official services. By the end of 1967, out of 23,192 more who had gone home, only 455 had applied. The very great majority regarded their return as temporary and did their best to find another job abroad. [19]

A major consideration of migration apologists who favour the maintenance of the status quo has been that work abroad helps to equip the Turkish labour force with useful skills against the day when migrant workers will have permanently resettled at home. The available evidence, however, does not support this claim; the numbers finding employment on their final return in the same category as that in which they worked abroad are very few. In many cases, migrants set up their own sole proprietorships, which, while providing some rewards in terms of personal satisfaction, often are inefficient from the standpoint of economies of scale. Many lose money and close after the first year, or continue to operate marginally until investment capital (i.e., the worker's savings) run out.

OECD specialists engaged in assessing the impact of returning migrants on certain areas of Spain, Greece, Italy, Portugal and Turkey found that

> returning emigrants tend not to go into jobs which are appropriate to the skills, or at least the specialised training or work-discipline, they have acquired abroad. Instead, they find themselves places in the traditional economy, in the craft trades or services, *and in any case prefer to set up for themselves*. [20]

Tuna's findings confirm this situation. He has determined that the occupations of returned migrants are usually different from those they had before departure and even more different from those they had abroad.

Further in the OECD study,

---

[19] Organisation for Economic Cooperation and Development, Manpower and Social Affairs Committee, *Cyclically-Determined Homeward Flows of Migrant Workers and the Effects of Emigration*, Paris: OECD, 21 February 1972), p. 20.

[20] "International Migration of Labour and Its Repercussions", *OECD Observer*, August 1970, p. 11 (emphasis added).

the rapporteurs had difficulty in finding any favourable factors in the process of re-integrating emigrants. None was able to quote any really conducive instance in which the returning labour was used in a manner at all conducive to development. In no way do the returning enigrants help to further their country's economic growth, whether by use of savings they have accumulated abroad or the experience they have acquired. [21]

In short, although exportation of manpower theoretically exposes unskilled workers to some on-the-job training and skilled workers to advancement potential in their particular fields, when considering that new employment opportunities are *not* being created for them in existing domestic industries, it may be concluded that experience gained abroad is not being fully utilised for the development and modernisation of Turkey.

The Turkish government would find itself ill-prepared to reaccept and provide meaningful employment for its migrant nationals were they soon to begin repatriation in large numbers. Such a possibility, though perhaps remote at present, is certainly not altogether unrealistic in the medium- and long-term given the potential uncertainty of future migration needs.

The results of the OECD study cited above are a serious indictment of Government in the face of what is perhaps the gravest of all the many problems facing a less developed country: the failure to create meaningful employment opportunities for so many of its citizens. Even more serious for Turkey is its failure to utilise those skills acquired by agricultural workers while they were working in manufacturing industries in western Europe. These returnees are a capital gain since Turkey did not make any investment to train them in industrial jobs. Although placing all of these workers would be impossible given the relatively narrow industrial base, the failure to use a significant number is especially disappointing.

Besides the attempt to increase absolute numbers of workers (in labour-surplus categories) going abroad, better prepare migrants prior to their departure, and assist them with their problems while they are abroad, Government must give top priority to efforts designed to re-integrate these workers successfully into what is for them a post-migration society. This would represent an important step for Turkey towards coming to grips with the

---

[21] *Ibid.*

structural weakness of its economy. The country's ability to adjust itself, in the short-term, to these returning workers is, in
large measure, indicative of its capacity to correct more fundamental imbalances in the medium- and long-term. The time to
begin working towards this end is now—while the number of
returning workers is still relatively small.

The Follow-up period—The capstone of any effect to discern
the cost-benefit balance to Turkey in the long-term will depend,
ultimately, on Government's continuing interest in, and contact
with, its returned workers. Migrants who return to their society
after having acquired new skills in the process of adapting to a
different standard of living and way of life must be actively
courted by Government so as to secure their effective participation in Turkey's development. These returnees, in fact, should
become the leaders of this process, examples for others to follow.

The present situation is, of course, quite different. It is almost
as though the experience had no meaning except to the individual and his family. Workers arrive back in the country quite
unnoticed. Returnees "disappear" and no government effort has
been successful in giving any indication of the location of more
than a handful within the country. For example, based on a 1968
OECD estimate that "in all probability" at least 70,000 of those
who had migrated had returned permanently to Turkey, the Turkish Employment Service conducted a nation-wide survey. In the
end, it was able to locate only 1,300 returned workers. [22]

While Directorate Representatives are responsible for workers'
needs in an overseas context, there are no specific agents to assist
migrants when they have returned to Turkish society. The need
for assistance in re-adjusting may extend beyond the first weeks
and months after return even into the first year. Has the returnee
been successful in locating a job commensurate with his aspirations and abilities? Is effective use being made of workers' savings? Are workers aware of Government's interest and concern
for their welfare? Does Government have a sound basis, for planning structural modifications and creating more jobs within the
economy, through a sure knowledge of what skills migrants bring
back with them? These are but a few of the hard questions de-

---

[22] *Migration Facts and Figures*, Statistical Supplement to the International Catholic Migration Commission's Magazine (Geneva: International Catholic Migration Commission, July-August, 1971), p. 3.

manding attention. Their answers remain clearly out of reach, however, as aids to national development as long as Government eschews interest in its returning manpower resources.

Understanding migration's contribution to the upgrading of labour force skills and assuring rational use of new and improved talents within the domestic economy can only be accomplished if contact is maintained [23] with workers who have returned permanently. Certainty will never replace conjecture until this goal is finally realised.

---

[23] It is not being suggested that *personal* contact be attempted with each returning worker. The task would be rather to provide service representatives to aid migrant workers who have returned if assistance were required. The real burden of contact lies in maintaining an accurate statistical framework.

THE FAMILY OF THE IMMIGRANT WORKER

MÜBECCEL B. KIRAY

Introduction

Throughout history people from rural areas have migrated to the cities where non-agricultural jobs were available. However, that has been taking place since the early 1960's in the Mediterranean Basin in general and in Turkey in particular is rather different in its volume, its form and in what happens to the immigrant and to his family in this movement.

Migration from Turkey to Western European countries started in 1960 with demand for labour from German industries.[1] At the time in Turkey an exodus from rural areas into the cities of the country was already in process. By the 1960's some of this flow had turned towards foreign countries where there were jobs for these immigrants. In this paper I shall try to discuss and analyse shortly who these immigrants were and what happens to their families in the type of migration that seems to perpetuate itself indefinitely. The family of the immigrant worker, its composition, the patterns of interaction among its various members, the way new cash income is used, the new values emerging about family, all seem to be rather different not only from the extended family from which the basic model from which it is assumed to stem, but also from the type that emerged in rural areas and among the urban immigrant families in Turkey after cash cropping.

To be able to understand where the immigrant and his family stands, it is essential to understand the process involved in the origins of the migration. Only then can one really see that migration is a consequence of a very basic structural change in the relative position of these people in the society. The main reason for their migration in the numbers they do nowadays is the rapid change in the pre-modern agricultural production system. With modern technology, new varieties of crops, and other related changes, the tenant looses his chance of share-cropping in large

---

[1] N. Abadan, *Batı Almanya'daki Turk Işçeleri ve Sorunları*, Devlet Planlama Teskila-ti yayinlari, Ankara, 1964.

land-owning areas and has to migrate out of the rural areas. For the small land-owning peasant the introduction of cash cropping requires considerable investment. Those peasants with less than 50 acres of land, in general in Turkey, end up with so much debt that in the course of fifteen to twenty years from one fourth to one fifth of the peasants lose their land and again have to earn their living outside agriculture. In areas changing to cash crops which did not require investments, indebtedness incurred for transportation and marketing could not be paid back. Such peasants also ended up by losing their land. Thus all three of these processes resulted in the de-peasantization of the rural population and this was further intensified by the high population increase rates. So migration today is not simply an accidental movement to gain cash for a single expenditure such as buying an ox or complementing the money for a house or just to save enough for bride-price. Now it is to start a new form of life and earn non-agricultural income permanently for this new life. Migration today indicates a process which is bringing basic changes in the form of production and in the basic structure of the society. Man-land relations have changed in such a fashion that the peasants are no more peasants and that is an irreversible process.

The ex-peasant, however, does not enter the new production relations as easily as he has been cut off from his land. They migrate. They migrate first, in general, to the urban centres in Turkey. But as industrial or complex organisational jobs are not created fast enough to absorb these immigrants, they acquire insignificant, unproductive occupations in so-called informal economies, ready to move again if and when there is a chance for more secure jobs. Then they migrate abroad to industrialised countries where there is a demand for labour and where they should be absorbed and integrated in expanding industry in a modern set-up. But since it is not their culture and because of other social, political and economic factors they cannot remain there permanently.[2] Thus the ex-peasant either in his village if he returns, or in the cities or abroad remains a "marginal man". The family of the marginal man, who is neither peasant nor farmer nor worker nor artisan, merges as his most important anchorage

---

[2] S. Castles and G. Cossacks, *Immigrant Workers and Class Structure in Western Europe*, Oxford University Press, 1973, London.

in society. The ambiguity of the situation creates its own strategies of adjustment, the main one of which is the flexibility and change achieved in the family.

In 1964 when Abadan first studied the Turkish workers in Germany their number had already reached 27,501. Among these workers 55.7 per cent were married (57.4 men and 44.8 of the women).[3] In 1973 the number had risen to 650.000 and the ratio of married had risen to 78.4 per cent.[4] As the process is still continuing, the family of the immigrant worker has become, indeed, very relevant. Below we shall discuss some of the more conspicuous aspects of changes in the structure of this family.

Composition of the Household

As far as the composition of households is concerned, the nuclear family, that is father, mother and unmarried children are neither novelty nor the minority of cases in Turkey, let it be in urban or rural environment. Although the model for Middle Eastern traditional families has always been, and is, the extended family, comprising father, mother, married son or sons and their wives, their children and the unmarried sons and daughters, with the domestic cycle and demographic factors such as low life expectancy, high infant and childhood mortality, as well as change that has been taking place has made the nuclear family the dominant form of its composition. In fact what has been shown by the analysis of Stirling in his article on the domestic cycle of the Turkish rural family[5] or by another major study of the Turkish family based on a national survey,[6] and case studies of individual villages before these changes,[7] have all shown that more than sixty per cent of the families have nuclear family households.[8]

---

[3] Abadan, *op. cit.*, p. 64.

[4] T. C. Devlet Planlama Teşkilati, *Kalkınma Planı*, Ueüncü Beş Yıl (State Planning Organisation, The Third Five Yearly Development Plan) 1972, Ankara, p. 626.

[5] A. P. Stirling, "Domestic Cycle in Turkish Villages" in J. P. Rivers (ed.) *Mediterranean Country Man*, The Hague, UNESCO, Mouton, 1963.

[6] S. Timur, *Türk Aile Yapısı*, Hacettepe Üniversitesi Yayınları, 1971, Ankara.

[7] I. Yasa, *Hasanoglu*, ODTAIE Yayınları, 1953, Ankara. Hinderink, J. and M. Kiray, *Social Stratification as an Obstacle to Development*, New York, Praeger, 1970, The case of the least developed village, p. 184.

[8] Prior to the publication of Goode's *World Revolution and Family Patterns* in 1963 and Levy's essay on "Aspects of the Analysis of Family Structure" in 1965, it had generally been supposed that the households composed of three or more gener-

However, this is a natural variation of the master model of the extended family and the influential role played by the male members of the older age groups can always be seen. With the change in agro-economic life of the villages as has been described briefly above, further increase in the nuclear households, with new interaction patterns have emerged. For example, in two villages, one with some possibilities for enterprise in agriculture have shown that extended family kin, although split into nuclear households in many ways share the agricultural cash income with informal arrangements in land and machinery.[9] Whereas in villages where the chance of joint enterprise is lost the nuclear family households interchange many forms of "help" with extended family kin by giving either cash or bought goods.[10] But in all of them whatever new formula has been devised to earn a living the composition of the household has dominantly become nuclear.

The villagers that move out to the cities from the villages and populate in ever-increasing numbers the squatter housing districts also show the nuclear family to be the basic composition of the households. The survey carried out in Ankara squatter housing districts[11] as well as a more recent study in Istanbul among the

ations were the typical household arrangements among a sizeable segment of the world populace. Goode and Levy raised serious questions about the validity of this view. Studies with such a view failed to consider the extent to which demographic conditions may limit opportunities to form and maintain extended family households. Empirical research on the influence of demographic conditions on the actual composition of the households in various societies has to differentiate it from the ideal one. K. K. Petersen, for instance, in her article explains why patrilocal extended family households embracing a man, his wife, his unmarried children plus his married sons with their wives and children have been uncommon in both rural and urban locales in Egypt. There is no reason to assume that the demographic situation in Egypt is unique in the Middle East. In fact with one possible exception, the rather advanced age at first marriage of males, low life expectancy at first marriage, high infant and childhood mortality and a lengthy childbearing period are characteristics of most pre-industrial societies. See W. J. Goode, *World Revolution and Family Patterns*, Glencoe, Illinois: The Free Press, 1963. M. J. Levy Jr., "Aspects of the Analysis of Family Structure" in A. J. Coale, *et al.*, *Aspects of the Analysis of Family Structure*, Princeton, Princeton University Press, 1965, pp. 1-63. K. K. Petersen, "Demographic Conditions and Extended Family Households: Egyptian Data", *Social Forces*, 46 (June 1968) No. 4, pp. 531-537.

[9] Hinderink and Kiray, *op. cit.*, pp. 183-189.

[10] *Ibid.*

[11] M. Kiray, "Squatter Housing: Fast Depeasantization and Slow Workerization in Underdeveloped Countries", Paper read in VIIth World Congress of Sociology, Varna, September 1970.

squatters employed in industry has ascertained that the father, mother and unmarried children are the main construents of the majority of the households. [12] However just as in rural nuclear families with wage income the interaction with extended kin is important, but is mostly carried on as exchanges of "gifts" and "help" without expressed obligations. With other behaviour patterns such as loss of authority by the father the urban immigrant family household composition seems to be the master model of a nuclear family and the variations from this form are situational or accidental. In such households the gravity centre has shifted in an obvious way towards the active age group male with his wife occupying a status close to the man himself.

The household composition of the family of the immigrant worker abroad has shaped itself not on the classic extended family composition but on the above forms emerged during the last 20-25 years in rural and urban Turkey. It is a household very much removed from the model of the extended family. But again in relatively close interaction with extended kin in new areas and in very new qualities, in variance with rural or urban extended kin interaction forms. [13]

---

[12] D. Kandiyoti, "Mobility Among the Industrial Workers of Istanbul: A Working Report", Paper read at the summer workshop on "Social Change and Mobility", September 12-14 1973, Marmaris, Turkey.

[13] In the 1920's Durkheim wrote about the law of contraction, meaning that all families are likely to change from large family associations to the restricted nuclear family. The same opinion is implicit in Zimmerman's theory of structure and family change, and the same view is expressed in Ogburn's writings. That the trend is towards a form of conjugal family detached from the larger circle of kin has more recently and formally been stated by T. Parsons. Parsons argues that the *isolated* nuclear family is a response to the demands of an industrial economy. That only this type of family unit permits the occupational, geographical and social mobility required by the system.

However much of the recent sociological research on urban social organisation in Western societies has demonstrated the significance of extra-household kinship ties for members of nuclear family households and the supportive functions of the kin group. Eugene Litwak, Marvin Sussman and Gerard Leslie assert that among the industrial urban groups, modified extended family structure consists of a form of coalition of nuclear families in a state of partial dependence. This dependence means that the members of various nuclear families exchange significant services with each other. Thus they differ from the isolated nuclear family, as well as retaining considerable autonomy, therefore also differ from the classical extended family. It seems that the difference between the interaction of extended kin in industrial and industrializing societies is a matter of frequency and intensity as in neither of them exist formal institutionalised patterns, but interaction is situational and takes place according to the needs of the moment. See: E. Durkheim, "La Famille Conjugale", *Revue Philosophique*, 1921, XX, p. 20. C. C. Zimmerman, *Family and Civilization*, New York, Harper and Brothers,

Abadan in 1964 reported that only 55.7 per cent of the workers in Germany at that time were married, [14] whereas in the last report published by the State Planning Organisation (SPD) the ratio in their sample has risen to 79.7 percent. In the case of the immigrant workers from the villages the ratio is as high as 87 per cent. [15] Obviously more and more married people are migrating as guest workers abroad. Among them the ratio of those who have family members together with them used to be rather limited, but increasing faster than the number of workers. In Abadan's report it was only 17 per cent whereas now in the SPD report it has risen to 28 per cent for men and 52 per cent for women. [16] However, whatever the ratio, the individual families abroad change their composition continuously. In August 1973 we were able to conduct a census-survey in one village on the Western Black Sea coast of Turkey from where an unusually large

---

1947. W. F. Ogburn, "The Changing Family", *The Family*, XIX (July 1938) pp. 139-43. T. Parsons, "Introduction to Part Two: Differentiation and Variation in Social Structures", in *Theories of Society*, T. Parsons, E. Shils, K. D. Naegele and J. R. Pitts, (eds.) New York, 1961, The Free Press of Glencoe p. 257.

For a more modified view of Parsons see: T. Parsons, "The Normal American Family", in *Man and Civilization*: The Family's Search for Survival Eds: F. Farber, M. Mustachi and R. H. L. Wilson, New York, McGraw Hill, 1965, p. 35. Gerard Leslie, *The Family in Social Context*, second edition, Oxford University Press, New York, 1973, pp. 221-310. Eugene Litvak, "Extended Kin Relations in an Industrial Democratic Society", in *Social Structure and the Family: Generational Relations*, eds. E. Shanas and G.F. Streib, Englewood Cliffs, New Jersey, Prentice Hall, 1965, p. 291. *Occupational Mobility and Extended Family Cohesion*, American Sociological Review XXV (Feb. 1960) pp. 9-21. Marvin Susman, "Relationship of Adult Children with their Parents in U.S.", in *Social Structure and Family Generational Relations*, ed. by E. Shanas and G. F. Streib, New Jersey, Prentice Hall Inc., 1965, pp. 65-92.

As examples of research reporting extended kin interaction in industrial-urban environment see: R. W. Firth, "Family and Kinship in Industrial Society", *Sociological Review* Monograph No. 8, 1964, pp. 65-87. G. S. Rosenberg and D. F. Anspash, *Working Class Kinship*, Lexington Books, D. C. Heath and Co. Lexington, Massachusetts, 1967. B. N. Adams, *Kinship in an Urban Setting*, Markham Publishing Co, Chicago, 1968. A. M. Mirande, "The Isolated Family Hypothesis: a Reanalysis", in *The Family and Change*, ed. by John N. Edwards: New York, Alfred Knoff, 1968. A. S. Dorian, "The Structure of Sibling Relationships", *American Journal of Sociology*, 1971, 76 (1: 47-56). Sylvia Vatuk, *Kinship and Urbanization*, University of California Press, Berkeley, 1972. B. D. Sebowirz, J. Fried, C. Madaus, "Sources of Assistance in an Urban Ethnic Community", *Human Organisation*, Vol. 32, Fall 1973, No. 3.

[14] N. Abadan, *op. cit.*, p. 64.

[15] State Planning Organisation, Yurt Dışından Dönen Işçilerin Sosyo-Ekonomik Egilimleri üzerinde bir çalişma. (A report on the socio-economic characteristics of the returning workers from abroad) Report No. 264, Ankara, 1974, Table 4.

[16] *Ibid.*, p. 63 and Table 5 respectively.

migration to Western Europe took place.[17] In this case-village of ours, out of a total of 132 married couples 28 men were abroad with their wives and children. A further 17 had only their wives with them, the children were staying in the village with the grandparents. Beyond this, as *the* dominant form, in 45 cases independent houses have been established for wife and children in the village while the men were abroad. In spite of the fact that the parents are in the village, the wife is not living with them, but has her own separate home where she takes care of her children and waits for her husband's return. Only in 25 cases were the wives and children staying with the parents reminding the households of classic extended family. There are a further 14 households where two generations of men are all abroad, the wife of the father stays with the wives of the sons and their children whereas in 12 cases there are no children yet, but mothers are with the wives, and all the husbands abroad. There are furthermore five cases where the wives are staying with their own mothers waiting for their husbands. It was particularly striking that there were no married sons and their wives and children living with parents. Similar or other variations may be observed in urban as well as in other rural areas of the country among the families of immigrant workers. What has to be stressed however is not only the fact that the tendency for nuclear form is dominant which is quite general for various types of families. This is only a very minor part of the specific characteristics that make up the structure of the family. For the immigrant family the discriminatory characteristic is the ultimate dispersal of the members of the nuclear family and the continuous change of its composition from one time to another as long as the men remain abroad. Although the immigrant family is basically a nuclear family, it splits itself into various parts, and composes itself in many ways with other kin as the conditions and possibilities of job, money

---

[17] The village of D is situated near to the mouth of Sakarya river on the Western Black Sea coast, on a very narrow strip of land. It consists of 172 households with a population of 926. One hundred and thirty five of the households have one or more members abroad. It is 26 kms from the sub-district (*Kaza*) to where there is daily transportation. There are two coffee shops in the commercialised centre of social interaction and two general stores (*Bakkal*) serve for the everyday needs of the villagers. There are also two primary schools. The village principally raises maize and vegetables for self-consumption and hazel nuts as cash crops. But since the terrain is hilly and there is considerable erosion, cultivatable land is scarce, hence the desire for migration.

and accomodation change for the worker himself during his stay abroad. From the case-village 40 per cent of the women now in the village stated that some time during their husband's stay abroad they had joined them for from 2 months to 2 years. A further 27 per cent added that they had also jobs there. Some came because of the children. Two turned back because they lost their jobs. When those wives who are at present with their husbands abroad come back, and when they are back whether they will join their parents or open independent houses, is not known. Any particular family throughout the years that one or more of its members are working abroad may change its composition and the place of its different members at any time. For instance if the man can find a suitable job and accomodation for his wife, when the wife and children are left in the village in a separate house, they may just change everything, leave the children with the parents and shift the centre of the nuclear family to the foreign country. This seems to have happened in our case-village numerous times. The following year the children are also brought over to Germany with a young girl of 14 or 15 to look after them. And when they think they are not saving enough all might turn to its first form with wife and children in a separate house and husband abroad on the third year.

A case from Istanbul, an urban centre, is very illuminating. S.H. lived in Istanbul with her husband and mother-in-law. Although they were of village origin both had cut their ties with the village and had nothing to do with the place. It was the wife who managed to get a job in Cologne first. She left immediately and in two months she was able to get a job and the necessary permission for her husband to join her. The mother remained in Istanbul. At the end of the year a boy was born to them. They asked the mother to come and look after the child while they both worked. The following year the mother refused to stay in Germany and returned home. That year the child was put in a paid institution in Cologne to join the family only during the weekends. During their fourth year abroad the boy was left with an elderly couple in Istanbul for which they paid more money than they did for the German institution. As far as they were concerned they did not yet intend to return to Istanbul and what would be the solution for the child during the following year was uncertain.

Into this turnover in the composition of the family one may even add the returning worker. In fact, there are men who had returned for good to their country and rejoined their families, but after two or more years, had applied again and went back to Germany to work, starting a new cycle of dispersion. In the case-village there were four men, two already gone, the others trying to go again. Or new members join the family and contribute to the turnover as in the case of new marriages. In the SPO report more than one percent of the single men married while they were abroad. In all the cases we observed the newly wed men took their wives with them when going back at the end of their vacations. Thus it emphasises neo-locality in marriage which was relatively rare in the middle of the sixties in the rural areas.[18] In fact as work abroad has great prestige with its better payment for the present and better prospects for the future, the single men coming back for vacation are considered more desirable suitors. When children are born, the child or both the child and wife are also brought back with one type of the above mentioned arrangements.

Some of the reasons for the type of splits and turnover in the possible composition of the households could be pointed out as the chances the women have in finding jobs where their husbands are, or whether the husbands can afford to have their families with them and can save at the same time. Another major factor seems to be the number and age of the children. Too young or too many children demand that their mothers stay behind with or without their grandparents living with them. When children are around primary school age (7-12) it is easy to leave them with grandparents. But at the same time to have children of 11-12 is a great asset for the mother. With their help she can manage a separate house with more facility. However, if children are grown above primary school age the tendency of the mother is again to leave them behind and go to work abroad. But if a son is reaching the age of 15, the family tries to see that he is over in Germany with his father as a dependent child so that he may reach the age of 16 in Germany and obtain a job there.

There have been a considerable number of cases where brothers out of other extended kin have stayed in the household of the

---

[18]   M. Kiray and J. Hinderink, "Agro-Economic Development and Social Change" *Journal of Development Studies*, IV, (July 1968) No. 4, pp. 497-528.

worker abroad. But such additions to the composition of the family is explained to be strictly as a visitor for a short stay, since accommodation is given to him only as a gift, until he finds a job or goes back to Turkey, since the conditions abroad such as the objection of landlords and extremely small quarters they live in makes it impossible to prolong the stay of the extended family kin.

Although we do not know exactly how many workers living abroad today had migrated first to a city and then acquired the chance to go to a foreign country, it is certain that they constitute a fairly large part of the immigrants. It should be noted that the adjustment of the family to migration to the city in Turkey has followed a pattern rather different from migration abroad as far as the composition of the household is concerned. The villager, arriving in a city, after spending some time in cheep hotels, in the houses of brothers, cousins, even friends from the same village or area, while he finds himself a way to earn a living, rents a squatter house and sends for his family almost immediately. Indeed in the squatter house areas the ratio of men without family is as low as three per cent. [19] In spite of the fact that the jobs he will find will never be good, secure, well-paid jobs, as the type of development taking place there does not create such jobs, still it is better than the village and the family achieves a sort of equilibrium in the form of a nuclear family with many "help" patterns evolved among the extended family members. At least the nuclear family perpetuates itself and the children are together with both their parents. Only in very rare cases and for short duration are children sent to their grantparents in the village, if they are still there. In fact for the great majority this is the last resort as almost none of the migrant families wish to go back to the village since the reason for their leaving in the first place was failure to earn a living in the village. This is expressed again and again in the great anxiety shown in building a house for themselves, even be it a squatter's house, as the most conspicuous part of their settlement and security in the city. However even this pattern is reversed when migration for work abroad for a man is achieved. In most cases the wife and children go back to the village, mostly to a separate house as mentioned above. The squatter house is sold to meet the expenses involved in this

---

[19]   Kiray, Squatter Housing ....

second uprooting of the family, and the relative equilibrium reached in the form of clear nuclear household with "help" patterns is indefinitely disturbed in a new and obviously longer territorial dispersal of the members of the nuclear family. So much so that today the nuclear family with members in more than one locality seems to be becoming the established form.

At one point in the sociological analysis the definition of membership to a family included, among other things, to be living under one roof as one of its determinants. [20] Obviously such a determinant is lost today for the family of the immigrant worker. Although one may say that to have multi-locality is only temporary, then one has to ask what is the length of duration of the splitting to be accepted as "temporary" or "permanent". There are cases now in the case-village who have been dispersed for more than ten years. Observations from other countries seem to show that the longer the stay away from the village the more chance for the wives to join their husbands. [21] When the migration is to a national city in Turkey the family unites almost immediately. But migration to foreign countries rejects every rule and pattern about the family and shows that the dispersal and composition is really a kaleidoscope where the pattern changes every year or with every vacation the man has. Obviously the territorial dispersal of the nuclear family and its incredible turnover of composition is the adjustment provided by the institution to meet the particular demands of the type of sucking of labour of the industries in foreign countries without allowing the worker to settle there. But it has to be remembered that the worker cannot obtain a living from agriculture in his village either. The result is the kaleidoscope effect we see in the composition of the nuclear family.

Women

The woman seems to be the crucial person from whom sacrifices are asked to be made to provide the best possible composi-

---

[20] G. Leslie, *op. cit.*

[21] S. B. Philpott, "The Implications of Migration for Sending Societies: Some Theoretical Considerations", in R. F. Spencer (ed.), *Migration and Anthropology*, Seattle, 1970, p. 16. H. Heisler, "The Patterns of Migration in Zambia", *Cahiers d'Etudes Africaines*, 13 (2) 1973, pp. 193-194. J. Connell, B. Das Gupta, R. Leishley, M. Lipton, *Migration from Rural Areas: The Evidence from Village Studies*, Institute of Development Studies, Discussion paper No. 39, The University of Sussex, 1974, Brighton.

tion of the family to meet the needs of the situation. Obviously the way the family splits itself and settles in more than one locality and changes all of it with some ease when the need arises, is one of the most ingenious adaptive strategies created as a reaction to the extraordinary constraints and contradictions produced by two diverse processes of our era, namely: the depeasantisation in not yet industrialised countries and the high demand for labour in advanced industrial countries. In this territorial dispersal it seems that, with the exception of cases where the wife is alone, by herself working abroad, the main base of the family is where the woman is living. The separate house for the wife and children in the village, the place where husband and wife live in the foreign country, or the house of the parents where the wife stays or whatever other type of combination has been achieved; the place where the wife lives presents itself as the main territory of the family. There the belongings of the family are kept and the place is referred to as "home". At this stage in the changes the wife seems to occupy a rather crucial place in the family. Her efforts are very important to hold the nuclear family as a unit. She herself seems to be going through great strains of change, pressure and deprivation; but in spite of all such overwhelming obstacles the women take the most important steps from a dependent subservient role in the family, vis-à-vis her husband and husband's extended family kin, and becomes an independent member of the nuclear family where she acts as the coordinator and decision-maker on almost every aspect of the affairs concerning her nuclear family.

Now whether it is in the separate house in the village or whether she is working with her husband abroad or whether she has another arrangement, apart from living with her in-laws, she is left very much to her own resources to deal with the day-to-day problems of the nuclear family. First of all the cash income of the unit sent from abroad is managed solely by herself. It is not only the cash income that is new—if there were no urban experience in Turkey before—but to be responsible for its expenditure is something that marks a new and important status. As will be discussed below with the financial matters concerning the family, money is sent to her usually at regular intervals or left in the bank to be drawn as need arises. Here starts the second cycle of important interactions for the woman, which usually took long years in the city or in the village in Turkey, to be a part of her daily life. These new experiences consist of dealing with institutions of society where relationships are secondary and anonymous, such as banks, post offices, payments in large figures for goods bought in large amounts, arrangements with agencies that these should be delivered to the home, trips to town to government agencies to have documents sent abroad to be used for fringe benefits. All types of new and unforeseen activities, definitely unknown in her previous life are encountered by the wife. It is certainly true that in almost all of these activities she is helped by her husband's or her own kinsmen or by the villagers, but she is also helped by other women who have learnt such formalities earlier. Furthermore, wherever there has been some land left in the possession of the nuclear family it is now the wife—instead of the father in the extended family or husband if they have split up—who decides what work is going to be done when and by whom. Such decisions used to be the source of authority in peasant families. Usually she has no one else to organise than herself and her children, but even so to decide what is going to be done at a specific time and what amount of money is to be spent is very emancipating. Her authority on her children is also not challenged by others, such as mother-in-law or husband. All such new roles for wives in the family bring them unforeseen sophistication. Today literacy is a felt need for women, whereas only seven years ago it was so dysfunctional that it was easy to find women who had forgotten how to write because they had had no chance to write since they left school. In our case-village, all women under the age of 35 were literate. Among the girls of school age the school attendance was 100 per cent.

That Turkish women have adjusted to working abroad with relative ease and that they have the consciousness of what is changing in their status has also been observed in other studies. Although the statement about "the migration of the women is less often caused by a desire to earn more than by a wish to enjoy more liberty in another country" is rather far-fetched, [22] it is not surprising that in one study carried out amongst Turkish workers in Germany a third of the male Turkish workers regarded family structure in the Federal Republic of Germany as decadent and worthy of utter condemnation whereas Turkish women

---

[22]   S. Castles and G. Cossacks, *op. cit.*, p. 362. H. Heisler, *op. cit.*, p. 196.

considered it rather suitable for themselves. They liked the equality of rights between husband and wife and appreciated the high status of women. [23]

There are many cases where the wife has gone abroad first, since jobs are easily arranged for women and she can find a job there for her husband and invites him as well. When this is the case, and she has learned the ways of the new country before her husband arrives fresh from the village, the husband submits to her protection and teaching for a long time. By the time he has also learnt what to do and what not to do, their relations have changed so much that it is never the same again. [24] It is interesting that some six years ago when the number of women workers was low and devoted mostly to single women from the cities, in newspapers one read interviews given by male workers abroad concerning their indignation that women should come to countries such as Germany and enjoy freedom there. [25] They even suggested that they should not be allowed to work abroad. The distance covered in the two situations hardly requires comment. It is obvious that the role of the woman as well as the concept of woman to man has changed incredibly and will keep changing. And one should perhaps stress that the change in the values and attitudes of the men indicates a very important stage of changes and now there may even be acceleration. The number of female workers in 1972 in Federal Germany reached 125.000. In 1967 it was 25.456, in 1968: 34.257, in 1969: 53.573, 1970: 82.500, 1971: 97.358; an increase of 500 per cent. More than two thousand of them married in Germany, of which close on 900 with foreigners. Besides 223 children out of 15.843 born to Turkish mothers in Federal Germany were born out of wedlock.[26] Obviously a new edition to chain reaction created by migration has started and it will have far-reaching effects not only in patriarchal family relations but in society at large.

One may assert that the separate house, the wife and children in the village, is the most conspicuous evidence and a good symbol of the type of emancipation we have indicated here.

---

[23] P. Granjeat, La Migration des Travailleurs en Europe", *Home and Migration Documents*, No. 771, 15 July 1969, p. 65.

[24] For the description of a case see the newspaper *Hurriyet*, June 21, 1973.

[25] See newspaper *Milliyet*, February 11, 1967.

[26] SPO, Report on workers abroad. ...

The-separate-house-in-the-village syndrome, if we may call these observations so, has to be considered as one of the most important functional changes in the role of women, brought by migration, in Turkey, as no law of the republican era could bring in such a scale.

It seems that women of Turkey adjust faster and better to unusual circumstances and hostile environments [27] because their traditional upbringing in the family is geared to prepare them to adjust to totally different environments. When a girl marries, she is uprooted from her own natural environment and goes to live in a different place among total strangers in close intimate and in some cases, basically hostile, circumstances. This is a very difficult experience for her. However, girls are brought up to accept the idea that they will have to adapt themselves to their husband's family, who may well be hostile towards them and that they will become second class members in that strange environment but still carry great responsibilities in human relations. As a result of this, women in general are always able to adjust to adverse circumstances far more easily than men in Turkey. And now in the second phase of the great changes in their lives (first being the split of the extended family in the village and migration to cities in Turkey) they are very much aware of their status vis-à-vis their husband and men in general and how it is changing.

As far as authority relations and decisions-making is concerned there is no doubt that women are still subservient to their husbands. But as she is now free from forbidding obstacles such as the proximity of the extended family kin from having an influence on her husband, and as they, the husband and wife, are living in trying circumstances, they are drawn together and act together. At least she is now the first person he consults. Furthermore all decisions about household affairs are left to her. When she is alone with the children, she is certainly under the general control of the community; but to whom she goes in times of crisis is rather interesting. In our case-village when the women who lived in separate houses with their children were asked to whom they would consult for advice in a case of crisis the great majority (60 per cent) said to nobody; 30 per cent said to their own mother and only 10 per cent to their father or mother-in-law. Contrary

---

[27] See M. Kiray, Eregli, Devlet Planlama Teşkilatı yayını, Ankara 1964, Chapter 7.

to the general impression that they are confused and helpless, they gave answers showing self-confidence and sophistication. How much our case-village observations can be generalised could not be said. But surely these observations do indicate a trend.

No matter how much the mistress of their own homes they become, wives do feel lonely by long years of separation from their husbands. All of them, wives and husbands, ultimately hope that they will join up some time soon. Two mechanisms seem to alleviate the desolation. One is to have children with great frequency. To be pregnant or have sucking infants keep many women emotionally satisfied. This brings up the question of the impact of migration on the number of children one family may have. It seems that it is not much. For the rural mother to have children is desirable and the average number both for the case-village as well as according to the last SPO report is very close to Turkey's rural average: 5.4 and 5.1 respectively. For urban families it is distinctly less and it is again close to Turkey's urban average (4.4 and 4.7). No adultery on the part of women was ever mentioned in our case-village.

The second mechanism is embedded in the social life for women in Turkish culture. Since the daily life of the sexes is traditionally well separated, they are accustomed to have well-established patterns of social life among the groups formed from the same sex. Thus to be without their husbands does not keep women from other social contacts and activities she would have with other women. So her activities in the ordinary course of the days is not very different from what it would be if her husband were around. To be able to participate fully in the ordinary daily life of the community also eases tension. [28]

As for the husband, extra-marital sexual relations abroad are considered "normal" and would not be considered a reason for separation. For workers however to venture into such relations is not very easy, as it would mean extra expense, and for the very much discriminated guest worker even the cheapest commercialised sex turns out to be expensive and unsatisfactory. As for possible alienation of the man, because of his experiences abroad, from his wife in the village, it may well be the situation. But as

---

[28]   L. Fallers and M. Fallers, "Men and Women in Egeli", paper read at the Social and Social Anthropological Meeting of Mediterranean Social Science Council on *Family Structure in the Mediterranean*, Nicosia, Cyprus, August 1970.

their relationships stand today, official and unofficial separation seem to be limited. In our case-village there was definitely no divorce, no gossip about any man having left his wife or not being in contact. As for the State Planning Organisation reports there is one case of divorce out of 342 observations of the sample. On the other hand there is rather high frequency of marriage among the single workers. During the last year 3000 have married in Germany alone and 101 of them with foreigners. Among the women workers as we indicated above the ratio of marriage with foreign workers is higher than among men. How the two sexes respond to conditions and changes created by migration, how solidarity is achieved or alienation occurs definitely needs further study with socio-psychological approaches. At this stage, according to our own observations, the human tragedy in terms of alienation does not seem to be as great as one would imagine.

Children

Children of the immigrant worker's family present different problems and questions. The dispersal of the nuclear family and the independence and sophistication acquired by its members through migration has also deep-rooted effects on the children since all the movements of the adults around the children also means frequent changes of rules of socialisation such as discipline and work for children. In the extended family households the most important relationship used to be the father-son relationship, since it served to perpetuate the family. Traditionally a family strongly desires sons. After childhood the father takes care to see that his sons learn to till the land or learn the family trade in towns or have a job, that suitable girls are found for them and that at the end of his active years the welfare of the family can be trusted to them, thus commencing a new domestic cycle. Today such relationships have completely broken down. However, as long as they continued, the woman's part in this set of relationships was again to emphasize the importance of the son. The boys were constantly reminded that they will eventually replace their father in his important role of control and decision-making. Indeed, from almost childhood sons were given a very privileged status. The extraordinary spoiling of male children by women compared with their treatment of girls, and the great tolerance with which both parents accepted the behaviour of their sons in extended families has to be explained in such a frame of reference. In such a set up the status of a boy of 10 or 11 years of age seemed to be higher than that of the mother and he could impose his wishes upon her. Now the immigrant family is composed of conjugal members, and the father is away in factory work where boys cannot be with and around him. The mother, in a separate house in the village, has to bring up her children in the absence of her mother-in-law and other close relatives who spoil the boys, and she faces the demanding responsibilities of the head of the family living alone. In such circumstances her attitude and behaviour about her sons changes very fast. She is much more strict with them and usually asks the boys of eleven-twelve to share her responsibilities of the household without the earlier spoiling. The change of the patterns of discipline and authority in early childhood and adolescence of the boys may well result in entirely different personalities in new generations.

To this, one also has to add, of course, the experiences: trips to foreign lands, anxieties, joys experienced now by the children in ever-changing form of the family life. Many of these experiences are not very pleasant. In extreme cases of dispersal, as in one of the examples given above, a very young child had gone through traumatic experiences every eleven months or so by changing the place at which he was left: with a grandmother or in a German institution, followed by an elderly couple, a stranger to the family or a Turkish institution. In another case two children aged 5 and 6, just could not be placed anywhere, both the mother and father were working in Germany. The last place they found with a rent within their reach refused to have the children. The solution they found on the spur of the moment was to send a letter to the parents of the husband now working as gardeners in Istanbul asking them to meet the children at the airport, and put the children on a plane. The children were met and taken home. But now the grandparents were not happy because the living quarters given to them were too small to have two growing children and they were afraid that they would lose their jobs. It took the grandparents only one week to send the children back to Munich. Again tickets were brought, letters were sent, hostesss of the plane were instructed and the children were packed off back to Germany. What the effect will be of such a shift of environment on their personalities is an open question, as is the case with parents who live in continuous anxiety because of their children.

Each serious constraint creates its institutions to absorb the shock. Where primary groups, nuclear family or extended kin failed to take care of children and similar cases became rather widespread in foreign countries as well as in Turkey, secondary institutions emerged to answer the need. With the increase of immigrants with young children and the discontinuity of the help of extended family kin, new anonymous commercial "houses", "nurseries" to take care of the children of workers have been established. [29] They are complemented by private boarding houses where school age children can be left and sent to government schools in the city—the cheapest arrangement. Certainly all such observations indicate the change in one of the most essential functions of the family, i.e. bringing up the children.

For the families who can have their children with them abroad to provide them with the primary school education seems to be a great problem. The latest figure for Turkish children in Federal Germany is 220.000. There are 300 Turkish primary school teachers appointed by the Turkish government for their primary education. This is obviously very inadequate. How many of the children attend German schools is not known. The conditions of education of children like the housing or other aspects of the life of the immigrant worker is very unsatisfactory.

The impact of migration on the education of the children at home is rather different. The necessity for the universal primary education, both for boys and girls, is very well understood and accepted in our case-village. But further education, particularly for boys, seems to have become less desirable in areas where almost mass migration abroad is taking place. It seems that the obssessive involvement with education seen in so many surveys made in rural Turkey in the 1960's, has lost its intensity. Now for boys above eleven or twelve years of age plans are to create a chance to go abroad as a dependent so that he will reach the age of 16 there and apply for a job. If his father is there it is the ideal situation. He will see that he comes and spends a year or so with him to learn the ways of the country and then obtain a job. Not

---

[29]   See newspaper *Cumhuriyet*, March 19, 1973.

much comment was made in the case-village as to acquisition of a vocation. Certainly nothing much is known in the village about whether it was possible to have any sort of training abroad while the son was waiting to reach the age to have a job. At the moment nothing can be predicted about how he will establish his family, what type of complex problems will arise when he returns home or when his compulsory military service is due. It is already not infrequent for families of two generations of males (fathers and sons) to be working abroad. Soon it may be three generations.

Family Finances

The composition of a family seems to be directly related to the source, form and amount of earnings of its members. In fact, in a sense the changes in the source of income bring the changes in the composition, thus cause the migration. The decrease in agricultural income, and impossibility to replace it with cash cropping, drives the peasant to possible sources of non-agricultural income outside his village. As the ratio of non-agricultural income increases the family becomes more and more alienated from its rural environment. As long as he migrates only to the cities around his village, this tendency ends with the nuclear family's final settlement with an income from urban sources in the city, from where they exchange "help" and "gifts" with extended family kin in the village if and when the need arises. As the family's income incorporates more and more cash income, particularly if it is obtained through a stable and secure urban job the relations with villages becomes less and less important. Whatever types of relationships are achieved with the extended or family kin it is always arranged on "help" and "gift" basis rather than on joint enterprise. Indeed now the financial interaction is something much more complicated among the different households of the extended kin. In other words the more the family becomes intergrated to its new class as worker or salaried man in urban centres the more its relations with the village and extended family members changes. Since the integration is not achieved overnight, but takes years, with the very slow development of industrialisation, such a process is prolonged taking many turns and forms as it proceeds. Sometimes as it reaches a standstill it is

possible to conceive it even as a distinct type as Epstein propo-
ses. [30]

Independent cash income in general, even if it is for instance
from agricultural wage work in the village, creates tensions in
extended family relations. [31] A much closer relationship is maintained if cash income is earned from a joint enterprise in agriculture. [32] The intensity is reduced if this enterprise is in urban
setting such as a shop in a city. But the moment it is wages and
salaries in urban settings from larger organisations, the split becomes more pronounced and relationship is reduced to "gifts"
and "help". Particularly significant is what is considered help
such as giving room and board until one finds a place to live, or
lending money on indefinite terms, or helping with the authorities, hospitals or similar places, is extended in cities among the
immigrants, not only to the extended family kin but to almost
anybody from the same village. So it is not something very special for the family.

Now that urban income is obtained in Western European countries, and its main source is proper industrial urban jobs, because
it is abroad and every policy concerning the immigrant worker
aims to have him there only temporarily, permanent integration
fails. But the main relationship between the source of income
and the composition of the family still works. In fact, because
the income is relatively large and the family from the beginning
sees that there will be no more peasant economy and self-suffi-
ciency in agriculture, it composes itself into the smallest unit and
modifies its relations with the extended family kin accordingly.
The most conspicuous form is observed where wives with their
children now remain in separate houses, even in the village.

The income earned abroad is always divided into three parts.
One is spent by the man for his expenses in the foreign country,
another is sent to his family for their daily needs. But as great a
part as possible is saved for future investment at home. The

---

[30] S. Epstein, *South India: Yesterday, Today and Tomorrow*, London, 1973,
pp. 200-211. Epstein prefers to give the name of "Share Family" to the extended kin
network which seems to establish itself in the place of joint or extended family in
India. Among such kin, close productive integration is accompanied by only a loosely
knit living arrangement. The share family is another example of different forms of
mutually beneficial adaptations.

[31] Hinderink and Kiray, *Social Stratification* .... p. 187.

[32] *Ibid.*, p. 188.

relative weight of all these three main allocations in the family's budget changes according to the special arrangements and needs of the family at a given time. Whether various members of the family are together, or when the wife is also working abroad or is alone with her children in the village, or the money has to be sent to grandparents because children are living with them, change the way and the ratio of the allocations from the income. When children are left with the older generation money is usually sent for their upkeep. In some cases where wife and children stay with the parents of the husband no money is sent. Even in such simple cases the finances of the family is rather complex. For example, our case-village raises maize and hazel nuts, in the cultivation of which the labour of women and children is valuable in hoeing and harvesting. Various inputs in the production such as the labour of women and children is obviously rationally assessed so that the worker does not feel himself obliged to send money regularly. In the case of families where wives and children live in separate houses, the upkeep is almost entirely provided by the money sent by the husband from abroad. If there is some land, not much effort is spent to increase production with new inputs such as changing the crop or technology by the women. Anyhow land will be of too small an area for this to be worthwhile. Whatever is produced from the land is consumed by the family as additional food. In fact women in the case-village said that they never sell the hazel nuts but let the children consume them as luxury food. Where it is vegetables and maize they see that these are properly cultivated for satisfactory home consumption.

Saving is the greatest concern. Their intentions from this saving change however, with the duration the man of the family spends abroad and the size of his income. At the beginning, since the immigrant's level of living is very low and even the most basic needs have to be met, the savings are spent for ordinary consumption items, apart from food, such as clothing, furniture and most important of all building a house. The house occupies a most important place in the life of the people who try to build up a life from almost nothing. It is the main source of security in ordinary times, and in bad times, as it can be sold for its worth at any moment, it is also a sort of investment. Among the consumption items bought by immigrant workers, durable goods such as refrigerators, radios, television sets, tape-recorders, shaving ma-

chines occupy a large place. Partly because they have become a
part of their consumption patterns. This particularly applies to
radios and tape-recorders. [33] But they can also be sold very easily
in Turkey at prices twice or more than those the worker originally
paid. Thus it is an easy way to increase his savings. Although it is
illegal to sell goods imported as personal effects, they do manage
to bring more than one. They keep one and sell the others.

Some conspicuous trends according to the marital status of the
workers have been observed in the savings habits in the survey
conducted by the State Planning Organisation in Turkey. For
instance rural men tend to save more than the workers from
urban centres (91.83 percent versus 83.46 per cent). Also more
married men save than single men (88.36 per cent versus 76.81
per cent), whereas it is the reverse for women: 100 per cent of
the single women saved as against 92.3 per cent of the married
women. Younger men save less than older men; and as far as
education is concerned, men with the least education saved most,
men with higher education came second and men with intermediary education were third. As for the amount of savings, married
men on average save 54.72 per cent of their income whereas for
single men the ratio is 46.50 per cent. For the married men from
villages the ratio goes up to 57.47 per cent and for urban men it
is 52.22 per cent.

These savings are basically kept in the banks (72.2 per cent).
But there are still people who keep it themselves (18.7 per cent).
The way they send it home varies. Only 38.9 per cent of the
respondents brought it home as cash, 49.4 per cent partly in
cash, partly in goods and 3.9 per cent only in goods. When it is
cash, less than half brought it themselves (42.6 per cent) without
using the services of banks or post offices. [34]

Later if the man manages to stay longer and save more than to
satisfy the most urgent consumption needs his attention is turned
towards genuine investment possibilities. Their first trial is land
and machinery in rural areas and real estate, trade or craft in
cities.

The SPO report shows that in rural areas 61 per cent of the
men invested their savings in some sort of enterprise and only 15
per cent on housing. For the cities the ratio of enterprise is 32.41

---

[33] SPO, *Report on Workers Abroad* .... Table 94.
[34] *Ibid.*, Table 72.

per cent and housing 28.97 per cent. The housing investments in cities surely constitutes also real estate development.

Among the expenditures, the money spent for ceremonies such as weddings, circumcision festivities and funerals are usually thought to be more important in villages where brideprice is still exercised. However the SPO survey has shown that while the immigrant from the villages spends only 2.24 per cent of his savings for them his urban counterpart spends 4.75 per cent of his. Particularly for villages it seems that ceremonial conspicuous consumption is at the level suitable to the local earnings, so that its ratio for foreign earnings remains low.

The income of the family before, during and after migration is rather interesting. In the SPO report 67.5 per cent of the immigrants from cities declared that they had less than T.L. 10,000 per annum income and 76.3 per cent of the immigrants from the villages had less than T.L. 5,000 before they went abroad. The average income during 1961-1969 abroad concentrates in the brackets of 1,500 and 3,000 where 65 per cent of the workers have put themselves. Among those who came back for good 55.2 per cent used to earn between T.L. 3,000 and T.L. 12,500 per year and only 2.49 per cent used to earn more than T.L. 45,000 per year. Another 12 per cent earn more than T.L. 20,000 per year. In general the income abroad for the workers from villages is around four times more than they earned before and twice as much as they would earn after their return. And the same is three times more abroad and twice as much after they return for urban immigrants. [35]

It seems that families always keep the income from abroad separate from the accounts of other extended family kin. When they venture into an enterprise together it is strictly in terms of rational partnership. As for our case-village, the women are very hesitant to comment on what will be done with the savings when the husbands return. First of all there is as yet no plan for coming back for good. What will be done afterwards is not much thought about. As a general rule they want to start a new enterprise but not necessarily with the brothers or other kin.

---

[35] *Ibid.*, Table 50.

Today, according to the last SPO report 78.2 per cent of those who came back permanently would like to go abroad again. The major reason they give is the inadequacy of the income they are able to earn here (56 per cent). More than seven per cent put the problem simply as unemployment. To these two categories one has to add dissatisfaction from work here (12.1 per cent). All three of them constitute more than 75 per cent of all those who came back, but would like to go again to work in Western Europe. [36]

Conclusions

This brings us to the question of when the migration and consequently the dispersal of the family will end and what will be the characteristic of the family at that time.

At this moment as everyone knows any economic crisis in Western Europe will cause the Turkish workers to loose their jobs there. When they come back there will be nothing much for them to do but to be a part of what is called informal economies in the cities. The integration to informal economies will make the family keep its nuclear composition with much "help" and "gift" exchange with other kin. However, assuming that economic crises will be followed by periods of expansion of economies and demand for labour, the flow of the workers and dispersal of the nuclear family will be resumed. This pattern will surely go on as long as one of the major contradictions of our era, i.e. the advance of cash cropping without industrialisation in under-developed countries and fast expansion of industrial economies will exist side by side. And perhaps in this process a very new status will emerge for women which might lead again to the formation of very different personalities of the man in coming generations.

---

[36] *Ibid.*, Table 110.

EDUCATIONAL PROBLEMS ENCOUNTERED
BY THE CHILDREN
OF TURKISH MIGRANT WORKERS

M. SITKI BILMEN

In regard to the migrant workers in Europe, the fact that strikes one most is the variety and diversity of the policies applied to them by various concerned parties such as: the countries of reception and emigration, regional or international lay organizations, church-affiliated bodies, labor unions, etc., all representing and pursuing different views and aims and, because of their very natures, usually in complete controversy with each other.

A. It is quite well-known that the problem caused by the migration of workers has become a constant matter of deep concern for both manpower-seeking and labor-exporting countries of the continent during the post-War era.

This particular problem has been a subject of major interest not only because it effects the present, but mainly because of the possible consequences it might present in the immediate and distant future.

However, no significant progress has yet been made in determining the effects of the problem on the social, cultural, economic and political life of Europe as a whole. What has happened, especially during the last decade, is that due to economic reasons, West European countries, rather small relative to their dense population, have been stormed by millions of foreign workers and their families.

The governments of the receiving countries, while exercising a policy to assimilate some select groups of migrants, are simultaneously exerting efforts to keep the bulk of the foreign masses away from their own people, who seem to sympathize with the latter part of this overall policy.

B. On the other hand, each one of the emigration countries tries to follow a policy of its own best suited to its own national interest.

The common aim of these policies exercised by the countries of origin, is to establish and maintain closer contact with their respective workers abroad.

The thought of their homecoming in voluminous proportions is just as much a matter of apprehension for their countries as would be their permanent residence in foreign lands.

C. It should be added that, besides the immigration and emigration countries, which are directly interested in the problem for obvious reasons, there are quite a number of non-governmental regional institutions and international organizations that are wholeheartedly dealing with the matter.

The extent of involvement in the subject by religious organizations should also be mentioned.

D. Of course, the other legitimate group involved in the problem is the migrant workers themselves.

Through observation, it has been noted that their relations with both the host countries and their own countries usually indicate some degree of instability and uneasiness.

Despite the fact that all foreign workers form an indivisible labor force, with the application of bilateral agreements between concerned governments, they become subject to different treatment within the same country.

The workers subjected to such discriminatory treatment may develop varied feelings toward their own and the host countries involved. This situation may cause the formation of masses which consider themselves either favorably or unfavorably treated.

Since bilateral agreements are always preferred by the big brothers of the European community, multilateral agreements usually have no binding effects applicable to all, but are merely recommendations as far as seeking solutions to the problems in the field are concerned.

E. So, in all this confusion and disarray, the problem of educating thousands of children in foreign countries is one that we are only lately beginning to conceive. I hope it would not be unjust to say that the educators of the European community have lagged exceedingly behind economists, sociologists and clergy in realizing their duties fully.

What this delay has cost thousands of children may never be learned.

It is worth mentioning that, even if the educators had realized the scope of the problem in time and put forth their recommendations to solve it, it would take at least ten years especially for the host countries to adjust their educational systems accordingly.

F. The issue of education of migrant workers' children, due to the tragic outcome of long years of neglect, has at last made an impact on the international arena.

The handling of this issue by the Council of Europe, should really be considered a renaissance in the field.[1]

The subject has been assigned to a "Sub-committee" at the request of the "Advisory Committee to the Special Representative" for the purpose of reviewing all its aspects and to recommend necessary measures to be taken.

This Committee[2] held its first meeting between 24 and 27 June 1971 at Strasbourg, and three more meetings have been organized for the following year.

The handling of the problem by the Council of Europe has been a cause for deep satisfaction among the member countries and great hopes were expressed especially by the countries of emigration.[3]

The endeavor by the Council of Europe's Committee has caused some immediate results:

a) It has contributed to the understanding that the subject in question is, by nature, a common European problem that can only be solved by the common efforts of the countries concerned.

b) It has been realized that certain countries have more common interests than they have interests peculiar to them.

c) The chaos and misunderstanding which prevails by the use of terminology and concepts has been radically reduced, and a new terminology enabling a better dialog among the interested parties has been adopted and developed.

d) Thus, a mechanism has been established to trace, collect and

---

[1] At its 17th meeting, held in Paris on December 7, 1966, the Advisory Committee, with the object of encouraging attendance by migrant worker's children at the schools and vocational training establishments of member countries, proposed that the Committee of Ministers include in the intergovernmental Work Programme of the Council of Europe, a study of school education for such children. This suggestion was approved at the 159th meeting of the Deputies, held in April 1967, and the activity in question was included in the Work Programme as Item XXI of the chapter on social matters. RS/SEMI (1968).

[2] "The Sub-Committee on School Education for the Children of Migrant Workers."

[3] "The National Association of Emigrant's Families is grateful to the Council of Europe for having taken up the important subject of school education for the children of migrant workers." RS/SEM-13 (1969).

disseminate both individual and common efforts and experiences in the field.

It can be claimed that the problem of educating the children of migrant workers is nothing but a tiny fragment when compared to the huge mosaic of complicated problems created by the total migration question. But the fact is that what motivates millions of workers to toil like slaves in faraway countries is the idea of feeding the minds as well as the stomachs of their offspring, for most of them, from their personal experiences, realize fully that a well-fed brain will prevent the stomach from going hungry as did theirs.

The most ironical aspect of the subject is that the countries striving to solve the schooling problem of thousands of their little citizens abroad, have, in fact, not yet been able to solve it for the children in their very homelands.

The Turkish Approach

A. Before 1960, it was only rarely possible to see the Turkish workers in Europe. They had stepped into the European market very quietly and almost one by one before that date.

However, in a short time, these industrious, durable, sober and discipline oriented men have formed one of the most sought-after labor forces by the countries with booming economies. [4]

Today there are about 700,000 workers from Turkey in West Germany, Belgium, France, Switzerland, Holland, Austria and Scandinavian countries. Together with their families, they number close to 1,000,000. The number of Turkish children in Europe is about 230,000, of whom approximately 125,000 are at the school age. Even so, it is obvious that all the children do not accompany their families in the host countries.

B. It is said that a Turkish father is almost always a father to more than one child. About 30,000 Turkish children are born each year in West Germany alone. 15 children are born each day just in West Berlin. (The Turkish population in West Berlin was on June 30, 1973 about 66.500). [5]

---

[4] "Who are they? Young, work hardened men, undismayed by the material conditions they encounter ...." F. Juge, "Turkish Immigrants in France", *Message du Secours Catholique*, No. 2401, April 1973.

[5] According official statistics, closed on January 31, 1973, there were a total of

Although the majority of these workers are at the most only primary school graduates, they are very keen on providing proper education for their children.

The table below indicates the results of a very interesting questionnaire on this particular point:

Table 1

Level of Education Desired by the Turkish Workers
in West Germany for their Children[6]

Level of Education Desired	For		%	
	Boys	Girls	Boy	Girl
Primary Education	5	94	1.0	19.0
Junior High School	17	154	3.5	31.2
S. High School and equivalent	105	21	21.3	4.2
Higher Education	343	194	69.4	39.3
School is not necessary	—	10	—	2.1
Response is not clear	24	21	4.8	4.2
Total	494	494	100.0	100.0

C. In trying to solve the schooling problems of more than a hundred thousand children scattered around in half a dozen foreign countries, it seems that the Turkish Republic has some apparent disadvantages and advantages in comparison to some of the countries.

Some of the disadvantages that render this problem more acute for Turkey are as follows:

1. Mass emigration was a new, unprecedented phenomenon for Turkey. For example, the first agreement dealing with the displacement of workers to West Germany, dates back only to October 1961. The flow of organized emigration has taken place only after that date. Consequently it may be said that Turkey was caught unprepared; inexperienced in regard to the problems of migrant workers as a whole, and even less to the problem of

---

66,521 Turks in West-Berlin with a very heavy concentration in two districts, namely Kreuzberg (Turks represented 30,8% of all foreigners) and Wedding (Turks represented 24.9 of all foreigners). It is expected that within six years every third school age child will be of Turkish nationality. J. Glowinski, Ausländer in Berlin (west) am 31. Januar 1973, Berliner Statistik, 27. Jahrg. 1973, H. 5, pp. 209-220.

[6] Nermin Abandan, Batı Almanya'daki Türk İşçileri ve Sorunları, T. C. Başbakanlık DPT, Ankara 1964, p. 218, Table 235.

the education of their children which is an area with special peculiarities.

2. Because Turkey has not previously established national minority groups in West European countries, it lacks voluntary non-governmental social, cultural and religious organizations. It is a bare fact that these kinds of organizations, in general, do their best to provide guidance and education for both migrant workers and their children.

3. Another major factor that should be taken into account is that the Turkish language has no relation whatsoever to the language of West European countries.

To this fact we certainly have to add the deep-rooted differences of the cultures. This, as can easily be understood, makes the adaptation much more difficult than superficial differences. [7]

4. The workers are sometimes scattered throughout the host country in small numbers. This is especially a hindrance in educational matters.

All these particular circumstances not only cause problems for children, but complicate their solutions as well as the solution of social, psychological and economic problems that Turkish workers are confronted with in Europe.

While reflecting on this issue, it would be well to list some of the advantages of Turkey along with these disadvantages:

1. The Turkish Republic has inherited a considerable number of minorities in various foreign countries from the Ottoman Empire. These minorities certainly are not temporary residents or communities like migrant workers, but still there are a number of similarities between the problems of the national education of the children of minorities and those of migrant workers. Consequently, keeping ties with the national culture is a practice with which the Turkish administration may be said to have much experience.

2. For many years Turkey has established and maintained close cultural ties based on bilateral cultural agreements with many of the European countries in which thousands of Turkish citizens

---

[7] When a Turkish child was asked what the kissing couple were doing in a movie, she was viewing during her first year in a foreign school, where sex education was given, she replied without hesitation that they were measuring their mouths to determine which one was bigger.

work at the present.[8] These agreements naturally provide ample opportunities not only to conduct cultural relations between the two countries in general, but also to secure a suitable base for discussing the schooling problems of the children of Turkish migrant workers, in order to seek proper solutions for them.

3. As a member of the Council of Europe, since the beginning, the Turkish Republic has taken an active role both in the committees related to the problems of migrant workers and in the special committees concerned with the educational problems of their children.

Hence, the opportunity has been found to closely observe and evaluate the opinions of the other member countries in relation to the problem, the measures that these countries have taken in accordance with their necessities and the results of these measures. This awareness has facilitated the analyzing of the problems, has helped to hasten the finding of their solutions and increased the effectiveness of the measures taken.

4. Turkey has been sending its youngsters to foreign countries for educational purposes for 150 years. Such being the case, Turkey has been compelled to take the necessary steps to facilitate the adaptation of these young people to a new foreign social and educational environment, to help them preserve their national culture, protect them from serious re-integration difficulties on their return.

For these reasons, Turkey has student inspectorships in some of the European countries such as France, West Germany, England, Switzerland. The main obligations of these offices are toward the Turkish students studying in foreign universities. They assumed additional functions in dealing with the education of Turkish subjects abroad—now, mainly the children of migrant workers in their regions.

I hope the explanations made so far, clarify somewhat the

---

[8] Cultural agreements between Turkey and some of the other European countries:
Turkey-France (6/17/1952) Date of Agreement.
Turkey-United Kingdom (3/12/1956) Date of Agreement.
Turkey-Federal Germany (5/8/1957) Date of Agreement.
Turkey-Norway (1/10/1958) Date of Agreement.
Turkey-Belgium (12/29/1958) Date of Agreement.
Turkey-Holland (5/12/1960) Date of Agreement.
S. Bilmen, *Türkiye Cumhuriyetinin Taraf veya Dahil Olduğu Kültür Anlaşmaları*, Millî Eğitim Bakanlığı, Ankara 1966.

conditions under which Turkey deals with the educational problems of the children of Turkish migrant workers.

Big Problems for Little Ones

A. One of the reasons why the problems concerning the education of children linger unsolved for hundreds of years is the
inclination of adults to think they can properly understand them.
For all the good intentions and endeavors, the success of adults
in this field is bound to be limited due to the very nature of these
problems.

This is true even in the case of children being educated in their
own country. Thus it is not hard to imagine to what degree the
difficulties expand if children are to be educated in an entirely
foreign environment. Other factors that have negative effects on
the child's education, and are almost entirely out of our control,
should also be recorded as reasons that limit our success in this
field.

Failure in educational matters of migrant workers children
may have drastic results such as an army of children unable to relate to any community whatsoever.

B. The most reasonable method for finding some effective
measures to meet this situation is, of course, to correctly identify
the causes of the educational problems encountered by the children of migrant workers and treat them accordingly.

Undoubtedly, proper treatment following a realistic diagnosis
is also fully valid as far as the education of Turkish children is
concerned.

In the following pages, I have tried to list, at least partially, the
educational problems faced by the Turkish migrant workers
children, their causes, measures already taken to solve them and
those measures it would be advisable to take.

C. Problems concerning the education of Turkish children
may be gathered under two main groups:

a. Problems arising from the peculiarities in the educational
systems of the receiving countries that prevent or reduce the
benefits of education.

The nature of the problems belonging to this category may be
related briefly to the facts outlined as such:

— Every child is entitled to the right to be properly educated to the full extent of his capacity no matter where he is. All concerned officials are responsible for providing the required conditions for the fulfillment of this right.

— Fostering, deliberately or unconsciously, conditions or situations that prevent or render diffucult the fulfillment of this right, or having indifference toward such circumstances, is a direct violation of this right.

— The primary outcome of a child's education is his adaptation to his social environment and his developing a constructive attitude toward it. Many of the positive values that the child thus gains may be transferred to another society; namely, his native country.

b. Problems that might cause maladaptation upon the childs return to his native land.

The characteristics of this second group of problems may be understood by taking the following facts into consideration:

— The child living in a foreign country usually returns to his own. From this second migration, even though he is returning to his original environment, severe adaptation difficulties will still be encountered by the child.

— If the child cannot easily overcome these difficulties, he will be either compelled to leave his homeland or, at worst, be a detriment to both himself and his country.

— Therefore, measures for reintegration should be taken before departure from the immigration country.

D. In the two categories above, of which I have tried to express the main characteristics, there are several problems.

Reasons that prevent, or render difficult, the child's ability to sufficiently profit from the educational system or other potentials of the host country follow.

1. To what degree migrant workers are aware of other conditions in the host country concerning themselves in general, may be said to be outside the bounds of our topic, but it has been noticed that they know little or nothing about the school system of the host country and their lawful responsibilities regarding the education of their children.

The lack of knowledge, especially in this area, keeps many parents out of school, when, in fact—in order to be helpful to their children—they are at least obliged to know:

— the potentials of the host country in connection with the education of pre-school age children;

— the special educational measures applied to the children of the migrant workers.

— It is also a must to enlighten the parents about the difficulties, and overcoming them, related to the reintegration of their children on returning to the homeland.

This knowledge, of course, may be provided through different means. An orientation book entitled, *"Education of Turkish Workers' Children in European Countries,"* prepared by the writer of this report, and published by the Ministry of National Education three years ago, may be mentioned as an attempt in this direction on the part of the Turkish government.

2. Some of the attitudes, although directly related to parents, still effect the education of their children:

— The migrant workers, in general, have no definite knowledge or personal decision regarding the duration of their stay in a foreign country. As a natural result of this uncertainty, they cannot choose the proper time, as far as their childrens education is concerned, in which to bring their children from, or to send them, or return together with them, to the country of origin.

— Quite a lot of workers, before returning home, go to another, a second or even third foreign country for a few years. As it may be imagined, this has a harmful effect on the education of their children.

The main problem arising from this particular situation is the improper evaluation or lack of appreciation of the children's previous education by the authorities in these respective countries.

In order to find a remedy for this kind of unfortunate situation, the Council of Europe has taken measures to develop a "School Career and Health Record."

This document is a complete school file to help the interested authorities get to know the child through his previous academic achievements, state of health and socio-psychological standing. [9]

---

[9] ".... Furthermore, the report will also deal with the standardisation of the "school career and health records" for these children, who will return to their homeland or go to another country and continue their education.

In both cases they are desperately in need of a complete school file, which may be termed as an educational passport, containing all the necessary information for the proper evaluation of their academic achievements, personalities and state of health."
S. Bilmen, *Education of Migrant Workers Children, Organization of Experimental Special Classes and School Career and Health Record for the children of Migrant Workers,* Council of Europe: RS 201 (1971), Strassbourg.

— It is also a known fact that some of the parents don't allow their children to attend schools at all.

There are several understandable, but unacceptable, reasons for that unfortunate attitude. In spite of the results of the previously-mentioned questionnaire, in practice, a sizeable number of the Turkish migrant workers' children at school age don't attend schools.

This intolerable situation is a common problem concerning all the other emigration countries. [10]

— Another problem faced by these children is that their parents cannot assist them in dealing with schoolwork to any degree.

It is true that most of the parents, due to their lack of education, cannot help their children scholastically even in their own language, let alone in a foreign one.

E. In addition to the problems caused mainly by the attitudes of the parents, we should now mention some others that may be related to the educational systems of the receiving countries which are not organized to satisfy the needs of thousands of foreign children.

1. There are more than one hundred thousand Turkish children in the European countries at pre-school age.

There is, of course, no need to discuss the importance of kindergarten for the children who will attend regular schools in a few years in a foreign land. [11]

In spite of this fact, the number of kindergartens are far from meeting the demand. Even if such schools were founded as mere buildings in sufficient numbers, it would still take years to provide them with competent staff. It is not possible to send teachers from Turkey to teach Turkish children in kindergartens, and it would not be a logical solution, either.

---

[10] ".... But everywhere there is a sizeable minority of immigrant children who for a variety of reasons, do not attend school." S. Castles, and G. Kosack, *Immigrant Workers and Class Structure in Western Europe*, Oxford University Press, London 1973, pp. ".... of these, about 21,000 are already of school age (between 6 and 15 years of age). It has been calculated however, that only 17,000 attend Germany primary school". Juan Manuel M. Aguirre, Children of Spanish Migrants in West Germany, *Migration News*, 1972, No. 5.

[11] "Kindergarden is a very important stage in the child's development. As a general rule he needs the company of other children of his age, i.e., he needs a community .... moreover, in the case of emigrant children, kindergarden has an important function to fulfill, as it teaches them the language of the country in which they are living ... Juan M. M. Aguirre, Children of Spanish Migrants in West Germany, *Migration News*, 1972, No. 5.

Consequently, the opportunity for learning the language properly and preparing for regular school is wasted for thousands of
children.

2. Difficulties confronting children, who started their primary
education in a foreign country and whose knowledge of the language will fall short of the required level are worth being noted.

As a matter of principle, like migrant workers' children of
other countries in schools where they total a considerable number, Turkish children attend "Special Classes" for about a year
before being accepted in regular classes with correspond to their
ages and former academic level.

These classes have been given quite a number of names such as
"special, admission, reception, introductory, transitional, preparatory" classes, etc.

In these classes, besides the target language, some lessons are
taught in Turkish. Unfortunately, even the teachers that give
language lessons are seldom citizens of the host country.

The majority of the children cannot acquire the required
amount of knowledge to be transferred to regular classes within a
year. [12]

The rate of failure of the migrant workers' children to be
accepted into normal classes is terribly high. [13]

The Council of Europe is convinced that these classes are necessary and beneficial, yet, in the course of application, serious
defects have been observed that are countrary to the principles of
education.

Although it would be very beneficial for children in these
classes to also attend normal classes for lessons that do not require an advanced degree of language ability, with a few excep-
tions, this is not the course taken; consequently, integration is
hindered even further. [14]

---

[12] "In 1970, one third of the pupils had been in the special classes for over two
years". Ollivier, Vingt-quatre nationalités, *Droit et Liberté*, 1970, No. 297, pp. 18.

[13] "Problèmes d'intégration des Jeunes Immigrés dans l'Enseignement Primaire et
Secundaire", Province de Liège, pp. 10-12.

[14] "It is also important that an immigrant child should take part in ordinary class
activities which do not require much knowledge of the language, such as foreign
languages, sport, music art and handwork and, of course, in various kinds of common
social activities in school." Comments by the Swedish expert, Mrs. M. Ek, on the
Secretariat Memorandum; R.S/SEM 7 (1968).

According to the definition above, the scheme of a well-organized special class can be drawn as follows:

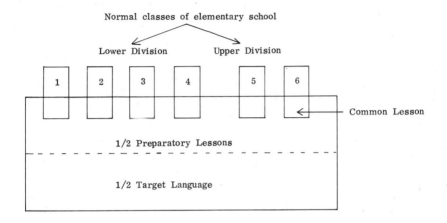

3. Still another crucial problem is that a proper evaluation of the education these children have received in their own country usually cannot be made in the immigration country. There are, of course, several reasons for the failures in this field. But no matter what the reasons, those that suffer in the long run are the migrant workers' children.

Taking this into consideration, the Turkish Ministry of Education has had a booklet published on the educational principles applied and the curriculum of the subjects taught in Turkish elementary schools. [15]

4. Another shortcoming is that, after a certain period of time, when it is thought fit to transfer the child into regular classes, measures aimed to make up for the child's deficiencies of language are lacking. There is not the slightest assurance that children accepted into regular classes, due to their success in special classes, will succeed there, also. As a matter of fact, the percentage of failure in regular classes is quite alarming. [16]

Since these children are deprived of parental assistance at

---

[15] Bilingual (Turkish and French) publication of the Turkish Ministry of National Education gives detailed information about educational opportunities for children of Turkish migrant workers. See: T. C. Millî Eğitim Bakanlığı, *Avrupa'da Türk İşçi Çocuklarının Öğrenim İşleri*, Ankara 1970.

[16] *Problèmes d'intégration des Jeunes Immigrés dans l'Enseignement Primaire et Secondaire*, Province de Liège, pp. 10-12.

home, there is the necessity of supplying complementary courses at school.

However, it seems probable that in a short period of time this service will be made available in all Western Europe through special television programs.

5. There is usually a scarce number of indigenous pupils in schools attended by immigrant workers' children. Since many educational drawbacks may arise from an abnormal proportion between the number of foreign and native children attending a school, some countries engage in a dispersal policy with the aim of correcting such a disturbing ratio. But this policy also has its complications.

6. It has been observed that for children who are older, of high school age, for example, the problems of educational integration are more severe, the main reason being that the amount of measures taken to assist children of this age group in learning the language is even more limited. There are no special classes for them, and since the number of children in these age groups is scarce, they have a limited number of friends, either native or foreign. It is not possible to properly evaluate their previous education and thus not possible to put them into classes coinciding with their level of knowledge. They usually do not feel at ease in classes for younger age groups. Consequently, they lose two or three academic years, a loss that the migrant workers, toiling under difficult conditions, cannot afford.

Problems Related to Re-Integration

A. It is, of course, not a prophecy to see that, sooner or later, upon their return to their homeland, migrant workers children are due to face another period of hardship—A period of reintegration. [17]

Many children return to their native countries just when they

---

[17] The intention of a great majority of the Turkish workers is to stay for only a few years in the receiving country. A survey carried out in Federal Germany, indicates that the national contingent with the lowest percentage desirous to stay permanently abroad are the Turks with 9%. The same survey reveals that from the Turkish workers in W.Germany, 20% stay less than two years, 37% of them between two and four years, 39% from four to seven years and only 4% stay abroad for more than seven years. Bundesanstalt für Arbeit, *Repräsentativuntersuchung'72*, Beschäftigung ausländischer Arbeitnehmer, Nürnberg 1973, pp. 34, 37.

have adjusted themselves to the social and cultural life of a foreign country causing innumerable difficulties, sometimes even grave psychological disturbances.

In many cases, another foreign country becomes a mid-stop, for some years, on the way home.

All this endangers a child in the same way a very delicate plant would be endangered by constant up-rooting, re-rooting and re-planting in entirely different soils.

Because everyone is aware of this fact, some measures are taken to facilitate the reintegration of the children while they are still in the host countries. [18] Otherwise, it would not be possible to protect these children from the harsh outcome of a second cultural shock.

However, since the effectiveness of these protective measures that are exercised by different countries has not yet been scientifically evaluated, it will, of course, not be possible to improve and develop these measures to get the best possible results.

B. From the measures taken to ease the reintegration burdens, arises still another category of problems for the children involved.

— The first reason for lack of adaptation on returning to the homeland will be the child's having almost forgotten the native language.

This inadequate knowledge of the native language is very likely to occur especially amongst those who have immigrated with their parents before they were school-age and have returned to the homeland within the school-age.

— The second reason for maladjustment is caused by the situation in which the child has become alien, or just aloof, to his inheritance of national culture and values.

— There is also the danger of the child's having completely abandoned his national values and replaced them with those of the immigration country.

— Still another inevitable cause for adaptation difficulties is the differences between the educational systems of the native and host countries.

---

[18] "A better way of solving the problem of reintegration in the home countries is the provision of special courses in the immigration countries, so that children whose parents intend to return home can learn to read and write in their own language and can be instructed in the history, geography and literate of their home countries." S. Castles and G.Kosack, *Immigrant Workers and Class Structure*, Oxford University Press, London 1973, p. 228.

The child on his return, will realize at once that the education of children of the same age is quite different than his own insofar as its substance and even level are concerned.

— Manners of dressing up, alien behavioural habits, a particular language accent that the child has brought with him from the immigration country, all give rise to his being regarded as a stranger by fellow school-mates.

These may seem to be trivial, but their effects are to the contrary.

Undoubtedly, every country anticipating these experiences of reintegration will seek remedies. But reintegration measures may be an additional burden placed upon the already trembling shoulders of the children of migrant workers. There is always the danger of this load becoming unbearable. [19]

C. The measures most liable to help reintegration are those that provide the child with a continuity of interest in his mother tongue and culture.

Since the family's contribution in this respect is very limited, taking the necessary measures and implementing them is more or less a job or responsibility assumed by the private, voluntary organizations established by the colonies of the respective emigration country.

I have stated before that Turkey lacks these kinds of supporting organizations, at least in any appreciable numbers; therefore, the main responsibility rests with the Turkish government, and Turkey, like some other countries in the same situation, has assigned elementary school teachers to the regions of some West European countries that are highly crowded with Turkish

---

[19] "We cannot overlook the fact that when dealing with the integration of migrant worker's children, we put on their shoulders an additional burden by requiring them to preserve their contact with their native language and national culture by attending courses designed for this purpose beside their regular school duties in a foreign country.

This may even be considered as applying the brakes when these children desire to go at full speed towards integration. This requirement, though unavoidable, as appreciated fully by the Council of Europe ("... conscious of the necessity of ensuring, in their own interests, that the children of migrant workers do not loose their cultural and linguistic heritage and that they benefit from the culture of the receiving country", *Committee of Ministers*, Resolution 70. 35), may be considered a cause of delay in getting fast results for the educational integration of these children. S. Bilmen, *Education of Migrant Workers Children*, Organization of Experimental special classes and school career and Health Record for the children of Migrant Workers, Council of Europe RS 201 (1971), Strassbourg.

migrant workers for the purpose of maintaining cultural ties.

These teachers instruct Turkish children, in groups, in supplementary classes secured in elementary schools for about four hours each week, in lessons such as Turkish, Turkish history, geography, civics and religion. These teachers have been trained in Turkey before undertaking this assignment and follow a curriculum especially designed for each subject.

They are all, naturally, responsible for periodically giving detailed accounts of their activities and the results obtained to the authorities concerned.

E. Some of the problems that Turkish migrant workers' children are confronted with concerning reintegration measures are the following:

1. These supplementary classes are not arranged to satisfy the needs of the children, who have not yet reached compulsory school age, nor for those, who already attend secondary schools, but only for children who are of primary school age and make up the majority.

Consequently, quite a number of children are denied this assistance.

2. These supplementary classes are far from providing the essential aid since there is an insufficient number of them especially in West Germany and Belgium, compared to the number of children.

Therefore, even those children at the proper age, who are theoretically within the scope of these classes cannot benefit from them totally.

3. It is quite a problem for children, who live in places far from the schools in which the supplementary classes are in existence to attend them once or twice a week or for the teachers to visit small groups of children and instruct them on the spot.

4. But the level of attendance is not totally satisfactory even amongst the children, who can more easily benefit from these classes, for some parents, in order to avoid (what they believe to be) the unnecessary fatigue of their children, will not send them. Parents reason that on returning to the homeland their children will learn the language easily anyhow. However, the purpose of these courses is not merely to teach the language, but to strengthen the bonds with the national culture.

5. It is not always possible to make satisfactory arrangements

concerning the timetables of regular and supplementary classes. But since getting positive results from the latter is dependent upon regular attendance at a time when the children are alert, the evening hours, and the later hours of the days and weekends are not advisable times for scheduling classes since all have tiring effects on both the children and the parents who accompany them.

6. These classes should be arranged so that they appeal not merely to the children but to the parents also, thereby helping the parents to tolerate and assume the difficulties arising from accompanying their children. Indeed, many fathers don't mind buying a costly toy for their children if they, too, can enjoy it during the absence of the real owner.

Some of the things that might be done to make these classes attractive and engaging may be the following:

> a. There should be special rooms, close to the classrooms, for parents bringing their children in which they may read or have a chat with each other. These rooms should contain books, newspapers, magazines from the homeland, and, if possible, tea or coffee should also be served. Thus a friendly, comfortable atmosphere may be created.
>
> b. The teachers should reserve at least an hour of their time for discussions with the parents, either privately or in groups.
>
> c. Attendance at these classes should be properly evaluated upon the child's return. The child should regain at least a year of the time that was lost in the course of his absence.
>
> d. There should be frequent presentations in these classes of films related to the motherland. The children should be given gifts such as books, photographs, etc., and the arrangement of leisure-time activities should take into consideration the purpose of these classes.

The operational cost of these supplementary classes should be equally divided between emigration and immigration countries. This is a matter which concerns not only Turkey, but many other countries as well, for these children may have the honor and responsibility of forming the nucleus of tomorrows united Europe.

SEGREGATION IN THE NETHERLANDS AND TURKISH MIGRATION

An explorative study on segregation of Turkish migrants in Rotterdam and Utrecht. [1]

GER MIK AND NIA VERKOREN-HEMELAAR

1. *Introduction*

With the arrival of large numbers of foreigners in the Netherlands during the past decade, problems of residential segregation seem to have entered this country.

The coming of temporarily attracted, so-called foreign workers from the countries around the Mediterranean, has led to concentrations of Mediterranean people in certain areas in Dutch towns. Because of the recency of this phenomenon, this residential segregation was hardly subject of research in the Netherlands, so there is every reason to go into some aspects of this problem. This study will be carried out with reference to Turkish migrants, the largest group of Mediterranean migrants in the Netherlands. Because of its explorative character the study will perhaps leave a lot of questions unanswered, but, as we hope, this will only stimulate further research in this matter. This article will give some insight in segregation in the Dutch context. The problem will be approached from two sides: part of this article is based on a selective study of literature, which is supplemented and illustrated with a comparative analysis of statistical data from Rotterdam and Utrecht. Both cities contain a rather large concentration of Mediterranean migrants and Turkish people;[2] the statistical data used are aggregated on town-district level.[3]

---

[1] In both towns research is done by the authors into segregation problems and the housing situation of foreign workers. As far as segregation is concerned up till now one study is published. This article relies as far as Rotterdam is concerned on data from this publication: P. Drewe, G. A. van der Knaap, G. Mik and H. Rodgers, Segregatie in Rotterdam, een vooronderzoek naar theorie, gegevens en beleid, Rotterdam, 1972.

[2] Henceforward, the juxtaposition of Mediterranean and Turkish migrants makes no distinction between those groups; Turkish migrants are only emphasized as a sub-group.

[3] A town-district is an administrative geographical region, which is normally used as the smallest spatial entity for the aggregation of statistical data (e.g. censusdata).

Map 1

The approximation by way of district data has the implicate danger of "ecological fallacy". This concept indicates that although in a district two phenomena both appear and a statistical relation between them is proved, this does not mean that both phenomena are in reality correlated in a direct causal relation. The validity of the statistical correlation can only be checked by way of exploration on the spot.

After a short look at the backgrounds of the international migration to the Netherlands, the phenomenon of segregation will be analysed more in detail; first the conceptual meaning of segregation is considered, as well as the present situation of segregation in both towns, secondly, some possible causes and consequences will be suggested.

2. The international labour migration to the Netherlands

The causes of the phenomenon of international labour migration are to be found in the polarity between the highly developed, industrialized countries of Western Europe and the countries around the Mediterranean, where the process of modernization and industrialization is still in development. They form a labour pool out of which the industrial countries can draw. After the second World War the Dutch government policy was aimed at coping with a rapid population increase by way of intensive industrialization, which had to create sufficient labour places to accomplish full employment. The decrease of employment in the agricultural sector made industrialization more necessary.[4] This policy led to an increase of export and was stimulated by an artificial low wage and price level.[5] As a consequence of this industrialization process, the Dutch labour market could no longer satisfy the continuous increasing labour demand by the prosperous developing national economy. From the middle of the fifties the situation turned out into labour shortage. In the Mediterranean countries an opposite situation exists; growth of employment doesn't keep pace with the growth of population

---

[4] Ministeries van Sociale Zaken and Volksgezondheid, Justitie, Financiën and Cultuur, Recreatie en Maatschappelijk werk, Nota Buitenlandse Werknemers, Session 1969-1970, nr. 10504, January 14th, 's Gravenhage, 1970.

[5] T, van der Grinten and H. Werker, Gastarbeiders 1970, Katernen 2000, 1970 no. 9, p. 6.

and manpower. Disguised and open unemployment go hand in hand with low incomes.

Therefore it is not astonishing that the migration of labour to Western Europe is mainly based on economic motives. A national survey showed that 50% of the Italians, Spaniards and Turks came to the Netherlands to earn (more) money; 29% gave as a reason saving money, while 13% mentioned unemployment in their own country as a motive.[6] These results are confirmed by the Turkish Neyzi-report, the Italian Vigorelli-report and the Greek Mitsos-report. In these reports economic motives for labour migration run as high as resp. 67%, 89% and 62.5%.[7] Although in 1949 Italians had been introduced into the Dutch labour market to fill up vacancies in mining, the great boom in immigration came during the sixties with only a slight decline in 1967 as reaction on the economic recession. In the meantime the Dutch government started to conclude agreements on recrutement with the emigration countries; the agreement with Turkey in 1964 resulted in a sharp increase of Turkish workers in the Netherlands[8].[9] At first most migrants came spontaneously but as a consequence of governmental action on this field in 1968, this kind of immigration was soon surpassed by official recrutement which only takes place with the permission and under the control of the governmental bureau of employment service.

In 1973 Dutch population counted 282,400 foreigners, of which nearly 150,000 from the Mediterranean countries. Of these almost one third comes from Turkey.[9]

Although the absolute number of foreign workers represents

---

[6] N.V. v/h Nederlandse Stichting voor Statistiek, De buitenlandse arbeider in Nederland; 's Gravenhage, 1971, pp. 137.
This national survey was carried out in 1968-1969, by way of interviewing a representative sample of 1003 foreign workers in the Netherlands. The results, which deal with all kind of aspects of the living and working situation of foreign workers, are published in two reports.

[7] T. van der Grinten en H. Werker, p. 16.

[8] In 1963 610 Turkish workers were registered, in 1965 7290. Figures from: Stichting Maatschappij en Onderneming, 'Gastarbeid in Nederland', 's Gravenhage, 1972, p. 78.

[9] Exact figures are: 3989 migrants (men and women, all ages) from Greece, 27901 from Morocco, 6952 from Portugal, 31362 from Spain, 732 from Tunesia, 46028 from Turkey, 1618 from Yugoslavia and 29269 Italians. See: Appendix VII of the 'Memorie van Toelichting van het Ministerie van Justitie', Vreemdelingenbestand; landelijk overzicht, 1974. To this total must be added an estimated number of 10,000 to 15,000 illegal migrants.

only a small share of the Dutch labour force, the migratory flow contributes about a quarter of the growth of the labour force since about 1965. [10] Though originally the attraction of foreign workers was seen as a short-term solution for the absolute shortage of labour, it appeared that this shortage was largely structural, for this labour shortage is caused by structural changes on the labour market, where the demand of unskilled labour is not fully matched by unskilled supply.

The industrial sector cannot as yet keep up with the rising educational level of the labour force. The labour market divides itself in several sub-markets of which the sub-market of unskilled labour, that often implicates unattractive and low-status jobs, shows great shortages. In the period 1960-1973 the demand for low or unskilled labour decreased with 118,000 man-years, while the total supply of low-skilled labour decreased with 183,000 man-years. [11] This gap is filled by foreign workers, who for the greater part are un- or low-skilled. The above mentioned survey showed that 63% of the Italian, Spanish and Turkish workers are unskilled. [12] The general low level of education, together with unfamiliarity with the labour market situation and inadequate verbal expression in the Dutch language tend to concentrate foreign workers in jobs, which are more and more left by the national workers in the process of vertical mobility.

The entrance of foreign workers on the Dutch labour market and in Dutch society brought with it many consequences of which segregation is one of the most striking.

3. Some concepts

Especially Anglo-Saxon literature has dealt with the problem of segregation of immigrant groups and other minorities. When making use of these experiences one has to keep in mind that there is a substantial difference in the character of the migrant groups

---

[10] Expressed in man-years. This estimated percentage is based on figures for the Netherlands in: Commissie van de Europese Gemeenschappen, 'Het vrij verkeer van werknemers en de arbeidsmarkt binnen de EEG–1970', Brussel, 1970, Appendix III, Statistics, p. 13.

[11] Centraal Plan Bureau, De Nederlandse economie in 1973, 's Gravenhage, 1970, p. 199. These figures are partly estimated.

[12] N.V. v/h Nederlandse Stichting voor Statistiek, p. 152.

who were in the Anglo-Saxon countries subject of segregation [13] and the Turkish migrants in the Netherlands. The Anglo-Saxon countries attracted mostly permanent migrants, while Turkish migration to the Netherlands has a temporary character. Whether this difference has specific consequences for the process and nature of segregation will be illustrated in the following analysis. Nevertheless the experiences elsewhere can offer us a good starting point for the analysis in the Netherlands. Considering the question what is understood by the concept of segregation, the following factors are of importance.

— Segregation is manifested in geographical space by the grouping of persons in certain areas of (urban) communities. In general the areas around the city centre appear to serve as a reception place for immigrant groups.

— The concept of segregation is applied to people, though concentration of enterprises and other activities is sometimes indicated as segregation

— In American literature, the concept is mostly limited to the concentration of racial minorities. However, we handle it in a broader context, viz. in all cases in which the grouping of people with common characteristics on a certain place is concerned. These characteristics can be racial, social-economic, cultural or a combination of these

— Segregation is not the description of a static situation but of a process, a continuous development going on until a, possibly provisional, static situation is reached. Especially the phases of infiltration, invasion and succession (first described in the twenties) [14], are often mentioned in this context.

In the process of segregation, described as the penetration of a population group in the residential area of another group, the phase of infiltration is characterized by a slow penetration, in which only a limited number of people of the incoming group

---

[13]   A.o. the European immigrants who went to the United States, the Commonwealth migrants to the United Kingdom and the internal migration of American negroes.
See a.o. R. J. Johnston, Urban residential patterns, an introductory review, London, 1971, K. and A. Taueber, Negroes in Cities, Chicago, 1965 and D. Ward, "The emergence of central immigrant ghettoes in American cities: 1840-1920" in L. S. Bourne (ed.) Internal structure of the city, readings on space and environment, New York, 1971, pp. 291—299.

[14]   See a.o. R. E. Park a.o. (eds.), The City, Chicago, 1925, especially: E. W. Burgess, "The Growth of the City".

settles down between the original inhabitants. This stage is followed by a fast moving in by the new population group (invasion), that goes on until the newcomers have replaced the original inhabitants (succession). Sometimes consolidation may occur in one of the stages of the proces as a whole, that may continue for a long time. If more than half of the population of the neighbourhood consists of newcomers with characteristics deviating from the original population group, a ghetto has developed.

Two concepts need to be mentioned here in the context of segregation: the self-fulfilling prophecy and the tipping point. The first phenomenon, which certainly plays a part in the American situation [15], occurs when people believe that a certain thing will take place, while that same belief causes these people to act in such a way that the expected result is made true. Applied to segregation, the process of self-fulfilling prophecy causes the original inhabitants to move out during and after the infiltration period, because of the belief that in the long run the incoming minority will occupy the whole neighbourhood with the effect of, for example, a lowering of the social status of the area. The minority occupies the places that become vacant (invasion), until eventually the phase of succession is reached: the belief in a high concentration of the minority in the neighbourhood has created this concentration. The tipping point indicates in this context the point in the infiltration- invasion- succession process, at which the original inhabitants start moving out of the neighbourhood on their own free will, or that newcomers of the same population group refuse to settle down in the neighbourhood. [16]

4. Segregation in Rotterdam and Utrecht

The entrance of temporarily attracted foreign workers from the Mediterranean countries in Dutch enterprises did not remain without consequences for the residential structure of especially

---

[15] See for example: R. L. Morrill, "The negro ghetto: problems and alternatives", *The Geographical Review*, vol. 55, 1965, pp. 339—361 and R. E. Forman, Black ghettos, white ghettos and slums, Englewood Cliffs, 1971.

[16] H. M. Rose: "The development of an urban subsystem: the case of the negro ghetto", *Annals of the Association of American Geographers*, Vol. 60, March 1970, no. 1, pp. 1—17.
See for some possible causes of "tipping": T. C. Schelling, "Dynamic models of segregation", *Journal of Mathematical Sociology*, 1971, Vol. 1, pp. 143—186.

the large cities in the three western provinces of the Netherlands: Noord-Holland, Zuid-Holland and Utrecht. These three provinces, out of the total of eleven, cover 20.8% of the territory of the Netherlands, are inhabited by 46.1% of its 13,3 million inhabitants,[17] while 51.2% of its labour volume is concentrated there.[18] Foreign workers tend to follow this concentration: 56% of the total number of mediterraneans is living in these three provinces.[19] Within this western part of the country immigration of foreign workers is directed especially to the agglomerations of Amsterdam, Rotterdam, The Hague and the city of Utrecht as important centers of economic activity. Rotterdam and Utrecht, both cities in the coherent circular town belt, the so-called "Randstad Holland", differ greatly in size, function and spatial structure (see map 1). Economic activities in Rotterdam have a strong international orientation, deriving from its position as the world's largest seaport, with all its industrial and commercial side-activities, while the central situation of Utrecht makes this city an important national and regional centre of trade and transport and industrial fairs. Another difference can be found in the spatial structure. Rotterdam lost its original inner city, dating from before 1870, in the second world war. Rebuilding after 1945 neglected the original parcel boundaries. As a result the inner city has a lower building density, a more rectilinear character, less residential population and a more luxury house-stock than before the war. In Utrecht the medieval inner city is still largely intact. Although parts of it are renovated and transformed in a mordern Central-Business District, it could maintain partly its original residential function, though this shifted partly to special groups as students, elderly and single people.[20]

Rotterdam   counts   670,060   inhabitants[21]   and   Utrecht

---

[17]   Centraal Bureau voor de Statistiek, Regional pocket year book 1972, 's Gravenhage, 1973, pp. 3–5.

[18]   J. A. v. Ginkel and H. F. L. Ottens: Wonen en Werken in en om het groene hart, een beschrijvende atlas, Geografisch Instituut Rijksuniversiteit Utrecht, 1973, p. 57.

[19]   Stichting Maatschappij en Onderneming, Gastarbeid in Nederland, 's Gravenhage 1972, p. 31. (in this case exclusive family members).

[20]   J. den Draak: De woonfunktie van de Utrechtse binnenstad (with summary: the residential function of the inner city of Utrecht, the Netherlands), Tijdschrift voor Economische en Sociale Geografie, 1966, no. 5, pp. 179–185.

[21]   Per 1 January 1972. For both Rotterdam and Utrecht is meant the number of inhabitants of the municipalities. The statistical data of Rotterdam used in this article come from the "Gemeentelijk Bureau voor de Statistiek" and the "Dienst Stadsontwikkeling" in Rotterdam.

269,591,[22] In Rotterdam 4% of the population is of foreign origin, in Utrecht 3.8%[23] (all nationalities). Both percentages are relativeley high in the national context. The majority of foreigners in both cities are migrant workers from the mediterranean countries, respectively 2.9% and 3.0% of the total residential population in Rotterdam and Utrecht (inclusive family members). The composition of the Mediterranean population group may be seen in the next table.

Mediterraneans by nationality in Rotterdam and Utrecht,
resp. per 1-1-1972 and 1-4-1973

	Rotterdam		Utrecht	
	absolute	percentage	absolute	percentage
Spaniards	5,736	29.7	1,256	15.6
Turks	4,964	25.7	1,761	21.9
Yugoslavs	3,319	17.2	199	2.5
Portuguese	2,042	10.6	25	0.3
Moroccans	1,671	8.7	3,139	39.0
Italians	1,164	6.0	543	6.7
Greeks	411	2.1	1,100	13.7
Tunisians	—	—	18	0.2
Algerians	—	—	1	—
Other North-Africans	—	—	9	0.1
Total	19,307	100.0	8,051	100.0

In Rotterdam the Spaniards form the largest group, in Utrecht the Morrocans, in both towns followed by the Turkish migrants constituting respectively 25.7% and 21.8% of the total number of Mediterranean people. But Turkish people have a low share in the total city population. In both cities 0.7% is of Turkish origin. Although the absolute size of the group Mediterranean and Turkish migrants is not very impressive, their presence determines the residential structure more than these figures might indicate.

To examine if, and to what extent residential segregation as a

---

[22]   Per 1 January 1973. The statistical data of Utrecht come from the municipal "Bureau voor Statistiek" and the bureau of "Sociaal-Economisch en Sociografisch Onderzoek" in Utrecht.

[23]   With "foreigners" or "foreign workers" is meant the whole foreign population group including family members, unless indicated otherwise.

phenomenon can be found in the residential pattern of Mediterranean and Turkish migrants, we analyse the distribution of both
groups over the different districts in both towns. [24] From this
broad pattern can be deducted if these people cluster together in
some districts, and if so, in what kind of districts. Because of lack
of sufficient adequate data we must confine the analysis to one
point in time, so that only the presence of the phenomenon of
segregation can be determined, not the process. An equal distribution of Mediterraneans among the several districts in each city
would give the same percentage in the district population as in
the total population. Distribution figures show that in both cities
both groups are overrepresented in some districts, underrepresen-
ted in others (i.e. positive or negative deviation from the average
percentage of 2,9 in Rotterdam and 3 in Utrecht). In 21 out of
75 districts in Rotterdam, and 28 out of 76 districts in Utrecht,
Mediterraneans are relatively overrepresented. In 14 Rotterdam
districts more than 5% of the population is Mediterranean, making up 63.9% of all Mediterraneans in that city. In Utrecht these
figures are 23 districts containing 69.8% of all Mediterraneans.
This concentration pattern is strengthened by the fact that in
6 Rotterdam districts and 8 Utrecht districts more than 9% of
the population comes from the Mediterranean Basin. The Turkish
people show in 19 Rotterdam and 21 Utrecht districts an above
average percentage (more than 0.7%), while they constitute in
7 districts of both cities more than 2% of the district population,
amounting to 46.3% in Rotterdam and 46.5% in Utrecht of the
total number of Turks. To check this pattern also the absolute
figures are considered, e.g. the internal spatial distribution of the
Turkish population group. The overall impression remains the
same: Turkish people are scattered over 48 districts in Rotterdam
and 52 in Utrecht, while about half of them are found in 6 Rotterdam and 7 Utrecht districts.

Maps 2-7 [25] show that this unequal distribution is characterized by the presence of clusters. Both Mediterranean and Turkish
people tend to concentrate in the districts around the city-centre.
The Turks even concentrate in a certain, more or less coherent
part of this belt: In Rotterdam in 2 groups of districts around the

---

[24]   Data for Rotterdam per 1-1-1972, for Utrecht per 1-4-1973.
[25]   The maps of Rotterdam are exclusive Hoek van Holland (district 00), which is
separately located westward along the North Sea, and district 99.

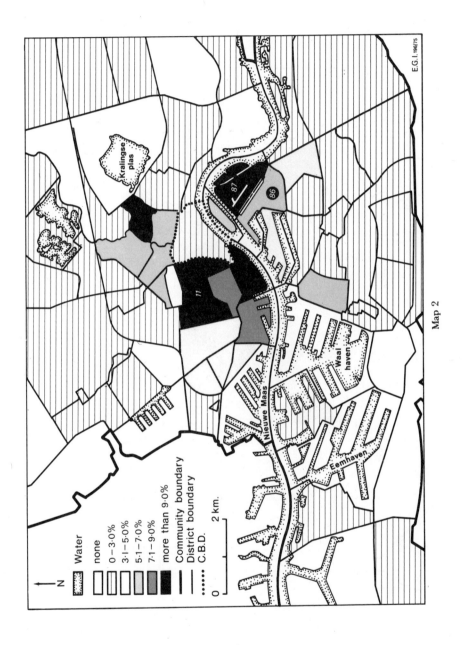

Map 2

Water

0–3·0%

3·1–5·0%

5·1–7·0%

7·1–9·0%

more than 9·0%

Community boundary

District boundary

C.B.D.

0   2 km.

Kralingse plas

Nieuwe Maas

Waal haven

Eemhaven

E.G.I. 196/75

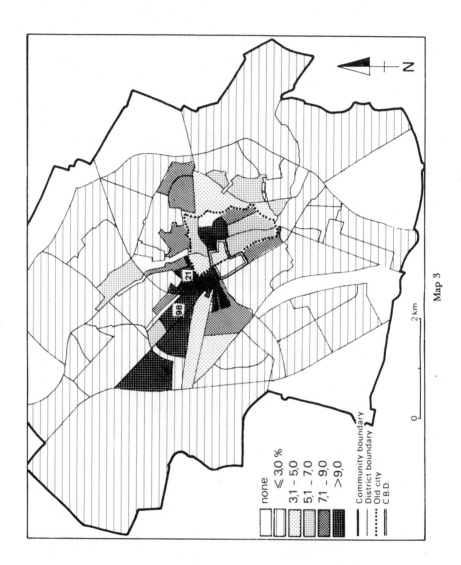

Map 3

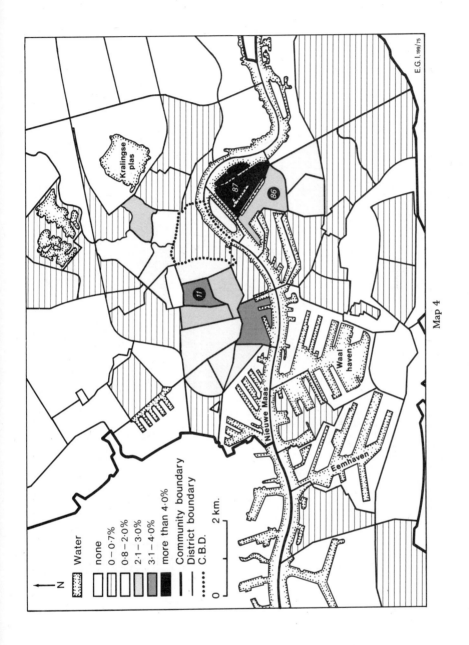

Map 4

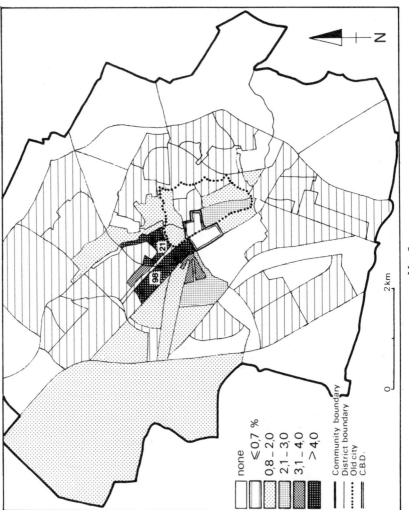

Map 5

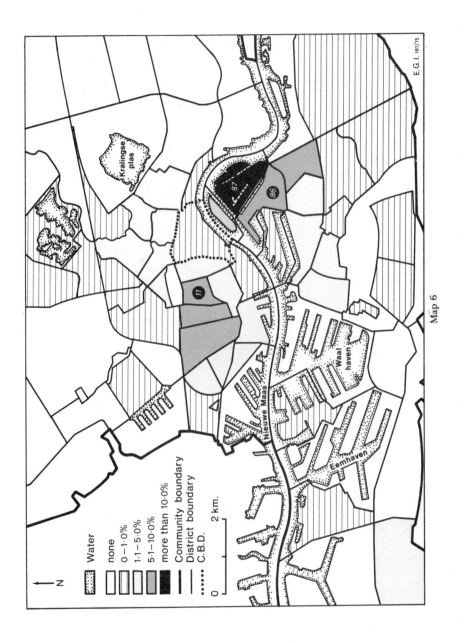

Map 6

Water

none
0 – 1·0%
1·1 – 5·0%
5·1 – 10·0%
more than 10·0%

Community boundary
District boundary
C.B.D.

0   2 km.

N

Kralingse plas

87

86

11

Nieuwe Maas

Waal haven

Eemhaven

E.G.I. 197/75

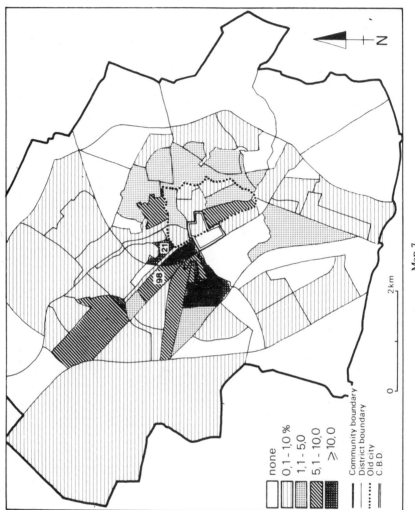

0,1 - 1,0 %
1,1 - 5,0
5,1 - 10,0
≥ 10,0

Community boundary
District boundary
Old city
C.B.D

Map 7

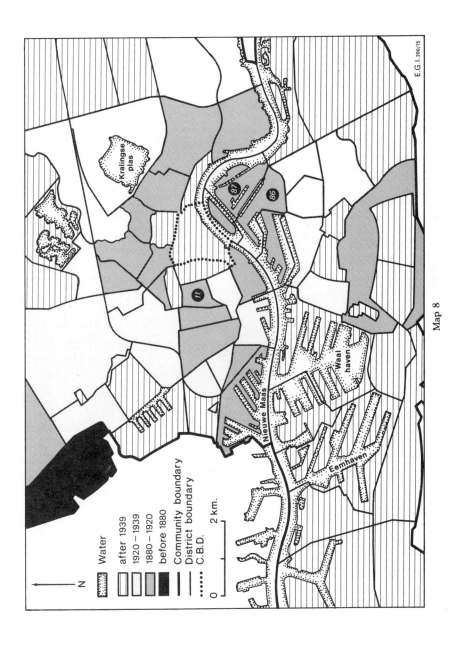

Map 8

Water
after 1939
1920 – 1939
1880 – 1920
before 1880
Community boundary
District boundary
C.B.D.

N

0   2 km.

E.G.I. 200/75

Kralingse plas

Nieuwe Maas

Waal haven

Eemhaven

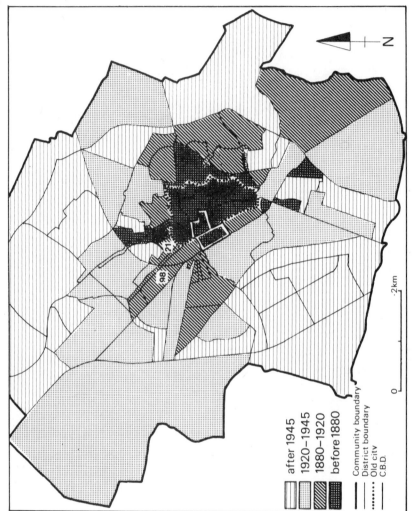

after 1945
1920–1945
1880–1920
before 1880

Community boundary
District boundary
Old city
C.B.D.

.2km

0

Map 9

town centre, in Utrecht in one group of districts north-west of the inner city.

The district in Rotterdam with both a high absolute and relative share of Turkish migrants is Feijenoord (district 87), located on the southern edge of the river "Nieuwe Maas" directly south of the city centre. The 516 Turks living in this district make up 5.7% of the total district population. Feijenoord is followed by Oude Westen (district 11), where 416 Turkish people form 3.5% of the total district population. It is striking that the Afrikaanderwijk (district 86), where riots arose between the Turkish and Dutch population in August 1972, has a relatively small share of Turks in its population, that is 2.5%, covering 345 Turkish people.

Also the number of Mediterraneans is not impressive: 903 or 6.5% of the district population. We will return to this subject later on in the article.

In Utrecht one finds the highest relative and absolute concentration of Turks in 2 adjoining districts north-west of the centre, 2e Daalsedijk (98) and Boorstraat-Kerkweg (21). In district 2e Daalsedijk Turks form 6.8% of the population. In district Boorstraat-Kerkweg the highest absolute number of Turkish people is found: 260.

Maps 8-9 offer some insight in the type of district in which Mediterraneans and Turks tend to cluster. As may be seen on these maps, most "concentration" districts of both groups are situated in the zone of older districts adjoining the town centre. These districts date from the period around 1900, when the industrial development in the Netherlands led to an extensive influx of people from the countryside to the towns as industrial centres. Around the turn of the century new quarters were built around the old town centre, to accomodate these migrants. Now the same quarters are in a transitional phase in which the original inhabitants who move out are replaced by other people such as labour migrants.

In Utrecht several districts within the original old town (within the moats) also contain a concentration of Mediterraneans and Turks, while in Rotterdam these districts from before 1880 are practically all substituted by modern buildings.

The distinction between old districts (from before 1920) and new ones (after the second world war) as residential quarters for Mediterranean migrants is striking.

This picture is sharpened when we consider the spatial distribution of non-Mediterranean foreigners in both towns. This group, mostly western nationalities, comprises 7.213 persons, or 1.1% of the total city population in Rotterdam and 2.248 or 0.8% of the total population in Utrecht. First of all these foreigners seem less to cluster together in certain districts, and, secondly, are relatively more found in the newer quarters of the cities. In Rotterdam 23.6% of this foreign group lives in "new" districts, in Utrecht 24.1%.

We may conclude that there is indeed a certain segregation of the migrants from the Mediterraneans in the old districts around the city centre. The Turkish migrants appear to concentrate within a smaller part of this belt, which would lead us to suppose that within the Mediterranean group different nationalities seem to keep together. The quantitative indications for this situation, both for the Mediterraneans and Turks, are strikingly similar for both towns, despite the large differences in size, spatial and functional structure between Rotterdam and Utrecht. This would justify the conclusion that there are general causes and circumstances which bring about segregation that are not completely dependent on the local situation. In the next part more light will be thrown on the subject.

5. The possible causes and consequences of segregation in Rotterdam and Utrecht

Before going deeper into the backgrounds of the ascertained segregation, first of all we must remark that there are few adequate research data on the local level available to support the following hypotheses and possible explanations. Often we have to illustrate our statements with national figures that at least can give some insight into the situation in Rotterdam and Utrecht, or secondary statistical data have to be brought forward. Following considerations have to be seen in this light. They give more a general impression of the direction in which causes and consequences of segregation have to be searched for than a complete explanation. Besides, other factors than the under-mentioned can play their part in segregation, that cannot be derived from the available data. Furthermore, it has to be emphasized that the causes dealt with do not operate separately, but in combination.

That is why they have to be checked and completed by more penetrating research. [26] Finally we will give a short look at some consequences of segregation.

5.1. *Possible causes*

5.1.1. *The temporality of presence*

As was indicated in the Introduction, one of the most important differences between earlier trans-oceanic migrations with the present international labour migration from the Mediterranean to Western-Europe, is the temporary aspect of the stay. A short duration of stay can have as a consequence the wish of the foreign workers to maintain their cultural identity which may result in a grouping together, a voluntary clustering. Although most foreign workers have the intention to return to their home country after a few years, a growing part of them stays for a longer period or even permanently. While 32% of the Italians who entered the Netherlands in 1961, 26% of the Spaniards and 31% of the Greek, Yugoslavs and Portuguese migrant group were still present in 1965, the percentages rose to resp. 41%, 39% and 39.6% for migrants of these nationalities who came in 1965 and were still present in 1969. For the Turkish migrants this percentage in 1969 was 48%. [27] From the above mentioned national survey it appeared that 25% of the foreign workers tend to stay in the Netherlands for such a long time that they may be considered as potential immigrants.

An important explaining factor for the trend to permanent settlement can be family reunion in the host country, in this sense that family reunion eliminates a strong motive to return to the home country. At the time of the national survey, 5.5% of the married Turkish workers was accompanied by their wive. A comparable figure is 26.9% in 1972 in Rotterdam. An indication for a further increase in family reunion, and probably longer stay can be found in Western-Germany. In the Netherlands and Western-Germany comparable percentages of foreign workers are

---

[26] An extensive explorative and explanative research is in preparation for Rotterdam.

[27] Stafbureau van de Statistiek van het Ministerie van Cultuur, Recreatie en Maatschappelijk Werk; Enkele gegevens betreffende de buitenlandse en binnenlandse migratie, Statistisch Cahier, nr. 11, 1970, p. 19. Figures for Turkish migrants are only available for the last period.

married, (resp. 71% and 73% in 1968), but in Western-Germany they come more often with their family or family reunion made more progress. 34% of the married Turkish workers in W.-Germany in 1968 lived there with his wife (Netherlands: 5.5%). Also the average duration of the presence in W.-Germany is longer: about one-third can be considered as long-staying (Netherlands: 25%). [28] Though the individual duration of stay increases, yet the greatest part of the Mediterranean workers are only for a limited number of years in the Netherlands, which can be the first cause for segregation. As is suggested by various authors, the temporarily attracted foreign workers will only partially go through the process of integration and assimilation. [29]

They are not primarily motivated to social and cultural adaptation but more to an instrumental modus vivendi, which leaves their identity undisturbed, but makes a functional participation quite well possible. [30]

Gordon indicates that integration and assimilation require a long time. The first generation of immigrants integrates only to a certain degree, while assimilation does not start at all until the second generation. [31] Although integration asks an effort from both sides, in this case, integration mainly has to come from one side because of the limited size of the foreign group with respect to the receiving population. [32]

To what extent can we expect the Mediterraneans to accomplish this effort when they only stay for a limited period in the Netherlands?

Nevertheless, most migrant labourers want to integrate to a

---

[28]   C. S. van Praag: "Buitenlandse werknemers in West-Duitsland; enkele cijfers, aantallen", *Nieuwsbrief buitenlandse werknemers*, 1970, no. 10, pp. 211—213.

[29]   For the meaning of these concepts we rely on the interpretation which Mrs. H. Verwey-Jonker gives in her introduction to "Allochtonen in Nederland" a publication from 1971. Integration indicates the process of which the final stage is a normal functioning of the foreigner in the receiving society, while the final stage of the process of assimilation means a complete absorbtion of the foreigner in the receiving society. This situation implicates that the foreigner no longer considers himself as a member of the immigrated group, and also is not considered as such by others.

[30]   R. Wentholt, (ed.), "Maatschappelijke achtergronden en factoren", in: *Buitenlandse arbeiders in Nederland*. Een veelzijdige benadering van een complex vraagstuk, Leiden, 1967, pp. 89-90.

[31]   M. Gordon, "Assimilation in American Life", New York, 1964, cited by H. Verwey-Jonker (ed.) in Allochtonen in Nederland, chapter 1.

[32]   J. J. M. van Amersfoort, Surinamers in de lage Landen, 's Gravenhage, 1968, pp. 23—24.

certain degree, as some results from the national survey show: 53% of the interviewed Italians, Spaniards and Turks wanted more contact with Dutch people, 39% thought they had enough contact, and only 3% did not want to make any contact at all. When asked with whom one preferred to associate, the same tendency appeared: 77% of them preferred the Dutch. [33] We can conclude from all this that the final stage of integration and assimilation probably will not be reached by the present Mediterranean and Turkish migrants, though this does not mean that they do not want any integration at all. A partial integration is pursued to make them function as flexible as possible in Dutch society. However, they hold on internal group relations, which is spatially expressed in their residential pattern, by way of some clustering or segregation.

5.1.2. *The location of low-rent housing*

The socio-economic position of migrant labourers determines for a great deal their position and their possibilities on the housing market. First of all the majority of foreign workers is low—or unskilled. [34] Because they are paid according to the same labour conditions as their Dutch colleagues, they belong in general to the group of lowest-paid productive people, which makes them dependent on low rent accommodation. Secondly, in most cases, their presence has strong economic motives [35] and this, together with their relative short stay, makes them want to save as much money as possible in a short time in order to meet the demands of their relatives at home, or to realise their material aspirations after their return.

In most Dutch cities cheap housing is mainly available in the belt of lower-class districts around the city centre, which is a second possible reason for segregation in this transitional zone. Some statistical base for this assumption is available for Rotterdam, but lacking for Utrecht. Out of the 21 districts where Mediterraneans are overrepresented in relation to the town-average, 19 districts have more than half of their houses in the class of less than f 100,— rent per month. Also in 18 out of 19 districts with more than the share average of Turkish people in the district

---

[33] N.V. v/h Nederlandse Stichting voor Statistiek, p. 229.
[34] See p. 257.
[35] id.

population, this cheap accommodation is dominating. This situation contrasts with the general level of housing rents of non-Mediterranean foreigners. In 16 of the 28 districts where they are overrepresented low-rent housing prevails, the other districts all offer
more expensive housing.

5.1.3. *The types of houses in the districts around the centre*

A Another differentiating factor of the houses in the concentration
districts with that in other parts of the town, apart from building
period and level of rent, is the size of the houses. Their rather
large size makes these houses extremely well suited as boarding
houses for collective lodging of the, mostly, single living migrant
labourers. Often these houses are transformed in so-called "pensions" where migrants, who, for instance, are recruited in the
same group, or have the same nationality, are crowding together.
This situation is characteristic for Rotterdam though illustrating
figures are not available. Some of the Utrecht districts consist of
one-storey houses that were set up as small working-men's
homes. It is a striking fact that clusters of Turkish people in
Utrecht are found first in these districts (districts 21 and 98). A
possible explanation is that some of these rather cheap houses are
bought by Turkish migrants in order to accommodate their family or relatives. [36]

5.1.4. *The chain-process*

The information sent home by the labour migrant makes people in the home country decide to follow their friend, relative or
fellow-villager— a mechanism which is called "chain-process".

On arriving in the host country they understandably prefer to
settle near their friends, on the one hand because their acquain-
tancy can be a support, on the other hand because those already
present can provide by themselves or help to provide accommodation for the newcomers. According to the national survey referred to, 62% of the Italians, Spaniards and Turks came here on
advise of relatives and friends or accompanied them to the
Netherlands after a holiday. [37] Moreover, 25% of these foreign

---

[36] One of the conditions for family reunion is that the head of the household
proves that he can provide suitable accommodation for his family.
[37] N.V. v/h Nederlandse Stichting voor Statistiek, p. 142.

workers acquired their accommodation with the help of coun-
try-men or friends. [38]

It is to be expected that those acquaintances find the accommodation in their own area because of the better overview there
and because of the other mentioned causes. The chain process
can provide the fourth factor that stimulates segregation because
it tends to attract people to those residential areas which are
already inhabitated by persons of the same group.

5.1.5. Prejudice

About the way in which prejudice can contribute to segregation even less empirical data are available than in the foregoing.
According to Wentholt prejudices are strongly negative and emotional loaded stereotypes concerning groups of people, by which
one member of the group is automatically judged on the ground
of his membership of that group and the negative characteristics
ascribed to that group. [39] In the foregoing we already stated that
in the infiltration-invasion-succession sequence the phenomenon
of the self-fulfilling prophecy is an important mechanism, while
this process itself may be inspired by prejudice against the
strange incoming group. It proved impossible to ascertain from the
available statistical data the part that prejudice played in the
situation of segregation in both cities. All that can be put forward in this context is, that in Rotterdam the group of Mediterranean foreigners saw its number increase in the old districts
around the centre during the last few years, while at the same
time the outmigration from these districts to other parts of the
city exceeded the outward movement from other districts. However, it is unknown whether this mobility is part of the general
shift to the new outer districts of the city, resulting from vertical
mobility and rising aspirations, or the direct consequence of the
entrance of Mediterranean people. But the existence of prejudices against minority groups of different ethnicity has been proved in a national survey [40] by way of the Bogardus-Scale. [41]

---

[38]   id. p. 173.

[39]   R. Wentholt, "Slotbeschouwing", in: "Buitenlandse arbeiders in Nederland",
pp. 193—196.

[40]   Nederlands Centrum voor Marketing Analyse, Rassenvooroordeel in Nederland,
1968. See also: J. M. Theunis, Gastarbeiders — Lastarbeiders, Hilversum, 1968.

[41]   E. S. Bogardus, "Measuring social distance", Journal Applied Sociology, 1925,
pp. 299—308. The method consists of a list of social relations grouped along a scale
that goes from a form of intensive contact to a form of little intensive contact.

5.2. *Possible consequences*

Up till now little attention has been paid to the consequences of segregation, even in foreign literature. Yet only a thorough analysis of the possible effects of segregation, for the minority as well as for the interrelated functioning of the minority and majority, together with the study of the causes of segregation, can give insight in the appropriate measures that could be taken to cope with the problems originating from segregation.

5.2.1. *Group relations*

Group relations which develop between members of the same nationality, e.g. between Turkish migrants, help to maintain the cultural and social identity of the group, as stated before. For newcomers the group serves as a kind of intermediary between the home and the host country.[42] Although in this way the group can have a positive function as a reliance for its members, especially for those who only stay for a short time, some negative aspects must not be neglected. For instance, frustrations and prejudices with respect to the autochtonous population, are easily transferred to new members of the group.[43] And it is also clear that membership of a coherent minority group might hamper a gradual integration of the individual in the receiving society.

5.2.2 *Prejudice*

Apart from the fact that prejudice can be a possible mechanism in the segregation process, it can also result from segregation. Of the sociological conditions which can lead to the development of prejudice, the existence of a competition situation between the native and the foreign population group, is one of the most important.[44] This principle operates the more when the foreign group is recognizable as such, which may be applicable on the Mediterranean population group, because of its ethnicity, language etc. There are reasons to believe that in Rotterdam and

---

[42] See a.o. J. J. M. v. Amersfoort, De Surinamers in de Lage Landen, 's Gravenhage, 1968, pp. 44–45.

[43] See a.o. J. J. M. v. Amersfoort, *op. cit.*

[44] M. Argyle: Psychology and social problems, London, 1964, pp. 93–94. See also: the research of Schrieke about the attitude against the Chinese in the United States, cited in: T. van der Grinten and H. Werker, Gastarbeiders 1970, Katernen 2000, 1970, p. 11.

Utrecht a competition situation exists on the housing market of low-rent accommodation, between foreign workers and Dutch people in the same socio-economic class. They are both committed to cheap housing. This competition situation becomes acute in the belt of old lower-class districts around the town centre, where this type of housing, which is relatively scarce on the Dutch housing market, is concentrated. Besides, Dutch people with rising wages and/or aspirations leave these districts for better (and more expensive) accommodation in other parts of the city, whereas the residual population sees itself confronted with foreign invaders. Some data concerning the social stratification [45] of the districts as well as population density and quality of the houses, will give an idea about the type of districts in which the competition situation develops. On the continuum of districts from a lower to a higher social status 4 out of the 7 Rotterdam districts with more than 2% Turkish people in the total population belong to the lower end of the scale and 3 to the upper.

The results for the 7 comparable districts in Utrecht are more striking: they all belong to the lower end of the continuum. Moreover these districts belong to the most densely populated areas in the city (see map 10-11), and show the highest concentration of low-quality accommodation. [46] In Rotterdam 14 out of the 19 Rotterdam districts where Turkish migrants are overrepresented, population density exceeds 150 inhabitants per ha., while in 13 districts more than 40% of the dwellings show six or more defects. Concerning the quality of the districts, the Rotterdam situation is approached in Utrecht: in most "concentration" districts the quality of the majority of the houses is called insufficient. [47] It will be clear that these more or less unattractive residential areas are resorts for "low-income" social groups of which labour migrants are only one example. The competition situation that arises between them can lead to severe tension which may find its climax in riots, such as in the Rotterdam Afrikaanderwijk in 1972. When it may seem surprising that such

---

[45] As indices for the social stratification of the districts are used: occupational level per district, educational level of the working population, number of telephone communications, in every district.

[46] The quality of the houses is based on the occurrence of defects. Six defects or more indicates bad housing conditions.

[47] Municipality of Utrecht: De toekomst van het wonen in oude woongebieden in de Gemeente Utrecht, Utrecht, 1972.

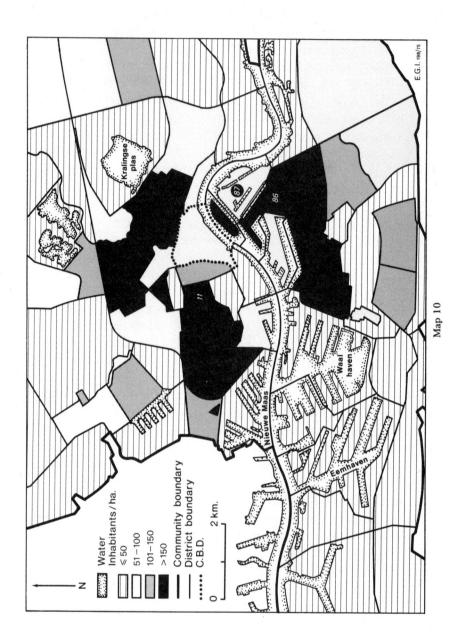

Map 10

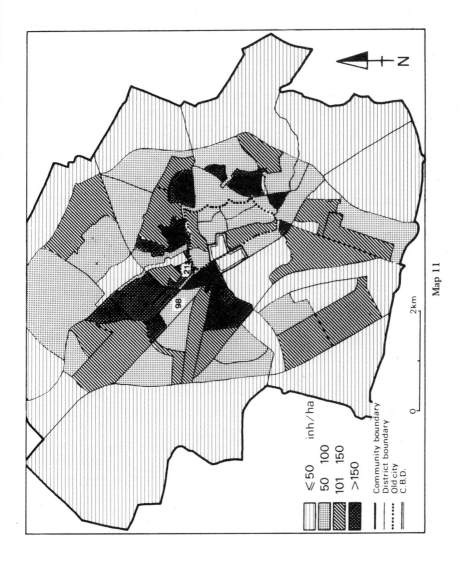

≤50   inh/ha
50   100
101 150
>150

Community boundary
District boundary
Old city
C.B.D.

0   2km

Map 11

an emotional outburst of xenophobia occurred in a district which is not even at the top of the segregation scale (see page 271) one must realise that exactly in those districts, people see the growing foreign influx as a worsening of their not too favourable situation (high density, high percentage of bad housing) and hence resist against further concentration of foreigners. In the sphere of mutual mistrust and competition prejudices are strengthened and sometimes lead to an explosion of feelings of dislike that only worsens the situation for all groups concerned.

6. *Conclusions*

Summarizing we can conclude that:

1) Mediterraneans tend to segregate in the lower class districts which surround the centre of both cities Rotterdam and Utrecht. The Turkish migrants conform to this picture and even show a concentration in a certain part within this belt. Other, mostly western foreigners, are more regularly distributed in both cities.

2) Both cities conform greatly in this situation, despite differences in function and spatial structure. This leads us to suggest that segregation, as a process and as an ascertained situation is not so much dependent on local, as well as on general spatial, economic and socio-psychological conditions.

3) Among these one can discern as possible causes: only partial integration, the location of low-rent housing around the city centre, the rather large size of the housing accommodation, the mechanism of the chain-process, and the operating of prejudice by way of the phenomenon of the self-fulfilling prophecy which plays its part in the infiltration-invasion and succession process.

4) Possible consequences refer to the emerging and strengthening of group relations between foreigners of the same nationality and to prejudices against them as an inevitable consequence of a situation of competition between those people a far from favourable environment and some autochtonous groups which can lead to most undesirable confrontations between the groups involved.

5) Segregation is not merely to be considered as a negative process, also positive aspects can be involved (group relation).

6) Segregation cannot be looked at as a unique development which adheres to the immigration of foreign labourers. The same old lower-class districts which are 'apt' to the segregation of these people, also accommodate Dutch people in the same socio-economic class.

7. *Epilogue*

The picture brought forward shows many gaps, which can only be filled by further detailed research in the matter of segregation. Only then, through a thorough weighing of the positive and negative aspects, responsible action can be taken. Mere indifference or opposal to segregation can create negative situations for all groups involved; the Turkish migrants were one of the first victims.

IMPACT OF TURKISH MIGRATION
ON EUROPEAN ECONOMIC AND SOCIAL STRUCTURES

The basic attitude of the German population toward foreign workers: "We need them, but they should not bother us!"
Karl Bingemer,
Leben als Gastarbeiter

"We should not allow those who stay in the present countries of employment to be treated as second class citizens, but rather as a factor which will help to unify the European community!"
Ivo Baucic, Temporary or permanent, the dilemma of migrants and migration policies

Since the Turkish migration represents only one facet of the large social post-war exodus from Mediterranean countries toward the highly industrialized countries of Central Europe, it seemed appropriate to complete this reader with an overall evaluation of this international phenomenon.

From the economic point of view, the major reason for this one-sided migratory move is the labour shortage and investment readiness of the European industrial nations. Every country with a predominant labour shortage has been able to improve the flexibility of its labour market. Foreign labour has permitted a more rapid adjustment to changes in the field of domestic or foreign trade, and increasing demands has helped to restructure certain sectors of the industry, to minimize price increases, to sustain the vitally important performance of unpopular services. Thus the social product of labour importing countries increased, their conjunctural development became stabilized and their competitive position in the world market improved.

However, a number of these advantages in favour of industrialized countries depend also to some extent upon entrepreneurial reactions. The less the qualifications of the additional acquired labour force, the more will the advantages of a flexible labour market decrease. Or, the longer the average stay of foreign labour and the greater the regional concentration of this labour force, the greater is the additional burden on the infrastructure and the less the advantages due to rotation and regional mobility. Or, the "older" a migratory movement, the more will the consumption and saving behavior of the migrant conform itself to the domestic norms; this means the disappearence of the initial low price levels. Or, the more enlargement investment projects are carried out and the more rationalizing measures are delayed, the more will the stabilizing effects decrease. Nevertheless, there is no doubt that upon comparison of the advantages and disadvantages of labour migration, the receiving countries are clearly in a more advantageous position.

One could certainly raise the question whether in the long run there are no definite negative structural consequences. Under this aspect it is appropriate to discuss the degree of innovation, the kind of production techniques and the international labour division. The facility with which labour importing countries obtained additional manpower until the outbreak of the energy crisis and the resulting weak pressure on wages may have led to insufficient capital-intensive investment, to a prolonged use of out-of-date installation and to a delay in the reorganization of labour intensive branches.

These general observations are confirmed to a great extent by the detailed article of H. Kok, who attempts to make a detailed analysis of labour migration from the point of view of the Netherlands. This comprehensive paper touches upon all the major fields affected by migration, presents an excellent criticism of cost-benefit analysis and governmental initiatives, reflects both the position of employers as well as of trade unions and culminates in trying to outline a developmental policy model which could provoke collective initiatives on the part of workers after their return.

The second paper, by G. E. Völker, presents in an almost parallel way, the balance of the import of foreign labour from the point of view of Federal Germany, without however touching upon the problems of the migrants themselves. Instead, Völker investigates the alternative of exporting capital to sending countries. He defends the point of view that the creation of low wage centres outside of Germany would be advantageous to all parties —a rather questionable assertion.

The third paper, by E. de Haan, representing the major charitable organization dealing with Turkish workers in the FRG namely "Arbeitwohlfahrt", helps the readers to grasp better the reluctance of various social groups and organizations to enlarge the field of activities related to foreign migrants, due to the almost endless chores, which ideally should be performed in order to create a harmonious, unexploited, yet heterogenous society.

The last paper, by G. Schiller, tries to disengage the mutual perspectives of migration. After dismissing the cost-benefit analysis method on the ground that a capitalist economy is not run at costs and benefits for a population, because it is an institutional arrangement to maximise production and consumption for the purpose of profit-making, G. Schiller devotes much attention to the center-periphery approach. He insists on the unequal character of this relationship by which the periphery, i.e. the sending countries, decay and must receive additional infusions of purchasing power, while the centre eventually might provide financial transfers for regional development programmes and subventions to agriculture. Furthermore, he points out that the excessive income differentiation forms in itself a system of exploitation. Certain high-level income groups live at the expense of low-paid groups. Thus G. Schiller comes to the conclusion that it is not an original labour deficit from which industrialized societies suffer, but the combined effect of capital surplus, a growing rate of inactivity and a rapid growth of unproductive activities. Quite pertinently, G. Schiller comes to the conclusion that only a strict adherence to the principles of democracy and social equality, of self-determination and human rights, and of international solidarity, especially of the workers can possibly help to build a bridge over the gap between the central and peripheral countries in Europe. Whether the global policy of the multi-national corporations with their transnational money market, advances in the techniques of centralization and superior bargaining power will ever permit any equalization between center and periphery remains to be seen.

LABOUR MIGRATION AND MIGRATION-POLICY IN THE NETHERLANDS

Developments and Perspectives

HANS KOK

1. *The developments in the Netherlands between 1949 and 1974*

In the context of post-war developments which surround the phenomenon of international labour migration, there are four dates which are especially important to the Dutch situation: the years 1949, 1967, 1970 and 1974.

Our observations of these developments shall group themselves around these dates.

In 1949 the first group of workers from abroad was employed in the mining industry. Italy, as a fellow-member of the European Coal and Steel Commission, provided the most appropriate area for recruitment. The Commission, brought about in 1948 by the Treaty of Rome, later made free travel possible for employees within the member states of the pact.

Spurred by the favorable experiences with these foreign workers several concerns in the metal sector, faced with an acute labour shortage, resorted to recruiting Italian workers.

Several large concerns such as Hoogovens and N.D.S.M. in the IJmond-area were at issue.

Italian workers were also sought for employment in the textile industry in the area of Twente.

The serious political and social-economic problems in that period of national and international "rebuilding" accounted for the fact that very little attention was paid to this labour migration.

Much more attention was focused on the large number of refugees who, influenced by political developments, came to Western-Europe from Central and Eastern Europe.

A number of countries—France, Great Britain and the Netherlands amongst them—received considerable numbers of repatriates from their former colonies in addition.

The Netherlands was faced with absorbing subsequently four

waves of repatriates from the former Dutch Indies along a persistant flow of migrant workers from Surinam and The Antilles.

From the end of the fifties onwards the gathering volume of migration was increasingly governed by the need which the expanding economy placed on manpower, whereas politico-idiological motives lost importance. The predominant labour aspect became more evident.

The need to provide the growing number of migrant workers abroad with a proper regulation was first felt around 1960.

The countries concerned made agreements (quite frequently bilaterally) in which a number of material issues such as the duration and contents of the labour contract and the obligation of the employers to provide acceptable housing were settled upon.

The Netherlands made agreements in that order with Italy (1960), Spain (1961), Portugal (1963), Turkey (1964), Greece (1966), Marocco (1969), Yugoslavia (1970), ending with Tunesia (1971).

The first agreement with Italy was thereby the model for the later ones.

Not until 1967 did international labour migration start to enjoy scientific attention.

In an early survey of this "complex" problem Wentholt termed the phenomenon of migration "international commuterism" and went on to describe it in detail by:

> "groups of (schooled and unschooled) workers from lowly industrialized countries with considerable (both apparent and concealed) unemployment and low wages, who (married or single, but primarily unaccompanied by their families) were attracted by the employment and higher wages of the highly industrialized nations of Western and Northern Europe to come and work there for a periode of time, without in the first instance (either intentionally or by prevention) permanently establishing themselves there."

Regarding both the push-factors in the countries providing labour and the pull-factors in the countries obtaining labour, economic causality was deemed primarily responsible for the appearance of the migration phenomenon.

A broad description turned out to be necessary because a lack of statistical data hindered illumination of components.

Numerous foreign and domestic publications would later point this lack out as one of the basic shortcomings. The main reasons behind the Dutch case were:

— the lack of a registration of relatives that accompanied the migrant workers.
— the most divergent estimates as to the numbers of "illegals" (the estimates differ between 15,000 and 25,000).
— cessation of the enumaration of permanent residence permits issued, and closely connected to that the detoriating insight into the amount of holders of these permits who had returned to their country of origin.

International comparison of available statistics was further impaired by the varying registration procedures amongst the countries involved and an ommission to register separately certain migrant populations, which, because of a special inter-relationship between a number of countries involved, had a distinctive character (e.g. Italians in the E.E.C., Algerians in France, Dutch nationals from Surinam and The Antilles).

From the data which were available at the time one could deduce that especially between 1960 and 1965 many concerns resorted to recruiting foreign manpower. Originally it was only the large companies but later on also the smaller companies which lured many foreign workers away from the larger concerns, especially towards the end of the annual contract with the foreign worker. This was most advantageous. The high costs of recruitment could thus be avoided, whilst the bare conditions which the recruitment agreements guaranteed, became inoperative.

An added difficulty in those years (1960 to 1965) was that a considerable spontaneous flow of migrant workers had got under way (with 2000 people per month on the average) which sometimes absolutely exceded official recruitment.

The resultant problems made it evident that the reception and welfare of the foreign workers could no longer be left over to the casual and frequently charitably tainted initiatives.

The existant institutions of the private welfare organisations were not up to this task either.

Strong advocations to coordinate the locally and regionally based activities, resulted in the establishment of the Foundation Netherlands Centre for Foreigners in Utrecht.

This Foundation actually coordinates the activities of 17 local and regional welfare organisations.

The government policy in the fifties and sixties was generally considered too passive. All kinds of ad hoc measures had to suffice in filling the gaps while the distinctive nature of the problem at issue was either briefly granted or entirely ignored.

The problems of foreign workers were dealt with within the framework of the regulations and procedures which applied to the autochtones.

At both the levels of social security, social services and housing, educational management etc. the aim and leading principle became an as equal as possible treatment of the Dutch nationals and the foreigners.

Such equality however, is only practicable as a principle if the autochtonous and allochtonous categories of the population do in fact enjoy equal positions! The structural disadvantages with which the foreign categories cope, and the continuing deprevation and discrimination under which they suffer daily, rather indicate the opposite.

The operative conception of equal treatment of Dutch nationals and foreigners appears not only to be marked by passivity but also substantially by *"weak universalism"*, i.e. by a glaring contrast between the advocated equality de jure and the existant inequality de facto. In that, the factual inequality is the cause as well as the result of the failing ideology of equality.

For that matter, the more noticeable the results of this unsuccesful policy became on several fronts, the greater the insistance became upon directives from the government.

Nevertheless, not until 1969 would the government intervene in the insatisfying situation.

The stream of unofficial recruited migrant workers was checked by coupling the issue of a temporary residence permit to the availability of a working permit. Working permits of course could only be obtained through the official channels.

The great number of illegal residents to reside in the Netherlands after that, however, attests the inadequacy of this measure in stopping the unofficial flow.

1970 is an important date to the Dutch situation because in that year the long awaited Government paper on international labour migration and its resultant problems appeared.

In it the economic necessity of increased labour importation was further examined. Thus the fact was established that there were more and more types of work for which the Dutch would not apply. In fact foreign labour made the imminent closing down of a number of enterprises or departments of enterprises avoidable.

This served the interests of not only national production but also the prospects of employment for autochtonous workers.

Furthermore, the possibility to engage foreign manpower was deemed an important asset in believing the pressure on the labour market.

En passant the paper remarked that the need for foreign labour had a structural character. This had become especially apparent in a period of serious economical depression (1967).

The conjunctural influences were heavily felt in that year and many foreign workers had to return prematurely. Nevertheless as the government paper mentioned despite the decrease of industrial activities a considerable demand for foreign workers remained.

The paper made an important point by rejecting any direct relation between the unemployment rates in certain sections of the Dutch working population and the employment supplied to foreigners.

The level of the work in question in its many qualitative aspects made such a direct relation impossible.

This, however, has nor kept certain parts of the Dutch population from emphasizing this relation in periods of conjunctural decline. Not unsuccesfully in fact when poorly informed or ignorant sections of public opinion were concerned.

The government paper did not only mention the advantages of the import of labour.

A much more alarming finger was pointed at the other, social, aspects of the situation such as the problematic relations between autochtones and allochtones in the areas where the foreigners were concentrated.

We should also mention the tendency towards increasing family reunion by which The Netherlands, as one of the most densely poulated countries, was faced in the sixties with an immigration instrad of an emigration surplus (Graph 1).

The main problem, however was the to Dutch standards very bad housing situation of the foreign workers.

Graph 1.   Growth of the population (per 1000)

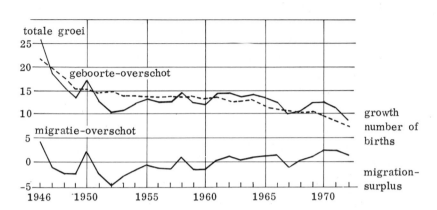

Source: C.B.S. Statistisch Zakboek 1973.

Especially these last reasons gave priority to studies which could provide alternatives.

In anticipation the government thought it advisable to let the short term aspect prevail, their main argument being that labour rotation, which is inherent to international commuterism, always allows one to attune the recruitment and admission policy to the actual situation.

The contents of this government paper justly loosed much criticism from various groups of the Dutch population.

Among the criticisers were the employers-organisations, the trade-unions and numerous national and local action groups.

Their criticism was especially aimed at:

— *The absence of vision in the government policy*: in the paper only a description was given of the existing situation and the measures which had been taken to date. No attention however was paid to either expected or desirable developments.
— *The biassed economic basis of the government policy*: The economic argumentation predominated whereas the social background, as a result of current policy, was ignored. The paper stood between an ad hoc (adjustment) policy and a short term (adjustment) policy.

— *The utterly national outlook on the problems*: the disadvantages for the countries of origin of foreign workers were ignored. Critical notes on the inequality which, both from an international and national point of view, had been growing between the population groups as a result of the mass migration got little attention.

It became clear that the Dutch governemental apparatus had hardly foreseen the developments. The paper showed how inconstructive the current directives were. Political measures strove only to reduce and bring under control the problems which had been arisen under much more liberal economic conditions.

The Council for the Labour Market had predicted this state of affairs when it remarked in a report that "it was a good thing to promote understanding in the current policies, although foresight was much more advisable".

Along with a continued study into certain aspects of the problem also the making of a cost-benefit analysis was advocated. Much of the criticism came to the attention of Parliament. After hearing several groups of the population, amongst them the foreigners themselves, parliamentarians posed more than 300 questions to the government.

As for the social changes about by 25 years of international commuterism a distinction will be made between social-demographic, social-economic ans social trends.

And as they are relevant to an understanding of the actual situation we shall go into a few aspects in a little more detail.

Table 1

Foreigners in the Netherlands

	1947	1960	1964	1966	1967	1968	1-1-1973
Total (x 1000) of which:	103.9	117.6	162.8	213.0	202.2	204.0	282.4
Belgian	25.3	19.2	20.4	20.0	19.9	20.0	20.5
German	27.9	29.5	26.0	27.4	28.1	28.7	36.8
British	3.1	4.7	7.9	9.9	9.5	9.3	13.5
Italian	3.4	5.0	11.4	14.2	14.5	14.5	19.3
Spanish	0.1	0.2	13.1	23.4	18.4	18.3	31.4
Turkish	—	0.1	4.3	14.5	12.3	13.5	46.0
Maroccans	—	—	1.7	14.3	12.6	12.8	27.9

Source: C.B.S. Statistisch Zakboek 1967, 1972 and 1973.

1.1. Social-demographic developments

Primary is the increase in foreigners in the Netherlands in the post-war period.

The following table shows the real number of foreigners present in the Netherlands by 1 january 1968 and 1 january 1973. The sub-divisions "Member-states of the E.E.C." and "Recruitment-countries" show whether alien traffic within the European Community or traffic from elsewhere is concerned.

Table 2

Foreigners in the Netherlands

Countries	1968		1973		children under 15	
	men	women	men incl. (6)	women (7)	boys	girls
1.	2.	3.	4.	5.	6.	7.
Member-states of the E.E.C,						
of which Italian	9737	4499	12880	6389	3766	3799
total	43339	33063	55859	40283	14682	13704
Recruitment-countries						
Greece	1882	403	2507	1482	724	622
Marocco	12544	43	25413	2488	1335	1286
Portugal	1857	737	4061	2891	837	865
Spain	14063	4370	21426	9936	3787	3752
Tunesia	142	30	626	106	71	63
Turkey	11912	412	34364	11654	5642	4977
Yugoslavia	1273	453	6690	4928	555	531
Total	43673	6448	95087	33485	12951	12096
Total General	181375		282361			

(including Europe, America, Africa, Asia, Australia, unknown, etc.)

Source: Rijksbegroting v.h. Dienstjaar 1973-1974 no. 12600 Part VI

The available statistics show the following noteworthy developments:

— *The growing tendency of family-reunion*, especially among migrant workers from recruitment countries.
— *The sharp increase in the amount of female migrants*, amongst them many non-working, married women.
— *The sharp increase in the amount of foreign children.* Many

(i.e. 8972) of them are under age of 10 (either born in the Netherlands under their foreign nationality or came with their parents).

— *The sharp increase in the amount of Spanish, Maroccan and Turkish migrant workers* (Appendix I).

— *The rising foreign labour surplus in proportion to the populationgrowth.* The ratio in 1973 was more than 25%.

— *The growing concentration of allochtones in the urban areas of the Netherlands,* partly caused by the concentration of labour migrants in the urban and industrial areas of the Netherlands (Randstad Holland, Twente, Utrecht and surroundings).

— *Overconcentration of allochtones in the most densely populated western part of Holland.* In recent years a process with a self-stimulating tendency has taken place in which a growing establishment-surplus of allochtones (blue-collar workers) juxtaposes a departure-surplus of autochthones (white-collar workers). The ratio of foreign labour surplus in proportion to the population growth in this area in 1972 was more than 40%.

— *The growing concentration of foreigners in the Dutch capitals.*

Table 3

Foreigners in the four main cities

year	Amsterdam abs.	Amsterdam in %	Rotterdam abs.	Rotterdam in %	Den Haag abs.	Den Haag in %	Utrecht abs.	Utrecht in %
1960	13816	1.59	8245	1.13	10885	1.80	2570	1.00
1964	21054	2.43	12187	1.67	14113	2.36	5466	2.05
1969	36584	4.40	21844	3.12	22538	4.09	12333	4.46
1971	—	—	32333	4.76	—	—	13903	4.99

V.T. Population Census 1960.

Source: Ministerie van Cultuur, Recreatie en Maatschappelijk Werk.
Statistisch Cahier no 11.

— *The overconcentration of foreigners in the C 19th inner cities.* Especially in the oldest quarters and neighbourhoods of these capitals. There is more and more a process of segregation by which the foreigners become spatially and socially

isolated. In many cases the allochthonous category constitutes more than 10% of the total population (e.g. in the Nieuwe Wijk neighbourhood of Rotterdam this is even more than 50%)
— *The increasing length of stay.* A growing number of foreign workers postpones the return to the country of origin.
— *The increasing permanent residence.* Approximately 25% of the migrant workers in the Netherlands are expected to establish themselves there. This can be seen in the number of naturalisation applications

Table 4

Naturalisations

	1963	1968	1969	1970	1971	1972
Total of which:	5389	5981	4182	3392	4213	4001
Spanish	—	41	67	32	79	101
Turkish	—	4	23	27	71	57

Source: Statistisch Zakboek 1972 and 1973.

This can also be deducted from the number of permanent workingpermits issued to foreign workers after more than 5 years of stay in the Netherlands. The data given are the most recent.

Table 5

Permanent working-permits per 15-6-1971

Greecs	Yugoslavians	Portugese	Spaniards	Turks	Maroccans	other	Total
578	207	576	4272	3205	2586	3725	15149

Source: Ministry of Social Affairs.

1.2. *Social-economic developments*

The main problem here is that labour migration has developed from an incidental, temporary into a permanent and structural phenomenon of Dutch society. Whereas the initial issue was the employment of *small numbers* of foreign workers by mainly the *large enterprises* in *certain sectors*, we are now concerned with large numbers in enterprises of all sizes in all sectors and branches.

Just as in the surrounding countries in the Netherlands the share of foreign workers is rising in proportion to the total working population.

Table 6

		Belgium	W-Germany	Luxembourg	Netherlands
Population (millions)	1971	9.7	61.3	0.34	13.2
Labour force (as in % of total population)	1971	41.2	43.2	41.7	35.2
Foreign workers (as % of wage and salary earners employed)	1958	–	0.7	–	0.6
	1969	6.6	6.4	29.0	1.8
	1971	6.9	9.6	30.0	1.8
	1972	7.2	10.5	34.0	2.6
	1973	–	–	–	3.2

Source: Verslag v.d. ontwikkeling van de Sociale Toestand in de E.E.G. 1972 Brussel 1973.
Verslag over de ontwikkeling van de sociale toestand in de Gemeenschap in 1973. Brussel, 1974.

Appendix II shows the increasing number of foreign workers in nearly all branches. Besides there is a concentration of foreign labour in certain branches such as Earthware, Building, Chemicals, Metals, Foods and Luxury goods, Commerce, Hotel and

Table 8

Proportion of foreign workers as in % of the Dutch working population in certain branches of industry

	1969		1972	
Earthware	1969	5.0	1972	7.5
Paper		4.4		5.0
Leather, Rubber etc.		5.7		9.2
Mining		3.6		4.9
Textile-industry		5.0		7.0
Foods and Luxury Goods		3.6		5.3

Source: C.P.B. Economische Effekten voor Nederland van de werving van buitenlandse arbeiders. Den Haag 1972.

Catering and Transportation over land. In some of these branches there is an over-proportion of foreign workers as compared to the average proportion of foreign workers to the Dutch working population. This average was 2.6% in 1972.

1.2.1. *Marginal branches*

The increasing need for foreign workers as well as the need itself can be explained by the recent developments in the Dutch economy. Especially important are the direct and indirect effects which these developments subsequently had on employment in various sectors, the nature of employment, size and composition of the labour force. First of all let us examine the structure of the employment supplied in various sectors and branches.

Industrially highly developed countries in their transition to the post-industrial era generally show a declining primary sector (i.e. agriculture and fishing), a large but gradually decreasing industrial sector and an increasingly labour-absorbing service sector.

Table 9

Agriculture	in %	Industry	in %	Services	in %
Turkey	72.2	W-Germany	47.4	Netherlands	52.0
W-Germany	10.0	Netherlands	40.2	W-Germany	42.6
Netherlands	7.7	Turkey	11.3	Turkey	16.5

Source: The Growth of Output 1960-1980. O.E.S.O./Parijs 1971.

This trend can be seen when we look at the developments which took place in the recruitment period of foreign workers in the Netherlands.

Table 10

Employment distribution per branch in the Netherlands

Year	Agriculture in %	Industry in %	Services in %
1947	20.2	34.0	41.0
1960	12.2	40.7	44.8
1971	2.0	47.9	50.1

Sources: Manpower and Social Policy in the Netherlands/Parijs 1967
C.B.S. Statistisch Zakboek 1973.

The developments in the industrial sector deserve special attention because of the considerable changes which took place in this sector in the sixties.

The following outline gives the absolute figures per branch between 1960 and 1970.

Number of workers decreased	↓	Textile-industry	—	32000
		Clothing and Shoes	—	13000
		Foods and Luxury-goods	—	7000
		Shipbuilding	—	8000
		Earthware, Glass, etc.	—	1000
Number of workers — equal →		Leather and Rubber		
Number of workers increased	↑	Metals industry	+	89000
		Chemical industry	+	27000
		Other processing-industry	+	18000

The distribution of foreign workers over the various branches of industry shows that allochthones are especially concentrated in the branches which offer poor prospects for autochthonous workers.

On the other hand ther are also strong concentrations in some branches with good prospects such as the Metals-industry.

More than 80% of the foreign workers in the Netherlands is concentrated in industry.

Foreign manpower concentrates itself more quickly in structurally weaker branches of industry than in the stronger ones. The employment of foreign workers has become a more or less permanent phenomenon of these weaker (marginal) branches, either in order to eliminate "bottlenecks" in production cycles or to guarantee the continuation of the branch itself or a section of it. Frequently heard criticism is that this unnecessarily postpones rationalisation of production in these branches.

The technically possible progress, measured not in terms of the G.N.P. increase but in income per capita, would supposedly be hindered by the labor intensive investment tendency (partly through the import of labour) rather than capital intensive investing (mechanisation and automatisation).

The fear for "technical conservatism" by the trade unions is rejected by the employers as being "difficult to prove" or "unfounded". The employers claim that in these weaker branches the possibility to substitute labour by capital is limited.

These marginal branches of industry are still strongly dependant, quantitatively as well as qualitatively, on foreign workers. A breach in the supply would inevitably lead to cessation of production or transfer of production to other countries.

Within the framework of the improvements necessary to the historically disrupted international division of labour, Tinbergen worked out the theory, that in the wealthy nations diminiution of production should be considered for several branches of industry in the primary and secundary sector. This would especially apply to the branches in which a choice is still possible between capital- and labourintensive ways of production.

According to Tinbergen, especially the labour intensive exporting branches of industry come into consideration for transfer to developing countries.

Some of these branches, e.g. textiles, ready made clothing, shoes, already started developing themselves in that direction in the sixties.

In that period the employment rate of labour intensive activities diminished by 3% per year.

Tinbergen and others believe it strongly advisable to incorporate these developments in an international reconstruction plan instead of leaving them to their obvious and chaotic fate. Such a plan should in turn be an integral part of future industrial policy at supra-national level. Economic and political unity within the European Economic Community in the first instance is considered essential. However political unity within the E.E.C. forms the main point of growing criticism.

What is more, doubts continually arise as to the effects of transferring certain branches of industry to developing countries. Not only far too little new jobs have been created as a result of transfers of production but also the profits from low-wage countries flow into developed countries instead of being invested in (expanding) industrial activities in developing countries.

Critics claim that the theory of international division of labour, which Tinbergen had set out roughly, functions as an ideological defense and fortification of the capitalistic and imperialistic system.

Allegedly the differentiation between capital and labour intensive investments is an artificial one because the two conditions often coincide. The two can be distinguished but not separated. The (high)ratio of capital investment in the Netherlands during the period if recruitment of foreign workers attests to this. In the service-sector the possibilities are limited, but most foreign workers do not work in this sector. On the contrary, the allochthonous workers shifted to the (labour intensive) service-sector whereas foreign manpower was attracted more and more for the (capital intensive) industrial sector, especially for the processing industry. Despite the predicted decline in employment on the long run the short term need in the industrial sector remained noticeably constant.

The discrepancy between supply and demand is much more at issue in this sector. This takes us to the quantitative and qualitative developments on the Dutch labour market.

1.2.2. *The Dutch labour market*

The labour market can be divided into a wage-market and a job-market.

We shall concentrate in the first place on the aspects of supply and demand of the job-market.

Supply

Compared to her surrounding countries, the Netherlands is characterised by a relatively small working population.

Still the Netherlands is one of the most densely populated countries in the world and the term "overpopulated" is heard more and more. Despite a sharply decreasing growth figure, mainly the result of a diminishing child constituent, the population is still growing considerably. The fact that the autochthonous working population does not keep up with the autochthonous population is especially striking. Both quantities are subject to the immigration-surplus by no means in the same degree. This can be explained by the fact that labour migration has more influence in the growth of the working-population than on the total-population increase (33% vs. 25%).

The small proportion of the working-population in the total population in the Netherlands is commonly explained by the lesser percentage of working married women as compared to other industrial countries.

Table 11

Degree of participation of women in the process of labour. (1968)

France	West-Germany	Belgium	Italy	The Netherlands
46.6	40.3	33.6	29.9	26.3

Source: V.N.O.

Between 1960 and 1970 when foreign manpower was being recruited the growth of the working population was strongly influenced by the willingness in women to participate in the labour process. According to provisional results of the Population Census in 1971 the percentage of participation had run up to 29.6%.

Women accounted for nearly a half of the total growth in the working population in that period (absolute amounts: 262,000 out of 530,000).

A decreasing participation percentage for men (in 1960—91%; in 1971—85,3%) however stood against the increase for women (in 1960—25,6%; in 1974—29,6%).

The higher degree in which women started entering the labour process was mainly the result of the increased participation of married women over 25. Three quarters of the increase in working women belonged to this category. Many of them work part-time. Not however in labour positions where they could replace the foreign workers.

The lag in the labour supply is largely the result of the strong expansion and higher level of education. Not only does the Youth enter the labour market at a later age, but also at a higher level.

Whereas 1/3 had no more than primary education in 1956, in 1966 this was less than 1/7, and in 1971 only 1/11.

The elderly (i.e. over 65) already make up more than 10% of

the total population. 75% of those leaving the labour market have had no more than primary education. The ever diminishing supply of unskilled labour on the Dutch Labour market explains the recruitment of foreign workers.

This clarifies the fact that the argument which is frequently heard in periods of lessening economic activities—namely that the Dutch unemployed should be employed to replace and/or reduce the number of foreign workers—must be rejected on social, economic, geographic and educational grounds of labour-allocation.

Demand

Despite the diminishing demand for unskilled labour under influence of technological developments, the national supply dwindles even faster. Between 1968 and 1973, according to the Centraal Plan Bureau, twice as fast in fact. The establishment of compulsory education till 17 years of age, which must be realised before 1980, shall hasten this development even more. For the Dutch labour market this means that there will hardly be any replenishment on the special job market for unskilled and unschooled labour. Invariably, nearly all predictions for the seventies show that continuation of the present tendencies can only lead to more import of labour.

Except for periodic conjunctural slumps the Centraal Plan Bureau even reckons with a regular increase of 15000 foreigners per year.

Thus the bogey of an ethnically layered labour market, with the situation in South-Africa as an extreme example, will near the Netherlands and the other labour importing countries of Western-Europe year by year.

Only an industry annex labour market policy at supra-national level (E.E.C.) can bend this critical line of development.

However the political motivation in the countries concerned is not equally strong and their outlook on development problems at international level also varies.

For the time bing all that can be done is to look for alternatives within the narrow boundaries of a Dutch development policy.

The present economic situation (because of energy problems)

does not encourage any experiments that could jeapordize the employment rate.

Especially the actual expected rise in the unemployment rate in the Netherlands calls for a most restrictive migration policy.

At this point we must bring into consideration that not only social-structural but also social-cultural factors determine the recruitment of foreign workers.

1.2.3. *The special job-market for foreign workers*

The jobs that are offered to the foreign workers are not only purely *unskilled* by nature but also *unattractive, without prospects* and of a *low social status*, not lastly because of the *poor wages* which characterize them.

The facts have given rise to a special job market for foreign workers featuring those labour positions which the Dutch can afford to avoid. The characteristics of this job market are:

(1) *Low occupational level*

According to the employment classification of the State Labour Office (Rijksarbeidsbureau) nearly 90% of the foreign workers are employed at levels 1 and 2 (i.e. unskilled and semi-skilled labour). An inquiry by the Regional Board for the Labour Market in the province of Utrecht showed that in 143 enterprises employing 19000 persons 6% of the foreigners, as to 54% for the Dutch, worked in a skilled labour position. 30% of the foreigners however believe themselves to be employed as skilled workers. Neither do the official statistics agree with the data in the countries of origin of the workers (especially Turkey and Yugoslavia) where it has become obvious that the skilled and routined workers tend to leave the country.

(2) *High degree of sensitivity towards wages*

Through this the foreign worker has acquired the image of a subject, who charged (or burdened) with "middle class ideas" is merely out to make as most money as possible in a very short time. Other motives for migration such as the escape from poverty, the need for adventure, self-fulfilment, progress, education for their offspring, a yearning to experience a modern way of live, a want for material elements of western culture and so on, are virtually unappreciated.

Especially these elements are ignored and detract attention from his social and cultural identity.

(3) *Instrumental attitude towards the job*

Dutch workers are becoming increasingly more conscious of those labour positions which allow an expressive attitude towards their job (in other words which content them to a certain degree with the labour contents, labour conditions and the labour situation.) As a result the foreign workers are left with the jobs which are purely instrumental (i.e. work as a means).

(4) *Unattractive jobs*

(a) Economicly unattractive, because these jobs are financially underappreciated and the changed market-value of these labour positions are in no way expressed in the wages.
(b) Socially unattractive, because these jobs are characterized by accumulations of inconveniences such as; heaviness, dirtiness, dullness and depression. It is routine work that alienates and is done irregularly and in shifts, where appeals to work over are frequent etc.
(c) Politically unattractive, because such jobs tend to emphasize the weak position of the manual workers.

(5) *High degree of horizontal mobility*

In other words the willingness to move geographically in order to get work. Migrant workers are sooner prepared and more capable of moving than the rooted Dutch.

(6) *High degree of functional mobility*

Or the willingness to move to take another job (most of the time within the same factory).

As a result of these developments the Netherlands is steadily nearing a point where there will be a "complete" special job market for foreign workers. The various possibilities which have been tried out to prevent this include: the adjustment of the supply of labour by making the unskilled jobs materially and immaterially more attractive and the promoting of horizontal as well as functional mobility of Dutch workers.

More capital intensive investments and a more restrictive migration policy must also influence the supply of labour.

Relevant too, is the fact that the sight of an enterprise can be influenced by imposing a tax and permit system.

As to the question of the effects of all these measures however, instead of a reduction of the need for foreign workers a stabilisation is more probable.

1.3. Social problems

1.3.1. Housing

The poor housing situation of many foreign workers in the Netherlands (especially the Turks and the Maroccans) has hardly improved up till now. The majority resorts to communal living in camps, obscure hotels and overcrowded private or company pensions with relatively high rents, where they "enjoy" a maximum of supervision and a minimum of privacy.

The hard facts have already been stated in numerous reports and inquiries taken on the spot, but without much effect.

There is however little evidence of active intervenience by the authorities. Stringency in the local lodging regulations is generally ineffective because of a lack of alternative accommodation.

The subsidy directives which the government issued to promote (re)building have fallen short of their aim. Unless these facilities are extended they can hardly even be taken seriously. The hard core of the problem of payable and acceptable housing for both the Dutch and the foreigners in the lowest income bracket cannot be solved without a strong government policy. This should include warranties and financial support from the government.

1.3.2. Education

(a) for migrant workers

The scant initiatives, which frequently have a private or voluntary background, boil down to tuition in Dutch for a small number of migrant workers. The facilities which are provided for them in the Netherlands, such as welding, elementary agriculture and market-gardening, have remained practically unused. The migrant workers are unwilling to follow these courses because they doubt the use of them upon their return. This will remain so until the opposite has been proved. Up till now the Dutch government has been unable to make adequate courses possible.

(b) *for the children of foreign workers*

The number of foreign children in Dutch primary schools has increased especially in the last few years.

Table 12

Number of foreign children in Dutch primary schools

Year	number	source
1966	± 1500	Ministerie C.R.M. Memorie van Toelichting 1966.
1972	9869	C.B.S. Afdeling Onderwijsstatistiek.
1973	12350	Ministerie van Onderwijs Afdeling Statistiek

There is a good number of foreign children which should be considered for education but nevertheless remain in need. In West-Germany only half of the children of foreign workers receive education. The Dutch situation is largely similar. By giving information more selectively the Dutch government hopes to improve the situation.

The core of the problem however, is the nature of the education. Purely Dutch tuition turns out to be unsatisfactory for several reasons:

(1) a good deal of the foreign children fall behind the Dutch children because of language difficulties. This in turn spoils their chances for secondary education.
(2) it purposes assimilation in Dutch society; as a result some of these children become estranged from their parents and their own culture.
(3) it gives the children great difficulties in adopting themselves upon return.

Appointing extra teachers helps to make up for the first problem but does nothing for the other two.

Bilingual and bicultural education are advocated as a means to meet the latter two problems as fully as possible. Apart from the obvious costs, which are considerable, the introduction of bicultural education faces the difficulty which 12350 children spread over 1400 of the Dutch primary schools present. In the urban conglomerations there is the added difficulty of the diversity of nationalities (e.g. Rotterdam-Rijnmond with 47 nationalities, Amsterdam-Bijlmermeer with 17).

Concentrating these children of foreign nationality in certain schools, appointing more teachers and recruiting teachers in the countries of origin of the pupils are measures which are intended to bring relief in the future. The problematical development of a deprived "second generation" may well then be brought back to more acceptable proportions.

1.3.3. *Medical Care*

The foreign workers in the Netherlands are still insufficiently assured of medical care. The provisions prove insufficient because of the language and culture barriers. These barriers often keep a foreign worker from getting their (often psycho-somatic) complaints across to the Dutch general practitioners, so that repercussions follow. The foreign general practitioners in the Netherlands can sometimes help in these cases. The disadvantage of employing professional people from the recruitment countries however is the worsening of the "brain-drain" or in other words the exodus of routined, skilled and highly qualified labour.

1.3.4. *Information*

Recently the many welfare foundations for foreign workers have been paying more serious attention to promoting more understanding, appreciation and tolerance in the Dutch and the foreigners for each others way of living.

Prejudices continually have to be eliminated, especially when they have been put there by the mass-media. As we have seen this is the case in periods of economic recession when the news administered is characterized by "manifest regulation of the latently present resentments".

The prejudice towards criminality is one of the most deeply rooted. The increase in criminality in the Netherlands is disproportionately attributed to foreigners. Neither the sort nor the seriousness of the delict are hereby taken into consideration. The actual statistical data by no means bear these prejudices out.

Providing foreign workers with specific information is also important for their safety on the job. The figures show that foreign workers have a much higher accident rate than their Dutch counterparts. Research done on the subject has shown that not only the type of work which is so characteristic of their position is to blame, but also their infamiliarity with industrial work(machines).

1.3.5. *Community Organisation for special groups*

Briefly, the welfare services in the Netherlands are passing from individual, charitable initiatives to more active forms. The foreign worker is seen no longer as an object of care, but as a participant and potential executive of welfare activities. The general function of community organisation thus influences the community organisation for special groups of the population. Much more emphasis is being placed on democracy and self-help activities.

By methodical groupwork and stimulating group processes foreign workers should be encouraged to voice their own opinions at policy makers' levels. Experience has taught that the best possibilities for activating and accompanying groups are to be found there were the situation allows for spontaneous gathering (in pensions, camps, in the neighbourhood, around specific interests, around political, economic or other goals and so on). The aspirations in this direction however are hindered by the fact that the welfare organisations are fairly well constantly engaged in dealing with basic-deficiencies in the welfare position of foreign workers (e.g. their rights by law, and their social and occupational security, housing, medical care, etc.)

This process by which the foreign workers start to say their part and actively participate in their communities has only just begun. Participation of foreigners in campains, strikes, neighbourhood committees, migrant councils and so on is becoming a more and more well known phenomenon.

2. *Pros and contras of international labour migration*

2.1. *Cost-benefit analysis*

The sharp criticism on the 1970 government paper prompted discussion throughout the Netherlands about the costs and benefits of international labour migration for both the labour providing and labour receiving countries.

Several German and Swiss studies were introduced in the Netherlands at that point. Amongst them were those by V. Lutz, A. Gnehm, H. Rüstow, and Mishan & Needleman.

Of these, Gnehm's study was the most encompassing because the consequences of the import of labour for productivity investment and infra-structural provisions were taken into consideration. A similar approach was thought of for the Dutch situation.

The above mentioned studies however, were biassed in that they only examined the consequences for the labour receiving countries. Zolotas and others would later improve upon this.

Despite the different purpose and visions that went into their studies, most of the authors agreed upon the thesis that in all the countries concerned with labour migration, the apparent short term advantages invariably turn to long term disadvantages. The most important argument employed was the prediction that the absorption and welfare of foreign workers and their families would force the labour receiving countries to make rather expensive infra-structural investments in housing, education, medical care, reception and guidance, information etc..

As to the Dutch situation one could draw a similar conclusion, and for this reason priority was been given to the making of a cost-benefit analysis.

N. Scott especially concerned himself with the development of a framework of such a cost-benefit analysis for international labour migration.

He differentiates two levels of analysis:

(1) The micro-economic level
     (a) for the individual migrant worker and his family,
     (b) for the enterprise.
(2) the macro-economic level
     (a) for the country receiving labour,
     (b) for the country supplying labour.

The analysis in 1972 in the Netherlands was made by the Centraal Plan Bureau (C.P.B.). This analysis was at macro-economic level and concerned only the labour receiving country.

The conclusions of this tentative analysis follow:

(1) The pressure taken off the labour market by employing foreign workers is micro-economically (enterprise-wise) important but macro-economically rather unimportant.

(2) There is definitely a downward pressure on wages and prices, but less than one would expect (in V. Lutz's terms: there is a relative wage effect on certain branches of industry and on certain groups, but hardly any general wage effect).

(3) The downward pressure that does result, principally lessens capital intensive investment, which implies a delay in the reconstruction process in the weaker (marginal) branches of industry.

(4) The real improvement for the own national dependant working population is negligible. The consequences for the real other income is more noticeably positive, either as a result of higher profits or smaller losses through underequipment.

(5) The national rentability of labour importation is positive. The differing consequences for both the real income (wages) available and the real other income (profits) make the advocation of labour migration from the employers' rather than the employees' side understandable.

(6) Positive national rentability results despite the stress on the social milieu (infra-structural provisions). Family reunion is relatively expensive so that national rentability is lowered; without, however, becoming negative.

(7) The social acceptability of family reunion therefore juxtaposes the economic consequences.

(8) On the other hand, the additional demand on the collective provisions should not be underestimated because of the pronounced concentration of foreign workers in Randstad Holland. A dispersal policy should therefore be backed.

(9) Because the results of labour migration are dispersed so widely throughout the national economy, it would be a rather discriminative measure to impose a tax for employing foreign workers.

(10) Despite the positive national rentability, increase in the own national labour supply is advisable.

(11) Proportionally greater participation by the Dutch working population should be encouraged and support to the weaker branches of industry should be disencouraged when this means:

- disagreement with the regional deliberations (given the small degree of mobility of the home supply)
- continuation of the existing labour shortage.

(12) When foreign workers become available it should be an impulse for investment activity. Added investment combined with labour importation means a considerable strengthening of the inflationary forces.

2.2. *Marginal notes*

This cost-benefit analysis by the C.P.B. was severely criticised. Neither the economic effects of labour migration for the supplying countries, not the social consequences for both categories of countries, nor the psychic consequences for the individual migrant worker and his family got any attention whatsoever.

Nor were the effects and results brought into connection with each other. The report gives little insight into the outcome of increased labour import on separate branches, occupations and areas.

The main objection however, is to the short-term character of the C.P.B. analysis. Such an attempt to weigh off the pros and contras of international labour migration can only be looked upon as a useable, but very incomplete and faulty instrument. Such a instrument should therefore be used with reserve.

Two conclusions from the C.P.B. report deserve special attention. The expectation of positive national economic rentability (point 6 above) does not necessarily detract from the plausability of Lutz's c.s. thesis that the short-term advantages are replaced by long-term disadvantages. When the existing (inadequate) infrastructural provisions are involved as a guiding principle in these deliberations, the expected benefit turns out to be mainly founded on the basic shortages to the well-being of the foreign workers and their families in the Netherlands.

A fully bodied welfare policy for this social category which has sufficient infrastructural provisions can thus serve the purpose of influencing and regulating labour migration. This brings us up to point 9 of the C.P.B. report because the minister who is directly responsible for community organization for special groups (Ministry of Culture, Recreation and Social Work) suggested that a tax should be imposed on employing foreign wor-

kers in order to help cover the costs of reception and guidance by
the welfare organisations.

The counsel sollicited by the National Board for the Labor
Market (S.E.R.) was brought out towards the end of 1973. Completely in accordance with point 9 of the C.P.B. report the board
made known its preference towards financing community organisation for special groups from the general means.

The rejected alternatives included taxing all industry and imposing a tax on specifically the enterprises that employed foreign
workers.

The joint welfare organisations share this point of view. Their
standpoint presupposes a sense of responsibility on behalf of the
whole Dutch population. The government cannot and may not
discard this collective responsibility.

2.3. *Employers*

The two employers' organisations in the Netherlands, the
V.N.O. (Verbond van Nederlandse Ondernemingen) and the
N.C.W. (Nederlandse Christelijk Werkgeversverbond), have repeatedly signalized in their periodicals "de onderneming" and
"de werkgever" the true importance of the import of labour for
industry.

Now that the aftermath of the lasting dependance upon foreign manpower is making itself felt and the government is being
faced with the responsibility for an adequate social policy, the
employers find themselves on the defense when they apply for
permission to import labour. In this, the question of whether
labour importation is intended to warrant the continuation of an
enterprise or to effect growth, can be decisive.

The social costs of labour migration are merely one of the
"external effects" on the recruiting enterprises, which through
their grip on investments, are in a position to determine the
nature, extent and level of the jobs that are offered in the Netherlands and thus the very need for foreign manpower.

It is especially these external effects which, inherent or not to
the system of enterprise-wise production, increasingly prompt
discussion on the social position of the enterprises.

Not only is the purpose of the enterprises (growth, profit,
continuity, employment) debated, but also their function, by
which is meant the side-effects (external effects) known or un-

known for society (e.g. pollution, tension between private and public consumption, emphasis on welfare and not on well-being, overestimation of economic purposes, inadequacy of social policies, widening gap between rich and poor countries and between rich and poor population groups).

The government has the mounting task of giving the social-economic developments a social twist.

An actual example of this is the problem of the "illegal" foreign workers. To the dismay of many, the government policy on illegal migrant workers had for years a remedial character; many of them were expelled as unwanted aliens.

Table 13

Aliens expelled between 1968 and 1972

year	1968	1969	1970	1971	1972
total	4147	5972	5320	6365	6375
of which Mediterranean	1870	2734	2096	2784	2948

Source: Rijksbegroting voor het dienstjaar 1973-1974, no. 12600. Hfdst. VI. Justitie Nr. 2 Memorie van Toelichting.

Early in 1974 an inter-departemental committee proposed to the Cabinet to have the illegal employing of foreign workers declared an economic delict.

Offenders should be sentenced to higher fines and imprisonment.

2.4. *Trade unions*

In the fifties and sixties the Dutch trade union policies towards foreign workers was similar to the German, being founded on the belief that international commuterism was a passing phenomenon.

The Dutch unions (N.V.V., N.K.V. and C.N.V.) refrained from making any official statements on the subject. The special relation between the trade unions and the foreign workers did not get the attention it deserved.

A certain degree of ambivalence in the attitude taken by the trade unions was noted. Generally they were in favour of recruitment of foreign workers but in concrete situations they found themselves unable to take a side. In most West-European coun-

tries labour importation was no more seen as a threat on wages
and the employment rate. On the contrary open boarders proved
to be necessary to maintain the existing wage structure and the
high employment rate. Not only was the economic growth, and
with it the improvement in the position of the autochthonous
workers, evaluated positively, but also the short term improvements which labour migration might have for the emigration
countries concerned. Some even thought that admitting foreign
workers from developing countries displayed international solidarity. As a first step in that direction was seen the equalizing of
labour conditions and position by law of the autochthonous and
allochthonous workers.

The trade unions however, have only recently expressed this
point of view in their various programmes. In the concept of
their campaign for 1971-1975 (Concept Aktieprogramma
1971-1975) which the consultation body of the N.V.V., N.K.V.
and C.N.V. brought out they state:

> "The trade union movement opinions that the employment rate
> should be raised in those countries which at present feature high
> unemployment and that investments should be attuned to this. When
> the recruitment of foreign workers is at issue, employment should be
> bound to conditions respective of the position by law, the guarantee
> of their means of existance, their reception and guidance, housing,
> improvement of education and skilledness.
>
> The Dutch trade union investment considers it its natural task to
> look after the interests of the foreign workers as well and to promote
> their equality of occupational and social rights."

Both the widely spread discussions on the 1970 government
paper and the persistant gap between the formal and factual
equality of rights of foreign workers in the Netherlands in the
seventies have caused the trade unions to alter their point of view
more and more. The structural nature of the need for foreign
labour made retrospection inevitable.

The trade union attitude is increasingly influenced by the expectation that mass labour migration will prove disadvantageous
for all countries involved. This explains why the Dutch trade
unions want to switch from a controlling policy towards the
admittance of foreign workers to a most restrictive one.

The following paragraph was included in both the *list of priorities for the 1973 government policy* as well as in the *programme
of priorities for 1974* from the trade unions.

"the immigration by foreign workers from outside the E.E.C. presents serious social problems. A policy should therefore be made in the near future in which interdependant conditions are laid down for the recruitment of foreign workers. On the one hand these conditions must bear on such circumstances as their position by law, the guarantee of their means of existance, their reception and guidance, housing, improvement of education and skilledmess, and information in their countries of origin. On the other hand the local situation and the feasability of absorbing foreign workers without serious social conflicts should be taken into account. In most cases careful appraisal of the social costs and benefits is highly necessary. A most restrictive admission policy is therefore essential."

In regard to the relation between trade unions and the foreign workers, some attention should be devoted to both the aspects of participation and representation.

Participation

The trade unions in Western Europe have not managed to persuade the foreign workers to take part in their activities. The degree of organisation amongst the foreign workers is by far inferior to the degree in the autochthonous population. Noteworthy is the fact that there are no exact figures on this because the trade unions are either unable or unwilling to produce them.

Research (De Buitenlandse Arbeider in Nederland, vols. I and II, The Hague, 1971) has shown that only 13% of the foreign workers in the Netherlands in 1968 belonged to a trade union. Especially the Turks and Maroccans have a much lower degree of organisation (respectively 10 and 1%). Grantedly there has been a certain improvement recently but according to present estimates the percentage of organised foreign workers is still about 20, as compared to 41 for the Dutch.

Representation

This small degree of organisation and participation is for a good deal due to the failure by the Dutch trade unions to come up directly for the interests of the foreign workers. The following factors however, represent at least equally major difficulties to the establishment of a relation between the foreign workers and the trade unions.

Not only are many foreign workers unacquainted with trade unions, frequently because of a rural background, but they also come from countries where trade unionism is either nonexistant or limited by political influences (Greece, Spain, Portugal and Turkey).

We should also mention here the difficulties the foreigners experience in the first years of their stay in adapting themselves because of the language and culture barriers, the social and spatial isolation they encounter in their working and living situation, their economic vulnerability, imperfect status by law etc.

The temporary stay and as a result of this the short-term outlook are often decisive here. Because of this many foreign workers can hardly identify themselves with the long-term purposes of trade unionism. This in turn is the reason why many of them shall never feel themselves represented by the unions.

This was made particularly obvious by the involvement of foreign workers in a series of wild cat strikes that took place in recent years throughout western Europe (e.g. Renault in Paris/ France, Hella in Lippstadt and Ford in Köln/West-Germany).

The failure by the trade unions to come up for the interests of the foreign workers provokes the foreigners to defend their rights.

The trade unions are accused of only being interested in the foreign workers who are their members and disregarding the rest.

For that matter, having the individual foreign members function properly in the Dutch trade unions is the source of many a problem. This is why the N.V.V. approach and its union activities are now aimed at groups.

Thus there are Spanish, North African and Turkish (Türk Irtibat Komisyonu) trade union groups.

Courses are being organised for the members of these groups in order to make them familiar with the organisation of Dutch trade unionism.

3. Migration and Development

3.1. Research

Concern for the effects of labour migration on supplying countries has been growing in the Netherlands over the past few years.

In this, the 1970 government paper and the cost-benefit analysis by the Centraal Plan Bureau have both clearly worked as a catalyser.

Especially the O.E.C.D. (organisation for economic co-operation and development) has done good studies in the field of "return" migration. Data on Italian, Greek and Yugoslavian return migration has also become available.

The Dutch from their side are putting more and more research into the effects of labour migration on the supplying countries.

3.2. *Evaluation*

We should note that the results of these studies must lead to a basic change in the public opinion that there is a positive relation between labour migration and development in the countries of origin. It is not feasible within the compass of this article to give the findings of the reporters on this the attention they deserve. We should therefore like to let Professor B. Kayser's conclusions suffice here as a very short summary:

> "The analysis of certain demographic trends gives reason to fear that emigration is ultimately a factor of impoverishment. At the outset it relieves congestion, but little by little it becomes erosive. In the short term there are signs that emigration is an obstacle to development where no deliberate and coordinated emigration policy exists. Since there can be no serious qualitative control of departures, it is almost certainly the most enterprising persons who leave. Moreover apart from diminishing the regional labour force qualitatively emigration enables a significant proportion of workers to subsist in a reserve which prevents labour from being efficiently employed. Furthermore it stimulates consumption of modern manufactured products which are in most cases imported".
>
> (Prof. B. Kayser, O.E.C.D. Observer no. 47 (1970) p. 9-13).

3.3. *Labour migration and development cooperation*

Based on the available data on the present rather negative relation between labour migration and development (Prof. N. Abadan speaks of the myth of labour migration as aid to developing countries), as well as the limited possibilities for the reception and guidance of foreign workers in the Netherlands more and more pressure was put on the Dutch government to revise its migration policy as expressed in the (criticised) 1970 paper. The realization of a clear connection between labour migration and development cooperation should be an integral part a newly conceived migration policy. The Nationale Raad van Advies inzake de hulpverlening aan minder ontwikkelde landen (a

national advisory board for the aid to developing countries)
brought out a note in which such a connection was deemed
feasible and advisable between the Netherlands and Marocco,
Tunesia and Turkey.

The Dutch government should outline a framework and express unequivocally the terms under which temporary residence
is beneficial to the foreign worker as well as his family and country of origin.

Mid-March the Dutch government brought out the long awaited Memorandum in Reply to the government paper of 1970.

4. Government Paper March 1974

4.1. Future Migration policy

In March 1974 the Dutch government made its point of view
towards future migration policy known in the memorandum in
Reply to the government paper of 1970.

A resumé of the main points follows:

The starting point to these policy was that they should concentrate on the interests of all parties: The Netherlands, the foreign workers and the countries of origin.

The unbalanced circumstances which are the cause of the arrival of great numbers of foreign workers in the Netherlands, namely the demand for foreign manpower on the Dutch labour market
and the lack of appropriate employment for the foreigners in
their own countries should find a more structural long-term solution. As long as the need exists to employ foreign workers their
admission and reception and guidance should be in close accord
with these long term goals.

For this purpose a bill is to be introduced governing the admission of foreign workers and their provision with employment.

In it several new elements for slowing down and controlling
labour migration are included:

(a) the possibility to limit the number of foreign workers;
(b) restricting labour migration to the recruitment countries
    (Greece, Marocco, Portugal, Spain, Tunesia, Turkey, Yugosla-
    via);
(c) introducing a license for providing foreign workers with em-
    ployment;

(d) extending the responsibility of employers towards proper housing;
(e) penalization under the Economic Misdemeanours Act for clandestinely providing illegal residents with employment;
(f) establishing a bonus-arrangement for foreign workers returning voluntarily for good to their countries of origin. An obligatory wait of one year was already imposed before first degree relatives could join a subject working in the Netherlands. In that period the latter will have to decide upon accepting the bonus. This bonus of around dFl. 5000 will be made available to foreign bonus. This bonus of around dFl. 5000 will be made available to foreign workers voluntarily returning for good to their countries of origin after a stay of 2 or 3 years.

A bill is also being prepared to assure foreign workers of free juridical help when necessary.

In the former bill the question of whether the foreign worker has given preference to the bonus or a prolonged stay in the Netherlands will determine the policy on reception and guidance which will apply to him.

Another point is that more information is to be given to foreign workers.

The government paper recognizes the fact that labour migration perpetuates the dependency by the supplying countries on the receiving countries. One means of lessening the inequality in this relation is to stimulate employment in the supplying countries while cutting down in western Europe on investments which augment the demand for foreign manpower.

Shaping, training and education of the foreign worker would be levelled on his prospects in his home country. This could be done within the duration of his contact. At a later stage development cooperation would justify post-contractual courses in either the Netherlands or the countries of origin.

As far as education for the children of foreign workers is concerned the starting point remains their integration in the Dutch school system without breaking the ties with their home countries.

The government is trying for better international division of labour through:

— a more free trade policy on the part of the wealthy countries.
— the stimulation of industrial activities in developing countries.
— adjustment of the Dutch production structure.

In the long run the policy will incorporate alternatives to eliminate the necessity of foreign labour recruitment.

4.2. *Critical remarks*

A positive aspect of the government paper is that at policy
makers' level the whole problem of labour migration is placed
within an international framework.

Not until now has attention been paid to the relation between
labour migration and development cooperation.

In this memorandum in Reply, the Dutch government to a
certain extent meets the need which was being placed on vision
in the migration policy. The paper marks the transition from a
short term (adjustment) policy to a long term (structural) policy.

The view that labour migration maintains the disruption of the
international division of labour justifies the wish in the countries
involved to slow down and control labour migration.

However, one cannot escape the impression that also short
term (conjunctural) deliberations have lead to the long term
(structural) point of view in future migration policy.

The economic problems in a period of recession, which is influenced by such factors as the international energy crisis, the
continuing oilboycott on the Netherlands, and the predicted
rise in the unemployment rate have undoubtedly lead to more
limitative measures.

The trade unions too have steadily insisted on a more restricted admission policy.

The paper makes it quite clear that the Dutch government tries
to avoid rather expensive infra-structural investments which
would otherwise be inevitable to guarantee future reception and
guidance of migrant workers.

It is therefore quite right to look upon the dFl. 5000 "departure" bonus as "an attack on acquired rights".

The emphasis in the government paper is placed here because
the settling of migrant workers and their families is unwanted.
Now by "subtile" rather than forceful means *rotation* of migrant
workers is sought after.

Particularly dew to a lack of such infra-structural provisions in the field of housing, education and medical care labour migration remains advantageous for the receiving countries.

The fact that the paper is not signed by the ministers responsible for these fields is understandably criticised.

This shows the role of utterly national considerations in migration policy making.

Another objection to the paper is that the resolutions are unelaborated. Therefore the introduction of the new bill should be awaited, which is why we shall not go into detail on this.

Besides it is not clear yet in what way the resolutions are to be concretized and how soon and whether they are feasible.

We should therefore prefer to concentrate on the main lines (perspective) of the policy and discuss the position that the government has taken in between labour migration and development cooperation.

The first reactions and comments on the government paper of March 1974 have shown that it will be widely met as uproarously as the government paper of 1970.

The voices of the migrant workers themselves will be heard far more distinctly this time.

4.3. *Perspective*

The memorandum in Reply, while advocating a restrictive admission policy grants that labour migration can only be reduced gradually.

A policy bent on removing structural barriers cannot be effective inmediately.

Nobody at present has any doubts to that there is a resting need for foreign labour. In fact if an overly stringent admission policy were to be enforced it would jeapordize the Dutch employment rate.

In the immediate future the proposed measures cause stabilisation rather than reduction in the need for foreign labour.

As labour migration is not an independent matter but part of a relation between wealthy and poor countries that is founded on structural inequality and dependency by the one on the other, obviously more attention should be paid on the relation between labour migration and development in the emigration countries.

Because of this the chapter "on the relation between problems of economic and social growth in the developing countries and the matter of the foreign workers" was in particular well received.

This chapter shows at least a little vision; it discloses the disadvantages of labour migration for the supplying countries, viz.

(a) Emigration by the male working population in the most productive years of their life and consequently a negative development in the formation of the remaining population (children and the aged).

(b) Unfavourable social effects of migrant labour dew to long periods of separation in families.

(c) The by effects of labour migration because of the depopulation of rural areas and the migration flow to the cities (so that "bidonvilles" or "geçekondus" arise).

(d) The ineffectiveness of savings on development because they are mainly used consumptively and not for investments to stimulate production.

(e) The returning migrant workers often end up, after they have gone through there money, in exactly the same position as before their migration.

(f) Many returning workers are forced to emigrate again after a lapse of time.

(g) The stay abroad seldomly leads to industrial experience and schooling which could be of use in the country of origin.

Based on the advice obtained from the Nationale Raad van Advies inzake de hulpverlening aan minder ontwikkelde landen, labour migration is deemed under certain circumstances an obstacle to the origination of more industry in the emigration countries and thus for the coming about of a better international division of labour.

If the labour supplying countries themselves consider labour migration as an immediate relief on unemployment and population pressure and a means of improving the balance of payments with more foreign exchange, these are advantages which are introduced to veil and thus prevent the realization of the necessary structural adjustments.

Not only does labour migration merely bring a temporary relief to structural unemployment, but also the country of emigration is bereaved of essential labour potential by the departure of the most enterprising and best skilled workers.

Moreover, in the developing countries labour migration can never be an alternative to setting up local-export industries. The origination of such industries is necessary for structural growth in employment rate and the realization of a more permanent and less one-sided inflow of foreign exchange.

Noteworthy too is the fact that labour migration leads to the importation of lasting consumption articles, and thus to a stimulation of the Western European growth.

Summarizing, we should note that labour migration is most disadvantageous for the emigration countries.

The Dutch government expresses its wish in this paper to establish a positive relation between migration and development of the emigration countries by relating labour migration to development cooperation, by;

(a) Promoting industrialization in the emigration countries and stimulating the establishment of labour intensive industries in these countries.

(b) Direct government support to projects in the Mediterrenean developing countries in which former migrant workers can find employment and use the schooling and industrial experience which they acquired during their stay in the Netherlands. Finances for development should be used for both technical and financial support.

(c) Reconstruction of Dutch industry in accordance with the improvement of the international division of labour.

(d) A search for possibilities to create facilities in which migrant workers can develop themselves upon return (e.g. shaping and schooling).

(e) Providing socially inclined credit banks in the emigration countries with the means to help returning migrant workers economically reastablish and socially develop themselves.

(f) Support to foreign workers returning permanently to their home countries in. for example, the form of facilities which encourage saving.

Especially the following considerations are important for the emigration countries;

Obviously there is the necessity of a permanent consultation structure between representatives of the migration countries so as to investigate the possibilities of the relation between labour migration and development cooperation.

The emigration countries should show a certain degree of initiative towards expressing the desirability of such a relation as well as its concretion.

If this is the case then priority should be given to formulating a relation between labour migration and the national (or regional) development policy.

Relief on unemployment and population pressure and also the positive effects of foreign exchange on the balance of payments are arguments which may and need not be tolerated as supposed advatages of labour migration.

When formulating such a policy attention should be paid to;

(a) Stating the preferable possibilities towards schooling and shaping of migrant workers while they are abroad.
(b) Promoting migration in groups so as to enable collective initiatives upon return of the members after they have been trained together while being abroad.
(c) Promoting migration through cooperatives in order to break up the "middle class ideology" and provoke collective initiatives in the workers after their return. These cooperatives in special should be enabled to get credit facilities if these make more employment available.
(d) Setting up projects in which returning migrant workers can be employed and use the industrial experience and knowledge they have acquired abroad.
(e) Informing the returning migrant workers on how to invest their savings in a more productive way.
(f) Advancing research that is socially relevant to the relation between labour migration and development cooperation.
(g) Creating an international research centre (e.g. by instigation of the O.E.C.D.) in order to attune the research activities in the various countries and to accumulate data.

With thanks to Christopher Mellen for his help in the translation.

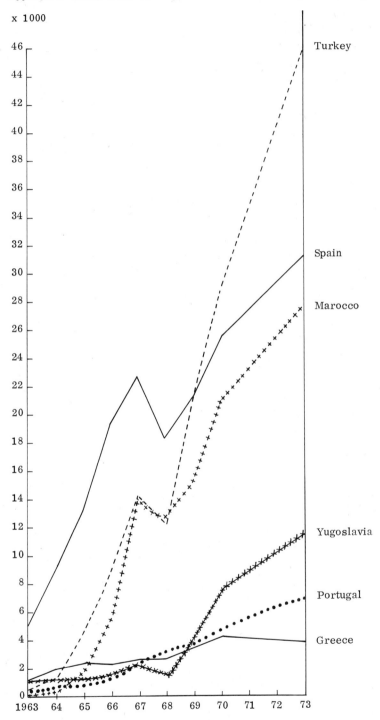

Appendix I. Survey of aliens from the reormitment countries (excl. Tunesia)

x 1000

Turkey

Spain

Marocco

Yugoslavia

Portugal

Greece

46
44
42
40
38
36
34
32
30
28
26
24
22
20
18
16
14
12
10
8
6
4
2
0

1963 64 65 66 67 68 69 70 71 72 73

Appendix II

Number of valid labour licenses issued to foreign workers per branch in the Netherlands.
situation at the end of

Branch	1958	1959	1960	1961	1962	1963	1964	1965	1966	1967	1968	1969	1970	1971
Earthware	399	470	596	816	897	1475	2165	2654	3017	2490	2699	2814	3798	3849
Diamond-industry	13	11	10	32	5	8	12	12	19	22	22	17	14	8
Graphic Trade	339	361	396	431	434	456	466	728	795	713	679	671	739	637
Building	1501	1409	1526	1501	1840	2226	2615	3741	3948	3447	3737	2959	3581	3926
Chemical industry	541	518	583	639	834	1045	1450	1841	2565	2067	2483	2709	3411	3486
Wood, Cork, etc.	277	277	293	336	347	462	845	1309	1733	1354	1517	1394	1673	1761
Clothing	1023	881	808	722	734	786	860	1092	1256	993	1274	1201	1114	1419
Cleaning	258	247	269	275	258	260	232	351	508	557	672	555	594	703
Artists, etc.	–	10	7	6	10	12	6	11	15	9	6	9	5	2
Leather, Rubber	422	388	562	757	1090	1410	2115	2508	2731	1956	2303	2259	2670	2975
Mining	3579	2347	1922	1840	2039	2854	4385	5002	2570	2097	2075	820	794	774
Metals-industry	4578	4310	5028	7810	9767	11088	17608	21408	19995	17115	18831	19556	22807	26493
Paper-industry	169	162	184	219	272	340	524	965	1296	1278	1451	1685	1950	1725
Textiles	1351	1404	1700	2554	2747	3456	5016	5370	5577	3331	4269	4727	4716	5492
Water, gas, etc.	179	144	150	151	301	291	443	515	287	359	179	57	43	25
Food, drink, etc.	866	793	869	1073	1155	1587	2165	3647	6096	5943	6483	7509	9948	10999
Agriculture	319	279	286	261	269	258	220	239	270	356	408	358	473	516
Chase, Fishing	6	7	5	20	10	17	14	13	23	6	15	6	8	9
Commerce	2255	2087	2289	2455	2570	2759	2807	3352	2715	2953	3235	2660	2979	2948
Aviation	63	71	124	171	227	358	452	451	507	639	692	395	456	485
Catering	909	802	1008	922	1153	1306	1477	1604	1491	2080	2212	1950	2384	3006
Ship-building	155	143	98	223	607	186	159	189	226	122	165	72	98	78
Transport	808	833	869	804	521	1220	1062	1243	1633	1575	1763	1612	1936	1686
Banks	236	206	290	391	293	298	333	349	202	225	239	113	180	146
Other	1913	1667	2699	2015	2158	2497	2858	3173	2805	3179	3215	3155	4210	144
Education	297	293	373	423	459	531	534	592	441	509	524	567	495	579
Religion	28	26	24	24	33	25	17	12	15	24	19	21	11	9
Domestic staff	1307	1091	1109	1119	939	822	771	728	326	329	303	191	165	137
Unknown	–	–	–	–	–	–	–	–	13210	16413	18869	18	–	4777
Total	23791	21237	24077	27990	31969	38033	51611	63099	76272	72141	80339	60070	71252	78794

Excluding:
Frontier-workers and Indonesian workers.
Workers from E.E.C. membership countries (Italy).
Workers from outside the E.E.C. in possession of a permanent labour license (after more than 5 years of stay).

Sources: Het Vrije Verkeer van werknemers en de arbeidsmarkt binnen de E.E.G. – 1969.
Het Vrije Verkeer van werknemers en de arbeidsmarkt binnen de E.E.G. ... 1972.

MORE FOREIGN WORKERS-GERMANY'S LABOR PROBLEM NO. 1 ?

GOTTFRIED E. VOELKER

In 1961 about 300,000 foreign workers, in 1965 about one million, in 1971 about two million, and in 1973 more than 2.4 million foreign workers were employed in Germany. If the development continues as in the last years, Theo Sommer envisions that about 20 per cent of the working population will be foreigners at the end of the decade.[1]

As of now, critical foreign-domestic worker ratios have been reached in Stuttgart with 24 per cent, Frankfurt with 21 per cent, Munich and Duesseldorf both with more than 15 per cent of the working population being foreigners.[2] However, in Germany the situation is not as dramatic as it is in Switzerland, where 25.7 per cent of the working population are foreigners.[3]

In August 1973, public opinion against foreign workers reached a peak, when about 10,000—mainly Turkish—workers at Ford AG. started a strike. Forced by economic necessity and public opinion, the government of the Federal Republic of Germany passed a program which is supposed to co-ordinate industries still growing interest in the employment of foreign workers with the ability of Germany's social infrastructure to accept and absorb foreign workers. As a side effect, it is hoped, that the program will motivate industry to substitute capital for labor. The additional investments are expected to be done in the less developed parts of Europe.[4] The problems of foreign workers in Germany will be discussed under four headings:

1. Foreign Workers in Germany.
2. The German Industry and the Foreign Worker.

---

[1] Theo Sommer, "Nigger, Kulis oder Mitbürger. Unser Sozialproblem No. 1: Die Gastarbeiter", *Die Zeit* (April 6, 1973).

[2] "Wohin zieht es Gastarbeiter", *Die Welt* (July 28, 1973).

[3] "Gastarbeiter in Europa", *Süddeutsche Zeitung* (March 28, 1973).

[4] Herrmann Buschfort, "Ausländische Arbeitnehmer—Prüfstein für den sozialen Rechtsstaat und die europäische Solidarität". *Die Neue Gesellschaft*, No. 8 (August 1973), 584.

3. Labor Migration and the Impact on the Economy.
4. Foreign Workers: A bone of Contention in Germany's Policy.

1. *Foreign Workers in Germany*

The employment of foreign workers in Germany is not a new phenomenon at all. In 1895, about 315,000 foreigners were employed in the "Deutsche Reich". In 1900, the number increased to about 500,000 and it reached a peak of about 950,000 workers in 1907. In relation to the German working population this made up 4.5 per cent.[5]

After World War II, Germany became again attractive for foreign workers. The vigorous economic growth achieved in the fifties quickly mopped up the unemployment which post war conditions had created. Up to August 1961, well-trained workers from the eastern part of Germany filled the gaps in the labor market. With the construction of the Berlin Wall, the influx of people from the East stopped almost completely. Germany's industries accustomed to the "easy" labor market of the fifties started searching for foreign workers.

In 1960 about 200,000 foreign workers were employed. The number rose steeply in the following years and reached the unprecedented level of over 1.3 million in September 1966, when the recession began.

During the recession the number of foreign workers declined and had fallen to about 900,000 by January 1968. In the following boom the employment of foreign workers rose again. By the middle of 1968, the million mark had been passed once more and the figure kept on rising at an extraordinary speed. In January 1973, the 2.34 million mark has been passed and the number goes on rising, but at a declining speed. By now 10.8 per cent of the working population is made up by foreigners in Germany.[6] Together with their families, it is estimated that presently more than 4 million foreigners are living in Germany.

Up to 1969, most foreign workers came from Italy. After the 1966/67 recession, more and more workers came from Yugosla-

---

[5] H. Wander, "Die Beschäftigung ausländischer Arbeitnehmer in der Bundesrepublik Deutschland", *Sozialer Fortschritt*, 9th Year, No. 10 (1960), 244.

[6] Der Bundesminister für Arbeit und Sozialordnung, *Arbeits- und Sozialstatistische Mitteilungen*. No. 3 (Bonn, March 1973), 76-77.

via and Turkey. In the years 1971 and 1972, Yugoslavia took the lead followed by Italy and Turkey. At the beginning of 1972, Turkey's group of workers was the largest. With the promulgation of Yugoslavia's new law to restrict the migration of highly trained workers, in 1972 the dominant role of Turkish workers became increasingly obvious.[7] In September 1972, the "Bundesvereinigung der deutschen Arbeitgeber" (Federal Association of Employers in Germany) estimated the number of Turkish workers in Germany being 511,600.[8,9]

There are two basic opinions why foreign workers leave their home countries, a "pull" and a "push" theory. The first one states that workers are pulled away from their home countries by wage differentials. According to this theory, workers will migrate if the differences in wages are large enough to compensate for the cost of migration. Industry favors this idea, since the paid wages are supposed to free them from any further obligations against the workers.

Wage differentials are, of course, an important factor for the workers' decision to migrate. Yet, most important seems to be the fact that within their home countries foreign workers have practically no chances for economic progress. Consequently, they are more pushed than pulled to migrate. This leads to the idea that possibly the paid wages do not fully compensate the foreign workers.

Contacts between foreign workers and Germans are few. Besides the languages barriers and the differences in social and religious background, main reason for the few contacts seems to be the residential segregation. John R. Clark pointed out that in the case of Cologne most foreign workers are either living in dormitories in out of the way corners of the city or in substandard housing in city areas generally avoided by Germans.[10]

The prejudice against Turks seems to be greater than against any other group of workers, since socially and culturally they are

---

[7] *Ibid.* 77.

[8] Bundesvereinigung der deutschen Arbeitgeber, *Jahresbericht der deutschen Arbeitgeberverbände* (Cologne, 1972), 86.

[9] On November 23, 1973, in a news dispatch of the Norddeutsche Rundfunk, the number of Turkish workers in Germany was estimated being about 650,000.

[10] John R. Clark, "Residential Patters and Social Integration of Turks in Cologne, West Germany". Paper presented at MESA meetings (Binghamton, November 2-5, 1972).

most different from the Germans. Turks, in general, expect Germans to be open and welcoming to strangers as it is custom in Turkey. This expectation of establishing friendly relations with the German population is normally rejected. [11] Reason might be an often seen attitude of Germans against foreign workers: cheap labor, good enough for street cleaning and garbage collection.

2. *The German Industry and the Foreign Worker*

In January 1972, most foreign workers (788,161) were employed in iron and metal producing industries, followed by manufacturing industries (533,154), and construction industries (336,121). At the same time, in regards to distribution of nationals, Turks were the largest group in iron and metal producing industries (533,159), manufacturing industries (116,467), and mining (32,873); Yugoslavs were the largest group in construction industries (119,693), the public sector (24.64), and agriculture (3,569). [12] On a percentage base, in September 1971, most foreigners were employed in construction industries (22.4 per cent) and hotel industries (19.1 per cent). [13] Although new figures have not been published, yet, it can be expected that construction industry has lost some foreign workers due to government policy; high interest rates and the stopping of the so-called 7b depreciation.

Between Oktober 1970 and September 1971, 600,259 new foreign workers started working in the Federal Republic of Germany. By this, the total number of foreign workers increased to 2,240,793, in September 1971. Most of the newcomers came from Turkey. [14] As a result of the oel crises and the decision of the Minister for Labor and Social Order, Walter Arendt, of November 23, to stop the inflow of foreign workers, it can be expected that the total number of foreign workers will decrease at a rate of at least 10 per cent per annum (fluctuation rate). In as much contacts will not be renewed at the day they expire is, at

---

[11]   Karl Bingemer, Neubert Meistermann-Seeger, *Leben als Gastarbeiter* (Cologne, 1970), 56-57.

[12]   Bundesministerium für Arbeit und Sozialordnung, *Arbeits- und Sozialstatistische Mitteilungen*, No. 4 (Bonn, April 1973).

[13]   Bundesanstalt für Arbeit, *Ausländische Arbeitnehmer 1971* (Nürnberg, September 1972), 11.

[14]   *Ibid.* 4.

the present, an open question, mainly since car industry and chemical industry are already talking about a decrease in the average working time per week.

The main problem for the newly ariving workers and their employers is the adjustment to each other. For workers, coming from backward rural areas and even for those coming from metropolitan areas, life in an industrial society is strange. In addition, the hard climate, the difficult German language, the strict and confusing laws, the fact that bargaining is taboo, together with the rules and regulations at the new working place, all require a great deal of adjustment from the arriving workers. In case of Turkish workers, it can be agreed with N. Abadan-Unat that the "speed, ease and willingness of adjustment within a totally different environment is surprisingly high. This fact is acknowledged and highly praised by all German official authorities and employers". [15]

For the employers the time of adjustment is difficult, too. New workers are coming. The only real information about them comes from questionnaires filled out by the recruitment offices of the Federal Republic of Germany in the different countries. Many questions remain open: the quality of the worker, his previous training, his actual health condition, his ability to manage the job, and his willingness to adjust.

In general, time and cost of adjustment can be assumed directly proportional to differences in culture, religion, and to the lack in formal and technical education. [16]

While for the worker the costs of adjustment are relative moderate, for the company the cost can be as high as three months salary excluding the cost of construction for living quarters. Besides the recruitment fee of 300 DM for workers from countries of the Common Market (for workers from other countries a fee of 1000 DM has to be paid), the firm has to pay the air or train fare from the German border to the new residence of the worker, the cost of medical check-ups, the cost for training on the job, and various fees for translators and the government. In addition,

---

[15] Nermin Abadan, "Turkish Workers in West Germany: A Case Study", *Ankara Universitesi*, Vol. 1 (Ankara, March 1969), 35.

[16] Fassbender, "Unternehmerische und betriebliche Probleme", *Probleme der ausländischen Arbeitskräfte in der Bundesrepublik Deutschland*, Beihefte der Konjunkturpolitik, Heft 13 (Berlin, 1966), 50-55.

firms are partly responsible for foreign workers' housing. Under the present law, at least 8 m² of living space per worker is required in dormitories. The cost, if newly constructed, run as high as 2,000 DM/m².

Despite the high initial cost for new foreign workers, industry demands more and more of them. Assuming industry minimizes cost, this seems to indicate that the employment of foreign workers is still less costly than the employment of German workers or the cost of investments in labor saving equipment. It may be argued this cost advantage, resulting from the employment of foreign workers, might have the effect to retarding the development of Germany's industry in the long run.

In 1967, Carl Föhl already mentioned this possibility. With a system of equations he seemed to prove that labor productivity with a purely German labor force would be higher than labor productivity with a mixed German-foreign labor force. He argued that without foreign workers new private investments would result in old companies being abondant by the workers. Attracted by higher wages, they would have to move to new modern firms. Given foreign workers, it is assumed there is a tendency for older industries operating with lower productivity to keep going. If Föhl's idea is assumed to be correct, the present share of nearly 11 per cent of foreign workers would have depressed labor productivity by about 10 per cent. [17]

The strikes at Ford AG. and Opel AG. showed how dependant Germany's car industry is on foreign workers. This is also true for construction industry, steel industry, and mining. Despite their vital importance to industry, foreign workers remain an isolated group, often pushed and misused by their German colleagues and firms.

The strike at Ford AG. is a good example for the last point. Initial reason for the strike was the firing of some Turkish workers. Turkish colleagues protested against the dismissals and, in addition, asked for better working conditions at the production lines. German workers symphasized with the demands and added a request for higher pay to compensate inflationary losses. IG-METAL, the workers' union and the workers' council at Ford AG took the workers' demands as their own and started bargain-

---

[17] Carl Föhl, "Stabilisierung und Wachstum bei Einsatz von Gastarbeitern", *Kyklos*, Vol. 20 (1967), 119-146.

ing with the Ford management. As soon as the management agreed to pay some compensation for the high inflation rate in Germany, the all workers' representatives were fully satisfied and asked the workers to continue working. There was no mentioning of the Turkish workers' demands. Turkish workers, who felt themselves tricked out, wanted to continue the strike. German police and some colleagues forced them to work or leave the plant. The strike ended in a battle. [18]

It seems as if foreign workers are quite welcome as working force, but just as a working force. Otherwise they are isolated and possibly discriminated. Nobody actually feels responsible for them, and the public should not overhear the warners believing that Germany is producing the "niggers" of Europe.

3. Labor Migration and the Impact on the Economy

From a macro economic point of view, the employment of foreign workers mainly effects national income, income distribution, wealth, labor mobility, the wage and the price level, the Balance of Payments, and the infrastructure.

3.1. Income and Income Distribution

An inflow of productive labor increases total production and thereby raises total income or Gross National Product (GNP). An increase in GNP may be considered as advantagerous for the economy, yet, a *sole increase does not* necessarily result into a higher standard of living. The possibly declining average labor productivity, as mentioned by Carl Föhl, may lead to a decline in GNP per capita, which is considered a more meaningful indicator to describe the standard of living.

The migration of foreign labor may promote a redistribution of income. Often foreign workers have to accept less skilled jobs, allowing German workers to move into more highly skilled and better paid ones. Thereby, it may be possible that a decline in the average per capita income, based on the total living population in Germany, may actually hide an increase in per capita income for the Germans but a decrease for the foreigners.

---

[18] "Türken-Streik. Faden gerissen", *Der Spiegel*, No. 37 (September 10, 1973), 28-33.

3.2 *Wealth*

The impact on wealth may be twofold. First, foreign workers may help to raise Germany's stock of goods, and secondly, they may effect the level of education and training.

H.J. Rüstow stated that the employment of additional workers demands certain additional investments. These investments require a sacrifice in consumption for the German economy within a certain time span. As long as more workers enter the country each year, higher additional investments are needed. Consequently, the total time of sacrifice will get longer and longer. [19]

Additional investments increase wealth. People may argue that the employment of foreign workers is an advantage for the economy. Yet, this result overlooks that most of the non-consumption leading to investments is done by the Germans and not the foreigners. In addition, the investments done to create working places for foreign workers might not be optimal from a long-run view point.

A positive impact on education and training by foreign workers is questioned by most authors. Much more, one can assume that the inflow of foreign workers with their families will lead to more scarce schooling facilities, which might depress the level of education and training.

3.3. *Labor Mobility*

Christoph Rosenmüller emphasises that the inflow of foreign workers improves Germany's overall labor mobility. [20] Improved labor mobility is considered to be advantageous to the economy since it may lead to higher labor productivity.

In their initial employment foreign workers are hired to places where labor is mostly needed. This may be called a temporary increase in labor mobility. However, as soon as the workers are settled in a job, their mobility is relatively low. Their contracts compel them to stay with the same employer for no less than one year. Total labor mobility may well decrease.

---

[19] H.J. Rüstow, "Gastarbeiter—Gewinn oder Belastung für unsere Volkswirtschaft", *Probleme der ausländischen Arbeitskräfte in der Bundesrepublik Deutschland*, Beihefte zur Konjunkturpolitik, Heft 13 (Berlin, 1966), 33ff.

[20] Christoph Rosenmüller, "Volkswirtschaftliche Aspekte der Ausländerbeschäftigung", *Ausländische Arbeitnehmer in der Bundesrepublik Deutschland*, Ed.: Der Bundesminister für Arbeit und Sozialordnung, Sonderdruck aus Bundesarbeitsblatt, No. 4 (Bonn, 1970), 6.

3.4 Full Employment

On November 26, 1973, the government of the Federal Republic of Germany ruled to close down all foreign workers' recruitment offices in non Common Market countries. The oil crisis resulting into a possible economic slow-down in Germany is named the reason for this decision. It seems as if the German government wants to use foreign workers as a safety valve against domestic unemployment.

W. Weidenbörner questions this view. He argues that foreign workers are treated as equals to German workers in respect to labor law. Foreign workers' contracts cannot be cancelled at will. It can even be argued that during recessions such one year contracts are a better protection than the period of notice prescribed by law for German employees. [21] In addition, it may be argued that in times of recession the recruitment fee for foreign workers (300.00 DM or respectively 1000.00 DM) may affect industry in such way to keep foreigners but to fire Germans.

The decision of the government is directive and hardly acceptable within the framework of a free and social market economy. Besides, economically it seems to be quite dangerous.

The Great Depression of the 1930's taught economists that anti-cyclical fiscal policy was the way to smooth economic ups and downs. If it is assumed correct that the German economy is gliding onto a recession, the decision of the government to stop the inflow of Turkish, Yugoslav, and Greek workers may turn out to produce cyclical effects.

Foreign workers' direct and indirect demand [22] for goods and services may be assumed larger than Germans'. [23] Therefore, a decrease in the total number of foreign workers will hit the domestic, and with a time lag, the export demand. The reduction in total demand may force industry to adjust production. More unemployment will appear. In the short run mainly German workers have to be dismissed, since they are only protected by the

---

[21] W. Weidenbörner, "Beschäftigung ausländischer Arbeitnehmer in der Bundesrepublik Deutschland", Ausländische Arbeitnehmer in der Bundesrepublik Deutschland, Ed.: Der Bundesminister für Arbeit und Sozialordnung, Sonderdruck aus Bundesarbeitsblatt, No. 4 (1970), 226.

[22] Indirect demand: export demand resulting from foreign workers' remittances.

[23] Gottfried E. Voelker, "Impact of Turkish Labor Migration on the Economy of the Federal Republic of Germany", The German Economic Review, Vol. 11, No. 1 (1973), 72-74.

period of notice granted by law. It follows that a decrease in the total number of foreign workers may possibly not help to keep a situation of full employment, but act in a cyclical way and increase unemployment, for German workers as well as for foreign workers back in their home countries.

3.5. *Wage and Price Level*

Labor migration may affect Germany's wage-price level in two possible ways:

(1)   A growing labor supply keeps wages down. This would improve price stability.

(2)   The greater number of workers inflates the demand for goods and services. This would tend to raise prices, which in turn would be a signal for labor unions to demand higher wages.

Labor statistics offer no evidence for the idea that between 1962 and 1971 an increasing number of foreign workers reduced wages. Whether wages were depressed has to be further investigated.

Competition is the major factor in keeping wages down. Consequently, more foreign workers competing with German workers for the same working place should depress wages.

C. Kerr points out that the German labor market is not homogeneous at all. It consists of a number of partial markets, which do not compete with each other.[24] Therefore it may be concluded that the growing number of foreign workers does not have a wage-depressing effect. In addition, the high degree of unionism in Germany will equalize wage-depressing effects if they would exist.

There is also no clear evidence in support of the second alternative. It is commonly known that foreign workers have a high propensity to save. In a closed economy this would dampen total demand and possibly depress prices, which may keep wage demands within acceptable limits. Yet, in an open economy and with a large number of foreign workers, the result has to be modified. Foreign workers' savings are sent as remittances to the workers' home countries. They are often immediately used by their governments to satisfy import needs. It follows that with some time lag foreign workers' remittances will reappear on the German market as additional export demand. The strength of this demand-pull effect has not been calculated, yet.

---

[24]   C. Kerr, "The Balkanisation of Labour Markets", *Labor Mobility and Economic Opportunity* (New York, London, 1954), 92 ff.

3.6. *The Balance of Payments*

The employment of foreign workers affects Germany's Balance of Payments mainly through the Current Account. Within this account the impact on the Balance of Trade and the Balance of Private Remittances and Government Transactions are most important.

On one hand, the employment of foreign workers increases Germany's export potential, which is a prerequisit for the positive Balance of Trade. On the other hand, in 1972, foreign workers have sent 6,700 million German Mark to their home countries. These remittances make more than 50 per cent of the deficit in Germany's Balance of Private Remittances and Government Transactions. [25]

In general, the huge deficit in the Balance of Private Remittances and Government Transactions would be dangerous for the German economy. Yet, taking into account Germany's long-time positive Balance of Trade, the deficit may, at the present time, be a welcome counter weight.

3.7 *Infrastructure*

Lately, an increasing number of scholars emphasize the growing cost of infrastructure due to the migration of foreign workers with their families. This change to more permanent migration will require considerable investments in housing, schools, hospitals, transportation facilities, and other forms of infrastructure.

In 1965, H.J. Rüstow estimated the cost for infrastructure (including housing) to be about 25,000 DM per worker. [26] This estimate was based on 1962 prices. Employing the cost of living index, for 1972 it was 130 per cent, the present value can be assumed at about 32,500 DM. Based on 2.5 million foreign workers, a total of 81,250 million German Mark should have been invested.

Only a small portion of this amount has actually been invested. Yet, the more workers that migrate permanently, the more pressing will be the demand for investments in infrastructure. Whether the German economy is able at all to do all these investments within an acceptable time span seems questionable. If we

---

[25] Monatsberichte der Deutschen Bundesbank, 25th Year, No. 10 (Oct. 1973), 72.
[26] H.J. Rüstow, *op. cit.*, 37.

take into account that in 1970, Federal and State agencies have spent a total of 78 billion DM for infrastructure and housing, and if investments in infrastructure would be equally divided between Germans and foreigners, it may take about 20 years to do all the investments for foreign workers.

This time period, of course, can be shortened, if industry and the foreign workers themselves are willing to carry a larger burden. Industry may provide more housing and contribute to the cost of children's schooling. Foreign workers may use some of their savings to be invested in Germany.

4. *Foreign Workers: A Bone of Convention in German's Policy*

In the last decade, the government of the Federal Republic of Germany regulated labor migration into Germany as little as possible. However, in the last two years, with the number of foreign workers skyrocking and the problems getting out of the hand, public opinion forced the government to search for acceptable solutions to the problems.

In June 1973, the government passed a so-called "action program". The main aim of this program is to limit the number of foreign workers in Germany. To reach this aim, seven guide lines have been given:

(1) All legally employed foreign workers have to be housed according to a specific housing law. For each new foreign worker the Federal Bureau for Labor has to check whether the requirements are met.

(2) In certain areas with high foreign worker concentration, (Frankfurt, Munich, Stuttgart), the migration of further foreign workers depends on the ability of the social infrastructure to accept additional workers.

(3) The recruitment fee payable to the Federal Bureau for Labor shall be increased for workers from non Common Market countries from 300.00 DM to 1000.00 DM.

(4) If these measurements do not slow down the inflow of foreign workers into Germany, the government reserves the right, to introduce a special tax payable by industries employing foreign workers.

(5) Industries who employ workers in an illegal way, will be punished more strictly.

(6) The government of the Federal Republic of Germany will not introduce a forced "rotation principle". Yet, it should be clear that Germany is no typical country for migration.

(7) The government of the Federal Republic of Germany believes that all problems arising from the employment of foreign workers, can only be solved within the whole European framework. From a political, social, and economical point of view, the government wants to motivate industry to increase the export of capital to south and southeastern Europe. [27]

Only a few ideas of a social and free market economy are left in this action program, and even those have been abolished lately by the decision of the Minister of Labor and Social Order, W. Arendt, to stop the inflow of foreign workers from non Common Market countries. Since associate members of the Common Market are not excluded from this decision, the European concept mentioned in point seven of the action program, seems to be just mere words. The action of the Federal Republic of Germany can be interpreted as a step backward to nationalism and away from the European concept.

4.1 Free Movement of Labor within the Common Market

Although the inter-country migration of labor is still regulated with-in the Common Market, it is expected by officials of the Common Market that freedom of residence for everyone in the Community will be fully realized soon. Into this freedom the associate members will be included at the end of the decade. From that time workers are free to move to places where they expect optimal return from their labor.

From a global point of view, the absolut free movement of labor may lead to socially unwanted concentration of labor in already over-populated areas. Problems arising out of such a concentration can best be studied in the United States, mainly in the areas of New York, Chicago, San Francisco etc. As long as the institutions of the Common Market do not have the power to regulate these unwanted flows of the labor force, each govern-

---

[27] Walter Arendt, "Konsolidierung der Ausländerbeschäftigung, Aktionsprogramm der Bundesregierung", *Die Neue Gesellschaft*, No. 8 (August, 1973), 587-589.

ment should act in the European interest. Thereby, the instru-
ments of a free and social market economy should be employed.

It has already been mentioned that the decision of the government to stop the inflow of foreign workers from non Common
Market countries is hardly acceptable under a system of a free
and social market economy. In addition, it is not in the interest
of a united Europe.

More market conform seems to be a system that would redistribute the cost of foreign workers employment. Industry, as
the main beneficiary, should carry as well the direct as indirect
cost arising from the employment of foreign workers.

Direct cost are mainly the wages paid. There, special pay
groups (Leichtarbeitslöhne) for foreign workers should no longer
be allowed, and equal pay for equal work should in the case of
foreign workers be more than just mere words.

In the field of indirect cost, industry should carry the full cost
of infrastructure due to foreign workers, less the taxes paid by
foreign workers. In addition, industry should pay the workers'
home countries compensation for the workers' education and for
the time after return. The last point seems to be of special interest. Foreign workers arrive in Germany within their best and
most productive years. Industry gets this advantage, but pays
only an average wage. Therefore, it seems justified that they pay
some compensation to the workers or their governments for the
years to come for the worker, when his productivity decreases.

The higher cost of production, possibly resulting into higher
prices, will force industry, if they want to remain competitive
within the world market, to look for other methods of production. On one hand, industry may try to substitute capital for
labor within Germany. On the other hand, industry may export
capital to places where labor cost are still low. The last possibility
if made even more attractive by the last up-valuation of the
German Mark.

The possibility to export capital instead of importing labor is
viewed as advantageous for all parties. The foreign workers may
return home and continue working there with a German company. This may solve the foreign workers problem in Germany.
From the industries point of view, the export of capital may
keep them competitive. Besides, this solution will bring industria-

lisation to the less industrialized parts of Europe. Thereby, income differential may be reduced.

Main problems for such a solution is the fact, that most European countries are not actually ready for the Common Market, they are all looking for their sole benefit. Yet, there are also actual problems. Industries decision to export capital and to produce a part or the whole production in a foreign country is not just a cost problem. It depends on many other points, as for example, the political situation within the foreign country, foreign ownership laws, import and export laws, the presence of supplying industry, the infrastructure, the cost of labor etc. From the German governments point of view, capital export is not without problems either. Capital export will lead to a decrease in tax revenues and a possible decrease in exports. Besides, the Balance of Payments will be affected. From the capital gaining country, capital import may conflict with domestic ownership laws, with the plans for development etc. There are lots of problems arising from the export of capital instead of importing labor. Yet, in the common interest they can and have to be solved.

Conclusion

The number of foreign workers skyrocked in the last two years in Germany. As a result various problems arose and the public demanded more and more that the government should act. The action program of the government was the first step to limit the total number of foreign workers in Germany. With the oil crisis, in November 1973, the government stopped totally the inflow of foreign workers from non Common Market countries. Besides, that the economic impact of foreign workers on the German economy in respect to GNP, wealth, price level, full employment, Balance of Payments, and Infrastructure are questionable, the decision of the government is directive and non market conform within a free and social market economy.

In respect to a united Europe, it seems best to redistribute the cost of foreign workers and to ask industry, as the main beneficiary, to carry the main portion. The higher cost for foreign workers may force industry to substitute either capital for labor within Germany or produce in low wage places outside Germany. The last possibility is seem as best solution, since it brings advantages to all parties.

FOREIGN WORKERS AND SOCIAL SERVICES IN FEDERAL GERMANY

EBERHARD DE HAAN

1. *Introduction Migration—An old Problem*

Manpower migration lead to societal conflicts of conscience. This seems to be the new aspect of migration, which itself is an old phenomenon, as people usually follow the standard advantages of production. If we deal with this problem in a larger framework, we might find in many periods of history such migratory movements. It has been pointed out repeatedly, that the present migration from the Meditterranean has been preceeded by a Polish migratory wave, which trickled down without almost any trace into the industrial center of the Ruhr—with the exception of family names.

Migration is not either a monopoly of Europe. In North Africa, Latin America, Central Africa and the Middle East, people are crossing bounderies toward productive centers, without the assistance of special organizations. Once they have to overcome sharp social and political cleavages, the character of migrations change.

2. *Democracy and the employment of foreigners*

It will be sufficient in our terms of the subject to define democracy as the existence of fundamental rights, the right to vote and of social solidarity.

According to their historical evolution, the European democracies did link up the usage of political rights to the status of citizenship, thus granting the citizen a privilege which remains denied to the inhabitant. Citizenship is awarded as is the title of nobility,—through birth or acknowledgement. The granting of citizenship—just as some time ago the bestowment of nobility—is tied up to complicated conditions.

At this point we should ask ourselves whether on the eve of European unification this historical result should be upheld. It seems that in a true democratic spirit, people should be entitled to participate in the shaping of governmental power in the place, where they are subjected to this power and not where they have been born.

The notion of foreigner (alien) is derived from the concept of citizen. A foreigner is any person, who is not citizen. He is subject to the laws of the host country, its criminal justice, its tax paying obligations, its specific legislation for aliens, which designs him a place in society, that clearly distinguished him from the normal citizen.

This proposition enables us to reduce the question related to any policy concerning foreigners to the following terms: how large should the discrepancy between citizen and foreigner be or has to be?

3. Foreigner and social services

Social services as well as services provided by private welfare organisations are elements of any modern social democracy. These services require constitutional guarantees, they represent in a sense the social conscience of society and help it to develop further. These services also claim to be a challenge to processes of elimination or marginalization, which are typical for all competitive societies. Indeed migrations may lead to a reduction of the individual or the group importance and in such societies the question of responsibility (fault) is not permitted to play an important role.

This is the reason why all kinds of social services are obliged in order to achieve something effective, to start from the real situation of human being, a group, to assess carefully the given situation of such individuals or groups, to test their legal status and measure the effectiveness of any assistance given. Only after a group has realized the scope of its situation, can it dare to make a step forward for additional changes. Under these circumstances, the lack of willpower represents very often the biggest problem.

I. The Federal German Republic and the Employment of Foreign Labour

1. The point of departure

The slogan of the "economic miracle" prevented many observers to realize that the Federal Republic of Germany has been able to create an equilibrium of its manpower market only since 1965. Until that date major handicaps such as the destruction due to World War II, the absorption of about 12 million people from East Germany and the stream of refugees from the DDR (a yearly average of 250,000) have to be solved.

It is during this very period that the German economy developed its tremendous capacity of expansion, which finally began in 1955 to strain the domestic labour market. The first agreement concerning manpower recruitment was signed with Italy in 1955, other agreements with Portugal, Spain, Greece, Turkey, Yugoslavia, Marocco and Tunesia followed.

At the end of 1973, roughly 2.65 million foreign workers were employed in Federal Germany, to this figure one has to add about 1,5 million family members among which there are about 850,000 children and young persons under the age of 21.

Comparing the great opportunities of open jobs in the FRG, one can not detect its counterpart abroad, what could be tantamount to heavy investments abroad. The jobs have not migrated, it is the people who have migrated and are continuing to migrate.

The reasons for this enormous capacity of open jobs has often been explained. The most relevant factors are the following:

— declining birth rate,
— abrupt end of the refugee stream from the DDR since 1961
— the expansion of the German army,
— the prolongation of schooling and vocational training.

It should be kept in mind above everything else, that all the initiatives in regard of the policy toward foreign workers are based upon one major point: the situation of the labour market. Reflections in terms of population policy have not been considered, foreign policy factors played a certain role only in regard of Marocco and Tunisia.

2. *The political framework*

The evaluation of the present day policy toward foreign manpower can only be done in terms of bilateral and supranational relations. The first agreement signed by the FRG in 1955 was concluded before the foundation of the E.E.C., others just at the time of its creation. Article 48 and 49 of the Treaty of Rome layed down the basis for the free circulation of the workers within the European community. Since 1964, these provisions have been put into effect, including regulation 1251/70, which grants foreigners a residence permit even after haven given up their regular work activity. Since these workers occupy an equal position with the Germans in regard to social and labour legislation, are not required to have a work and residence permit and are entitled to benefit from all social services, they can be defined in brief as citizens without political rights.

The general public has not so far become conscious of the "Europeanisation of the labour market". The migratory intentions of Europeans—with the exception of the Italians—remain minimal. Foreigners from E.E.C. countries in the Federal Republic of Germany constitute a small minority of the large bulk of foreign workers at large. In addition, it should be noted that a successful conjunctural policy permitted Germany to avoid a sharp competition for open jobs between Germans and Italians.

The German policy toward foreigners has to be evaluated from this particular perspective. If the thesis: the European Common Market evolves on two levels, bilateral and supranational—, is valid than the employment of a foreign labour force acquires a rank, which reaches far beyond the national labour market policy. In that case bilateral agreements represent the first phase of further commitments which can only be interpreted within the framework of a future European labour market.

This point of view is certainly justified in the case of Spain and Portugal, which for the time being, can not belong to the E.E.C. due to structural weaknesses. Greece and Turkey have associate memberships treaties with the E.E.C. Only Yugoslavia represents an exception.

It seems quite relevant to describe these interactions, since West Germany, blinded by its own success, treated its foreigners and adopted a policy which for a long time was tantamount to an arrangement to be carried out within a limited time as if the problem was a temporary one. Only in 1973, due to a formal statement of the Chancellor, did this discussion gain some new dimensions and constructive elements.

Social services, which are supposed to meet the social consequences of migration must be embedded into a political framework. Without the constellation of societal goals, social welfare degenerates into charitable, paternalistic and planless individual help.

With the cristallization of the political framework, two important consequences became visible: a) The realization that the employment of foreign manpower may acquire a permanent, unpredictable character, b) The necessity to shape its social security aspect. Provisional measures, which are based upon the assumption that the end of these temporary arrangements is approaching, have to be eliminated for good.

3. *The stratification of interests*

The politics which have characterized the organization of the labour force recruitment in eight countries, reflects clearly different economic, political interest positions, but certainly not the individual interests of the workers. Their position and the social, political minimum to be granted to them, will be treated under a separate heading.

The sending countries are saving through mediation of excessive manpower, the compensation of social burdens, produced by underemployment and a tight labour market. Remittances sent to the families of the migrant workers are representing for weak economies, an important source of foreign currency. Whether beyond this point their activity in the FRG secures at the same time a vocational training, is a hotly debated issue.

In the Federal Republic of Germany available jobs are filled, industrial capacities enlarged, capital intensive investments saved. In addition it should also be mentioned, that the workers savings, which are deposited in German banks, help also to promote the German capital market.

II. *The social basic facts*

1. *Recruitment procedures*

According to German jurisdiction the recruitment of manpower is given in form of an absolute monopoly to the Federal Employment agency and its local branches. The private mediation of manpower, whether German or alien, is strictly forbidden by law.

Thus the recruitment of foreign labour is regulated by German laws and bilateral agreements. The placement of a foreigner in the FRG requires the employer to fill in a placement request. So far the only important criterion in regard to the recruitment of foreign workers has been the interest of the management. Any other reflections of social or structural nature, are not taken into account, but these considerations are now beginning to be explored.

The employer offers to the foreign worker, whom he does not know, a one year working contract. This contract can not be repealed by either side and guarantees the foreigner a living arrangement. (Lodging, actually a vacant place in dormitories). The contract with its addendum, is signed by the foreign worker abroad.

This procedure, as depicted, commits a foreigner toward an unknown employer in a totally strange working place, with unknown working conditions. As the contract ends within one year, the future remains dark.

2. *The status of foreigner*

Foreigners, who are permitted legally to work in the Federal Republic, are required to have a work as well as a residential permit. For the first year, these permits are issued together with the recruitment procedure.

After the first year, the work permit is given or refused by the Employment Agency, the same is true for the granting of residential permits, which are issued by a special security agency, dealing solely with foreigners. Both agencies are functioning according to different laws. The working permit can be issued, if unemployed citizens of the E.E.C. countries are not waiting for a vacant job. This limitation is valid for the first five years for any foreign worker, who belongs to a country outside the E.E.C. After five years the working permit is granted unconditionally, leaving all labour market considerations aside. However the granting of any working permit, even after five years, depends upon the granting of a residential permit. The latter is subject to a large extent to the discretion of the agency dealing with foreigners. If this agency suspends an issued residential permit, the priorily accorded to the working permit automatically ceases to be valid.

The dualistic structure of these agencies potentially jeopardizes the social existence of the foreign worker. It creates a typical atmosphere of unsecurity, fear and anxiety, as well as the feeling of temporary living, a strain under which most of the families are suffering.

3. *Additional legal dispositions*

If the non-typical yearly contract is not taken as a rule, the status of the foreign worker in terms of labour law and social security is placed on an equal footing with the German worker. Any foreign worker has the right to participate in collective bargain agreements and to receive illness, old age, invalidity, accident and unemployment insurances. He can petition for the granting of housing financial aid and state sponsored saving premiums, however, his social services right are still limited.

Society expects him to get acquainted with his rights and to use them on given occasions, although he is not a citizen born in the country and has not been brought up within its social structure. On the contrary, he has been suddenly pushed into a new environment and the education he has received does not help him to adjust himself painlessly.

4. *The impact of the home countries*

Within the framework of various bilateral agreements, special articles stipulate that the first selection of the candidates for migration should be carried out by the responsible authorities of the emigration country. These agencies are not obliged to undertake a selection based upon the criteria of fitness for emigration, but are fully entitled to use other criteria, which may be deducted from the prevailing conditions of their domestic policy. These criteria are, of course, the very understandable desire to keep the skilled labour force at home and exclude it from governmental exchange as well as a preference for recruitment in regions with a weak social structure. Since usually residents of such areas also come from an underdeveloped educational system, very few, if any at all, informed and industrial minded workers, are sent to the Federal Republic.

The structure of motivation with these emigrants varies also strongly in accordance to the pattern of domestic politics in their home country. Especially all questions related to the expectations of their stay abroad and their intentions to return depend upon the prevailing economic conditions of the home country.

The expectation in regard of their stay is almost always limited with a certain time ceiling. However surveys and inquiries related to this subject must be interpreted with great caution. Not only because foreigners might change their intentions and opinions, but also because a permanent residence, in other words, a total emigration has so far always been turned down by German authorities. Empirical evidence shows that the desire to stay for a longer period is growing with the actual time spent abroad. Skilled workers wish to stay longer than unqualified labour and families would like to prolong their stay more than bachelors.

This intentions related to return are even vaguer. According to a survey carried out in 1971 by the Friedrich-Ebert Stiftung, only 13% of Turks wanted to return home as industrial workers, whereas 33% were intending to establish themselves as independent artisans or small enterprise owners.

A similar uncertainty reveals itself also among those, who so far have no opinion when they would like to return to their home country. According the above cited survey, only 5% of Turks want to stay less longer than intended, 27% are decided to stay as long as they planned, 31% want to stay longer in Federal Germany and 37% have no opinion.

This collected empirical data is proving once again that the feeling of uncertainty and anxiety can be largely explained by the precarious legal status of the foreign workers in Federal Germany.

III. *The Politics of the Federal Republic of Germany*

1. *Premises*

The Federal Republic laid down the basic elements of its policy in February 1970, when a document entitled "Principles for the integration of foreign workers and their families" was published and publicly defended. These principles were elaborated and formulated in February 1970 by a special commission attached to the Federal Ministry of Labour. Three years later, on April 20, 1973, a new version, which is based basically on the first draft, was adopted as the binding regulation for foreign workers and presented to the German parliament by the Federal Minister of Labour. In these principles, it is formally and repeatedly stated, that the economy of the Federal Republic of Germany can not give up the practice of employing foreign manpower. This statement represents at the same time a legal basis upon which a series of social and political demands are built, which all have as their goal the realization of an effective integration of the foreign workers. It mentioned in particular the imperative necessity to contribute to the reunion of families, the need for professional and language educational program, social counseling and assistance, provisions of adequate housing and the school education of children and adolescents.

All these discussions, so far, have been centered around the assumption that the employment of foreigners is advantageous in terms of the national economy. It has been claimed that this flow is positively influencing the age structure of the population and thus contributing to an advantageous income source of social security. Since they save a considerable amount of their wages, which diminishes their purchasing power on the German market, they are also preventing to a certain extent a too rapid rise in prices and are slowing down the price conjuncture.

Against these clearcut and very optimistic appraisals, there has been some voices of dissent. These critical voices expressed their concern in regard to a prolongued stay of the foreign workers and the family reunion, which is its logical consequence. They claim, that this development will weaken regional mobility, obstruct the stream of technical investments and thus cause a fall in productivity. In addition they maintain that a rising number of foreign workers and a longer stay in the country requires very important investments from both the public and the private sectors, that new housing and school units have to be built and additional infrastructures added for the realization of full integration.

A concrete measuring of the negative and positive factors involved with emigration cannot be carried out at this point of Germany's social and economic policy. Only one fact can be stressed: with increasing social expenditure a point may be reached, when an additional growth of foreign manpower employment will no longer secure further growth in the increase of the per capita income of the population.

This question has been raised for the first time officially, when the German Chancellor referred to the question of the employment of foreign manpower within the context of the new government program in January 1973. Taking this declaration as a point of departure, the Minister for Labour and Social Order added during this debate, that each day the evidence is showing that the social infrastructure is unable to make a parallel adjustment with the increasing volume of the labour market, which gains in volume and credibility. The danger that the foreign manpower will produce a relevant marginal group in German society, is very great. Thus, it seems imperative to investigate carefully what kind of measures are necessary to combine the interest of foreign workers with the necessity of their due integration into Germany's society. In other words, the flow of foreign manpower cannot be left solely to the demands of the labour market, it has to be monitored according to the degree of receptivity and absorption of the social infrastructure.

In his speech the German Chancellor of the time, stressed also the fact, that the task of integrating foreign workers, requires also a spirit of solidarity and will provide a daily testing ground for the degree of democratic consciousness of German citizens, through which they will prove their tolerance and willingness to offer good neighbourhood relations to these minorities.

All these pronouncements are stating explicitly, that there is a definite need for a long range concept of integration for the foreign workers and their families, which at the same time must be compatible with the principles of a modern social rate. Such a new concept must embrace the following four major requirements:

— The right of the foreign worker to live with his family in the FRG,
— The right of residence, which takes in account their integration,
— Unconditional equality of changes in terms of social mobility,
— The right for foreign children to obtain full chances for education professional training.

The temporary interruption of further recruitment, a decision taken in November 1973, provided the first opportunity to implement a necessary social welfare policy and close the gap created within the social infrastructure. The bulk of the discussion hereby is focussed on those region, where industry created an undue degree of concentration, resulting in an overcrowding of foreign workers. According to the statistics of the Employment agencies, 50% of all the foreign workers in the FRG are living in a highly concentrated pattern on 4% of the total area of the country.

On June 6, 1973 the Federal Government issued an "action oriented" program related to the employment of foreign manpower. Although the stream of new emigrants has been brought to an abrupt stop in November, the importance of this document has not diminished; on the contrary, its meaning has been further enhanced.

This program demands the realization of the following points:

1. A careful assessment of all housing units for foreign workers and their adjustment to meet the requirements of prevailing legal provisions;
2. The elimination of recruitment requests from heavily concentrated industrial regions until their social services provide adequate proof that due to additional population increase of foreign workers, no stress of the existing structures is happening;
3. The administrative fees charged for the recruitment of foreign labour will have to be drastically increased. The additional income secured from this rise is to be used for educational measures, oriented toward a more effective method of teaching the language and the acquisition of new professional skills;
4. If the above mentioned measures are not followed by the expected changes, the introduction of a special tax may be considered. It will have to be paid by all enterprises employing foreign manpower.
5. The illegal employment of foreign labour shall be more effectively fought. It is planned to reform the penal code and to provide penalties for the deprivation of personal freedom in cases if illegally recruited foreign manpower.
6. The Federal government will refuse on ground of social and humanitarian considerations to bring to an end the residence of a foreign worker after the completion of a given period. On the contrary, in cases of a prolonged stay, the legal status of foreign worker should be improved.

It is certainly not erroneous to state, that with the acceptance of this new action-oriented program a new epoch is marked down in the employment of foreign labour. It is only now that consid-

erations based upon the assumption that the employment of foreign manpower is not solely the responsibility of the employer,
but carries with it numerous consequences, has won wider acceptance. This explains why only now serious efforts are displayed
to relieve these groups from the one-sided influence of their employer in order to reorganize their life on the basis of social and
political criteria.

IV. *The achievments of private voluntary associations*

1. *Work division and scope of activities*

The welfare organizations functioning within the boundaries
of Federal Germany as charitable voluntary associations have until now largely contributed to the solution of a great number of
social problems afflicting foreign workers. The Federal government did support these efforts by financial contribution. The
work division so far has been carried out by the Federal government in way of grouping together certain ethnic groups and placing them under the competence of a given charitable association.
Accordingly the various national contingents are benefiting from
the support and aid of the following organizations:

Arbeiterwohlfahrt
Turks, Yugoslavs, Maroccans, Tunisians

Caritas (Catholic Church)
Portuguese, Spaniard, Italian

Diakonisches Werk (Protestant Church)
Greek

This work division is still in force, there are only a few instances where some overlapping is occuring. Thus the Catholic
Church is also counceling a relatively small number of Greeks and
a somewhat greater degree of Slovanians and Chroatians. The
Diakonisches Werk has set up in two different places, counselling
agencies for Yugoslavs. The German Trade Union Federation
(DGB) started to create for all foreign workers special councelling bureaus to deal solely with issues related to labour and social
welfare legislation. These bureaus are open also to any foreigner
not affiliated with any trade union. The Jugensozialwerk, rough-

ly the equivalent of the Red Cross, carries out a special program
for future returnees among the Turkish workers abroad.

The task of the Arbeiterwohlfahrt, which we intend to describe in more detail, embraces five gravitation points:

— Social counseling bureaus,
— Cultural centers,
— Cultural events,
— Language courses,
— Aid in the preparation of homework for foreign children.

Obviously neither the Arbeiterwohlfahrt, nor the other participating voluntary associations can meet all needs. It can also not
be maintained that these associations are making full use of their
capacities. Especially social counselling and help for the homework of school children as well as language courses can and
should be further improved and enlarged. On the other side,
cultural activities and leisure time centers need a critical reappraisal.

The "Arbeiterwohlfahrt" was sustaining on January 1, 1974,
some 139 counselling bureaus, which were set up theoretically to
meet the needs of 1,5 million workers from Jugoslavia, Marocco
and Tunisia. These bureaus have been established in 136 industrial concentration points of smaller and larger density and dispose a staff of 214 persons. According a recommendation of the
E.E.C., which proved to be right, these tasks are exclusively carried out by national representatives of the diverse contingents.
This measure proved to be absolutely necessary as significant
linguistic and cultural barriers between German authorities, employers and foreign workers can only be surmounted successfully
with this kind of approach. The cited counselling bureaus are
from the view point of space not large enough, their personnel is
definitively unsufficient, which prevents them to meet growing
demands.

The positive development in terms of societal interest displayed toward foreign workers and the desire to integrate selected
nationals has, instead of alleviating it, increased the burden of
foreign social counsellors. This is due to the fact that because of
their familiarity with the specific problems of the workers, their
ability to communicate with them, they became the initiators of
almost all official and social actions.

These councellors are held responsible for an adequate information, for counselling individuals and groups in specific situations, for administering technical help in social welfare and finally for mediation between the German authorities and the foreign workers, who are facing each other many times in a kind of helpless dilemna.

This explains also why a clearcut professional profile of these social workers could not be developed. The multitude of their obligations creates a kind of blurred image. In order to understand better the situation it seems useful to compare the major fields of activities of these counsellors in the light of the official policy defined by the Federal government and the "de facto" situation these social workers are confronted in their daily life. The previously cited guiding principles for social work are tracing the major fields of activity around the concepts of information, counselling and assistance as follows:

The information, counselling and assistance to be given to foreign workers and their families should contribute to the awareness of their particular situation and to the enumeration of the given possibilities which might help to solve their problems.

The foreign worker need above everything:

— Information about the living conditions in the FRG.
— Counselling and assistance to meet the requirements of daily life,
— Counselling about the housing market, assistance in location and furnishing of lodgings,
— Assistance in regard of creative use of leisure time.
— Individual assistance in the realms of social, family and health problems,
— Legal councelling, especially in regard to labour laws and social welfare provisions.

The above stated major fields of assistance and counselling are brought together in the form of a comprehensive program. In reality the social workers themselves have built up an empirical catalogue of various tasks and duties, which are producing a much more detailed and diversified field of activity.

The social workers themselves are making a clear distinction between assistance and councel given in the bureaus and the rather dominant type of assistance, which means counselling on the spot and in the field. No doubt, this second type of activity is much more time consuming.

According this second type of classification, elaborated by the social workers themselves, the various types of social services are much more diversified and can be enumerated as follows:

Employment agencies

Assistance for the obtainment of working permit, unemployment insurance, clarification of disputes about work contract, allocation of children allowances, translation of legally required documents, guidance to obtain new jobs, vocational training or change in occupational activity.

Special agency dealing with foreigner affairs

Information concerning the rights and obligations of foreigners, assistance in filling out various legal documents (residence permit, registration for domicile, change of domicile), personal and phone contacts with various agencies, information related to conditions for family reunion, procedures used in cases of expulsion.

Insurance

Information concerning health and social security, translation of medical prescriptions prepared in their home country, mediation in case of dispute about social security, assistance for the continuation of medical care in the home country, availability of social insurance for family members on the home and host country, maternity indemnity, information concerning voluntary illness, old age and accident insurance, family pension rates.

Judiciary

Translation of judiciary formalities and personal appearance with the worker involved at administrative, labour and social courts; consultation in questions related to legal disputes.

Criminal justice

Assistance for workers under detention or inmates in prisons. Assistance in cases related to criminal justice. (Police, trafic violation).

Educational agencies

Assistance for the registration of school age children, changing school helping worker's children to obtain special aid for the preparation of homework, special tutoring.

Youth agencies

Assistance in cases involving the establishment of parenthood ties or the search for foster parents for children born out of wedlock, securing vacant places in nurseries, kindergardens and childcare centers.

Special assistance agencies

Information about possibilities and limits of the usage of social welfare.

Civil marriage registry

Assistance in questions related to civil marriage, delivery of birth certificates.

Treasury department

Information and assistance on questions related to income tax refund and similar problems.

Hospitals

Visits to patients, assistance in clearing disputable situations related to the length of stay in hospital and hospital discharge.

Housing and rental agencies

Assistance in locating suitable lodging, settling rent disputes.

Contact with employer

Companies, which are employing foreign manpower, should be visited in regular intervals by social workers. During those contacts it is the duty of the social worker to represent the interests of the foreign worker, to act as a mediator, in case of misunderstanding and to establish the necessary good understanding between employer, employee and the workers councils. It seems imperative that especially in the case of newcomers, there should be a close collaboration between employers, social workers in regard of information about the new living and working conditions. An additional obligation for the social worker is to provide the foreign worker with ample information in the form of printed material in his native language.

Contact with embassies and consulates

The social worker should also be able to establish useful contact between the official diplomatic representatives and the host country's agencies in questions related to specific laws and regulations concerning foreigners.

Cultural activities, language courses, lectures

The social worker should encourage the establishment and continuation of sport, music and dance groups. In order to avoid the malfunctioning of such groups, the social worker should also participate in the organisational activities of any special events.

2. Foreigners and social services

All services provided by social welfare organisations are assuming to be demanded by the foreigner. Counselling and other forms of aid are pursuing the goal of contributing to promote societal integration. The administration of ghettos is neither a political goal, nor a duty of social associations.

All these considerations indicate, that before a foreigner enters a counselling center, attends a language course or registers his child for help with homework, important decisions have to be taken. These decisions have to be well planned, coordinated, regularly re-evaluated in order to perform its basic function: to help the adjustment of individuals in unaccustomed harsh environments. The beneficial results of social work performed thus depends as much from the capacity and scope of the various organizations as from the policy decision of the host country and its supporting measures.

MUTUAL PERSPECTIVES OF DEVELOPMENT AND UNDERDEVELOPMENT IN EUROPE

DR. GÜNTER SCHILLER

I. *Introductory Remarks*

The movement of workers from the countries of the underdeveloped periphery of Europe to highly industrialized centers has become a salient feature of the European pattern of development. By their very nature, international migrations connect different countries. There is no doubt, however, that contemporary European labour mobility, its volume and its forms, are determined to a great extent by the receiving countries. For where, how many, and under what conditions foreign workers will be accepted depends on what the industrial countries regard as requirements, useful assets to their economies, a state of affairs clearly reflected in the reactions of governments to changing economic conditions.

To be sure, this reveals a factor of unilateral dependency between both groups of countries involved: the countries of emigration can refuse to supply labour, if they do not agree with the terms proposed, but this has rarely happened, the only example being Greece which has brought emigration nearly to a stop. We feel justified therefore to focus this analysis on the countries of immigration, even in a publication which concentrates on an emigration country, because it is the policy of the former which determines largely that of the latter.

The interpretation of European labour mobility suffers frequently from a historical short-windedness. As far as the Federal Republic of Germany is concerned the phenomenon itself has only recently become apparent. It has been preceded by comparatively much larger dislocations of population, in the case of Germany e.g. the compulsory exodus from former German territories in the East or the refugee movement from the German Democratic Republic until 1961. France received a backflow of white settlers from Algeria, the Netherlands absorbed returning natives or emigrants from former colonies like Indonesia. Great

Britain, finally, faces today a serious immigration pressure from naturalized coloured citizens.

Furthermore the pattern of migration resumes for many countries as a result of historical events. The Ruhr district in Germany received a large inflow of Polish and Silesian farmers during the past century. In 1907 population statistics registered already 3,4% foreign workers in the labour force. Historical accuracy makes it necessary to also mention here the millions of enslaved laborers who kept production running during the Second World War in Germany.[1]

A strict interpretation of present labour movements in the framework of European capitalism has not yet been formulated. It would probably have to start from the realization that the growth mechanism inherent in capitalist systems can principally take two forms:

1. An outward-oriented variety which means that capital, labour, technical know-how, i.e. economic resources, pour out of the developed countries and open up—maybe in a selective way—hitherto economically underdeveloped spaces. This strategy may be related to historical processes like the colonization of the New World and—with certain qualifications—to colonialization.
2. An inward oriented growth pattern which brings about a rapid increase in the internal production capacity by continually offering new and ample investment opportunities. This process usually results from an accelerated pace of technical progress. The period of industrial revolution but also—at least in Europe—the unparalleled economic boom of the past decades may both be recalled here.

This is not the place here to discuss both models in detail, nor to indicate the general conditions of change from one pattern to another. Nevertheless we may list if only in an eclectic way some reasons for the recent expansion of the European economy:

1. The destructions of World War II which opened up vast opportunities of economic activity.
2. The inflow of dynamic and hard-working groups of population.

---

[1] Wirtschaft und Statistik, 1965, p. 93-94.

3. The breakdown of the liberal world economy. This change was marked by two world wars and the Great Depression. The nation-states had to rely on their own resources to secure the economic survival of their peoples. Simultaneously, John Maynard Keynes offered an economic philosophy, which enabled governments to stimulate economic activities and foster economic growth.

4. The loss of colonies which withdrew from venture capital and from possible emigrants the political security which are preconditions of an engagement in foreign countries.

5. An undervaluation of European currencies with respect to the US, which favoured the expansion of production and exports and attracted foreign capital to Europe instead of channelling it to less developed regions.

6. The foundation of the European Economic Community, which generated considerable growth impulses. Furthermore the high internal capital accumulation was further accelerated by capital imports by means of which the United States tried to establish a firm position in the Common Market.

Import of labour was another element in the interaction of various growth factors, after increasing discrepancies had arisen between a rapid capital accumulation and a slackening population growth.

But we should emphazise once more the relative brevity of this process. In our opinion, it would be erroneous to extrapolate the course of recent economic development in a linear way and to forecast giant armies of foreign workers in the industrialized countries for the future. At the same time the elasticity and adaptability of the economic system seems to be underestimated in view of the fact that a renunciation of foreign manpower may lead to breakdowns. But we also question the notion which politicians like to entertain that employment of foreign labour is a safety valve, that can be opened or closed at will and combined freely with any economic strategy.

The thesis, which we are going to elaborate here, is that labour migration forms a distinct element in a growth process, which has certain structural features and has developed out of certain historical conditions. We can ask now two basic questions:

1. What are the rules and norms which have governed the tradi-
    tional growth process in regard of migration?
2. What are the prospects for the future: in concrete terms,
    what changes in the socio-economic environment may react
    upon the pattern of migration?

II. *The Effects of Labour Migration:*
The Center-Periphery-Model

The number of publications which attempt to clarify the effects of migration is impressive. Frequently so called cost-benefit-
schemes have been applied or a number of economic key aggregates have been analyzed to find out how they have been influenced by migration: Prices and wages, the balance of trade and of
payment, the business cycle, the growth rate, the structure of
employment. The objective was to find out how the economies
involved were affected by the inflow of additional labour (and
population), and whether the welfare of the populations was
raised or not.

We shall not try to give an overview of this debate. In fact, and
this is perhaps its most characteristic result, it has not led to very
definite and unquestioned conclusions. This may shed a significant light on the state of economic science. Typically for many
such studies, the following summary may be quoted: "Although
an exact synopsis of all single effects is not possible for reasons
already quoted, we feel justified to defend the thesis that the
employment of foreign workers has affected the growth of national income per worker unfavourably in the shorter term"[2]
That the theoretical analysis is still in such an unsatisfactory state
is highlighted by the fact that official judgments of migration and
migration policies are subject to frequent fluctuations. Until
some years ago the official position in the Federal Republic of
Germany was that the take-in of foreign workers was not only
beneficial to the German population but also to the countries of
emigration. It was even classified as the most efficient form of
development aid.

Today public opinion holds the view that a permanent stay of

---

[2] S. Bullinger, P. Huber, H. Köhler, A. Ott, A. Wagner, *Die volkswirtschaftliche Bedeutung der Beschäftigung auslandischer Arbeitnehmer in Baden-Wurttemberg*, Tübin-
gen 1972, p. 392 (translation by the author—G.S.).

foreign workers overburdens the social infrastructure. This is certainly true if we merely compare the total existing infrastructure with the total demand of places in schools, kindergardens and hospitals, of teachers, medical doctors and social workers. This becomes highly misleading, however, whenever we compare the contributions of foreign workers to the public budgets with the expenditures which they require.

In our opinion we miss the point in looking at labour migration from the perspective of such a cost-benefit-comparison. A capitalist economy is not run at costs and benefits for a population; it is an institutional arrangement to maximize production and consumption for the purpose of profit-making. The physical aspect of profits is investment and hence expansion of production. The growth process (of which two types have been outlined earlier) could not have been sustained in Europe on the basis of nation states separated by political and economic frontiers. Consequently what we see as a determining force in Europe today is the amalgamation of national economies into a (more or less) unified economic space. This enlargement has been a life and death necessity in order to compete with the US-Economy which is more advanced and disposes of immense resources.[3]

The formation of this uniform economic space follows a pattern which has characteristics strikingly close to those of the development of national industrial economies in the past.

1. Internally the freedom of movement and exchange is increased. Goods as well as capital and labour can commute freely within the community.
2. In contrast to the internal economic liberalization a certain separation from outside takes place. The Common Market has surrounded itself with a relatively high wall of tariffs. Trade policy has come already under the competence of the Community.

Economic growth does not affect a regional space uniformly, but leads to typical forms of differentiation.

---

[3] We do not underestimate, of course, the frictions still existing in Europe. There are countries, which have not at all joined the EEC like Sweden, Austria, Switzerland or Norway. Some are not (yet) admitted like Spain and Greece. Turkey finally has the status of an associated member with the perspective of a full membership. It is nevertheless characteristic of Europe today that many economic barriers have been removed for the economic sector—while a central political power is still lacking.

1. Normally economic growth takes place primarily in some central places, but most frequently in one center of gravitation, thereby creating a dualism of center an periphery. Resources, the factors of production follow a trend of agglomeration. Manpower and capital move towards the center. Increasing production and investment stimulate savings and profits. The demand for training, science and research increases likewise. Growing production creates prosperity and optimism in all branches of economic activity. Furthermore, production, income and demand are the most important sources of taxation. Rising yields of taxes enable the government to increase the level of public services, infrastructure and amenities, which again stimulate further development.

2. The periphery on the other hand decays. Firms (or corporations) cannot keep up against the competition of the central regions. There, close linkages of production units, a highly developed infrastructure and easy access to big markets give rise to "external economies", that are not compensated by somewhat lower wages in the periphery. It is very difficult to find productions where the peripheral regions have comparative cost advantages. One reason is that the periphery has to import a lot of input materials; another that the output goods have to be transported again to outside markets. Hence the periphery suffers from a serious lack of originally created value added, i.e. goods and services with which it can compete against the center.

3. One important export item of the centers are highly qualified services. At the national level, both public and private administration are concentrated in the capital and the big cities. They produce bureaucratic work the costs of which are collected by taxes throughout the national territory (in the case of government administration). On the international level the central nations have an overall monopoly of sophisticated tertiary functions, i.e. in planning, marketing, designing, researching, financing, insuring. In the division of labour the periphery takes over those parts which receives little payment. Agriculture is normally the most important item, and through various mechanisms producer prices for agricultural products are in effect kept low. Another economic function is tourism. But here as well only low paid jobs are created

which in many cases give only seasonal employment.

4. In order to maintain the viability of the periphery it must receive additional infusions of purchasing power. They may, in fact, be much lower than the outflow of resources but it is one of the inherent features of domination that while the latter are hidden in the forms of economic exchange the former are explicitly shown as subventions, aid or compensatory policy measures. These transfers increase the purchasing power over the regional social product. Most of them, however, flow immediately back to the developed regions where they are spent for the import of goods.

Such center-periphery-models can be applied at various levels from a single town to the world economy. We think that it describes adequately the structural background of labour migration, on the national as well as on an international level:

1. Emigration is the most striking feature of depressed regions from Ireland to Galicia, Andalucia, Sicilia, (North) Greece and Anatolia. The redundant population moves not only into the industrialized countries of Central Europe, but, also, into the national growth centers: the capital, big ports and metropolitan regions.

2. There is not much capital to leave, because the formation and accumulation of capital takes place in the centers. Nevertheless there is a general consensus that depressed areas lose most of their internal savings. Collection and withdrawal of savings can happen in two forms:

   a) through the banking system. Banks are normally strongly centralized and command over a network of branch offices. These offices collect savings which are put at the disposal of the headquarters. Obviously most of the capital is invested in areas where industry is expanding.

   b) through transfer of rents. Many—although not all—underdeveloped emigration areas are marked by a strong concentration of land property. Big estates dominate which are run by administrators or by means of various forms of leasing. The owner normally does not live in the place—on the estate—but resides in the provincial or national capital where he lives on the rents.

The main sources of financial transfers from the center to the periphery are:

1. Regional development programs

    They rely on two major mechanisms:
    a) transfer of income in order to stimulate demand,
    b) reduction of cost of production through public invest-
        ments in infrastructure. Both objectives are often connec-
        ted so that such investments are incorporated in employ-
        ment programs.
    c) A third measure of regional development policy consists
        of tax holidays and other forms of subvention. They,
        however, are not directly connected with financial flows
        to the region.

2. Subventions to agriculture

    Today many Mediterranean countries have massive subven-
    tions programs for the agricultural sector. They may include
    assignments from the public budget, price stabilization mea-
    sures for certain products or tax exemptions. In many cases
    these programs work in favour of the strong and powerful
    landed interests.

3. The social security system

    Institutions of social security may have a redistributive char-
    acter in favour of depressed regions too because these schemes
    are normally organized on a national level. Contributions
    and out-payments are generally fixed. But because of relativ-
    ely lower yields the underdeveloped areas receive net pay-
    ments on balance. We would like to emphasize, however, that
    these effects do not always occur. Old age insurance systems
    e.g. exclude frequently the rural population as well as daily
    paid workers.
        These systems work on the national as well as the inter-
    national level. As far as the latter are concerned, workers' re-
    mittances are an important component. But also in other
    respects supranational programs come to the fore: credits of
    the European Investment Bank, the agricultural policy of the

Common Market, or the regional development policy which is now under discussion.[4]

III. *Structural Features of the Countries of Immigration*

Even this center-periphery-model is only a formal description of a specific pattern of economic interaction between units characterized by a differing level of development. It does not explain how the center-periphery dichotomy arises nor indicate factors which modify its structure.

According to traditional economic theory economic interactions are governed by equilibrium tendencies. Factors of production which are abundant in one place should be channelled by the price mechanism to places where they are short in supply. Low wages in overpopulated regions should attract capital by high rates of return. The center-periphery-model now demonstrates why regional imbalances may have reinforcing effects. High incomes in developed areas result in boosting consumer demand which in turn stimulates expansion of production. Increasing tax receipts permit the authorities to improve the social infrastructure so that profit conditions remain attractive.

Of course, this reciprocal stimulation is finally counterbalanced by disfunctional side effects, which can be clearly recognized in the highly industrialized European countries.

The expansion of production in the industrialized countries was closely linked with a fast capital formation. At the same time, however, a whole range of factors were limiting the labour potential available in particular for the production process. Here are some constituent parts of the development:

a) Decreasing population rate
b) Prolonged education time
c) Decreasing participation rates (e.g.: women)
d) Increasing young age infirmity
e) Lowering of retirement age
f) Reduction of weekly working hours
g) Growing number of non-productive activities, in particular public services. This last point needs some explanation.

---

[4] A more elaborate description of the center-periphery-model is given in: H. Salowsky und G. Schiller, Ursachen und Auswirkungen der Ausländerbeschäftigung, Koln 1972 (special edition—not on sale).

The highly developed economies are showing a built-in neglect of social welfare. The natural environment is unhesitatingly exploited and destroyed (theoretically justified by the notion of free goods like water, air, etc.), the social communities are fragmented in small families and individuals. The consequences of the process of economic growth, new social requirements, the scattering of population and social isolation have created a need for public services. New schools and universities, homes for old-aged people and kindergartens, highways and filtering work maintenances, etc., increasing criminality and natural environment pollution require an increasing rate of labour potential and deprive industry from a corresponding part of the labour market.

Swiftly growing productive capital and stagnant labour potential lead to factor imbalances. These are usually identified as the labour gap. From another point of view, which is more appropriate, they appear as an excess of capital. In the industrialized countries, there are continually too many jobs offered than can be filled.

Furthermore as the production process becomes more and more hazardous and risky, a tendency arises to acquire an increasing part of the national product by forms of speculation. A comprehensive analysis of these trends cannot be given here. So we have to restrict ourselves to a few empirical illustrations.

1. Monetary crises which have happened frequently during the past years allow for the acquisition of fortunes within hours at the expense of the national economies.
2. The gold boom and hoarding of raw materials are stimulated by expectations of rapid price increases.
3. A very important factor is real estate speculation. In the countryside fortunes are created just by changing the use of land. In the cities the old centers become monopolized by big capital groups, which destroy the housing space in order to use the land more profitably for commercial purposes.
4. Another destructive factor is over-extended income differentiation. Economic and social rewards do in no way accord with the heaviness, the unpleasantness and alienation of work. Those jobs which are performed in an agreeable atmosphere, which permit at least a relative degree of satisfaction

are paid much better than others which are dangerous, monotonous, dirty, strictly regulated and deprivating. The income
differentiation forms in itself a system of exploitation. Certainly high level income groups live at the expense of low
paid groups. But even within the workers' stratum which may
on the whole be on the loser's side this system of discrimination and privileges also works: men against the women, the
semi-skilled against the unskilled. In the Federal Republic of
Germany we find a range of 40-50 wage groups among workers only, not to speak of clerks, professionals, entrepreneurs
or politicians. And the fact that it stretches very far into the
lower social strata (hence the fight for its persistence takes
place on all levels of the social hierarchy) gives an amazing
stability to the hierarchy of income. It is in this context that
the phenomenon of migration must be understood, and it
becomes immediately clear how functional migration has
been for the maintenance of the social processes described
above. Foreign workers more and more formed the productive basis on which the system of exploitative and speculative
appropriation of the social product was based. They take the
unpleasant jobs; they are in the low wage groups. The demoli-
tion of living conditions in urban centers, the transformation
of living space into business space, are pushed ahead by concentration of foreigners, a process which leads to the often
lamented slums and ghettos. Foreign workers also formed a
suitable remedy for the growing labour deficit.

In order to cope with this imbalance, the industrialized countries have obviously taken the easiest road. The inflow of labour
force made it possible to pursue without a break the pattern of
growth that had been hitherto practiced. The immigration of
workers first of all eliminated crucial barriers of growth and made it possible to avoid the difficult and often painful processes of
adjustment and adaptation a labour shortage normally entails.
Today, it clearly seems that employment of foreign workers had
been a sedative medicine only. Problems of economic structure
have been covered for a while until they break out, more serious
than before or appear in another sector of activity.

Labour immigration is the direct consequence of the *absolute*
shortage of productive labour supply. The *relative* decrease of

productive employment leads to a progressively mounting volume
of income distribution.

Here again, the two tendencies feed each other: a generally
decreasing participation rate and the incomes of that part of the
labour force which is engaged in either parasitic activities or
compensatory social services.

The volume of income redistribution either lowers the person-
ally available incomes or pushes up the costs of production depending on whether the constrributions are charged to the enterprises or paid out of gross personal incomes. Finally it jeopardizes
international competitiveness.

The analysis so far leads to some important clarifications.

1. It is not an original labour deficit from which the industrial-
    ized societies suffer but the combined effect of a capital
    surplus, a growing rate of inactivity and a rapid growth of
    unproductive activities. The latter aspect is concealed by a
    misleading definition of productivity in the national account-
    ing system.

2. It is not the foreign workers who cause the appearance of a
    ghetto- and a housing problem. On the other hand, they form
    an strategic element in the speculative conversion of cities.

IV. *The Change of Migration Policy in the FRG*

In the preceding section the usefulness of labour immigration
for the continuation of a certain growth pattern was analyzed.
Some authors even consider it indispensable for the survival of
the capitalist system. [5]

But also in public opinion, in the mass media or in (some)
scientific studies foreign workers were welcomed as contributing
to our welfare. They allowed our workers to leave the lowest
ranks of the social hierarchy, they took over the low paid and
unpleasant jobs, they paid normal taxes and social insurance fees
although they utilized public services to a lesser extent and their
rent claims are in a very distant future.

It will be all the more puzzling for the reader to see that, most
recently, the usefulness of labour immigration has been question-

---

[5] Cf. e.g. M. Nikolinakos, Politische Ökonomie der Gastarbeiterfrage, Reinbek
1973.

ed by the receiving countries themselves. About three years ago, the German government's official position became increasingly skeptical of the economic and social value of labour import. Chancellor Willy Brandt referred to this problem in the inauguration speech of the small-coalition government on January 18, 1973, saying, after referring to some positive effects: "It has become necessary, however, to consider very carefully where the absorption capacity of our society is exhausted and where social reason and responsibility demand a stop!"[6]

In June 1973 an "action program" was announced by the government, postulating a "consolidation" of foreign employment; and at the first signs of an economic recession, in autumn 1973, a complete stop of recruitment of foreign workers of countries outside the EEC, was imposed.

The key argument in this new debate is that foreign workers, especially when accompanied by their families, overburden the social infrastructure. It is widely held now that it is no longer worth fostering economic growth by recruiting foreign workers and that possible private profits would be paralyzed by increased "social costs". The notion of "social infrastructure", however, is not clear at all. Usually sporadic references are made to the schooling situation in some ghetto areas with predominant foreign population or to the difficulties of migrants to get adequate housing. A paper submitted to a discussion group invited by the Minister of Labour and Social Order (Sozialpolitische Gesprächsrunde), lists the following sectors where the social care of foreign workers is in the most critical phase: housing, kindergartens, education at pre-school and primary school level, vocational training, social assistance and counseling as well as medical care.[7] While deficiencies in these services are evident, it is surprising, however, that there has not been any thorough investigations of the real impact of foreign employment. It seems, in any case, that the argument of an overstrained social infrastructure is at best superficial. This does not mean, that we should necessarily overlook it and advocate an unlimited inflow of foreign population.

In order to clarify the term "social infrastructure", we must first distinguish between investment and the permanent absorp-

---

[6] Translation by the author—G.S.
[7] Vorlage zur Sozialpolitischen Gesprächsrunde beim Bundesminister für Arbeit und Sozialordnung, 6.4.73, hektographed.

tion of manpower for the operation of social institutions. Obviously the problems of providing an adequate public infrastructure are not caused by a lack of investment capacity. Huge funds invested in roads and highways in the FRG and 150,000 non-occupied flats from only last year's building boom (714,000 flats), reveal that the problem is not one of volume, but of proper distribution. On the contrary, high public investments are necessary to keep the level of final demand up. The difficulties arise from the described fact that social services withdraw manpower from other activities and have to be alimented by income redistribution, resulting in an increased proportion of non-productive people who must be supported whilst activity in the productive field is reduced.

The essential specific shortcomings of the creation of a social infrastructure reveal the priority scales that are valid in a society, where primary schools, care for children, old age people and foreign workers occupy only lower ranks, while the army, preservation of law and order, are given higher priorities.

The idea of relating the acceptance of foreign workers to the capacity of the social infrastructure often seems to go along with the conception that higher space capacities are available outside the big centers of agglomerations. But there are reasons to doubt this. As an example we could mention medical care, which is already a most critical problem in remote areas. An increased geographical dispersion of foreigners cannot solve the difficulties in providing social services. On the contrary, new burdens can be created if the reduction of foreign resident population is linked with an increase in daily commuting.

In the same way provision of social assistance, the creation of leisure centers, etc. are facilitated in towns. The problem of social services is thus reduced to a question of burden sharing between local entities.

A number of difficulties do not result from the concentration of foreigners as such, but from the structural change, to which the big towns are generally subjected:

a) Exodus of the original population from the center of the cities toward the suburbs,
b) Transformation of housing zones into shopping and traffic zones.

The foreign population often has the function of connecting and accelerating both processes. It seems that up to now the general structural problems of the agglomeration process as well as of supplying social services have been related directly to the inflow of foreigners. By reducing labour import, it may well happen, that instead of raising "our" standard of social welfare, we will just remove the productive basis on which our wealth had rested.

We can imagine another alternative as a further expansion of the "social infrastructure". It is often suggested that the problem could be solved by means of "supplementary efforts" and "in the course of time". We fear that there is a danger of nursing false hopes. The new demands to increase the proportion of the national budget alloted to investments or to check the "staff explosion" in the public sector, clearly delineate limitations.

V. *The Search of Alternatives*

If migration policy in the past was based on insufficient economic analysis, then caution is advised now as well when the question of alternatives will be discussed. If we conceive of the imbalance of factor proportions as the underlying fundamental problem, the remedies may come from two sides:

a) adjustment of the capital stock to the existing labour supply
b) increase of manpower availability by means of other than immigration.

As far as the latter is concerned, possibilities are generally regarded as limited.

As to the capital side, three principle adjustment processes can be distinguished:

a) reduction of capital formation (problem of zero-growth)
b) increase of capital intensity of the production process.
c) capital export.

We note that the general interest concentrates on capital export. Transfer of production is the message today as labour immigration was that of the past. The rapidity with which the first strategy superseded the second, the lack of any in depth studies of real consequences of a greater capital export on employment

and regional development cloud with uncertainty the factual results of such a policy.

It is not yet possible to indicate precisely the structural reasons which have caused this change of views. So the following
considerations are only tentative and need further research:

1. Massive variation of exchange rates have modified the calcul-
    atory basis of production costs in international comparison.
    The undervaluation of European currencies and the overvalu-
    ation of the US $ made production in the European countries
    relatively profitable for a long time. This point demonstrates
    on the other hand to which extent arbitrary manipulations of
    the currency system determine the spatial allocation of pro-
    duction, of employment and growth.
2. The developments in the industrial centers indicated above
    have raised the cost of production to an extent that competi-
    tion with low wage countries is no longer possible. The cloth-
    ing industry, e.g. complains that apart from wage differences
    indirect wage costs are 9 per cent in Singapore, while they are
    54 per cent in the FRG. [8]

The growth strategy of the industrialized countries so far fits
very well into the center-periphery-model: they retain the well paid
operations which need highly sophisticated knowledge, while low
paid jobs are transferred to other areas. In addition the developed
countries will concentrate their industrial production into some
capital intensive branches which allow a high degree of automa-
tion.

At first sight this alternative looks quite attractive for the
population in industrialized countries. It should not be overlook-
ed, however, that it creates immediately a number of new problems. It would be all too easy, to consider capital export as an
automatic mechanism to solve a disequilibrium in the supply of
factors of production.

1. Firstly, the transfer of production does not start in the over-
    industrialized agglomeration centers but in the peripheral and
    underdeveloped problem areas of the industrial countries.
    Many labour intensive branches had been allocated there by
    granting various forms of incentives. Now their definite exo-

---

[8] Cf. Handelsblatt, 12.2.74, p. 9.

dus leaves behind unemployment again, calling for even higher subventions to create new working places.

2. Secondly, there is the question of volume. In an economic
system where activities are based on independent decisions of
enterprises there is no guarantee that capital export can be
kept within those limits which are regarded as socially toler-
able. What may be accepted in the case of clothing industry
would have disastrous effects in the case of the car industry.

3. For the labour force the consequences of such a strategy
would be either that of qualification and social rise or that of
unemployment. But not all workers can qualify, because they
are too old or for other social reasons. The United States
offer an example for this development. While on the one
hand there exists a large middle stratum with elevated incomes there it as well an unemployed labour force of 5 per
cent which is composed of redundant unskilled workers.

Furthermore this strategy succeeds only as long as the developed countries have the factual monopoly of sophisticated organization, of science and technology. At present this advantage is
perpetuated by a strong concentration of these countries on
education and research complemented by a deplorable neglect of
these functions by the less developed countries. If, however, those
countries manage to bridge this gap, multinational enterprises
would certainly not hesitate to transfer high-skilled activities,
too, if that would reduce costs of production.

So, the new situation will be as ambiguous as the old one. The
belief that blind operations of formal mechanisms would lead to
optimal and "equilibrium" situations should be discarded from
economic reasoning once and for all.

Instead the situation calls for fundamental social reforms
which attack the problems at their roots. We have tried to point
out that the present practice of economic theory and policy
primarily deals with the symptoms instead of the real problems.

One effect is that now labour migration is blamed for defects
which are not caused but only highlighted by it.

Among the reforms which are most urgent the following may
be mentioned:

a) a drastic reduction of income differences which are no longer
(if they were ever) in line with the heaviness of work.

b) putting an end to speculative forms of income acquisition.
   One important point here is to eliminate housing and real
   estate speculation.

c) Developing and applying social utility criteria to measure the
   desirability of general social developments as well as social
   services. The extension of social services and public administration are not measures of success. Instead it should be tried
   to reduce their necessity. Concerning migration policy application of the same principles would lead to surprising results.
   Paradoxically measures which seem to imply an increase of
   the social burden would in fact lead to its reduction. Housing programs e.g. would have an easening effect on housing
   rents. Language training would reduce the number of accidents
   at the working place and the demand of interpreters and social
   workers (at least relatively). So these measures are not only
   desired for reasons of humanity but also for their economic
   effects.

The reader may complain that these considerations are unduly
restricted to the problems of the industrial countries and do not
take into account properly the much more urgent problems of
the countries of emigration. Such a view cannot be accepted,
however. It would be misleading to assume that the peripheral
countries would gain from a rise of social and economic frictions
and tensions in the developed ones. Furthermore, much of what
has been said before applies to emigration countries as well.
There, too, income differentiation is certainly too high to be
socially acceptable. Real estate speculation has become a social
issue and the expansion of public administration burdens the
productive sector.

It should no longer surprise anyone now that most of the
countries of the European periphery are themselves confronted
with the existence of a foreign work force. A recent publication
of the International Labour Office quotes alarming figures:
100,000 in Spain, 30,000 in Greece, and the number of foreigners in Italy is certainly higher than the 40,000 officially registered.[9]

So, the separation of "socially undesirable jobs", which are

---

[9] Migration of Workers as an Element in Employment Policy, International Labour
Office, Doc. 22/1973, Geneva 1973, p. 83.

rejected by the native population, starts long before full employment has been achieved.

VI. *Perspectives for the Emigration Countries*

Which are now the development perspectives for the European periphery? Which are the social processes, which have been set in motion by emigration?

First it should be reminded that every advantage produces its negative correlates. Thus the transfer or foreign exchange may be an important source of inflation. Or, while on the one hand unemployment is reduced, on the other hand the outflow of young and motivated workers may cause an economic setback, which creates new unemployment. Apart from that a considerable group of emigrants is not unemployed at the time of departure.

Even political effects are not so plain. Whether emigration leads to a stabilization of traditional social structures, because of the export of discontent population groups or whether the returning migrants bring with them new mobilizing ideas and attitudes is very uncertain. We should not attribute much importance to either of these alternatives.

Of course, the outcome could be improved, if the countries of emigration conceived of a more clear-cut migration policy, also closely associated to developmental efforts. But here, too, caution is necessary, because of possible social repercussions. Very certainly conflicts would arise, if the governments of emigration countries granted additional privileges, to those, who are considered as having already chosen the better lot.

Finally, the position of governments of emigration countries is not itself very clear. On the one hand, they like to stress the disadvantages their countries suffer from the loss of a potentially active part of their labour force and they insist on the final return. On the other hand, they would like to send out as many unskilled workers as the receiving countries are able to assimilate. The contradictory position of the emigration countries coincides very well with the interests of the receiving countries governments which use this argument to defend their own restrictive

naturalization policy. Taking, however, the practically implemented measures as indicators one can certainly not speak of a
consistent return-migration-policy.

Another contradiction is emphasized by Livi-Bacci: "The existence of an excess supply calls for efficient population policies as
a first step. The aim of these policies would be to lower the rate
of population growth and to eliminate the differences between
the sub-national areas. Immediate steps have to be taken in the
sense, though a liberalization of legislation (almost everywhere
very restrictive) concerning family planning. It is conceivable that
the emigration countries (except for Turkey) still maintain an
official position condemning emigration as evil, together with an
anti-liberal, reactionary and absurd legislation making it difficult
(and sometimes impossible) for the couple to plan their family
size efficiently." [10]

But returning to our analysis of migration we cannot merely
list a number of unrelated economic, social or political effects
classified as advantages or disadvantages. Economic and social
development is not properly described as a mechanistic reaction
of macro-economic aggregates nor as a mental process, the adoption of development-mindedness, by a number of individuals. It
results from social groups taking over political power and drawing their strength from certain forms of industrial and economic
development while basing their legitimacy on economic progress.
Generally speaking in less developed countries the distribution of
social power is more heterogenous than in the developed countries. There, economic growth is the common denominator which
satisfies the interests of trade unions and entrepreneurs, of farmers calling for subventions and politicians who try to promote
themselves by increasing social expenditure. For less developed
countries the situation may be quite different. The establishment
of a growth-oriented milieu may well hurt the power interests of
important social groups e.g. the landed interest. All the more
there exist different growth patterns: one which is based on a
strong national industrial capitalism, another which relies more
on the industrialization by international capital. The latter may
be favoured, by those capital groups who have interests in inter-

---

[10] M. Livi-Bacci and H.M. Hagmann, Report on the demographic and social pattern of migration in Europe especially with regard to international migrations, Council
of Europe, 2nd European conference, Strasbourg, 31.8.-7.9.71, CDE (71) T. IV, S. 80.

national trade, banking and branches of the service sector. It may find other supporters as well, e.g. the army and the technocrats in administration and professions. And there is no reason why trade unions should object to it. Of course, both strategics require different measures: advocates of the first one will support stronger protection of national enterprises, and austerity and autarky, keeping foreign capital out of the country. The others will plead instead for opening the country to foreign capital, for free trade and mobility of the factors of production.

This, of course, is a very sketchy outline of the political structures of Mediterranean countries. It does not reproduce the reality in any of them. Nevertheless it would be interesting to analyse political decisions in Turkey with this model. In fact, the approach of autonomous industrial capitalism faces practically unsurmountable difficulties nowadays. For the countries of the European periphery a fundamental step towards the internationalization of the economy has been taken with the establishment of various relations with the Common Market.

The apparently rather contradictory effects of labour migration may be seen now in a more consistent way. The withdrawal of an underemployed labour force from the countryside may deprive the traditional agricultural sector of the manpower basis on which its social and economic influence rested. So, a change in rural areas is effected, not by a clear-cut and open agrarian reform but by the passive elimination of an indispensable element. Also the complaints of industrial enterprises of high fluctuation rates and of lack of skilled manpower due to emigration will have to be seen in a new light.

VII. *Concluding Remarks*

Finally we may ask what consequences the countries of the European periphery will have to face if a real change of economic policy is introduced by the industrialized countries. One crucial question will be, whether and how much of the capital exported from the centers will flow into this region. Frequently the complaint is voiced that the wage level in those countries is already too high in comparison with other regions in the world. If one excludes now the alternative of reducing the wage level which may well be regarded as unduly low, an improvement of labour productivity will be required. But if some countries like Greece have practically closed down their frontiers for workers wanting to emigrate to European countries an important reason may be to avoid labour shortages leading to wage increases.

Another problem is that of the political stability demanded by foreign investors. At present we see that the attractiveness of countries to foreign capital is quite inverse to the democratic and social appearance of their governments. Here again we hit on a very important factor of influence emanating from the centers to the periphery.

So a change of strategy will create a number of new problems for the peripheral countries too. Only a strict adherence to the principles of democracy and social equality, of self-determination and human rights and of international solidarity especially of the workers can possibly gain a victory over all tendencies to perpetuate a welfare gap between the central and the peripheral countries in Europe.

APPENDIX

STATISTICS

Table 1

Turkish Workers Sent Abroad By The Turkish Employment Service

Countries	1961=1967			1968			1969			1970			1971		
	E.M.	K.W.	T.T.	E.M.	K.W.	T.T.	E.K.	K.W.	T.T.	E.M.	K.W.	T.T.	E.M.	K.W.	T.T.
F. Germany	144685	31505	176190	30099	11310	41409	77472	20670	98142	76556	20380	96936	52162	13522	65684
Australia	—	—	—	106	1	107	962	8	970	1172	14	1186	833	46	879
Austria	5848	168	6016	668	5	673	918	55	973	10511	111	10622	4285	335	4620
Belgium	13917	—	13917	—	—	—	—	—	—	430	1	431	578	5	583
France	88	—	88	—	—	—	184	7	191	8992	44	9036	7856	41	7897
Netherland	6634	12	6646	874	1	875	3404	—	3404	4840	3	4843	4790	63	4853
Great Britain	8	—	8	—	—	—	—	4	4	512	51	563	1232	57	1289
Switzerland	598	121	719	73	24	97	162	21	183	1458	140	1598	1227	115	1342
Others	458	—	458	43	—	43	108	—	108	4328	32	4360	1279	16	1295
Total	172236	31806	204042	31863	11341	43204	83210	20765	103975	108799	20776	129575	74242	14200	88442

Countries	1972			1973			1961-1973 Toplamı			From 2/1/1974 to 8/11/1974		
	E.M.	K.W.	T.T.	E.M.	K.W.	T.T.	E.M.	K.W.	T.T.	E.M.	K.W.	T.T.
F. Germany	48911	16964	65875	79526	24267	103793	509411	138618	648029	1037	31	1068
Australia	478	162	640	659	227	886	4210	458	4668	626	319	945
Austria	3291	1181	4472	4943	2140	7083	30464	3995	34459	1830	507	2337
Belgium	111	2	113	256	9	265	15292	17	15309	515	15	530
France	10572	38	10610	17467	77	17544	45159	207	45366	10434	33	10467
Netherland	670	74	744	1980	14	1994	23192	167	23359	1442	16	1458
Great Britain	69	13	82	106	10	116	1927	135	2062	79	9	88
Switzerland	1134	178	1312	845	264	1109	5497	863	6360	461	202	663
Others	1339	42	1381	3003	27	3030	10558	117	10675	1494	12	1506
Total	66575	18654	85229	108785	27035	135820	645710	144577	790287	17918	1144	19062

Source: Turkish Employment Service, Bulletice 8.11.1974

E.M. = Male   Toplam = Total

K.W. = Female

Table 2

Migrant Workers In Germany By Country Of Origin
(as of January)

Country of Origin	1963	1964	1965	1966
Italy	216,593	215,367	250,380	304,371
Greece	89,419	124,566	164,125	186,005
Spain	97,465	114,355	149,146	167,501
Portugal	1,857	2,584	6,893	15,231
Yugoslavia	36,442	42,904	48,827	68,673
Turkey	22,054	44,953	94,975	133,000
Total	668,969	'764,230	952,461	1,126,593
	1967	1968	1969	1970
Italy	272,455	227,654	282,166	330,049
Greece	171,891	132,655	155,822	206,819
Spain	141,515	106,429	119,997	149,190
Portugal	19,035	16,745	22,107	32,802
Yugoslavia	90,474	84,805	148,439	296,970
Turkey	136,255	123,386	171,018	272,423
Total	1,068,025	903,591	1,136,899	1,575,072
	1971	1972	1973	
Italy	362,704	384,303	409,448	
Greece	250,971	264,427	268,408	
Spain	170,382	175,998	179,157	
Portugal	47,387	57,180	68,994	
Yugoslavia	415,461	434,893	465,611	
Turkey	373,019	449,676	528,414	
Total	1,964,213	2,158,680	2,346,800	

Source: 1968-1971, Bundesanstalt für Arbeit, Ausländische Arbeitnehmer, pp. 54
1972-1973, Bundesanstalt für Arbeit, Ausländische Arbeitnehmer, pp. 11

Table 3

Distribution of migrant workers in Federal Germany
according nationalities in percentage

Nationality country	End of January			End of September		
	1973	1972	1971	1972	1971	1970
Turks	22,5	20,8	19,0	21,7	20,2	18,2
Yugoslavs	19,8	20,1	21,1	20,2	21,4	21,7
Italians	17,5	17,8	18,5	18,1	18,2	19,6
Greeks	11,4	12,3	12,8	11,5	12,0	12,4
Spanish	7,6	8,2	8,7	7,8	8,3	8,8
Portugese	2,9	2,6	2,4	2,8	2,6	2,3
Marrocans	0,7	0,6	0,5	0,7	0,3	0,5
Tunisians	0,5	0,5	0,4	0,5	0,5	0,3
From countries with recruitment agreement	82,9	82,9	83,4	83,3	83,7	83,8
Other nationalities	17,1	17,1	16,6	16,7	16,3	16,2
Total	100,0	100,0	100,0	100,0	100,0	100,0

Source: Bundesanstalt für Arbeit, *Ausländische Arbeitnehmer 1972-73*,
p. 11.

Table 4

Migrant Workers By Region Of Origin In Turkey

	1973		1972		1971		1970	
	No.	%	No.	%	No.	%	No.	%
Marmara	18,301	18.0	14,529	23.3	14,278	22.4	20,445	21,4
Central Anatolia	26,892	26.5	14,740	23.6	14,793	23.2	21,951	22.9
Black Sea Coast	14,602	14.4	8,486	13.6	8,821	13.8	15,977	16.7
Aegean	23,888	23.6	13,787	22.1	15,938	25.0	25,337	26.5
Eastern Anatolia	8,158	8.0	4,980	8.0	4,971	7.8	4,090	4.3
Southern Anatolia	9,585	9.5	5,872	9.4	4,976	7.8	7,885	8.2

	1969		1968		1967	
	No.	%	No.	%	No.	%
Marmara	19,949	20.3	9,953	24.0	3,154	43.6
Central Anatolia	23,384	23.8	9,536	23.0	1,156	16.0
Black Sea Coast	15,790	16.1	5,983	14.4	782	10.8
Aegean	23,382	23.8	8,161	19.7	798	11.0
Eastern Anatolia	7,797	8.0	4,095	9.9	722	10.0
Southern Anatolia	7,840	8.0	3,722	9.0	621	8.6

Source: Bundesanstalt für Arbeit, *Ausländische Arbeitnehmer,* 1967-1968, p. 29
Bundesanstalt für Arbeit, *Ausländische Arbeitnehmer,* 1969-1971, p. 36
Bundesanstalt für Arbeit, *Ausländische Arbeitnehmer,* 1972-1973, p. 49

Table 5

Total Remittances Of Migrant Workers In Germany
(Million DM)

Country of origin	1973	1972	1971	1970	1969	1968	1967
Italy	1.350	1.300	1.300	1.150	950	850	850
Spain	850	750	500	450	350	300	350
Greece	900	850	600	500	400	300	350
Yugoslavia	2.200	1.900	1.250	950	550	250	200
Turkey	2.500	2.100	1.200	900	550	350	300
Total	8.450	7.450	5.300	4.300	3.100	2.150	2.150

Source: Ausländischer Arbeitnehmer, 1972-1973, p. 19

Table 6

Migrant Workers In Germany — Age Groups By Sex And Nationality
1968 and 1972

	Males							
	Under 25		25-35		35-45		45 and over	
Nationality	1968	1972	1968	1972	1968	1972	1968	1972
Italians	27	25	32	31	26	24	15	18
Greeks	7	8	54	42	32	38	7	11
Spaniards	11	12	38	35	40	36	11	16
Portuqgese	—	4	–	45	–	38	–	12
Yugoslavs	11	17	50	47	29	28	10	7
Turks	7	9	60	54	29	32	4	4
Others	–	22	–	38	–	21	–	18
Averaqe	16	16	42	43	29	29	13	11
	Females							
Italians	36	38	35	28	11	21	—	12
Greeks	30	25	44	44	23	26	–	–
Spaniards	23	25	39	31	27	28	11	16
Portuqese	–	27	–	46	0	21	–	–
Yugoslavs	39	39	39	39	11	17	–	5
Turks	32	32	41	44	17	19	–	–
Others	–	30	–	25	–	–	–	–
Average	32	32	38	39	21	20	9	8

Source: 1968 — Bundesanstalt für Arbeit, Ausländische Arbeitnehmer, 1969, p. 48
       1972 — Bundesanstalt für Arbeit, Repräsentativ-Untersuchung, '72, p. 16

Table 7

Migrant Workers In Germany By Economic Sector And Nationality
1965 and 1969-1971

1965

	Italians	Greeks	Spaniards	Yugoslavs	Turks
Agriculture	1.0	0.4	1.2	1.1	0.8
Mining	5.3	3.1	4.1	3.3	11.9
Metals	29.6	48.1	41.0	23.2	40.7
Manufacturing	23.3	36.6	30.6	16.6	19.4
Construction	29.6	5.6	10.9	28.9	18.8
Trade	2.7	1.8	2.4	4.3	1.5
Transport	3.1	0.6	3.8	0.7	2.7
Services	5.3	3.7	5.9	21.9	4.2

1969

	Italians	Greeks	Spaniards	Yugoslavs	Turks
Agriculture	0.9	0.3	1.4	0.8	0.7
Mining	3.3	1.4	2.4	2.2	6.2
Metals	35.7	51.1	42.8	34.2	43.4
Manufacturing	28.1	35.5	31.7	17.4	25.8
Construction	18.5	3.5	6.9	29.6	15.5
Trade	3.6	2.4	3.5	2.7	1.9
Transport	2.6	0.7	4.0	0.7	2.1
Services	7.2	5.1	7.4	12.6	4.3

1970

	Italians	Greeks	Spaniards	Yugoslavs	Turks
Agriculture	0.9	0.2	1.5	0.9	0.7
Mining	3.1	1.3	2.6	2.1	7.0
Metals	36.5	52.4	43.5	34.5	44.5
Manufacturing	26.6	34.1	30.3	16.7	24.2
Construction	18.8	3.7	7.3	31.1	15.2
Trade	4.0	2.6	3.7	2.9	1.9
Transport	2.6	0.7	4.2	1.3	2.2
Services	7.4	5.1	7.1	10.5	4.3

1971

	Italians	Greeks	Spaniards	Yugoslavs	Turks
Agriculture	0.9	0.2	1.6	0.9	0.9
Mining	3.1	1.3	2.6	2.2	7.3
Metals	34.8	50.1	41.2	31.9	41.0
Manufacturing	26.0	33.7	29.7	16.6	24.5
Construction	19.8	4.3	8.4	31.9	15.9
Trade	4.5	3.3	4.2	3.8	2.6
Transport	2.6	0.9	4.5	1.2	2.3
Services	8.3	6.1	7.9	11.4	5.4

Source: Bundesanstalt für Arbeit, Ausländische Arbeitnehmer, 1970, pp. 62-69.

Table 8

*Migrant and Domestic Workers By Sector Of
Economic Activity (Percent)*

	Premigration[1]		Migrant Workers in Germany[2]		Domestic Labor Force[3]	
	1967	1971	1965	1970	1965	1970
Agriculture	30.2	40.7	0.8	0.7	71.4	65.8
Mining	2.5	5.2	11.9	7.0	0.6	0.8
Manufacturing						
— metals	—	—	40.7	44.5	0.9	1.6
— other	8.4	4.5	19.4	24.2	7.2	7.2
Construction	16.5	11.7	18.8	15.2	2.6	2.9
Trade	3.4	4.7	1.5	1.9	2.9	5.0
Transport	3.7	3.0	2.7	2.2	2.2	2.7
Services	5.2	2.3	4.2	4.3	6.3	11.9

Source: 1. İş ve İşçi Bulma Kurumu, *Yurt Dışındaki Türk İşçileri ve Dönäs Eğilimleri,*
1969, p. 11, 1971, p. 12.
2. Bundesanstalt für Arbeit, *Ausländische Arbeitnehmer,* 1970, pp. 62-69.
3. State Institute of Statistics
— 1965 Population Census, Table 43.
— 1970 Population Census, Table 14.

Table 9

*Foreign Employees As A Proportion Of Total Number
Of Employees In German Industries, September 1969*

Industry	Foreign Employees as Percentage of All Employees	
Extractive industries	3.7	
Agriculture, forestry, fishery	4.5	
Metal industry (including metal production, engineering, electrical goods)	11.0	
Non-metal manufacturing industries	9.7	
Of which: Chemical industry		7.6
Plastic, rubber, and asbestos processing		16.5
Earth, stone, ceramics, glass		11.9
Wood, paper, printing		7.9
Leather, textiles, clothing		12.1
Food, tobacco, drink		6.4
Building	12.4	
Services, commerce, transport	2.8	
Of which: Catering		12.7
All industries	7.0	

Source: Bundesanstalt für Arbeit, *Ausländische Arbeitnehmer* 1969, p. 12.

Table 10

Migrant Workers In Germany By Selected Industries, By Nationality, By Sex

Men	Nationality						
	Italy	Yugoslavia	Turkey	Greece	Spain	Portugal	Others
Number in Employment	262,348	152,120	165,954	100,261	91,391	18,779	178,473
Industry	%	%	%	%	%	%	%
Metal production and engineering	31.2	29.2	38.9	41.9	40.9	36.4	23.2
Building	24.5	44.5	19.7	6.0	10.0	10.8	1.6
Other manufacturing	9.9	4.6	8.4	15.8	14.6	14.9	7.9
Textiles and clothing	6.1	3.8	7.9	9.0	5.2	14.2	4.8
Electrical goods	4.7	4.7	5.0	10.7	5.3	2.3	6.9
Total 5 industries	76.4	86.8	79.9	83.4	76.0	78.6	44.4
Women							
Number in Employment	77,896	74,170	46,997	74,087	44,155	7,600	77,818
Industry	%	%	%	%	%	%	%
Textiles and clothing	24.5	15.2	22.7	17.6	16.8	22.8	13.3
Metal production and engineering	21.3	10.9	17.0	27.4	23.6	19.8	9.3
Other manufacturing	18.1	11.7	19.4	18.0	23.0	21.4	10.8
Electrical goods	11.3	18.6	23.9	21.4	12.9	7.5	6.6
Public services and administration	4.6	16.0	5.2	4.7	8.4	9.3	22.6
Private services	9.0	19.2	5.0	3.1	7.0	9.7	16.4
Total 6 industries	88.8	91.6	93.2	92.2	91.7	90.5	79.0

Source: Bundesanstalt für Arbeit *Ausländische Arbeitnehmer* 1969, Table 6, pp. 110-11.

Table 11

Distribution of Turkish Worker's Children According Age Groups
(Percent)

Countries	1973	Pre-School 0-6	%	School Age 6-18	%	Total	%
Federal Germany		65,000	82	110,000	88	175,000	86
Netherland		4,557	06	6,062	04	10,619	05
Austria		235	00	890	00	1,125	00
France		392	00	712	00	1,104	00
Switzerland		3,444	05	2,271	02	5,715	03
Belgium		4,029	05	2,511	02	6,540	03
Denmark		75	00	175	00	250	00
Australia		726	00	1,124	01	1,850	01
Sweden		433	00	1,610	01	2,043	01
Great Britain		23	00	52	00	75	00
Norway		38	00	62	00	100	00
Others		178	00	672	00	850	00
Total		79,130		126,141		205,271	

Source: Ministery of Education, *Yurt Dışında Çalışan Türk İşçilerinin (0-16 Yaş) Çocuklarının Eğitimi Sorunları*, Ankara 1974, Yayın No. 74-20, p. 6, Table 4

Table 12 (A)

Numerical Distribution of Children of Migrant Workers
Attending Primary and Secondary Schools in Federal Germany

School Year	Greece	Italy	Yugoslavia	Spain	Portugal	Turkey
1965/66	4.051	9.337	—	7.066	—	2.956
1966/67	5.802	13.562	—	9.273	—	5.119
1967/68	7.570	16.429	—	9.956	—	7.191
1968/69	10.965	21.207	3.649	11.061	1026	10.402
1969/70	16.702	26.502	6.051	13.190	1082	15.868
1970/71	25.503	32.438	11.025	15.866	1718	25.950
1971/72	34.109	40.579	15.806	19.812	3586	41.397

Source: Bayerisches Staatsministerium für Arbeit u. Sozialordnung, cited in G. Mahler, *Zweitsprache Deutsch*, 1974, p. 180

Table 12 (B)

Numerical Distribution of Children of Migrant Workers
Attending Primary and Secondary Schools in Bavaria

School Year	Total	Greece	Italy	Yugoslavia	Spain and Portugal	Turkey
1968/69	6.695	1436	2270	412	814	1.763
1969/70	9.478	2293	2864	755	960	2.606
1970/71	13.570	3446	3582	1350	1152	4.040
1971/72	18.662	4713	4505	2054	1465	5.925
1972/73	22.778	5066	5435	2724	1508	8.045
1973/74	27.688	6688	5827	3170	1685	10.067

Source: Bayerisches Statistisches Landesamt, Bayerisches Staatsministerium für Unterricht und Kultus, cited in G. Mahler, *Zweitsprache Deutsch,* 1974, p. 181

Table 13

Savings of Migrant workers in FRG

Country of Origin	% of persons with saving account in FRG	Average of savings per household in FRG April 1972, in DM
Greece	64	7911
Italy	34	5533
Spain	39	5400
Yugoslavia	44	5110
Turkey	49	4260
Portugal	32	3484
Mediterranean countries	45	5400
Other countries	47	5475

Source: Monats Bericht der Deutschen Bundesbank, April 1974, p. 26.

Table 14

Savings of Turkish Workers in FRG

Length of sejourn	% in terms of duration of stay	% in terms of savings in FRG	Average amount of savings in FRG in DM (until 31.2.72)
0-1 year	2	—	—
1-3 year	42	45	3.095
3-5 year	27	53	4.110
5 and more	29	53	6.045

Family conditions	Marital status	% in terms of savings in FRG	Average amount of savings in FRG in DM (until 31.2.72)
Bachelor	18	39	2.700
Married:			
Husband abroad	45	48	3.773
With wife abroad living in FRG	34	55	5.475
Other	3	—	—

Occupational activity of spouse and number of children	Occupational status	% in terms of savings in FRG	Average amount of savings in FRG in DM (Until 31.2.72)
Spouse works:			
Without children	29	57	4.297
With children	30	60	7.160
Spouse does not work:			
Without children	13	45	4.513
With children	28	50	4.840

Source: Monats Bericht der Deutschen Bundesbank, April 1974, p. 29.

Table 15

Remittances of Turkish Workers According Duration of Stay,
Family Conditions and Occupational Activity of Spouse
Number of Children

Length of sejourn	% in terms of duration of stay	% in terms of remittances of each group	Average amount of remittances in DM (until 31.2.72)
0-1 year	2	58	....
1-3 year	42	87	4.332
3-5 year	27	93	5.521
5 and more	29	90	5.692

Family conditions	Marital status	% in terms of transfer of each group	Average amount of remittances in DM (until 31.2.72)
Bachelor	18	66	2.726
Married:			
Husband abroad	45	98	5.910
With wife abroad			
living in FDR	34	88	4.642
Other	3	91	5.370

Occupational activity of spouse and number of children	Occupational status	% in terms of tranfer of each group	Average amount of remittances in DM (until 31.2.72)
Spouse works:			
Without children	29	93	5.132
With children	30	83	4.726
Spouse does not work:			
Without children	13	96	5.223
With Children	28	86	4.055

Source: Monats Bericht der Deutschen Bundesbank, April 1974, p. 28.

BIBLIOGRAPHY

This bibliography has been compiled by Nermin Abadan-Unat with additions taken from the bibliography attached to Tufan Kolan's dissertation, title: "International Migration and Economic Development: the Turkish Case" as well as the selected bibliography, attached to the article of Duncan Miller.

FOREIGN LANGUAGE

BOOKS

Bibliography

Bertelli, L., Corcagni, G., Rosoli, G. F., *Migrations*, Catalogue of the Library of the Center for Migration Studies, Rome, 1972.

Glaser, W. A., *Bibliography about the Migration and Return of Professionals*, UNITAD and BASR, Third Edition 1973.

OECD, *Bibliography*, International Migration of Manpower, Paris 1969.

Thomas, B., *International Migration and Economic Development*, A Trend Report and Bibliography, UNESCO, 1961.

General Works

Baucic, I., *The Effects of Emigration from Yugoslavia and the Problem of Returning Emigrant Workers*, European Demographic Monographs II, The Hague: Nijhoff, 1972.

Beck, R. H., *The Changing Structure of Europe: Economic, Social and Political Trends*, Minneapolis: University of Minnesota, 1970.

Beijer, C., *Rural Migrants in Urban Setting*, 1963.

Beijer, F., Hofstede and Wentholt, *Characteristics of Oversea Migrants*. The Hague, 1961.

Bingemer, E., Meistermann-Seeger, E., Neubert, E., *Leben als Gastarbeiter*—Geglückte und missglückte Integration, Köln u. Opladen, 1970.

Borrie, W. D., *The Cultural Integration of Immigrants*. Paris: UNESCO, 1959.

Bouscaran, A. T., *International Migration since 1945*. New York: Praeger, 1963.

Böhning, W. R., *The Migration of Workers in the U.K. and the European Community*. Oxford University Press, 1972.

Braun, Rudolf, *Sozio-kulturelle Probleme der Eingliederung italienischer Arbeitskräfte in der Schweiz*. Erlenbach-Zürich, 1970.

Breitenbach, D. u. Dankwortt, D., *Probleme der Ausbildung und Anpassung von Praktikanten*. Saarbrücken, 1966.

Brody, E. B., *Behavior in New Environment*, Sage Publications, 1969.

Calame, P. and Pierre, *Les Travailleurs étrangers en France*. Paris.

Castles, S. and Kosack, G., *Immigrant Workers and Class Structure in Western Europe*. London: Oxford University Press, 1973.

Cinnani P., *Emigration und Imperialismus*. Zur Problematik der Arbeitsemigranten. München: Trikont Verlag, 1970.

Claes, B., *De sociale integratie van de italiaanse en poolse migranten in Belgisch-Limburg*. Hasselt 1962.

The Committee on the International Migration of Talent, *The International Migration of High-Level Manpower*. New York: Praeger 1970.

Cuisenier, J.–Aron, R., *Problèmes du développement économiques dans les pays méditerranéens*. Paris–La Haye, 1963.

Dahnen, J., Kozlowicz, W., *Ausländische Arbeiternehmer in der Bundesrepublik*. Stuttgart, 1963.

Delgado, J. M., *Anpassungsprobleme der spanischen Gastarbeiter in Deutschland*. Köln, 1966.

—, *Die "Gastarbeiter" in der Presse—Eine inhaltsanalytische Studie*. Opladen, 1972.

Descloitres, R., *Le Travailleur étranger, son adaptation au travail industriel et à la vie urbaine*. Paris: OECD 1967.

—, *The Foreign Worker*. Paris: OECD 1967.

Dincer, N. *Emigration and Immigration in Holland*. Policy and Organization TODAIE, Publ. No. 12, Ankara, 1962.

Eisenstadt, S. N., *The Absorption of Immigrants*. London: Routledge and Kegan Paul, 1954.

Ex, J. *Adjustment after Immigration*, The Hague: Martinus Nijhoff.

Friedlander, S., *Economic Migration and Economic Growth: A Case Study of Puerto Rico*. Cambridge, Mass. The M.I.T. Press, 1965.

Gani, *Syndicats et Travailleurs Immigrés en France*. Paris: Edition Socials 1972.

Gavett, T. W., *Migration and Changes in the Quality of the Labor Force*. 1967.

Geiselberger, S. *Schwarzbuch: Ausländische Arbeiter*. Frankfurt a. Main: Fischer Verlag 1972.

Girod, R. *Travailleurs étrangers et mobilité sociale en Suisse*. 1965.

Glass, D. *Cultural Assimilation of Immigrants*. London: Cambridge University Press, 1950.

Gnehm, A. *Ausländische Arbeitskräfte*. Ihre Bedeutung für Konjunktur und Wachstum, dargestellt am Beispiel der Schweiz. Bern, 1966.

Goldthorpe, J. H. Ed. *The Affluent Worker in the Class Structure*. London: Cambridge University Press, 1969.

Grandjeat, P. *Les Migrations de Travailleurs en Europe*. Paris: Institut Internationale d' Etudes Sociales. 1966.

Granotier, B. *Les Travailleurs Immigrés en France*. Maspero, Paris, 1970.

Hagen, E. *Arbeitsmotive von Gastarbeitern*. Bern: Verlag P. Haupt, 1973.

Hagman, H. M. *Les Travailleurs étrangers—chance et tourment de la Suisse*. Lausanne: 1966.

Hampel, G. *Einwanderungsgesetzgebung und innereuropäische Wanderung*. Kiel: Institut für Weltwirtschaft, 1957.

Handlin, O. and Thomas, B. Ed., *The Positive Contribution by Immigrants*. Paris: UNESCO, 1955.

Hernandez-Alvarez, H. J., *Return Migration to Puerto Rico*. Berkeley: 1967

Hoffman-Nowotny, H. J., *Migration*. Stuttgart: Verlag F. Enke 1970.

—, *Soziologie der Fremdarbeiterproblem. Eine theoretische und empirische Analyse am Beispiel der Schweiz*. Stuttgart: Verlag F. Enke, 1973.

Houte, H. van and Melgert, W. Eds., *Foreigners in our Community*. Amsterdam-Antwerpen: Keesing Publ. 1972.

Huffschmid, J. *Die Politik des Kapitals*. Konzentration und Wirtschaft in der BRD Frankfurt a. Main. Suhrkamp, 1969.

Hurst, M., *Zur Ich und Identitätsentwicklung des Fremdarbeiterkindes*. Zürich: 1970.

Isaac, J. and Beld, C. A., *The Effects of European Migration on the Economy of Lending and Receiving Countries*. The Hague 1953.

Jackson, J. A., *Migration*. London: Cambridge University Press, 1969.

Kaltenstadler, W., *Migration und Integration von Gastarbeitern*. Auswirkungen auf die heimische Wirtschafts und Sozialentwicklung. Augsburg, n.d.

Kayser, B., *Manpower Movements of Labour Market*. Paris: OECD, 1971.

——, *Cyclically Determined Homeward Flows of Migrant Workers*. Paris: OECD, 1972.

Klaassen, L. H. and Drewe, P., *Migration Policy in Europe: A Comparative Study*. Lexington, Mass.: Farnborough Saxon House, 1973.

Klee, E. *Die Nigger Europas. Zur Lage der Gastarbeiter*. Düsseldorf, 1971.

——, *Gastarbeiter, Analysen und Berichte*. Frankfurt a. Main: Suhrkamp Verlag, 1972.

Kindleberger, C. P., *Europe's Postwar Growth—the Role of Labour Supply*. Cambridge, Mass.: Harvard University Press, 1967.

Koch, H. R., *Gastarbeiterkinder in deutschen Schulen*. Königswinter, 1970.

Leudesdorff and Zillessen, Eds., *Gastarbeiter—Mitbürger*. Gelnhausen und Berlin, 1971.

Livi-Bacci, Ed. *The Demographic and Social Pattern of Emigration from the Southern European Countries*. Firenze, 1972. Dipartimento Statistico Matematico dell Universita di Firenze.

Livi-Bacci and Hagman, H., *The Demographic and Social Pattern of Migrants in Europe*. Strassbourg, 1971.

Lohrmann, R. and Manfrass, K., *Ausländerbeschäftigung und internationale Politik*. Bonn 1974, Verlag R. Oldenburg.

Lucassen/Penninx/Van Velzen/Zwinkels, *Trekarbeid*. Van de Middellandse Zeegebieden naar West-Europa, Sunschrift 84, Nijmegen: 1974.

Marshall, A., *The Import of Labour: The Case of the Netherlands*. Rotterdam: 1973.

Mahler, G., *Zweitsprache Deutsch*. Die Schulbildung der Kinder ausländischer Arbeitnehmer. Donauwörth: 1974, Verlag L. Auer.

Maturi, G., *Arbeitsplatz: Deutschland*. Mainz 1964, Verlag O. Krausenkopf.

Mehrländer, U., *Beschäftigung ausländischer Arbeitnehmer in der* BRD *unter spezieller Berücksichtigung von Nordrhein-Westfalen*. Köln und Opladen: 1969, Second Edition 1972.

——, *Soziale Aspekte der Ausländerbeschäftigung*. Friedrich Ebert Stiftung, Bd. 103, Verlag Neue Gesellschaft, Bonn 1963.

Minces, J. *Les Travailleurs Etrangers en France*. Paris: 1973, Ed. du Seuil.

Michel, A. *Les Travailleurs Algériens en France*. Paris, 1956.

Musgrove, F., *The Migration Elite*. London: Heineman, 1963.

Müller, G., *Gutachten zur Schul und Berufsbildung der Gastarbeiterkinder*. Verband Bildung und Erziehung.

Nelson, J. M., *Migrants, Urban Poverty and Instability in Developing Nations*. Harvard University, Center for International Affairs, No. 22.

Neubeck and Fischer, *Gastarbeiter—Eine neue gesellschaftliche Minderheit*. Zur sozioökonomischen und politischen Situation der Gastarbeiter in der BRD. München, 1972.

Nikolinakos, M. *Politische Ökonomie der Gastarbeiterfrage: Migration und Kapitalismus*. Reinbeck bei Hamburg: Rowohlt, 1973.

Panayotopoulos, M., *La Sécurité Sociale des Travailleurs Migrants.* Genève: 1973.

Papalekas, J. Chr., *Strukturfragen der Ausländerbeschäftigung.* Herford, 1969.

Pepelasis, A. A., *Labour Shortage in Greek Agriculture, 1963-1973.* Athens: Center of Economic Research, 1963.

Reiffers, J. L., *The Role of Worker Immigration in the Growth of the Federal Republic of Germany.* Geneva: ILO, 1970.

Rose, A. M., *Migrants in Europe.* New York: Harper and Row, 1968.

Salowsky, H., *Gesamtwirtschaftliche Aspekte der Ausländerbeschäftigung.* Köln, 1971.

Sampson, A., *Anatomy of Europe.* New York: Harper and Row, 1968.

Schiller, G., *Europäische Arbeitskräftemobilität und wirtschaftliche Entwicklung der Mittelmeerländer.* Eine empirische Untersuchung über die Wirkungen der Gastarbeiterwanderungen auf die Abgabeländer. Darmstadt: Bläschke und Dreher, 1971.

Siebrecht, V., *Die ausländischen Arbeitnehmer.* München, 1964.

Somers, G. C. and Wood, W. D., *Cost-Benefit Analysis of Manpower Policies.* Kingston-Ontario: Industrial Relations Center of Queen's University, 1969.

Stirn, H. *Ausländische Arbeiter im Betrieb.* Frechen und Köln, 1964.

Striso, W., *Zur betriebswirtschaftlichen Integration der ausländischen Arbeitnehmer.* Köln, 1967.

Thomas, B, *Economics of International Migration.* Proceedings of a Conference held by the International Economic Association. London: MacMillan, 1958.

——, *Migration and Urban Development.* A Reappraisal of British and American Long Cycles. London: Methuen, 1972.

——, *Migration and Economic Growth.* A Study of Great Britain and the Atlantic Economy. Second Edition, Cambridge, 1973.

Trebous, M. *Migrations and Development: the Case of Algeria.* Manpower requirements in Algeria and vocational training in Europe. Paris: OECD, 1970.

Verwey-Jonker, Ed. *Allochtonen in Nederland.* Den Haag, 1971.

Wentholt, R. Ed. *Buitenlandse arbeiders in Nederland.* Leiden, 1967.

Zieris, E. *Wohnverhältnisse von Familien ausländischer Arbeitnehmer in Nordrhein-Westfalen.* Düsseldorf: Diehl Verlag, 1971.

Zolotas, X. *International Labor Migration and Economic Development.* Bank of Greece Papers and Lectures. Athens: Bank of Greece, 1966.

Specific Books on Turkey

Ansay, T. and Gessner V., *Gastarbeiter in Gesellschaft und Recht.* München: 1974, Ch. Beck.

Benedict, P., Tümertekin, E., Mansur, F., *Turkey: Geographic and Social Perspectives.* E. J. Brill, Leiden: 1974.

Bozbağ, A. T., *Das kemalistische Entwicklungsmodell und seine Bedeutung für die politische, wirtschaftliche und sozio-kulturelle Entwicklung der Türkei.* Frankfurt a. Main: 1970.

Cohn, E. J., *Turkish Economic, Social and Political Change: the Development of a More Prosperous and Open Society.* New York: 1969, Praeger.

Graevenitz, A. V. and Ergun, I., *Entwicklungspolitische Förderung der Rückgliederung türkischer Arbeitnehmer in die Volkswirtschaft ihrer Heimat.* München: 1971, WIP-Wirtschaft-Infrastruktur.

Hershlag, Z. Y., *Turkey, the Challenge of Growth.* Second Edition of Turkey, An Economy in Transition. Leiden: 1968, E. J. Brill.

Hinderink, J. and Kiray, M., *Social Stratification as an Obstacle to Development.* A Study of Four Turkish Villages. New York: 1970 Praeger.

Haex, J., *Emigratie van Turkse arbeiders, 1961-1971*. Van Leuwen: 1972, Katholieke Universiteit, Sociologisch Onderzoeks Inst.

Jackson, D. A. S., *The Political Economy of Collective Bargaining, the Case of Turkey*. Cambridge: 1971.

Karpat, K. H. Ed., *Social Change and Politics in Turkey*. A structural-historical analysis. Leiden: 1973, E. J. Brill.

Kiray, M. Ed., *Social Stratification and Development in the Mediterranean Bassin*. Paris/den Haag: Mouton, 1972.

Miller, D. and Çetin, I., *Migrant Workers, Wages and Labor Markets*. Emigrant Turkish Workers in the Federal Republic of Germany. Istanbul University, Institute of Development, 1974.

Robinson, R. D., *High Level Manpower in Economic Development: the Turkish Case*. Cambridge, Mass.: 1967, Harvard University Press.

Tezel, S., *Wachstumprobleme der türkischen Wirtschaft unter besonderer Berücksichtigung des ersten Fünfjahresplan*. Köln: 1965.

Ürgüplü, H. S., *Die Auswirkungen einer Assozierung der Türkei mit der Europäischen Wirtschaftsgemeinschaft auf die türkische Wirtschaft*. Köln: 1965.

Werth, M. et al., *Türkische Arbeitnehmergesellschaften in der BRD: Struktur, Leistungen, Aktivierungsmöglichkeiten*. ISOPLAN, Saarbrücken/Bonn: 1973.

Yücer, I., *Bevölkerungswachstum und wirtschaftliche Entwicklung in der Türkei nach dem Zweiten Weltkrieg*. Bamberg, Rodenbusch, 1969.

ARTICLES

General

Abraham-Frois, G., "Capital Humain et Migrations internationales" *Revue d'Economie Politique*. Mars-Avril 1964.

Agapitides, S. "Internal Migrations in Greece and Turkey" UN, *World Population Conference-1965*. V.IV., pp. 471-474, UN Publ.1967.

Allaya, M., "Les Migrations internationales des travailleurs du Bassin Méditerranéen, Caractéristique démographiques et socio-économiques", *Options Méditerranéennes*. Avril 1973, No. 18, pp. 83-97.

Appleyard, R. T., "Determinants of Return Migration: A Socio-Economic Study of United Kingdom Migrants, who returnes from Australia", *The Economic Record*. No. 9/1962. pp. 352-368.

——, "The Return Movement of United Kingdom Migrants from Australia" *Population Studies*. (London) Vol. XV, No. 3 (1962), pp. 214-225.

Bain, T. and Pauga, A., "Foreign Workers and the Intraindustry Wage Structure in West Germany", *KYKLOS*, V. XXV, No. 4 (November 1972), pp. 820-824.

Barkin, S., "The Foreign Worker in Europe" in *Britannica Book of the Year 1966*. Chicago: Encyclopedia Britannica 1966.

——, "Trade Union Policies and Programmes for National Internal Rural Migrants and Foreign Workers", *International Migration*. 4 : 1 (1966).

——, "The Economic Costs and Benefits and Human Gains and Disadvantages of International Migration", *The Journal of Human Resources*. V. 2 (1967), pp. 495-516.

Bartoli, H., "Les migrations de la main d'oeuvre", *Esprit*. Avril 1966.

Baucic, I., "Some Contemporary Characteristics and Problems of the Migration of Yugoslav Workers", *Sociologica*. No. 2 (Beograd 1973), pp. 183-216.

Becker, D., Dörr, G. Tjadden, K. H., "Fremdarbeiterbeschäftigung im deutschen Kapitalismus", *Das Argument*. H. 9/10, 1971.

Beijer, G., "The Brain Drain from the Developing Countries and the Need for the Immigration of Intellectuals and Professionals" *International Migration.* 4 : 1 (1966).

Bestermann, W. M. "Immigration as a Mean of Obtaining Needed Skills and Stimulating Economic and Social Advancement" in *UN: World Population Conference— 1965.* Vol. IV, UN 1967, pp. 196-198.

Ben Sassi, "Les Travailleurs tunésiens dans la région parisienne" *Hommes et Migrations.* No. 109, Paris: 1968.

Berry, R. A. and Soligo, R., "Some Welfare Aspects of International Migration" *Journal of Political Economy.* V. 77, Sept.-Oct. 1969, pp. 778-794.

Bilmen, M. S., "Special Classes Proposed by the Council of Europe for Migrant Children", *Migration News.* No. 5, 1972.

Bodenhofer, T., "Zur Theorie der Arbeitskräftebedarfsschätzung für eine wachsende Wirtschaft", *Schmollers Jahrbuch.* Jhrg. 90, 1970, H. 11, pp. 149-168.

Botsas, E. N., "A Note on Migration and the Balance of Payment" *Economica Internazionale.* V. XXII, (1969), pp. 247-251.

Bowles, S., "Migration as Investment: Empirical Tests of the Human Investment Approach to Geographical Mobility", *The Review of Economics and Statistics.* V. LIII, (November 1970), pp. 356-362.

Bowman, M. J. and Myers, R. G., "Schooling, Experience and Gains and Losses in Human Capital through Migration", *Proceedings of the American Statistical.* 1966, pp. 210-225.

Breton, R., "Institutional Completeness of Ethnic Communities and the Personal Relations of Immigrants", *American Journal of Sociology.* V. 70, September 1964, pp. 193-205.

Böhning, W. R., "The Social and Occupational Apprenticeship of Mediterranean Migrant Workers in West Germany" in LIVI-BACCI, Ed. *The Demographic and Social Pattern of Emigration from the Southern European Countrie.* Firenze 1972, pp. 175-259.

——, "The Differential Strength of Demand and Wage Factors in Intra-European Labour Mobility with Special Reference to West-Germany" *International Migration.* No. 4, 1970.

Caporale, C. "Côuts et profits des migrations internationales", *Revue de l'action populaire.* (January 1965), pp. 45-60.

Cerase, F. P., "A Study of Italian Migrants Returning from the USA", *International Migration Review.* 1967, No. , pp. 67-74.

Comay, Y., "Determinants of Return Migration: Canadian Professionals in the U.S.", *Southern Economic Journal.* Vol. 27, No. 3 (1971), pp. 318-322.

Danieli, L., "Labour Scarcities and Labour Redudancies in Europe by 1980: an Experimental Study" in LIVI-BACCI, Ed. *The Demographic and Social Pattern of Emigration from the Southern European Countries.* Firenze 1972.

Dell'Angelo, G., "Under-Employment in Agriculture", in Economic and Social Studies Conference Board, *Agricultural Aspects of Economic Development.* Istanbul: 1965, pp. 321-331.

Descloitres, R., "The Problems of the Return of Young Adults who have Acquired Skilled Training", in Churches Committee on Migrant Workers in Western Europe, *Migrant Workers in Western Europe.* Geneva 1968, pp. 32-42.

Dietzel, K. P., "Die Rolle der rückkehrenden Arbeiter in der Entwicklungsstrategie des westdeutschen Imperialismus", *Das Argument.* V. 13, 1971, pp. 764-781.

Dreyer, H. M., "Immigration of Foreign Workers in the Federal Republic of Germany", *International Labour Review.* V. 84, No. 1/2, 1961, pp. 1-25.

Ebersbach, G., "Berufsförderung ausländischer Arbeitnehmer als Chance zu beruflichem Aufstieg und sozialem Aufstieg", *CARITAS*. H. 1, 1972.

Eldridge, R. H., "Emigration and the Turkish Balance of Payments", *The Middle East Journal*. 20 : 3, Summer 1966. "Research Priorities of the World Employment Programme", *International Labour Review*. May 1972.

Emmerij, L., "Research Priorities of the World Employement Programme", *International Labour Review*. May 1972.

Fischer, H., "Wege zur wirtschaftlichen Erfasung der Situation der ausländischen Arbeitskräfte in der Schweiz", *Industrielle Organisation*. 6, 1961.

Franck, P. G., "Brain Drain from Turkey" in The Committee on the International Migration of Talent, *The International Migration of High-Level Manpower*. New York: Praeger 1970, pp. 299-374.

Federici, M., "Women Migrant Workers Possesses only certain Rights", *Migration News*. No. 5, 1968.

Frucht, S., "Emigration Remittances and Social Change", *Anthropologia*. Vol. 10 (1968), pp. 193-208.

Glatzer, W., "Bildungsnachfrage und Bildungsdefizit der Kinder ausländischer Arbeitnehmer" in Leudesdorff R. and Zillessen H., *Gastarbeiter–Mitbürger*. 1971, pp. 61-68.

Grubel, H. G. and Scott, A. D., "The International Flow of Human Capital", *American Econmic Review*. 1966, pp. 268-274.

de Haan, E., "Soziale Beratung und Fö rderung ausländischer Arbeitnehmer durch die Arbeiterwohlfahrt", *Bundesarbeitblatt*. No. 4, 1970, pp. 255-260.

Harris, J. R. and Mitchell, F., "A Further Note on Labour Migration", *Kyklos*, Vol. XXIII, 1970, pp. 585-592.

Hernandez-Alvarez, "Migration, return and Development in Puerto Rico" *Economic Development and Cultural Change*. V. 16 No. 4 (1968), pp. 574-587.

Hofstede, B. P., "The Motives of Emigration", *International Labor Review*, 81 : 1, 1960.

Hume, I. M., "Migrant Workers in Europe", *Finance and Development*. V. 10, No. 1, 1973.

Isaac, J. "International Migration and European Population Trends", *International Labour Review*. V. LXV, 1952.

Jelden, H. "Entwicklungspolitische Rückgliederung ausländischer Arbeitnehmer vor dem Start", *Entwicklungspolitik*. No. 2, 1971.

——, "Rückgliederungsprogramm für Arbeitnehmer aus Entwicklungsländern" *Entwicklungspolitik*. No. 5, 1971.

Johnson, R., "The Concept of Marginal Man, a New Approach", *International Migration*. 1965, 3 : 47-49.

——, "The Assimilation of Immigrant Women in the Workforce", *International Migration*. (1966), No. 4, pp. 35-99.

Kade, G., "Arbeitskräfteverlust und wirtschaftliche Entwicklung in Griechenland", *Konjunkturpolitik*. No. 6, 1965, pp. 341-356.

——, "Die Bedeutung der Arbeitskräftewanderung für die planmässige Entwicklungspolitik einiger Mittelmeerländer", in Probleme der ausländischen Arbeitskräfte in der *BRD, Beihefte der Konjunkturpolitik*. H. 13, Berlin: 1966, pp. 113-143.

Kade, G. and Schiller, G., "Gastarbeiterwanderungen, ein neues Element in der Wirtschaftspolitik der Mittelmeerländer", *Weltwirtschaftliches Archiv*. V. 102, No. 6, 1969, pp. 333-355.

Kindleberger, C. P., "Mass Migration, Then and Now", *Foreign Affairs*. 1965, pp. 647-658.

——, "Emigration and Economic Growth", *Banca Nazionale del Lavoro Quaterly Review*. V. XVIII, No. 74, 1965, pp. 235-254.

404　　　　　　　　　　　　　BIBLIOGRAPHY

Kruse, M., "Der deutsche Arbeitsmarkt und die Gastarbeiter", *Schmollers Jahrbuch*. V. (1966), pp. 423-434.

Lambiri, J., "The Impact of Industrial employment on the position of Women in a Greek Country Town", *British Journal of Sociology*. 14 (1963), pp. 240-247.

Lee, E. S., "A Theory of Migration", *Ekistics*. V. 23, 1967, pp. 211-216.

Leggewie "Export von Arbeit—ein Entwicklungs-faktor", *Die Dritte Welt*. 1. Jhrg., No. 1, 1972, pp. 50-77.

Levine, U., "Old Structure, new Culture", *Social Forces*. V. 51, 1973, pp. 355-368.

Lutz, V. "Some Structural Aspects of the Southern Problem: The Complementarity of Emigration and Industrialization", *Banca Nazionale del Lavoro Quarterly Review*. V. 14 (1961), pp. 367-402.

McDonald, J. R., "Labor Immigration in France, 1956-1965", *Annals of the Association of the American Geographers*. V. 59, 1969.

McKinnon, R. I., "Foreign Exchange Constraints in Economic Development and Efficient Aid Allocation", *The Economic Journal*. V. LXXIV, No. 294 (1964) pp. 388-409.

Mahler, G., "Gastarbeiterkinder brauchen ihre Chance", *Schulreport*. 1973/2, p. 5.

Malhotra, M. K., "Die soziale Integration der Gastarbeiterkinder in die deutsche Schulklasse", *Zum Nachdenken*. No. 49, Mainz.

Mangalam, J. J. and Schwarzweller, "Some Theoretical Guidelines toward a Sociology of Migration", *International Migration News*. V. IV, Spring 1970.

Massell, B. F. and Yatopoulos, P. A., "A Note on Labour Migration". *KYKLOS*, V. XVII, 1969, pp. 331-333.

Menendez, J. M., "Children of Spanish Migrants in West Germany", *Migration News*. No. 5, 1972.

Merx, "Ausländische Arbeitskräfte im deutschen Reich und in der BRD", *Wirtschaftspolitische Chronik*. Bd. 1967/1968.

Michalopoulos, C., "Labour Migration and Optimum Population", *KYKLOS*, V. XXI, No. 1 (1968), pp. 130-144.

Miracle and Berry, "Migrant Labour and Economic Development", *Oxford Economic Papers*. V. 22, No. 1, 1970, pp. 86-108.

Mishan, E. J., "Does Immigration confer Economic Benefit on the Host Country", *Economic Issues in Immigration*. London, Institute of Economics Affair 1970.

Moldofsky, N., "Language—A Passport to Successful Immigrant Adjustment? The Quebec Experience", *International Migration*. V. X, No. 3, pp. 131-139.

Nesswetha, W., "Der ausländische Arbeiter in arbeitsmedizinischer Sicht", in H. Stirn, Ed. *Ausländischer Arbeiter im Betrieb*. Frechen, 1964, pp. 82-107.

Niederer, A., "Überfremdung und Fremdarbeiterpolitik, Wirtschaftsförderung", *Stimmen zur Staats und Wirtschaftspolitiek*. No. 46, 1969.

Nikolic, M. "Yugoslav Skilled Labor Temporarily Employed Abroad", *Yugoslav Survey*. V. 14, No. 2, 1973, pp. 15-38.

Nikolinakos, M., "Zur Frage der Auswanderungseffekte in den Emigrationsländern", *Das Argument*. V. 13, No. 9-10, 1971, pp. 782-799.

——, "Wanderungsprozesse und ihre ökonomischen Determinanten" in R. Mackensen and H. Werner, Eds. *Dynamik der Bevölkerungsentwicklung*. München 1973, pp. 152-166.

Petersen, W., "A General Typology of Migration". *American Sociological Review*. 23, 3, 1958, pp. 256-266.

Philpott, S. B., "The Implications of Migrations for Sending Countries: Some Theoretical Considerations" in R. F. Spencer Ed. *Migration and Anthropology*. Seattle, 1970.

Power, J., "Europe's New Proletariat" *The Progressive*. 1972, pp. 33-36.

van Praag, Ph., "Aspects économiques à long terme des migrations internationales dans les pays de la CEE", *International Migration*. V. IX, No. 3/4 1971.

Rabut, O., "Les étrangers en France", *Population*. No. 3, 1973.

Reithoffer, "Arbeitsmarktpolitik—ein internationaler Vergleich" *Das Recht der Arbeit*. 13. Jhrg., 1963, pp. 358-360.

Rey, M. "An Experiment in the Social and Linguistic Integration of Migrants" *Migration News*. No. 2, 1972.

Richter, H., "Probleme der Anwerbung und Betreuung ausländischer Arbeitnehmer aus Sicht der Gewerschaften", *Bundesarbeitblatt*. No. 4, 1970, pp. 251-255.

Rideau, R., "Young Migrant Workers", *Migration News*. No. 2, 1972.

——, "L'Enfant, élément positif dans l'immigration", *Migration News*. No. 1, 1969.

Rocheau, G., "The Free Movements of European Workers and its Limits", *Migration News*. No. 2, 1968.

Rodgers, A. "Migration and Industrial Development. The Southern Italian Experience", *Economic Geography*. V. 46, 1970, pp. 111-135.

Rosen, B. C., "Social Change, Migration and Family Interaction in Brazil", *American Sociological Review*, 1973, pp. 198-212.

Rosenmöller, C. "So verschwenden sie ihr Geld", *Der Arbeitgeber*. No. 6, 1966, pp. 151-153.

——, "Volkswirtschaftliche Aspekte der Ausländerbeschäftigung", *Bundesarbeitblatt*. No. 4, 1970.

Rotschild, K. R., "Arbeitskräfteknappheit und ausländische Arbeitskräfte", *Gewerkschaftliche Monatshefte*. 13 Jg., 1962, pp. 229-233.

Rüstow, H. J., "Gastarbeiter—Gewinn oder Belastung für unsere Volkswirtschaft", *Beihefte der Konjunkturpolitik*. No. 13, 1966.

Schiller, G., "Die Auswanderung von Arbeitskräften als Problem der wirtschaftlichen Entwicklung", *Das Argument*. V. 13, No. 9-10, 1971, pp. 800-809.

Scott, F. D., "The Study of Effects of Emmigration", *Scandinavian Economic History Review*. V. 8, (1960), pp. 161-174.

——, "Towards a Framework for Analyzing the Cost and Benefits of Labour Migration", *Bulletin of the International Institute for Labour Studies*. No. 2, (1967), pp. 48-63.

Sills, D. L., "Migration, II. Economic Aspects", *International Encyclopedia of the Social Sciences*. V. 1o, Second Ed. 1968, pp. 292-300.

da Silva "Geopolitics and the International Migration of Workers", *Migration Today*. 1970, No. 15, pp. 43-53.

Sjollema, B. Ch. "Return Migration and Development Aid", *Migration Today*. No. 5. 1965.

Stark, T. 'The Economic Desirability of Migration", *The International Migration Review*. I, 2, 1967, pp. 3-22.

——, "A Further Step towards the Protection of Migrant Family Rights", *Migration News*. No. 1, 1968.

——, "Difficulties of Migrants and Refugees in Professional Categories", *Migration Today*. No. 6, 1970.

—— "Migration and Development", *Migration News*. No. 1, 1973.

Stephan, G. 'Einstellung und Politik der Gewerkschaften", in J. Chr. Papaleka, *Strukturfragen der Ausländerbeschäftigung*. Herford, 1969, pp. 34-46.

Stirn, H. "Ausländerbeschäftigung in Deutschland in den letzten 100 Jahren", in Stirn, H. Ed. *Ausländische Arbeiter im Betrieb*. Frechen und Köln: 1964, pp. 9-69.

Tapinos, G., 'Le rôle de l'émigration dans la phase de démarrage de la croissance économique", *Migration dans le monde*. No. 4, 1969.

Taliani, E., "Der Gastarbeiter auf dem Wege zur Emanzipation", in Leudesdorff and Zillessen, *Gastarbeiter—Mitbürger*. Gelnhausen and Berlin, 1971, pp. 69-96.

Tinbergen, J. "Migration Labour and the International Division of Labour", in H. van Houte and W. Melgert, Eds. *Foreigners in our Community*. Amsterdam and Antwerpen, Keesing 1972, pp. 16-20.

Thomas, B., "International Movement of Capital and Labour since 1945", *International Labour Review*. V.LXXIV, No. 3, 1956, pp. 225-238.

——, "The International Circulation of Human Capital", *Minerva*, V. V, No. 4, 1967, pp. 479-506; *Minerva*, V. VI, No. 3, 1968, pp. 423-427.

Vigorelli, P., "Returning Migrants Re-Employed in Italian Industry", *Migration News*. No. 2, 1969.

Wallner, E. M., 'Vorurteile und Gesellschaft. Zur Problematik der Sozialarbeit zugunsten ausländischen Arbeitnehmer", in *Ausländische Arbeitnehmer: Hilfen im ausserbetrieblichen Bereich*. Frankfurt a. Main, 1970.

Wander, H., "Social and Economic Importance of Overseas Migration from Europe", in *International Migration*. V. X, 1/2, 1972.

Watanabe, "International Subcontracting Employment and Skill Promotion". *International Labour Review*. V. 105, No. 5, 1972, pp. 425-449.

Weber, R., "Die Beschäftigung ausländischer Arbeitnehmer aus der Sicht der Wirtschaft", *Bundesarbeitblatt*. No. 4, 1970, pp. 246-251.

Weicken, H., "Anwerbung und Vermittlung italienischer, spanischer und griechischer Arbeitskräfte im Rahmen bilateraler Anwerbevereinbarungen", in *Ausländische Arbeitskräfte in Deutschland*. Hessisches Institut für Betriebswirtschaft, Rüsseldorf 1961.

Werner, H., "Freizügigkeit der Arbeitskräfte und der Wanderungsbewegung in den Ländern der Europäischen Gemeinschaft", *Mitteilungen aus der Arbeitsmarkt Berufsforschung*. 6. Jhrg. 1973.

Wolf, E., "Probleme und Methoden der Einordnung in den Aufnahmeländern", in J. Chr. Papalekas, *Strukturfragen der Ausländerbeschäftigung*. 1969, pp. 23-33.

Zieris, E., "Anlernung und Ausbildung" in J. Chr. Papalekas, *Strukturfragen der Ausländerbeschäftigung*. Herford, 1969, pp. 60-63.

Zingaro, R., "Re-Integration of Returnees in Andria", *Migration News*. No. 2, 1969.

Articles on Turkey

Abadan, Nermin, "Studie über die Lage und die Probleme der türkischen Gastarbeiter in der BDR", in *Arbeitsplatz: Europa*. Europäische Schriften des Bildungswerks Europäische Politik, Heft 11, Köln 1966, pp. 102-124.

——, "Turkish Workers in West Germany: a case study", *Siyasal Bilgiler Fakültesi Dergisi*. 1969, C. XXIV, No. 1, pp. 21-50.

——, "Immigrants and Migrant Labour: Turkish Workers in the FRG", *Wilton Park Journal*. Winter 1969, No. 42, pp. 12-22.

——, "Le non-retour à l'industrie, trait dominant de la chaine migratoire turque", *Sociologie du Travail*. No. 3, 1972, pp. 278-293.

Abadan-Unat, Nermin, 'La Récession de 1966/67 en Allemagne Fédérale et ses répercussions sur les ouvriers turcs", *The Turkish Yearbook of International Relations*. 1971.

——, "Turkish External Migration and Social Mobility", in Benedict, P., Tümertekin, E., Mansur, F., (Eds.). *Turkey: Geographical and Social Perspectives*. Leiden: 1974 E. C. Brill.

——, "La migration turque et la mobilité sociale", *Studi Emigrazione*. Anno X, No. 30, Giugno 1973, pp. 236-253.

Alpat, S., "The Effects of Turkish Workers going Abroad as Labor Force", in R. G. Riddker and H. Lubell (Eds.), *Employment and Unemployment of the Near East and South Asia*. Vol. II, India Vikas Publ. 1971.

Ansay, T. and Wuppermann, M. "Das Vaterschaftsanerkenntnis in den türkisch-deutschen Rechtsbeziehungen", *Das Standesamt*. 27. Jhrg. No. 5, 1974, pp. 113-123.

Baade, F. "Die türkischen Gastarbeiter als Wirtschaftsfaktor", *Deutsch-Türkische Gesellschaft Mitteilungen*. H. 75, Bonn: 1968.

Bartels, D. "Türkische Gastarbeiter aus der Region Izmir. Zur raumzeitlichen Differenzierung der Bestimmungsgründe ihrer Aufbruchsentschlüsse *Erdkunde*. 22, pp. 313-326.

Barthel, G., 'Das Auslandskapital in der Türkei", *Wirtschaftswissenschaft*. 15 Jhrg., Heft 8, Berlin 1967.

Cillov, H. 'Population Increase of Turkey and Economic Development", *Istatistik Dergisi*. C. 1, No. 3, 1969, pp. 3-12.

Dağlier, E. "The Flow of Turkish Workers to Common Market Countries and its Significance to Turkish Economy", *Turkish Review*. V. 1, No. 8, pp. 12-24.

Denis, F. "Les Travailleurs turcs et nord africains", *Nouvelles de la Commission Internationale Catholique pour les Migrations*. Sept.-Oct. 1965, No. 5, pp. 1-5.

Dirks, S. "Un problème social dans les campagnes turques: la famille", *Cahier de l'Orient Contemporain*. 24 (1967) pp. 26-28.

Eldridge, R. H., "Emigration and the Turkish Balance of Payment", *The Middle East Journal*. 20:3, Summer 1966.

Ersoy, T., "Mobility of Rural Labour in Turkey: An Econometric Approach", *Istatistik Dergisi*, Vol. 1, No. 6-7, 1969, pp. 51-85.

Franck, P. G., "Brain Drain from Turkey" in The Committee on the International Migration of Talent, *The International Migration of High-Level Manpower*. New York: Praeger 1970, pp. 299-374.

Gökalp, E., "L'émigration turque en Europe et particulièrement en France", *La Population*. Mars-Avril 1973, No. 2, pp. 336-350.

Haar, R., "Türkische Arbeiter in der Betreuung durch die Arbeiterwohlfahrt", *Die Arbeiterwohlfahrt*. 1963-64, pp. 56-60.

——, "Experience with Turkish Workers in Germany", *Migration News*. V. XIV, No. 17-19, (1965), pp. 17-19.

Habermeier, E., "Türkische Arbeiter in Deutschland", *Orient*. (1966), 4: pp. 121-125.

Kiray, M., "Restructuring of agricultural enterprises affected by migration in Turkey", in C.A.O. van Nieuwenhuijze, *Emigration and Agriculture in the Mediterranean Bassin*. Institute of Social Studies, The Hague 1972.

Miller, D., "Emigrant Turkish Workers—A Framework for Analysis", *Studies in Development*. Fall 1971, pp. 529-541.

Oğuzkan, T., "Migratory Behaviour of the Turkish Ph. D's working abroad", in R. E. Krane, Ed. *Manpower Mobility Across Cultural Boundaries Social, Economic and Legal Aspects*. Leiden: 1975, Brill.

de Planhol, "Les émigrations du travail en Turquie", *Revue de Géographie Alpine*. 40: pp. 583-600.

Schachbazian, K. and Wilke, H., "Bewusstseinselemente türkischer Arbeiter in der BRD", *Das Argument*. 68/1971, pp. 757-763.

Yaşer, Y. "Industrial Relations and Social Problems of Turkish Workers Abroad", in CENTO, *Seminar on Industrial Relations*. Teheran 1972.

DOCUMENTS, REPORTS AND STATISTICAL YEARBOOKS

General

Arbeiterwohlfahrt, Bundesverband: Denkschrift zur Reform der AusländerPolitik, Sondernummer, *Theorie und Praxis der Sozialarbeit.* Z 21 441 F Bonn.

Baucic, I., *"Some Economic Characteristics of the Yugoslav Foreign Migration of Worker".* International Conference of the Development of the Meditterranean Area, Cagliari-Nuoro, 19-21 January 1973, (Mimeo).

——, "Temporary or permanent—the Dilemma of Migrants and Migration Policies" European Conference on Migration Problems, Catholic University of Louvain 31 January-2 February 1974, (Mimeo).

Antwort der Bundesregierung, *Kleine Anfrage der Abgeordneten Hussing, Giesinger, Ruf, betreffend die Politik der Bundesregierung gegenüber den ausländischen Arbeitnehmern in der BDR.* Drucksache IV/3085, 31.1.1972.

Bundesminister W. Arendt, *Aktionsprogramm für Ausländerbeschäftigung.* Bulletin, Presse und Informationsamt, No. 70, 8.6.1973, pp. 693-694.

Bundesanstalt für Arbeit, *Ausländische Arbeitnehmer 1969.* Ergebnisse der Repräsentativ-Untersuchung vom Herbst 1968, Nürnberg, 28.8.1970.

——, *Ausländische Arbeitnehmer 1970.* Nürnberg, 27.8.191.

——, *Ausländische Arbeitnehmer 1971.* Nürnberg, Sept. 1972.

——, *Ausländische Arbeitnehmer 1972/73.* Nürnberg, July 1974.

——, *Repräsentativ-Untersuchung '72.* Beschäftigung ausländischer Arbeitnehmer, Nürnberg, November 1973.

Bundesminister für Arbeit und Sozialordnung, *Eingliederung ausländischer Arbeitnehmer.* Bonn, 1972.

Bundesvorstand des Deutschen Gewerkschaftsbundes (DGB), *Die deutschen Gewerkschaften und die ausländischen Arbeitnehmer.* 2.11.1971.

Bourguignon, F., *Emigration ou l'Investissement Etranger: Une Eventuelle Alternative pour Certains Pays en voie de Développement.* Working Paper, Seminar on Demographic Research in Relation to International Migration, Buenos Aires, 5-11 March 1974 (Mimeo).

Cerase, F. P., *Migration and Social Change: Expectations and Delusions.* Reflections upon the return flow from the U.S. to Italy, 1973 (Mimeo).

Churches Committee on Migrant Workers in Western Europe, *Relation between Migration Economic Development.* Report given at Geneva: World Council of Churches, 14-18 October 1968.

Commission des Communautés Européennes, *La Libre Circulation de la Main d'Oeuvre et les Marchés du Travail dans la CEE.* June 1970.

Council of Europe, Secretariat, *Problems Raised by the Return Home of Migrant Workers.* Strasbourg, RS 84, 1966.

——, Consultative Assembly, *Report on the Integration of Migrant with the Society of their Host Countries.* 3322, Strasbourg, 12.9.1973.

Glaser, W. A. and G. C. Habers, *The Migration and Return of Professionals.* Report for UN Institute for Training and Research, 1973 (Mimeo).

International Labour Office (ILO), *Employment and Economic Growth.* Geneva: 1964.

——, *Manpower Aspects of Recent Economic Developments in Europe.* Geneva: 1969.

——, *Migrant Workers.* Report VI, ILO Conference, 59th Session 1974, Geneva: 1973.

——, *Some Growing Employment Problems in Europe.* Report II, Second European Regional Conference, Geneva 1974. Geneva: 1973.

Kudat, A. and L. Wakeman, *Migration, Disintegration and Salvation.* International Institute of Management, West Berlin, 1973 (Mimeo).

Livi-Bacci and Hagman, H. M., *Report on the Demographic and Social Pattern of Migrants in Europe, especially with Regard to International Migration.* Report for the Council of Europe, Second European Population Conference, August 31-September 7, 1971.

McLin, J., *International Migration and the European Community.* Fieldstaff reports. American Universities Field Staff, West Europe Series Vol. VII, No. 1, 1972.

Manganara, L., *A Study of Returnees to Rural Areas in Greece,* 1973 (Mimeo).

Maselli, G., *Confrontation of Migration Policies: Results of the Preliminary Inquiry.* Paris, OECD, 1967.

Miudin, P., *Governmental Measures for Attracting Emigrant Workers Savings and Guiding them towards Economic Investment.* Paris, OECD, CT/5745, 29.11.1972 (Mimeo).

Nelson, J.N. *Migrants, Urban poverty and Instability in Developing Nations.* Harvard University, Center for International Affairs, Occasional Papers in Int. Affairs, No. 22.

Organisation for Economic Cooperation and Development, *Emigrant Workers Returning to their Home Country.* Final Report, International Management Seminar Athens, 18-21 October, 1966, Paris: OECD, 1967.

Poinard, M., *Rapport sur les retours du Portugal.* Paris: OECD, MS/M/404/366, 9.8.1971, (Mimeo).

Polyzos, N.J., *Conséquences des Retours en Grèce des Emigrants.* Paris: OECD, MS/M/404/365, 28.7.1971, (Mimeo).

Schiller, G., *Mobilität der Gastarbeiter in Westeuropa. Mikro und Makroökonomische Aspekte.* 1973, (Mimeo).

—, *The Problem of Savings of Migrant Workers in Europe.* Paris: OECD, MS/M/404/443, 19.9.1973.

—, *Auswirkungen der Arbeitskräftewanderungen in den Herkunftsländern,* Bonn, 1973, (Mimeo).

—, *Economic and Political Dimensions of Labour Migration* European Conference on Migration Problems, Catholic University of Louvain, 31 January—2 February 1974, (Mimeo).

Sönmez, N., *Problems Raised by the Return of Italian Migrant Workers* Strassbourg: Council of Europe, RS 114 (1967), (Mimeo).

Statens Offentliga Utredninger 1974: 69,

Arbetsmarknadsdepartment, *Invadrarutedningen 3,* Invandrama och Minoriteterna, Stockholm 1974.

Travis, W. P., "*The Relationship among the International Movements of Workers, Capital and Goods,* Working Paper No. 16, Seminar on Demographic Research, Buenos Aires, 5-11 March 1974.

United Nations, *The Determinants and Consequences of Population Trends: A Summary of Findings on Studies on the Relationship Between Population Changes and Economic and Social Conditions,* UN Population studies, No. 17, New York: UN, 1953.

United Nations, *Economic Survey of Europe, 1969. Pt.: Structural Trends and Prospects in the European Economy.* New York: 1970, UN.

—, *Investment in Human Resources and Manpower Planning.* Papers presented to the eight Session of Senior Economic Advisers to ECE Governments, New York: UN, 1971.

UN, Office of Social Affairs of the European Office, *European Seminar on Social Welfare Programmes for Migrant Workers.* April 2-10, 1965, Geneva.

UN, Population Conference 1965, Vol: IV, *Migration, Urbanization, Economic Development.* UN 1967.

Vlachos, E., *Worker Migration to Western Europe: The Ramification of Population Outflow for the Demographic Future of Greece*. Colorado State University, 1972, (Mimeo).

Wilder-Oklader, *Research on Return Migration and the Concept of "Intention of Permanence in Migratory Theory"*. (Mimeo) 1973.

Specific on Turkey

Akre, J., *Turkish Labor Migration in Western Europe: Maximization of Short Term Benefits*. Unpubl. Master Thesis, University of Pittsburgh, 1972.

Altuğ S. M. *Turkish Aspects of Migration for Employment in Europe*. Symposium on Migration for Employment in Europe, Geneva, ILO, 13 pp.

Barişik, A., *L'Emigration des Ouvriers Turcs vers les Pays du Marché Commun. Situation Economique et Sociale*. Thèse, Strassbourg, 1970.

Börtücene, I. and Ersoy, T., *Labour Migration in its Relationship to Industrial and Agricultural Adjustment Policies*. Paris: OECD, CD/AG(74)825-8.

Clark, J. R. *"Residential Patterns and Social Integration of Turks in Cologne, W. Germany"*. Paper presented at the Middle East Studies Association Meeting, Binghamton, New York, November 2, 1972.

Demirgil, D., *"Factors affecting the Choice of Technology in Turkey and Implications for Levels of Employment"*. Paper presented at NESA Employment Seminar, Kathmandu, 1969.

van Dooren, P. J., *"Kapitaalvorming door Turkse Gastarbeiders b.v. Kooperatieve Projekten"*. Unpublished Paper, Jure 1972, N.A.R. Netherlands.

Gökmen, O., *"Die türkischen Gastarbeiter in Europa"*. Paper Presented at the European Conference on Migration Problems, Catholic University of Louvain, 31 January-2 February 1974, (Mimeo).

Hamurdan, Y. Ö., *"Surplus Labour in Turkish Agriculture"*. Paper presented at NESA Employment Seminar, Kathmandu, Nepal, 1970.

Kapil, I. and Gençağa, *Migration and Urban Social Structures*. AID, Ankara, Economic Staff Papers.

Kaupen-Haas, H., *Reintegration Problems among Turkish Workers*. Paris: OECD, DD/PO/6.107 and MS/M/503/251.

Kölan, T., *International Labor Migration and Economic Development: the Turkish Case*. Doctoral Dissertation, University of Colorado, 1973.

Krahenbuhl, R. E., *L'Emigration et le Marché du Travail en Turquie*. Paris: OECD, 1969, MS/M/404/301.

Krane, R. E., *"Cyclical Cross-Cultural Migration as a Mobility Multiplier. A Case Study from a Society in Transition"*. (Mimeo) 1973.

Kudat, A., *International Migration to Europe and its Political and Social Effects on the Future of Turkish Society*. Paper presented at the Hacettepe Conference, Ankara, 10-15 June 1974, (Mimeo).

Miller, D., Ed. *Essays on Labor Force and Employment in Turkey*. AID, Ankara: 1971, (Mimeo).

Miller, D. R. and Çetin, I., *"The International Demand for Brawn Power and Wealth Effect of Migration: A Turkish Case Study"*. Paper presented at the Middle East Studies Association Meeting, Binghamton, New York, November 2, 1972.

Monson, T., *"A Comparison of Industrial Learning Behavior of Turkish Workers at Home and Abroad"*. Paper presented at the Middle East Studies Association Meeting, Binghamton, New York, November 2, 1972.

Neuloh, E., Krämer, H. L., Endruweit, G., *Industrialisierung und Gastarbeit als sozioökonomische Faktoren für die Überwindung struktureller Arbeitslosigkeit in der*

Turkei. Institut für Empirische Soziologie, Saarbrücken, 1969, (Mimeo).

OECD, *Economic Surveys: Turkey.* Paris: OECD, 1972.

Özelli, T., *Economics of Education in a Developing Country: The Case of Turkey.* Unpublished Ph.D. Dissertation, Columbia University 1966.

Özkan, Y., *The Legal Status of Foreign Workers in the FRG with special Focus on Turkish Laborers.* Free University of Berlin, 1973, (Mimeo).

Özşahin, Ş., *Turkish European Manpower Movements.* AID, Ankara, Staff Paper, 1970, (Mimeo).

Rodie, R., *Turkey: Workers Abroad and their Reintegration and the Local Economy under the Second Five Year Development Plan (1968-1972).* Paris: OECD, 1968, (Mimeo).

Saver, E. Z., *A Socio-Economic Appraisal of Turkish Emigration, (1965-1972).* Ankara, 1973, (Mimeo).

Selçen, I., *Berufliche Wertmuster der türkischen Gastarbeiter.* Unpublished Ph.D. Dissertation, University of Köln, 1966.

Şengölge, Ö., *Turkish Workers in Europe.* Paper presented at the CENTO Symposium, Teheran 1969.

Tapan, E., *Change in Manpower with Special Reference given to the Turkish Workers in the Netherlands.* Skriptie Rotterdam, 1973, (Mimeo).

Tavernini, U., *Problems Raised by the Return of Turkish and Greek Migrant Workers to their Home Countries.* Council of Europe, Strassbourg, RS/111/, 3.5.1967.

Tuna, O., *"Labour Force and Employment Problems in Turkey".* Papers read at the RCD Collogium on Common Problems of Economic Growth, Karachi, 28-30 June 1965.

Republic of Turkey, State Planning Organization, *Second Five Year Development Plan, 1968-1972.* Ankara: 1969.

Üner, H., *The Economic Impact of the Outflow of High-Level Manpower from Turkey to the U.S.* Unpublished Master Thesis, George Washington University, 1968.

van Velzen, L., *Internationale Trekarbeid en Ontwikkelingsprocessen in Yugoslavie en Turkije, een Trendrapport.* Rotterdam, 1974, (Mimeo).

Verband Türkischer Lehrer in der BDR und in W. Berlin, *Zur pädagogisch-politischen Funktion der türkischen Priester und Koranschulen in der Türkei und im Ausland.* Paper presented at the Meeting for Foreign Workers and their Children, 1-4 June 1971, Theoder Heuss Akademie, Gummersbach, Niedersachsen.

Yaşer, Y., *The Turkish Workers Abroad and Their Problems.* Paper presented at the CENTO Symposium, Teheran, 1972, (Mimeo).

Zadil, E., *Auswirkungen der Arbeitskräftewanderungen in den Herkunftsländern: Fallstudie für die Türkei.* Bonn: 1973, (Mimeo).

TURKISH

BOOKS

Abadan, Nermin, *Batı Almanya'daki Türk işçileri ve sorunları*, DPT, Ankara, 1964, p. 278.

Aker, Ahmet, *İşçi göçü*, Sander Yayını, İstanbul 1972, p. 95.

Aksel, Lütfullah, *Dış Ülkelerde Çalişan Türk İşçilerinin Sosyal Güvenlik Hakları*, Anka Yayını, Ankara 1968, p. 86.

Araslı, Oya and Araslı, Doğan, *Almanya'daki İşçiler Hak ve Menfaatları*, Ayyıldız Matbaası, Ankara 1973, p. 207.

Ekin, Nusret, *İşgücü ve Ekonomik Gelişme*, Fakülteler Matbaası, İstanbul, 1968.

Ekin, Nusret, *Gelişen Ülkelerde ve Türkiye'de İşsizlik*, İstanbul 1971.

Ecrimen, Orhan, *Yurt Dışında Çalışan İşçilere 499 Sayılı Kanun ve Sair Döviz mevzuatile sağlanan Menfaatler*, Türkiye Emlâk Bankasi Yayini No. 4, Ankara 1970.

Gökmen, Oğuz, *Federal Almanya ve Türk İşçileri*, Ankara: Ayyıldız Matbaası, 1972.

Heper, Niyazi, *İş gücünün değerlendirilmesi ile ilgili olarak Alman İş ve İşçi Bulma ve İşsizlik Sigortası Kurumunun Plasman (İşe Yerleştirme) mesleğe yöneltme ve İşsizlik Sigortası*, Eskişehir Iktisadî ve Ticarî Akademisi Yayınları, No. 18, Eskişehir 1963.

Oğuzkan, Turhan, *Yurt Dışında Çalışan Doktoralı Türkler: Türkiye'den başka ülkelere yüksek seviyede eleman göçü üzerinde bir araştırma*, Ankara: Orta Doğu Teknik Üniversitesi 1971.

Reisoğlu Seza, *Ortak Pazar Hukuku, Özellikle İşçi dolaşım, yerleşme ve hizmet edimi serbestisini düzenliyen kurallar*, Ankara 1973, Huk. Fak. Yay. 316.

Reisoğlu, Seza, *Yabancı İşçiler yönünden Alman İş ve Sosyal Güvenlik Hukuku*, Ankara, 1973, Huk. Fak. Yay. 317.

Şenel, Şengün, *İşçi Tasarruflarını Değerlendirme Rehberi*, İş+İşçi Bulma Kurumu, 1974 Yayın No. 110.

Timur, S., *Türk Aile Yapısı*, Hacettepe Üniversitesi Yayınları, Ankara 1971.

Tuna, Orhan, Ekin, N., and Yazgan, T., *Türkiye'den F. Almanya'ya işgücü Akımı ve Meseleleri. I. Rapor. F. Almanya ve Türkiye'nin Emek ve Arz Talebi bakımından Tetkiki*, İstanbul, Sermet Matbaası, 1966, p. 117.

Tuna, Orhan, Ekin, N., and Yazgan, T., *Türkiye'den F. Almanya'ya İşgücü Akımı ve Meseleleri. II. Rapor. F. Almanya'ya İşgücü Akımı ile İlgili Organlar ve Meseleleri*, İstanbul Sermet Matbaası, 1966, p. 118.

Tuna, Orhan, *Dış Ülkelerde İnsangücü Akımı ve Sorunları*, Yakın ve Ortadoğu Çalışma Enstitüsü, İstanbul, 1968.

Tuncer, Baran, *Nüfus artışı ve Turkiye Ekonomisi*, Ankara, Hacettepe Universitesi, 1967.

Tümertekin, Erol, *Türkiye'de Iç Göçler*, İstanbul 1968.

Türkiye Ticaret Odaları, Ticaret Borsaları Birliği, *Yurt Dışındaki İşçilerimizin Tasarruflarının Değerlendirilmesi Semineri*, 15-16 Mayıs 1972, Ankara, 1972.

Türkiye İşçi Sendikaları Konfederasyonu, *Ortak Pazar İşgücü Hareketleri*, Türk-İş Yayınları, No. 66, Ankara: Başnur Matbaası, 1970.

Bibliyografya

İş ve İşçi Bulma Kurumu Genel Müdürlüğü, *Yurtdışı İstihdamla ilgili Bibliografya*, Ankara 1974, No. 11.

ARTICLES

Abadan, Nermin, Federal Almanya'nın 1966-1967 de geçirdiği ekonomik buhran açısından yabancı işgücü ve Turk işçilerinin durumu, *SBF. Dergisi*, 1971, Sayı 4, 159-180.

Abadan-Unat, Nermin, Yurtdışına göçen Türk İşgücü ve dönüş eğilimleri *SBF. Dergisi*, C. XXVII, 1972, No. 2, 183-207.

Aksöz, İ, Türkiye Ziraatindeki Atıl İşgücü ve bunun değerlendirilmesi, *İktisadî Kalkınmanın Ziraî Cephesi*, Ekonomik ve Sosyal Etüdler Konferans Heyeti, İstanbul 1965, s. 272-290.

Ansay, Tuğrul, Almanya'da boşanan Türklerin hukukî sorunları, *A.Ü. Hukuk Fak. Dergisi*, XXVII, 1972, No. 3, p. 353-369.

Ansay, Tuğrul, Alman yabancılar kanunu ve Türk işçileri, *A.U. H.F. Dergisi*, Cilt XXXI, No. 1-2, 1974, p. 223-243.

Ansay, Tuğrul, İşgücü ve yabancı ülkelerdeki işçilerimizin aile hukuku sorunları, *Hacettepe Semineri*, Ankara, 10-15.6.74.

Çavdar, T., "Türkiye'deki istihdam sorununun nüfusun nitelikleri açısıdam görünümü", *Çalışma Dergisi*, V. I, No. 2, 1972, pp. 127-141.

Dalsar, Fahri, Müşterek Pazar Karşısında Türk İşçisi *Türkiye İktisat Gazetesi*, Ankara, No. 350, 1960.

Denek, Turgut, Türk İşverenlerinin dış ülkelere işçi akımı karşısındaki davranışı, *İst. Ü İkt. Faküt. Sosyal Siyaset Konf.* 18, 1966, p. 229-258.

Ecevit, Bülent, Dış ülkelerdeki işçilerimizin problemleri, *İst. Ü İkt. Fak. Sosyal Siyaset Konf. 18*, İstanbul 1966, p. 47-74.

Ekin, Nusret, "Türkiye'de Sanayileşmenin bazı Sosyal Problemleri", *Sosyal Siyaset Konferansları*, V. XXI, pp. 135-154.

Ekin, Nusret, "Ekonomik Gelişme ve İşgücünün Sektörler İtibariyle dağılışındaki değişmeler", *İktisat Fakültesi Mecmuası*, V. XXIV, No. 3-4, p. 109-133.

Ekin, Nusret, "Türkiye'de Ekonomik Gelişme ve İstihdam meseleleri". *İktisat Fakültesi Mecmuası*, V. XXV, No. 3, pp. 90-104.

Ekin, Nusret, "Türkiye'nin Sanayileşmesinde Köylü-Şehirli İşçiler". İktisat Fakültesi *Mecmuası*, V. XXVII, No. 3-4, pp. 225-264.

Ekin, Nusret, "Ortak Pazarda Calışma Meselesi ve Türkiye". *İst. Ü. İktisat Fak. Sosyal Siyaset Konf. 18*, İstanbul 1966, p. 279-314.

Erker, Turhan, "Dış Ülkelere İsansangücü Akımı ve İ.İ.B.K.", *İst. Ü. İkt. Fak. Sosyal Siyaset Konf. 18*, Ankara 1966, p. 85-104.

Garipoğlu, Burhanettin, "Dıştaki İşçilerin Ortak olduğu Fabrikalar", *Milliyet*, 22.174.

Gürtan, Kenan, Az Gelişmiş Ülkelerde İşsizlik Yönünden Nüfusun Bünyesi ve Türkiye'deki Durum, *Sosyal Siyaset Konferansları XX*, 17-36.

Karahasanoğlu, Taner, Yurtdışı İşgücü Gönderilmelerinin Türkiye Yönünden Değerlendirilmesi, *Eskişehir İktisadi ve Ticari İlimler Akademisi Dergisi*, Cilt IX, Ocak 1973, Sayı 1, 170-200.

Karahasanoğlu, Taner, Türkiye'de Ekonomik Gelişme Açısından İşgücünün Tahlili, *E.İ.T.İ.A. Dergisi*, VIII, sayı 2.

Köksal, Bülent, Yurt Dışındaki İşçiler, *Çalışan Adam*, Sayı 19, 1973, 16-17.

Kulin, Muhittin, "Dışarıya Giden İşçilerimiz", *Milliyet*, 1.7.1964.

Öktem, Bengü, "Almanya'da Türk İşçilerinin Suçluluk Durumu ve İlgili Meselesi", *İst. Ü. İk. Fak. Sosyal Siyaset Konf. 18*, İstanbul 1966, p. 178-198.

Özakman, Turgut, Dış Ulkelerdeki İşçilerimize Hitap Eden Radyo Yayınları, *İst. Un. İkt. Fak. Sosyal Siyaset. Konf. 18*, İstanbul 1966, p. 141-158.

Pehlivanoğlu, Sadi, "Dış ülkelerdeki işçilerimizin sosyal, kültürel meseleleri", *İst. Ün. İkt. Fak. Sosyal Siyaset Konf. 18*, İstanbul, p. 75-84.

Tokcan, Çetin, "Türkiye'de İnsangücü Açısından İşsizlik", *Sosyal Siyaset Konferanslari*, XX, 37-43.

Ünver, O., "Yurtdışındaki işçilerimiz ve ekonomik sorunları", *Ankara İktisadî ve Ticarî İlimler Akademisi Dergisi*, Vol. I, 1969, pp. 107-147.

Ünver, O. "İşçi Dövizi ve Kalkınma", *Ankara İktisadî ve Ticarî İlimler Akademisi Dergisi*, V. III, No. 1, 1971, pp. 1971, pp. 105-129.

Yasa, İbrahim, and Bozkurt, Ömer, "Orta Anadolu'dan Batı Avrupa'ya Göç ve Toplumsal Değişme", *Amme İdaresi Dergisi*, Cilt 7, p. 3, 1974 45-72.

DOCUMENTS, REPORTS AND STATISTICAL YEARBOOKS

Bilmen, Sıtkı, *Yabancı Memleketlerdeki Türk İşçi Çocuklarının Eğitimleri Meselesi*, Milli Eğitim Bak. 1971, Rapor III (Mimeo).

Börtücene, İ., *Uluslararası İşgücü Hareketleri ve Türkiye*, DPT Yayını 450, SPD 103, Ankara 1966, p. 64 (mimeographed).

Börtücene, İ, *Dış Ülkelere İşgücü Göndermede Kooperatif Kuran Köylülere Öncelik Tanınması Projesinin Uygulanması Üzerine Bir İnceleme*, DPT Yayını 499, SPD198, Ankara 1968.

Ecevit, Bülent, *Yurt Dışındaki Türk İşçileri*, Çalışma Bakanlığı, Aralık 1964, (mimeographed).

Ege, Ünal, *İş ve İşçi Problemleri*, DPT No. 331, SPD No. 80, 1965 (mimeographed).

Erker, T., *Belçika'daki İşçilerimizin Durumları ve Sorunları*, İş ve İşçi Bulma Kurumu Yayını, Ankara 1964.

Evrenesoğlu, I., *Federal Almanya–Türkiye İşgücü İlişkileri*, DPT, Ankara 1971 (mimeographed).

Gökçen, Ahmet M., *Kırdan Şehire İşgücü Göçleri, 1965-1982 ye ait Tahminler*, DPT 1107, SPT 240, Ankara 1971 (mimeographed).

Gülsün, İlhan, *Sanayileşme Politikası ve Yurtdışındaki İşçi Tasarruflarının Değerlendirilmesi*, T. Ticaret ve Sanayi Oda Borsalar Birliği, Ankara 1972, p. 29.

Gülsün, İlhan, *Sayılarla Yurtdışındaki İşçilerimiz ve Sorunlarına Ait İstatistikler*, İş ve İşçi Bulma Kurumu, Ankara 1974, p. 120.

Hamurdan, Y., *Sayılarla İstihdam Sorunu (1965-1982) Geçici Tahminler*, T.C. Devlet Plânlama Teşkilâti, Ankara 1971 (mimeographed).

Hamurdan, Y., *Türkiye'de İşgücü Arzı, Talebi ve İşgücü Fazlası Tahminleri*, DPT: 964, SPD: 216, Ankara 1970 (mimeographed).

İktisadi Kalkinma Vakfi, *Türkiye ve AET'de İşgücü Ücretleri*, İktisadî Kalkıinma Vakfı Yayınları, No. AET/21, İstanbul 1968.

Köksal, I., *Ortak Pazar İşgücü Hareketleri ve Türkiye*, T.C. Devlet Plânlama Teşkilâtı, Ankara 1966 (mimeographed)

Tuna, Orhan, *Yurda Dönen İşçilerin İntibak Sorunları*, DPT/SPD, Ağustos 1967, Ankara p. 80 (mimeographed)

T. C. Devlet Planlama Teşkilâtı, *AET Düzenine ve Türkiye Yönünden Getireceği Sorunlara Genel Bakış* Yayın No. DPT: 580, İPD: 233, Ankara 1968.

T. C. Devlet Planlama Teşkilâtı, *Yurt Dışından Dönen İşçilerin Sosyo-Ekonomik Eğilimleri Üzerinde Bir Çalışma*, DPT: 1342 SPD: 264, 1974, teksir.

T. C. İş Ve İşçi Bulma Kurumu Genel Müdürlüğü, *Avrupa Memleketlerinde Türk İşçileri ve Problemleri: İsviçre, Hollanda, Belçika, F. Almanya ve Avusturya'da Yapılan Bir İnceleme Gezisinin Notları*, 10 Haziran 1968-9 Temmuz 1968, Yayın No. 49, Ankara, Başbur Matbaası, 1968.

T. C. İş Ve İşçi Bulma Kurumu Genel Müdürlüğü, *Fransa'da Çalışan Türk İşçileri: Bir İnceleme Gezisi Raporu*, Yayın No. 79, Ankara 1970.

——, *Yurt Dışındaki Türk İşçileri ile İlgili Sorunlar ve Çözümleri*, Yayın No. 33, Ankara 1967.

——, *Yurt Dışındaki Türk İşçileri ve Dönüş Eğilimleri*, Yayın No. 43, Ankara 1968.

——, *Yurt Dışındaki Türk İşçileri ve Dönüş Eğilimleri*, Yayın No. 59, Ankara 1969.

——, *Yurt Dışındaki Türk İşçileri ve Dönüş Eğilimleri*, Yayın No. 85, Ankara 1971.

——, *Sayınlarla Yurtdışındaki İşçilerimiz ve Sorunlarına İlişkin İstatistikler*, Ankara 1974, Yayın No. 111.

Yener, Semira, *1960-65 Döneminde Köyden Sehire Göçler*, DPT: 932, SPD: 212, Ankara 1970, (Mimeo).

Yurtdışında Çalışan Isçilere Konut ve Küçük Sanat Kredisi Açılması ve Ödünç Para Vermilmesi Hakkında Kanun, No. 499, 14/7/64, Yayım Tarihi: 22.7.1969.

ADDENDA

Publications which have become available since this book went
to press

R.E. KRANE, Ed., *Manpower Mobility Across Cultural Boundaries*, Social, Economic
and Legal Aspects, The Case of Turkey and West Germany, E.J. Brill, Leiden
1975.

Suzanne PAINE, *Exporting Workers*, The Turkish Case, Cambridge University Press,
1974.

Georges TAPINOS, *L'Economie des Migrations Internationales*, Fondation Nationale
des Sciences Politiques, A. Colin, Paris 1974.

AUTHOR INDEX

SUBJECT INDEX

AUTHORS

Nermin ABADAN-UNAT, Professor of Political Behaviour, Faculty of Political
Science, University Ankara. Former consultant at OECD and ILO, Turkey

Otto NEULOH, Professor of Sociology, Director of the Institute of Empirical Sociology, University of Saarbrücken, Federal Germany

Turhan OĞUZKAN, Chairman of the Department of Education, University of
Boğaziçi, Istanbul, Turkey

İsmail Hakkı AYDINOĞLU, Former Minister of Village Affairs and Cooperatives, Consultant at the Central Bank, Ankara, Turkey

Tufan KÖLAN, Research Director of the AFL-CIO Appalachian Council, Washington,
D.C., United States

Duncan R. MILLER, Economic Analysis Staff Member, AID, Ankara. At present Manpower Division — OECD, Paris, France

Ruşen KELES, Professor of Urbanism, Institute of Settlement and Urbanization,
Faculty of Political Science, University of Ankara, Turkey

James E. AKRE, Consultant, International Labour Office, Geneva, Switzerland

Mübeccel B. KIRAY, Former chainman of the Social Science Department, Middle East
Technical University. At present Faculty of Architecture Technical University,
Istanbul, Turkey

M. Sıtkı BİLMEN, Former Turkish Educational Attaché, New York. At present Ministery of Education, Ankara, Turkey

Ger MIK, Lecturer in Urban Geography, Department of Economic Geography Erasmus
University, Rotterdam, Holland

S.G.M. VERKOREN-HEMELAAR, Research Assistant, Department of Geography,
State University of Utrecht, Holland

Hans KOK, Research Assistant of the Netherlands Foundation, Center for Foreigners,
Utrecht, Holland

Gottfried E. VÖLKER, Department of Economics, Middle East Technical University,
1971-1973. At present German Director, Clearing House for Social Development
in Asia, Bangkok, Thailand.

Eberhard de HAAN, Director of the Section for Turkish Workers, Arbeiterwohlfahr
Bonn, Federal Germany

Günter SCHILLER, Associate Professor of Economics, Institute for Social and Economic Planning, Technische Hochschule, Darmstadt, Federal Germany